Dedicated to my father, Mani van der Spuy,
without whom this book would not have been written.
Thanks, Dad, for always believing in me.

CONTENTS AT A GLANCE

CONTENTS

ABOUT THE AUTHOR

Rex van der Spuy is a freelance interactive media designer specializing in Flash game design, interface design, and ActionScript programming. He programmed his first adventure game at the age of 10 on his Commodore VIC-20. He went on to study film production, graduating with a BFA in Film/Video from York University (Toronto) in 1993, and spent a number of years working as an independent producer and freelance cameraman.

Rex has designed Flash games and done interactive interface programming for clients such as Agency Interactive (Dallas), Scottish Power (Edinburgh), DC Interact (London), Draught Associates (London), and the Bank of Montreal (Canada). He also builds game engines and interactive museum installations for PixelProject (Cape Town). In addition, Rex taught advanced courses in Flash game design for the Canadian School of India (Bangalore).

In his spare time, Rex does a considerable amount of technical and fiction writing, and he maintains a semiprofessional musical career as a performer on the sitar. He currently divides his time between Canada, India, and South Africa; and he works on consulting and software development projects for clients in India, North America, and the UK. He also maintains the game design learning and experimental lab http://www.kittykatattack.com.

ABOUT THE TECHNICAL REVIEWER

 **Josh Freeney** is currently an instructor for the Digital Animation and Game Design program at Ferris State University in Grand Rapids, Michigan. He likes board games, hiking, sleeping in, and anything Lego. He teaches Flash game development classes focused on rapid agile production with maximum reusability. Josh has spoken at the Michigan Flash Festival and continues to consult anyone, anywhere with a Flash problem that needs fixing.

ABOUT THE COVER IMAGE DESIGNER

 **Corné van Dooren** designed the front cover image for this book. After taking a break from friends of ED to create a new design for the Foundation series, he worked at combining technological and organic forms, with the results now appearing on this and other books' covers.

Corné spent his childhood drawing on everything at hand and then began exploring the infinite world of multimedia—and his journey of discovery hasn't stopped since. His mantra has always been "The only limit to multimedia is the imagination," a saying that keeps him moving forward constantly.

Corné works for many international clients, writes features for multimedia magazines, reviews and tests software, authors multimedia studies, and works on many other friends of ED books. You can see more of his work (and contact him) at his web site: http://www.cornevandooren.com.

If you like Corné's work, be sure to check out his chapter in *New Masters of Photoshop: Volume 2* (friends of ED, 2004).

INTRODUCTION

So you want to make a video game. Where do you start? What do you need to learn? To whom can you look for help?

If you've ever asked any of these questions, you'll know how difficult it is to find the answers. I asked myself these same questions many years ago in a little village outside of Bangalore, India, where I was teaching programming and interactive media at an international school. All my students were playing games and they all wanted to create games, but there were no comprehensive books or online resources available on how to do this.

A little bit of research turned up something surprising: not only did basic game design require relatively little programming knowledge but the same set of techniques could also be used over and over again in different contexts to create completely different kinds of games. It was fun to do, the results were immediate, and it was a great creative outlet. The result of this research was an in-house textbook on game design that formed the basis of three high school–level courses and inspired the writing of this book.

That was back in the now almost prehistoric days of Flash 4 and 5, when the ActionScript programming language was still in version 1.0, and Flash had some wonderful built-in interactive tutorials that guided new users every step of the way. It seemed as if everyone was a beginner in those days, so it was relatively easy to find books and tutorials that assumed the reader had no background knowledge.

ActionScript is now in version 3.0, and things are not so easy. The ActionScript language has become much more powerful but also much more complex. Many of the resources that you'll find for AS3.0 are focused on that complexity, and it's harder and harder for beginners with little previous programming experience to get a comprehensive foothold to start learning. The irony of all this is that AS3.0 actually makes it much *easier* to build games than in the days of AS1.0. What this book does is to strip away the apparent complexity of AS3.0 and get to the core of what you need to know to make games. It's fun and easy, and anyone can do it.

Game design is a fantastic thing, and what you're about to learn is one of the closest things you can get to creating magic that the real world allows. Hang on for a wild ride—you'll be amazed by what you'll start producing very quickly.

Layout conventions

To keep this book as clear and easy to follow as possible, the following text conventions are used throughout.

Important words or concepts are normally highlighted on the first appearance in **bold type**.

Code is presented in `fixed-width` font.

New or changed code is normally presented in **`bold fixed-width font`**.

Pseudo-code and variable input are written in *`italic fixed-width font`*.

Menu commands are written in the form Menu ➤ Submenu ➤ Submenu.

Where I want to draw your attention to something, I've highlighted it like this:

> *Ahem, don't say I didn't warn you.*

Sometimes code won't fit on a single line in a book. Where this happens, I use an arrow like this: ➥.

```
This is a very, very long section of code that should be written all on ➥
the same line without a break.
```

Source files

All the programming code used in this book is available for download at `http://www.friendsofed.com/downloads.html`.

Most of the book's chapters make reference to these source files, which contain working examples of games, completed projects, and additional sample programs and utilities.

To make use of these source files, you need to "create a project" using Flash's CS4's new Project panel. Here are the steps you need to follow:

1. In Flash, make sure that the Project panel is open. If it isn't, select Window ➤ Other Panels ➤ Project.

2. In the Project panel, select Open Project from the drop-down menu.

3. Find the folder that contains the source files and select it. The source files are organized by chapter, and the folder you're looking for will usually be a subfolder of the chapter folder.

4. Click the Choose button.

5. All the files required for the project will be loaded into the Project panel.

6. You now need to assign an FLA file as the default document. The default document is the file that Flash uses to create the SWF file, which is the file that actually runs your program or game. If the project's default document has already been assigned, it will be indicated by a yellow star on the FLA file's icon. If the default document hasn't been assigned, you need to assign it manually. To do this, right-click the FLA file and select Make default document from the context menu. (Sometimes this option won't appear the first time you select the file. If it doesn't, select the FLA file again.)

7. After the default document has been assigned, you can click the Test Project button to see the result of the program. Double-click any of the files to open them to make changes.

Chapter 1

PROGRAMMING FOUNDATIONS:
HOW TO MAKE A VIDEO GAME

Congratulations on picking up this book! Video game design is one of the most interesting and creative things you can do with a computer. You're about to embark on a remarkable journey, and this book will guide you every step of the way.

So how do you make a video game? Although there are probably as many ways to make games as there are readers of this book, a good place to start is with a piece of software called **Flash**. Not only is Flash very easy to learn but you can also use it to produce games of great complexity and professional quality if you have time and imagination. The other great thing about Flash is that the skills you'll acquire while learning game design with Flash can be directly applied to game design on many other platforms if you want to take your learning further. Flash is a completely comprehensive software tool for building games. It's now in version 10 and is part of Adobe's Creative Suite 4 set of design software (although it can be purchased and used as an individual product).

Learning game design with Flash is really a two-step process. You need to learn Flash's visual work and graphic design environment, and also its built-in *programming language* called **ActionScript**. A programming language is a kind of language, similar to English or French, that we humans can use to communicate with computers. To make games with Flash, the game characters and objects are designed in Flash's visual design environment and they're then told how to behave using ActionScript. The big advantage of using Flash to learn game design over other methods is that the visual design and programming elements are completely integrated. This greatly speeds up the simplicity and efficiency of the game-design process and makes it a whole lot of fun as well.

Tens of thousands of people around the world have made a career out of designing games with Flash. With this book and a little bit of practice, you could become one of them.

Basics you need to have

Surprisingly, video game design can be a relatively low-tech affair. Here's the basic equipment you need:

- A reasonably up-to-date computer, either running Windows or the latest version of Mac OS X.
- An installed copy of Adobe Flash CS4 (version 10). You can download Flash directly from the Adobe website: www.adobe.com. Although it requires an initial investment, it's a bargain for such a powerful piece of professional software. Adobe also offers upgrades from previous versions at an extremely reasonable cost. You can try Flash for a free 30-day trial period if you want to make completely sure it's for you.

Things you need to know

This book assumes that you haven't had any experience using Flash—or any experience with computer programming. You'll go on a step-by-step journey through these fascinating worlds. If you want to learn to design games from scratch, this book is all you need to get started.

That said, Flash and the ActionScript programming language are huge topics that you could easily spend a lifetime studying, and no one book will be able to provide all the answers to all the questions you might have while you're learning. If you've never used Flash before, I highly recommend that you spend a bit of time reading through the documentation and working through some of the exercises and sample projects in Adobe's online Help system. (To access them, select Help ➤ Flash Help from Flash's menu.) You might also find it very beneficial to spend a weekend with a good introductory book on Flash, such as one of the excellent books for Flash beginners published by friends of ED. These resources will answer some of the more basic questions that you might have about how to use Flash and what it's capable of without the added complexity of having to absorb some of the conceptual issues of game design and ActionScript programming at the same time.

But, hey, if you want to dive into the deep end right away, I'm with you! This book is a great a place to start and is the only resource you need.

And the things you don't need to know

Perhaps even more enlightening is what you *don't* have to know to be able to make use of this book:

- Math (not much, anyway!)
- Computer programming
- Website design

- Graphic design
- Practically anything else!

In fact, I'll even allow you to say, "I hate computers," or let you indulge in a fantasy of hurtling a particularly heavy blunt object at your monitor. Rest assured that I have shared exactly those same feelings at some point or another!

It's all about programming

What most of the content of this book deals with is how to write computer programs. **Computer programs** are like movie scripts that tell the characters and objects in your games what they should do and how to behave under certain conditions. For example, suppose that you designed a game in which the player must use the arrow keys on the keyboard to guide a duck through a pond infested with hungry snapping turtles. How will the duck know that it must move when the arrow keys are pressed? You would need to write a program to tell the duck to do this.

ActionScript is the name of the computer programming language that you'll be using to write the programs for your games. It's a very sophisticated and powerful language, closely related to Java. ActionScript is currently in version 3 and is known as AS3.0 for short. It's a wonderful language for learning to program because of the following:

- It is completely integrated into Flash's graphic design environment, so you can create visually rich games much more quickly than with most other programming languages.

- For the same reason, you can often see the results of your programs on the screen right away. This makes the experience of programming very concrete, very satisfying, and far less abstract than learning to program in many other programming languages.

- Adobe has done a lot of work to make the experience of programming with AS3.0 extremely user friendly. It has simplified the technical hurdles to getting programs up and running as a one-click process.

- AS3.0 is a "real" programming language like Java or C++. It's been in development for many years and complies with an open source programming language called EMCAScript. The great thing about learning to program with AS3.0 is that the skills you learn will be directly applicable to the study of other programming languages, and you'll be able to build on these skills for years to come. ActionScript is here to stay, and you can grow with it.

- Games and programs created with AS3.0 are **cross-platform**, which means that they run on any computer operating system (Windows, Mac OSX, or Linux) as long as that system has Adobe's free Flash Player software installed. The Flash Player is one of most widely installed pieces of software in history, so you're guaranteed a potentially huge audience for your games without having to rewrite the programming code from scratch for each system.

- There is a huge community of friendly AS3.0 developers on the Internet who have devoted vast amounts of time to writing tutorials and helping others in online forums and discussion boards. If you get stuck while writing a program, just ask a question on one of the many Flash and ActionScript discussion boards, and you'll surely get a helpful reply.

Programming? But I'm terrible at math!

So is the author of this book! One of the biggest misunderstandings that nonprogrammers have about computer programming is that programming is some kind of math. It's not. It might look the same on the surface, and some of the syntax has been borrowed from mathematics for matters of convenience, but the whole underlying system is completely different.

That's not to say you won't be using any math in these lessons—you will. How much? You'll use addition, subtraction, multiplication, division, and some very basic algebra (the kind you might remember from fifth grade). That's as complex as the math gets, and AS3.0 actually does all the calculating for you.

It can get as complicated as you want it to. In a later chapter you'll use a bit of trigonometry to achieve some specific motion effects. However, you won't need to necessarily understand the mechanics of how trigonometry is achieving those effects—just how to use it in the context of your game. This book is written largely from a nonmath point of view, so mathophobes of the world are welcome!

> *Although you certainly don't need to use much math to start building great games right away, acquiring a deeper understanding of the mathematical possibilities of programming with AS3.0 will definitely give you many more options as a game developer. Two very comprehensive and highly readable books that cover this area in much more detail than the scope of this book allows are* Foundation ActionScript Animation: Making Things Move!, *by Keith Peters; and* Flash Math Creativity, *by various authors. Both books are published by friends of ED and are perfect companions to* Foundation Game Design with Flash. *You can apply all the techniques they discuss directly to the game projects in this book.*

I already know how to program!

This book has been written to be as accessible as possible for beginners and doesn't assume any programming background. However, many of you might be experienced programmers who are reading this book to find out how you can use your existing AS3.0 skills to create games. Don't worry; although the earlier chapters are definitely geared toward people new to Flash and ActionScript, later chapters deal with fairly advanced areas of object-oriented programming that provide quite a bit of meat for you to sink your programming teeth into.

What I recommend is that you flip ahead to Chapter 5, which is the first chapter that uses programming techniques to build a complete game from beginning to end. If it seems a bit complex or there are some terms and concepts you don't understand, step back by a chapter or two until you find your comfort level. Otherwise, if Chapter 5 seems like a good level for you, go for it! From a programming point of view, things get quite a bit more interesting from that chapter onward.

Many of the techniques involved in game design are quite specialized, Even though you might know quite a lot about ActionScript or programming, it's not always obvious how to use those skills to build games. The focus of this book is on the architecture of game design instead of the specific nuts and bolts of programming. If you have a lot of programming experience, this book will show you how you can use those skills within the context of completely developed games.

Some of you might be new to Flash CS4 and AS3.0, but have used previous versions of Flash and have programmed in AS1.0 or AS2.0. To ease the transition process, this book will also point out the major differences between the new AS3.0 way of doing things and the way it used to be done in earlier versions of the language.

What kind of games can I make?

The focus of this book is on two-dimensional action, adventure, and arcade games; it also touches on puzzle and logic games. Flash is a fantastic medium for creating these types of games. Each chapter guides you through every step of the design process, but the projects are very open-ended and encourage you to come up with your own original ways of using the techniques in your own games.

Flash CS4 is actually pretty good at 3D, but 3D is quite a large topic that deserves a whole book in its own right. The great thing is that most of the game design techniques you learn in the context of 2D, particularly how games are structured, can be applied directly to 3D games with little or no modification. To simplify the learning process and make sure the material is as focused and clear as it can be, however, I decided to stick to 2D games in this edition.

Learning some new terms

Like any large specialized field, programming comes with a lot of new terminology to learn. This book will try to sidestep as much of the jargon as possible in favor of slightly longer and concrete descriptions. Some terminology is so widely used that you should learn it, and this book will explain all new terms in the text.

Laying the foundation

As a game developer, you can think of yourself as an architect. All buildings of any size or shape have some fundamental things in common: they all have a foundation, walls, and a roof. No matter how big or small, humble or grand your house is, you need to dig a foundation, erect some walls, and put up a roof. After that you can start the really fun stuff: designing the interior layout, doing the landscaping, buying the furniture, and throwing a housewarming party.

Over the course of the rest of this chapter, you'll write a very simple program that will lay the foundation for all the games and programs you'll be creating in the rest of the book. If you haven't done any programming before or are just starting to get to grips with AS3.0, this chapter is for you.

If you have prior programming experience, you might want to jump ahead to the end of the chapter to see how much of the technical and conceptual material looks familiar. Make sure that you become acquainted with the structure you'll be using to build your games and programs, but feel free to skip this chapter if it all looks pretty straightforward.

In a tip-of-the hat to the history of computer programming, you'll write a program called a **Hello World program**. It is traditionally the first program that novice programmers write when learning a new programming language because it's the simplest complete program that can be written. It does something very simple; it just outputs the words Hello World! in Flash's Output panel.

The program might seem modest, but you will achieve two very important things by learning to write it:

1. You'll build a robust and flexible system for programming that will become the core of all the projects in this book and probably hold you in good stead with your own projects for years to come.

2. You'll complete a crash course in programming with AS3.0 that will lay the foundations for some of the very important concepts and techniques covered in later chapters.

Scared of programming? Ha! Not you! In this chapter, you'll grab the programming beast by the horns and wrestle it to the ground!

Files you'll need

When you create a game with Flash and AS3.0, you don't work with only one file; you'll need at least the following two files:

- **AS file**: This file contains all your AS3.0 programming code—the brains of your game. AS files are simply text files with an .as file extension (you'll learn more details in a moment). If you have used earlier versions of Flash and are migrating to AS3.0 from AS2.0 or AS1.0, you might have done most or all of your coding directly in frames on the timeline and used only one file: an FLA file. You *can* actually still use timeline code, but now is the time to bite the bullet and say goodbye to it for good. Don't worry; you'll soon see that keeping all your programming code in a separate AS file is actually much more efficient and in fact *much easier* than keeping track of what invariably turned into an unmanageable sprawling mess of timeline code in earlier versions of Flash.

- **FLA file**: This is an ordinary Flash file and has an .fla file extension. This file is where all the visual objects for your programs will reside, such as game characters and environments. The AS file is actually the one that does all the "thinking," but it depends on the FLA file to do all the administrative work of interpreting and running the programming code (turning it into a playable game), displaying it on the screen, and allowing players to interact with it. The FLA file can also contain **embedded assets** (such as animations, sounds, videos, and graphic artwork) that your game might need.

After you finish designing your game, the FLA and AS files will work together to produce a third file known as a **Flash movie file**. The Flash movie file is your finished product; it's the file that you can upload to the Internet to share with the rest of the world. Flash movie files have the file extension .swf, so I'll call them SWF files throughout the remainder of the book. To create a SWF file, you need to publish it from Flash. You'll see how to do that in a moment.

Setting up the work environment

Before you start writing your Hello World program, you need to organize the work directory and create blank FLA and AS files that you need to start programming with. You'll use this same format for all the projects in the rest of the book.

1. Find a convenient spot on your hard drive and create a project folder called Hello World Program.

2. Open Flash. Select File ➤ New and choose ActionScript File from the New Document dialog box (see Figure 1-1).

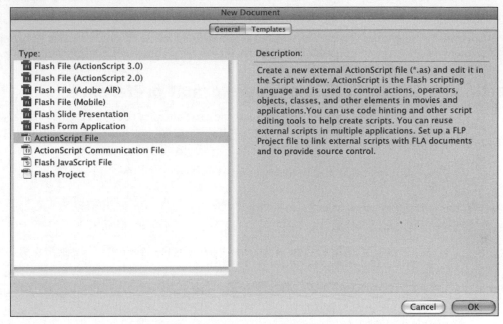

Figure 1-1. Create an ActionScript file.

3. Click OK.

4. A new ActionScript file will open called Script-1. Select File ➤ Save As. Enter the new file name Main.as. Save it in the Hello World Program folder that you created in step 1.

This new file, Main.as, is the AS file in which all the programming will take place. (Make sure that you spell the name with a capital letter *M*; your program might not work otherwise.) At the end of this chapter, I'll discuss a feature of programming practice called naming conventions, which explain some of the odd capitalizations that you might notice in this project. For now, just make sure you follow the suggested names exactly.

5. You now need to create an FLA file. Select File ➤ New and choose Flash File (ActionScript 3.0) from the New Document dialog box.

6. Click OK.

7. A new Flash file called Untitled-1 will open. Select File ➤ Save As. Enter the new file name helloWorld.fla. Save it in the Hello World Program folder, along with the Main.as file.

8. Check the Hello World Program folder and make sure that it looks something like Figure 1-2.

Figure 1-2. Check to make sure that the FLA and AS files are in the same folder.

Setting up the Flash Developer workspace

Flash allows you to customize your work environment so that the various windows and panels you'll be working with are comfortably arranged. These areas are called **workspaces**.

You'll set up a **Developer workspace**, which is recommended for doing programming. (Programmers are sometimes referred to as **developers** because they *develop* software applications such as games.)

Setting up the ActionScript code format preferences

You'll set up Flash's preferences so that it formats the programming code to be easily readable. You won't necessarily notice the benefit of doing this at this stage, but you'll use the same format for the rest of the projects in this book, so it makes sense to set it up now.

1. Select Flash ➤ Preferences if you're using Mac OSX or Edit ➤ Preferences if you're using Windows.

2. In the Category menu, select Auto Format.

3. Select the options so that the Preferences window looks like Figure 1-3.

   You're free to choose any code format you're comfortable with, but for learning and debugging purposes, this suggested format is the most clear.

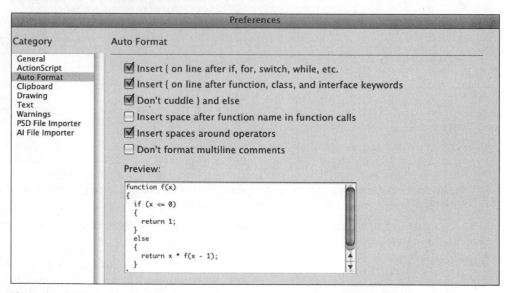

Figure 1-3. Set the code format preferences to make the code easy to read and debug.

4. Click OK to save the changes.

Flash now automatically formats the code according to these selected options.

Writing your first program

You now have most of the pieces in place to begin writing your first program. In the next few steps, you'll do the following:

1. Create a **package** that groups all the code neatly together.
2. Create a **class** that is the first building block of your program.
3. Create a **constructor** method that triggers the first actions in your program to run.
4. Create a **directive** that is the actual action that you want your program to perform.
5. Import Flash's built-in MovieClip class to help your program display its output.
6. Publish the SWF file to see the actual output of all your hard work.

This process might seem like a lot of work, but at the end of it you'll have a complete system in place that will form the basis for all the projects in the rest of the book and a flexible foundation for you to build any of your own programs and games.

I'll take that to go!

To make sure that Flash understands which bits of AS3.0 programming code you want to keep separate or together, you need to wrap all the code in a **package**, which consists of three parts:

- **Keyword**: This keyword is called, conveniently enough, package. Keywords are special words that AS3.0 understands and that do a special job (such as creating a package!). When you type keywords in your program, Flash turns them blue so you can spot them in the code.
- **Identifier**: An identifier can any be any name you want to give the package. It is optional, and you won't be using package identifiers until much later in the book.
- **Curly braces**: Curly braces ({ }) are used to keep whatever is inside them together. You can think of them as the string that ties the package together.

Creating a package could not be easier:

1. Open the AS3.0 editing window that contains the blank Main.as file that you created in the previous steps.

   If you are new to Flash, you can find this file by clicking the Main.as tab in the tab bar just above Flash's stage. (The **stage** is the white rectangle in the middle of the Flash workspace in which you design the visual elements and layout for your games.) Figure 1-4 shows you what the tab bar looks like. You can move back and forth between the AS and FLA files by clicking these tabs.

2. In the Main.as file, enter the following text into the editor window:

   ```
   package
   {
   }
   ```

Figure 1-4. Use the tabs above the stage to move between the AS and FLA files.

Your ActionScript editor window should now look something like Figure 1-5.

What you just created is something programmers call a **block statement**. Block statements define a particular section of the program and are used to group together all the code between the curly braces. In this case, the package block statement is completely empty because there's nothing between the curly braces. But don't worry; it won't remain empty for long!

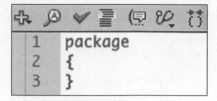

Figure 1-5. Create a package in the Main.as file.

Before continuing, however, it's worth taking a closer look at exactly what you created.

As you started typing the code in the ActionScript editor window, you noticed that the word package was automatically colored blue by the editor. This is Flash's helpful way of telling you that what you've just typed is a keyword—a word it understands. Keywords are also known as **reserved words**. This means that those words belong to ActionScript and ActionScript alone; you can't use them as names you choose to give your packages, classes, variables, or methods (more on them soon). The package keyword simply tells Flash, "Hey, I'm creating a package!" Not too hard, is it?

After the package keyword come our dear little friends, the curly braces:

```
{
}
```

Cute, aren't they? At the moment, they're completely empty, but that's about to change very quickly. Soon you'll put something inside them {like this!}.

Don't skip class!

Now that you created a package, the next step is to create a **class** inside that package. You can think of a class as a basic building block for creating an ActionScript program.

3. With your ActionScript editor window still open, add the following text in bold, directly inside the package's curly braces. Notice that this new text is indented from the left margin. Use the Tab key on your computer keyboard to indent it when you add it to your program. The code in this book uses indent levels of two spaces, but the ActionScript editor window indents your code by four spaces when you press Tab, which is just fine. Very soon you'll see how important it is to indent your code like this.

```
package
{
  public class Main
  {
  }
}
```

You've just created a class called Main. (Make sure that the *M* is uppercase.) Both the words public and class will be colored blue to show you that they're reserved keywords that AS3.0 understands.

It doesn't look like much, does it? And what is a class?

If you take a car as an example, each component of a car (such as the steering wheel, the engine, and the ignition switch) performs a single specific function. If you were building a car with ActionScript, the steering wheel would be one class, the engine another class, and the ignition switch yet another class. Each of those classes is a perfectly useful, self-contained unit in its own right, but also works with the others to create the single bigger and better unit called a "car."

> *There is a subtle but extremely important difference between our car example and an actual class that I'll touch on briefly (it will become much clearer in the chapters that follow). A class is also a blueprint for other objects that share its same properties or behaviors. If that sounds confusing, think of the wheel of a car. Most cars have four wheels that look exactly the same and do exactly the same thing: they roll. In fact, the only difference between them is their names: "left front wheel," "right front wheel," "left back wheel," and "right back wheel." Other than that, they're completely identical. So if you're designing a car, why go to the all the trouble of designing four wheels from scratch? Why not just design one wheel and make four copies of it?*
>
> *That's exactly the convenience that classes provide. A class is like a master template or a cookie cutter that you can use to make as many copies as you want. That is, in fact, exactly what the word* class *literally refers to—a master category of things that share the same properties.*
>
> *For example, a car designer might create one wheel called* Wheel*. The designer could then make new copies (or* **instances***) of that parent* Wheel *class called* leftFrontWheel*,* rightFrontWheel*,* leftBackWheel*, and* rightBackWheel *In all four cases, the wheels' behaviors and properties are exactly the same as their parent* Wheel *class; only their names are different.*
>
> *You'll encounter the word* instance *a lot in this book. If a class is like a printing press, an* instance *is the printed paper the press produces. Instances contain exactly the same properties as the original, but are individual objects in their own right. When an instance of a class is made, it's said to be* **instantiated***.*
>
> *This example is a slight oversimplification, but the important thing to remember is that when you create a class, you're also creating a master template that you can use to make as many individual instances of that class as you need, without having to rebuild from scratch each time.*

Any ActionScript program you write must have at least one class, but most of the programs and games you'll be building in this book will have many. Take a quick look at the new code:

```
public class Main
{
}
```

This code is called a **class definition**. Just like the package, a class definition is a type of block statement. You can tell this by the class's own pair of curly braces, hanging there in space. (Those braces are empty at the moment, so the class can't do anything yet. That will change very soon.)

A class definition does three main things:

- It creates the class. The keyword class tells Flash that you are creating a class. Simple enough!

- It gives the class some rules to follow. This should be obvious: how many of you have been in a class without rules? This code tells Flash that the class you're creating is public. That means that the information it contains can be shared by any other classes that are part of the same package or part of any other packages your program might be using. The information the class contains is freely available to all. (Although most of this book uses public classes, sometimes you'll want to prevent classes from sharing information, much like a school football team would not want to share its strategy with a competing school. In a case like that, you would define a class as internal. Internal classes share their information only with other classes that reside in the same package.)

- It gives the class an identifier, a name, which can be any name you choose. In this case, the class is called Main. The *M* is capitalized because, by convention, all class names begin with a capital letter.

> *You're not experiencing déjà vu! You have seen the word* Main *before. It's the name of the AS file that you're working on:* Main.as. *This is no coincidence. When you create a class, it has to be saved in a file that has an identical name to the class name. For every new class you create, you must create a new AS file that shares the same class name.*
>
> *The choice of the name* Main *is an old programmer's convention for the first file that gets the program up and running. Like the ignition switch on a car, it fires up the program and kick starts any other files you might be using. And when eventually you're working on big game-design projects with hundreds of files, you'll always remember that your main file is called* Main. *You'll see how all this works in later in the book, but for the first few chapters you'll be doing all the programming exclusively inside the* Main *class.*

The class definition's poor little curly braces are still empty. Let's put them to use!

Using the constructor method

The constructor method. That sounds daunting, doesn't it? In fact, it has the ring of science fiction–like doomsday peril about it. Like a kind of interdimensional quantum death ray used by a race of robotic drones to crush the spaceships of rival empires into the tin can–sized condiments they sell in their cafeteria vending machines. But before you put this book down and tiptoe quietly from the room, take a small step back and look at what you've done so far.

First, you created a package. But the package was nothing more than an empty container for the class. So next you created a class. But that was nothing more than an empty container. Lifeless! What to do? It seems so hopeless!

This is where the **constructor method** comes in. It makes things happen. Specifically, it throws the class into action as soon as the class is called upon by being instantiated, and any programming code it contains is run instantly. If the class definition alone is just an empty shell, the constructor method is like its heart and lungs. Fear not; you can come back into the room now. The constructor method is on your side!

4. Now create the constructor method for the Main class. Add the code in bold to the code you already wrote:

```
package
{
  public class Main
  {
    public function Main()
    {
    }
  }
}
```

As you can see, the constructor method is simply a block statement that looks an awful lot like the class definition. In fact, it has the same name: Main. This is no accident: all classes need to have constructor methods that are named exactly the same as the class name.

The other thing you'll recognize is the keyword public. As with the class definition, using the word public tells Flash that the constructor method is freely available to be used by different classes from different packages. (A strange quirk of the AS3.0 language, however, is that constructor functions can only ever be public.)

One new thing is the function keyword, which tells Flash that you're creating a **function definition**. Function definitions are simply block statements that perform actions. They do all the heavy lifting for your program. You can think of function definitions as dutiful servants who snap to attention with a prearranged set of chores as soon as you call on them. The constructor method, which will always be the first function definition you write when you create a class, has the special job of running any actions it contains immediately—as soon as the class is called upon and before any other methods you might be using are put to work. The constructor method is a bit like the head servant who's up at the crack of dawn, gets all the other servants out of bed, and greets you with a fresh pot of tea and the morning paper before you've even found your slippers.

The last thing you should notice about the constructor method is the set of parentheses after the method name:

```
Main()
```

Those empty parentheses allow you to provide the method with extra information, known as **parameters**, if the method needs it. You'll look at method parameters in detail fairly soon, but for now you just need to know that you must provide a set of parentheses when creating a function definition, even if those parentheses are empty.

Aligning code

You might have noticed an interesting pattern developing in the format of the code. Like a set of hollow wooden Russian dolls, the Main constructor method is inside the Main class, which is inside the package block statement. Each item sits inside the outer item's pair of curly braces, and you now have three levels of block statements. The only way that you can tell where one ends and the other begins is by whether the block statement's curly brace is open or closed.

As you can see, this could easily result in a confusing tangle of curly braces. If you weren't absolutely sure which pair of braces belonged to which block statement, you could start adding new code in the wrong place, and you'd get all sorts of errors when you tried to run the program.

The code format that you set in Flash's Preferences, and that I recommend you use for the projects in this book, helps solve this potential confusion somewhat. Figure 1-6 shows that you can draw an imaginary line between a block statement's opening brace and its closing brace. It very clearly shows you at which indentation level you should be adding code.

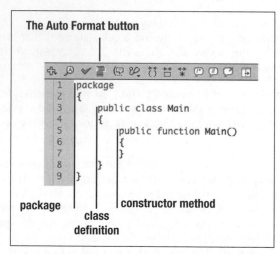

Figure 1-6. You can make sure that you're adding code in the right place by keeping each block statement's opening and closing braces aligned along an imaginary line.

A frequent confusion when writing code is not being certain where one block statement ends and another begins. If you use this suggested format and can see these imaginary divisions while you write, it will really help to prevent accidentally adding a line of code in the wrong place.

The ActionScript editing window toolbar also has a special button called Auto Format that will automatically format all your code according to the options you set in Flash's Preferences. If you get a bit lazy about keeping things neatly aligned, just click it and it will figure out all the indentation and spacing for you.

What's your directive?

The next bit of code that the program needs is a **directive**. One of the great pleasures of computer programming is being able to bandy about terms like *constructor method* and *directive* as though you were the captain of your own personal galactic cruise liner. Very simply, a directive is a single action that you want the program to perform. Methods are made up of one or more directives, and with them the program springs to life.

5. The directive you'll add to the constructor method will tell Flash to display the words "Hello World!" in its Output window when the program runs. Add the following text in bold to your program:

```
package
{
  public class Main
  {
    public function Main()
    {
      trace("Hello World!");
    }
  }
}
```

trace is a method built into the AS3.0 language that's used to send whatever is in parentheses to Flash's output window. If you want to send the Output window some text, that text needs to be surrounded by quotation marks. AS3.0 has lots of built-in methods, such as trace, that you can use to do all kinds of interesting things, and you'll be looking at many of them in detail over the course of this book.

Directives end in a semicolon like this one:

```
;
```

The semicolon is a basic piece of punctuation that lets Flash know that "The directive is finished!" It's like a period at the end of a sentence.

> *If you forget to add a semicolon at the end of a directive, Flash will still give you the benefit of the doubt and assume that you intended to add one. Your program will still run flawlessly without it. Thanks, Flash! But in the interest of good programming style, you should always add a semicolon. If you go on to learn other programming languages that aren't as lenient (and most aren't), you'll have already developed an excellent habit.*

Importing and extending the MovieClip class

All the code you've written so far is perfectly ready to go, except for one small technical detail. Your program needs an extra bit of code to help it actually output the words "Hello World!" onto the screen. To do this, you need to do two more things:

- Import Flash's built-in Sprite or MovieClip class.
- Use the new imported class to extend your own Main class.

When you **extend** a class, the class you're extending inherits all the properties and methods of that class without having to program them all from scratch. What does extending a class really mean? Maybe the following analogy will help.

Let's say you've spent a few months designing and building a car for a client with deep pockets but a rather difficult reputation. The car works perfectly well, gets good mileage, and you're particularly proud of the paint job. But on the day of delivery, the client comes by to pick it up and says, "Hmm . . . looks good, but I'm in Los Angeles and I really need to get to Ulaanbaatar by tomorrow morning for the World Cappuccino Tasting finals. So thanks, but I don't need the car anymore; I'm going to fly instead."

Before you panic and call the bank to make sure that the deposit cleared, consider this: a plane is merely a kind of car with wings. You've already done all the hard work: a good engine, a nice set of wheels, a cozy interior, and a really stellar paint job, if you do say so yourself. How much more work would it be to slap on a pair of wings and maybe add a navigation system? With the magic of AS3.0, not much at all: you just have to create a new class called plane that simply imports and extends your original car class. The new plane class inherits all the properties of the original car. That means that you can just take your car as is and do only the little bit of work you need to make it fly without having to redesign all the original parts of the car that are already working.

The reality of programming is similar, but also slightly different. Programmers usually build a class that is very general. In the previous example, suppose that the workshop has a class called Vehicle. It's a very general class, but it includes all the properties that are common to both planes and cars, and maybe even boats. If you want to make a Car class, all you need to do is import and extend the Vehicle class and add those components that make cars unique.

Importing and extending a class to make a new class is called **inheritance**, which is extremely useful and a huge time-saver. Flash has loads of built-in classes that you can import and use. I'll introduce many of these built-in classes over the course of this book.

The most important of these built-in classes for game designers are the Sprite and MovieClip classes because they contain special directives for getting the output of your program onto your screen. Which one should you use?

In the current program, you'll import the MovieClip class. The MovieClip class contains a **timeline**, which is particularly useful for making objects for games. (I'll be discussing Movie Clip timelines a bit later in the book.) The little Hello World program doesn't make use of a timeline, but because you'll be using the MovieClip class as part of almost every class you create in the rest of this book, you'll use it here for consistency.

One drawback of the MovieClip class is that its inclusion of a timeline adds slightly more size to the file and consumes a little more of the Flash Player's memory when the program runs. It's not much more (about 30 bytes), but the general rule of thumb is that if you're creating graphic objects that don't use a timeline, you should instead import and extend the Sprite class. The Sprite class is the same as the MovieClip class, but it doesn't include a timeline. If you use the Sprite class wherever you can, you will probably find your larger-scale programs and games run more quickly and smoothly because they won't be consuming as much memory or processing power.

> As your programs and games become bigger and more complex, they'll start to run sluggishly or become less responsive as you add more and more code. The responsiveness of software is something programmers call **performance**. In game design, in which lightning-quick response time and feedback from a game is essential for making the game fun to play, performance is the keystone around which your game will be built. Imagine playing Missile Command, hitting the fire button, and then having to wait for a second or two before your rocket launches. Wouldn't be much fun to play, would it? It doesn't matter how good or bad your sounds or graphics are; if your game lags and limps along like a tired racehorse en route to the glue factory, I guarantee that its performance is the only thing the players will notice and they'll be demanding their money back en masse. Performance is the vengeful deity to which game designers bow down and sacrifice their virgins, and you will certainly find yourself making many difficult decisions about what to sacrifice in your own games in the interest of performance. By using the Sprite class instead of the MovieClip class wherever you can, you'll save a slight bit of processing power that can add up to a lot of improved performance over the long run (and maybe spare the lives of a few horses and virgins along the way).

6. Importing a class to use in your program is conceptually identical to importing images or sounds into the Flash Library (which you might have done if you've worked with Flash before). The only difference is that you use a directive directly in your program instead of selecting an option from the Flash menu. Also, the imported class must be imported into the package *before* your class definition. To import the MovieClip class into your program, add the following bold text (I also added a blank line between the import directive and class definition so the program is a little easier to read):

```
package
{
  import flash.display.MovieClip;

  public class Main
  {
    public function Main()
    {
      trace("Hello World!");
    }
  }
}
```

The keyword import does the importing for you. The MovieClip class is part of another package called display. The display package contains a number of classes that—logically enough—help you display things on the screen. The display package itself resides in another folder called flash. All of Flash's built-in classes are in the flash folder, so you must use the keyword flash to remind Flash of this. The dots (.) that separate flash, display, and MovieClip indicate their relative positions in the directory structure. You're simply saying, "Hey Flash, I need the MovieClip class from the display package that's in the flash folder." This translates rather prosaically to this:

```
flash.display.MovieClip;
```

And don't forget the semicolon! You don't need to worry about where Flash actually goes to get all this, but you do need to remember that if you need to borrow any of Flash's built-classes, this is the format you have to use. Later in the book, when you start working with more than one package, you'll use this same format to import your own classes into other new classes that you'll have written from scratch.

> If this seems like suddenly a lot to absorb, don't worry! Importing classes to use with your programs is very routine, and you don't need to feel that you have to memorize all these technical details right now. You'll do a lot of importing of many different classes throughout the course of this book and you'll soon become comfortable with this format.

7. The next step is to tell your Main class to use all the properties and methods of the newly imported MovieClip class to help it display things on the screen. This is called **extending** the class, and you can extend your Main class by modifying the following line in bold:

```
package
{
 import flash.display.MovieClip;

  public class Main extends MovieClip
  {
    public function Main ()
    {
      trace("Hello World!");
    }
  }
}
```

It's very simple; you just need to add the keyword extends, followed by the class you want to use; in this case, the MovieClip class.

As discussed, importing and extending a class is called inheritance. It will not be at all obvious to you how it works at this stage, so don't worry too much if you don't really understand what's happening or why you need to do this. Later in the book you'll see some detailed examples of exactly how this works and learn what a thing of heady and terrifying power inheritance can be. It will be fun!

Adding comments to your code

When you're writing a program, it is often useful to write a short note about what a particular section of code does. This is especially helpful if you've solved a complex programming problem that you're not certain you'll actually understand the next time you look at it. It also helps other people who might be looking at your code to understand it better.

There are two ways to add comments to your code. The first is by using two forward slashes:

```
//
```

Any text you add on the same line after these forward slashes will not be interpreted by AS.30 as programming code. You can write anything you like, and the AS3.0 compiler will ignore it when your program runs. Here's an example:

```
// Hi mom!! This is a comment and you can write whatever you like here.
```

Sometimes you might want to write a comment that contains more text than you can easily fit on one line. You can do this by creating a multiline comment. Multiline comments look like this:

```
/*
Anything between the opening and
closing multiline comment characters
will not be interpreted as
programming code.
*/
```

Multiline comments start with the character sequence /* and end with the character sequence */. You can write anything you like between them, over any number of lines.

In addition to leaving notes to yourself, comments are especially useful for disabling sections of code if you want to test how your program behaves without them

8. To get used to using comments, add one to the Hello World program. Modify your code with the following line in bold:

```
package
{
 import flash.display.MovieClip;

  public class Main extends MovieClip
  {
    public function Main ()
    {
      //The next line outputs text
      trace("Hello World!");
    }
  }
}
```

Before you go any further, ensure that your program looks like Figure 1-7.

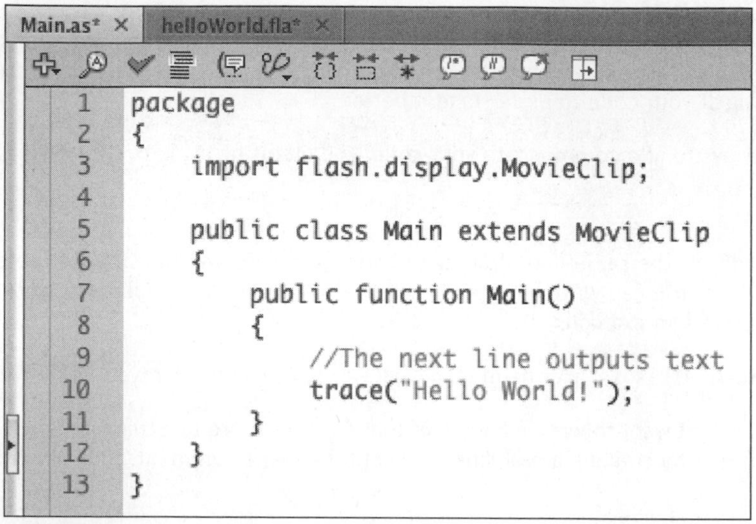

```
1  package
2  {
3      import flash.display.MovieClip;
4
5      public class Main extends MovieClip
6      {
7          public function Main()
8          {
9              //The next line outputs text
10             trace("Hello World!");
11         }
12     }
13 }
```

Figure 1-7. Add a comment to your code.

The ActionScript editor window colors comments gray so that you can easily differentiate them from your code.

9. Finally, if everything looks good, save the Main.as file.

You're now ready to see result of the program in action.

Publishing the SWF file

Earlier I mentioned that the FLA and AS files work together to produce a SWF file. The SWF file is your finished product, and you need to create one to see how your program works. The act of creating a SWF file is known as **publishing** it.

The first step is to bind the AS file with an FLA file. You need to do this because the SWF file will be created by software components that are part of the FLA file; the AS file contains the logic that will control these components.

You'll set the Main class as the FLA file's **document class.** Any class that's assigned as a document class is automatically run when the SWF file runs. This is a vital step in getting your program to work. Follow these steps:

1. Click the helloWorld.fla tab near the top of the editing window to return to the helloWorld.fla file. You'll know you've done this when you see your program replaced by the FLA's empty stage.

2. Check to see whether the Properties panel is open. If it isn't, display it by selecting Window ➤ Properties.

3. In the Properties panel there's a field (a box where you can type text) called Class. In the Class field, enter Main (this links your Main class with the FLA file). Your Properties panel should now look like Figure 1-8. (If the Class field does not appear in the Properties panel, select the black arrow Selection Tool in the Tools toolbar and click the empty white rectangle in the middle of the workspace, which is known as the stage.)

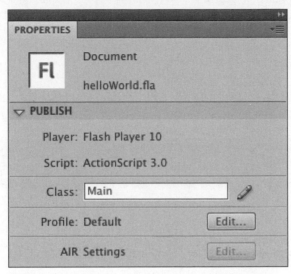

Figure 1-8. Enter Main into the Class box of the Properties panel.

4. Save the helloWorld.fla file.

5. Finally, select Control ➤ Test Movie. Flash will publish the FLA file and automatically generate a SWF file (a Flash movie file) called helloWorld.swf in the same directory as the FLA and AS files. You should see the Output panel appear, displaying the words Hello World! (see Figure 1-9).

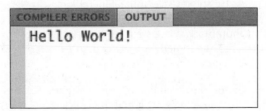

Figure 1-9. If you've followed the instructions correctly, you should see the words Hello World! displayed in the Output panel.

Although selecting Test Movie from the Control menu is usually the quickest and easiest way to publish a SWF file, you can also select File ➤ Publish. The difference is that the Test Movie option runs the SWF file immediately after publishing it. This is great if you want to test how everything is working while you're still writing your program or making your game. You'll usually use the Publish option only when everything is finished, and you just want to publish the latest version of the SWF file without needing to run it as well.

You can change many parameters that determine exactly how the SWF file is published from the Flash SWF publish settings. To access the publish settings, select File ➤ Publish Settings and then select Flash. You won't be looking at any of these custom settings in this book, but you should know that they exist because you might find yourself working on a project when you'll need to make some changes to them.

It didn't work?

There might be an unlucky few of you who did not see the output shown in Figure 1-9. Instead, you saw a Compiler Errors window, showing you an error message you probably don't understand, such as the example shown in Figure 1-10.

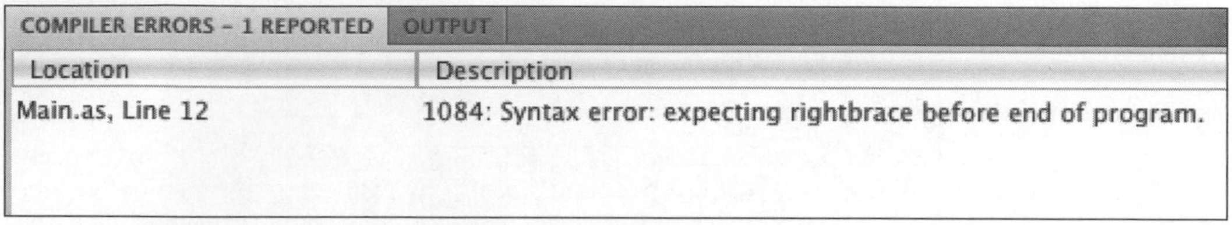

COMPILER ERRORS – 1 REPORTED	OUTPUT	
Location	**Description**	
Main.as, Line 12	1084: Syntax error: expecting rightbrace before end of program.	

Figure 1-10. If you made a small mistake in your code, such as forgetting to close one of the curly braces as in this example, you will receive an error message in the Compiler Errors window.

This error message means that somehow, somewhere, there is a mistake in your code.

When Flash creates the SWF file, it **compiles** your AS3.0 code. Compiling the code is the job of a software component that's part of Flash called the **compiler**. It checks to make sure that your code is okay; if it is, it creates the SWF file. If it finds a problem, it gives you an error message.

Unfortunately, Flash's compiler doesn't know what you intend your code to do; it can only tell you what it expects and what it doesn't understand. If you're lucky, it precisely pinpoints the problem. But more often than not, it will just be able to give you a general idea of where to look and what to look for. It's a bit like a two-year-old yelping with pain and pointing to his big toe. You know where the problem is, but whether it's a thumbtack, a bee sting, or just another way of saying, "The last time I did this you gave me some chocolate," the remedy will depend on experience, skeptical investigation, and a thoughtful diagnosis.

The Compiler Error window tells you on which line of your program it thinks your problem lies. If you click the error message with the mouse to select it and then click the Go to Source button, it will actually highlight the spot in your code for you. For the rest, it's up to you to intelligently analyze what you think Flash is looking for and what you might have to fix or change to get your program running properly.

If you're not sure where the problem with your program lies, ask yourself whether one or more of these might be the issue:

- Did you save the `Main.as` file before you published the SWF file?
- Did you spell everything correctly and use the correct case?
- Did you save the files in the correct location, and do the spelling and case of your folders and files match the package and class names?
- Are all the AS3.0 keywords (such as `import`, `package`, and `function`) a dark blue color? If one of them isn't, that's a clear indication that you might have spelled or capitalized it incorrectly.
- Have you closed all your curly braces and parentheses?
- Did you enter the correct class name, `Main`, in the Class field in the `helloWorld.fla` Properties panel?
- Did your cat jump on the keyboard while you were in the kitchen getting another cup of coffee?

And here are some more general pointers that you should always keep in mind while debugging:

- If you receive more than one error message, always try and fix the first one first. Subsequent errors are usually the result of bits of code that depend on the earlier bits of code working correctly. Fix the first one, and the correction will cascade through the code and often magically correct the rest.
- Check the line of code that's *just above the line that Flash thinks is the problem*. Often, small mistakes in the line above, which might not be big enough in themselves to generate a compile error, could be enough to trip up the code in the next line down.
- *Always save the AS file you're working on before you republish it!* I can't stress enough how common an oversight this is. A programmer will find an error and fix it, but then gets exactly the same error message when the SWF is republished. This is because the file wasn't saved after the fix was made, so the earlier saved version of the file is the one that Flash is actually compiling.
- Make only one single change at a time between republishing. If your program worked and then suddenly stopped working after you made that change, you know exactly what is causing the problem. If you republish it only after making five changes and it doesn't work, you won't know which of those five things is tripping you up.
- Finally, the programmer's universal mantra: Test Early; Test Often. Do lots of testing and solve lots of tiny manageable problems early on to avoid having to deal with hulking intractable problems that can grind your project to a halt later.

Except for a few exceptional cases, this is the last discussion of debugging issues in any detail in this book. You'll be on your own from here on out, but the sooner you gain practice debugging your own code, the better. Experience counts for everything in this realm, and there is no better whetstone upon which to sharpen your skills as a programmer than a tricky debugging problem.

Also, get used to the Compiler Errors window—you'll be seeing a lot of it! It will become your closest ally in finding and tracking down problems.

Project Panel

A new addition to Flash 10 is a great feature called the Project panel, which allows you to manage all your project files and folders from one convenient place.

When you're working with only two or three files (as you will be for the next few chapters), the usefulness of the Project panel might not seem all that apparent, but it certainly will by Chapter 8 (you'll be juggling a small army of AS files). It's also extremely useful if you're working on a number of different projects at the same time because simply selecting the project name from the menu will make all the project files readily accessible. It also includes some more advanced features such as the ability to automatically create classes based on templates. You can also add and delete files and folders directly from the comfort of the Project panel without having to open Windows Explorer or OSX Finder.

You'll notice the Project panel on the left side of the Flash workspace. (If you are not using the Developer workspace or if it's not visible, select Window ➤ Other Panels ➤ Project.) Let's create a project for the Hello World program.

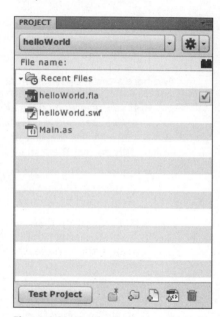

1. In the Project panel, click the Projects drop-down menu and select Quick Project. All the files you're currently using will be added to the project, and the project will be named after the FLA file; in this case, helloWorld. Your Project panel should look now like Figure 1-11. (Depending on your monitor resolution, the right side of the Project panel might not be entirely visible. Drag the right edge of the window to increase its width if you need to.)

2. When you create a Quick Project, Flash automatically uses the FLA file as the **default document**, which it indicates by a check mark next to it. The default document is the FLA file from which Flash creates the SWF file. The Quick Project option also automatically gives the project the same name as the default document.

Now that your project has been created, you can test your program and publish the SWF simply by clicking the Test Project button. You can also browse and edit each of the files just by clicking their names in the Project panel.

Figure 1-11. Use the Project panel to help you keep your files organized.

> *In most cases, using* Quick Project *will serve you perfectly well, but if you want to create a project from files or folders that aren't already open, you should use the* Open Project *option. Selecting* Open Project *allows you to browse to a folder that you want to use as your project root, assign a project name, and then manually assign a default document.*

For game development, the Project panel will become an extremely useful tool to help keep all your projects organized and will speed up your development time. Try to get into the habit of using it with each project.

A little more about AS3.0 and the Flash Player

At the end of this process, you have a SWF file that you can take to any computer and run, as long as the Flash Player is also installed on that same computer. The fact that the SWF file needs the help of the Flash Player to run is very important. As a game designer, you need to know why this is and the kinds of limitations it might impose on you. Let's take a closer look at what's going on behind the scenes when you publish a SWF file.

AS3.0 is a type of **high-level programming language**. High-level programming languages, such as Java, C++, and Visual Basic, are designed so that humans can easily read, write, and understand them. They use real English words such as *function* and *class*, and use elements of English grammar such as quotation marks and semicolons. But computers don't understand English. Try asking your computer for help with the dishes this evening, and I expect you'll get nothing but a stony silence (if not, let someone, hopefully a professional, know about it!).

At their most basic level, computers, understand only a binary language of 1s and 0s. So all the AS3.0 code has to be translated into binary code so the computer can understand it. Fortunately, you don't have to do that manually, so you can put away that pencil and paper. Flash has a built-in compiler (a software component that translates code) to do the job for you.

Keep in mind that, unlike writing a program in a language such as C++ or Visual Basic, Flash's compiler doesn't compile your code so it's directly readable by your computer's central processing unit (CPU), which is your computer's main "brain." It compiles it only so that it can be read by the Flash Player software.

Before you can run any of your AS3.0 programs, the Flash Player software has to be installed on your system because it's the job of the Flash Player to interpret your code to the CPU. Because of this, AS3.0, like Java, is known as an **interpreted programming language**. Interpreted languages use a piece of software known as a **virtual machine**, which acts as an interpreter between the CPU and your program. The Flash Player is AS3.0's virtual machine.

Interpreted languages have a number of advantages over languages that compile directly to the CPU. Most importantly, it means that your programs will run flawlessly and exactly the same way on any operating system (Windows, Linux, or OS X) that has the Flash Player installed. You only need to write your code once, and the Flash Player, which is written for each operating system that it's available for, will take care of the job of making sure your code runs properly. The other advantage is that the Flash Player protects the computer it's running on from any code that you might have written that could accidentally freeze or crash your system. All this tends to make interpreted languages very convenient and reliable languages to program with.

One major disadvantage with interpreted languages, however, is in the area of performance. Imagine visiting a foreign country where you don't speak the language, but instead are accompanied by a translator who painstakingly translates every word you say and then translates each reply back into English. It would be a very slow and tedious process. Unfortunately, this is exactly what's happening between the Flash Player and the CPU when you run your AS3.0 programs. How slow is it? Exact numbers are hard to come by, but a reasonable estimate might be 10 to 20 times slower than if the code were compiled as binary machine language and running directly on the CPU. (By "slow," I mean exactly how quickly the CPU can process each instruction or calculation your program asks it to perform.)

Adobe has done a great deal with each successive generation of the Flash Player to improve performance, but this is a major handicap for game developers who depend on squeezing every iota of processing power out of a system to maximize performance in their games. This is why 3D Flash games, which require a vast amount of processing power to calculate geometry, struggle to compete with the rich graphic splendor of 3D on the game consoles (such as the Xbox, PlayStation, and Wii.) The consoles use custom compilers that optimize all the game code to run directly as machine language on their specific processors.

If you're thinking of eventually getting into game design for the consoles, however, you're still in pretty good shape with Flash: the skills you'll learn by programming in AS3.0 can be directly applied to programming for consoles when you're ready to take that step. The AS3.0 programming environment is also probably the most user-friendly programming environment you can learn in. And, hey, make a game with Flash, post it on the Web, and you've got a potential worldwide audience for it—that's power!

Naming conventions

Before this chapter closes, let's take a quick look at an aspect of programming practice called **naming conventions**.

You might have noticed something peculiar about the kinds of names that you gave the file, class, and method names. Have a look at the choice of file name for the FLA:

```
helloWorld
```

Does it look a little strange to you? It should. You'll notice that the *h* is lowercase and the *W* is uppercase, and there's no space between the two words. This is a style of giving things names that programmers affectionately call **camel case** (also known as humpBackNotation). Can you guess why it's called that? I'm sure you can!

With camel case you can write a compound phrase using more than one word. The words are not separated with blank spaces, and the phrase is still easily readable you and by AS3.0. Blank spaces in the middle of compound names are the programming equivalent to foxes in a chicken coop—avoid them at all cost! The AS3.0 code compiler throws its hands in the air when it encounters a blank space where there shouldn't be one, so camel case was developed by programmers as an efficient way of writing compound words or phrases without spaces.

Camel case is an important feature of naming conventions, which are rules that programmers decide on before they start a project about the style they'll use for creating package, variable, class, object, method, and file names. By strictly sticking to these naming conventions, programmers are better able to dodge the easy-to-make errors that come from misspelling or incorrectly capitalizing any elements in their code. They can also easily see what kind of programming object they're dealing with simply by the way it's been capitalized.

There are two types of camel case that you'll be using throughout this book:

- **Lower camel case**: startsWithLowerCaseLetter. You'll be using this case for package names, variables, methods, and instances. You'll also be using lower camel case for the names of the FLA files (for example, helloWorld.fla).

- **Upper camel case**: StartsWithUpperCaseLetter. You'll use this case for class names and constructor method names. You'll also use it for the names of AS class files such as Main.as, which must be named exactly like the class they define in the file.

Because ActionScript is a case sensitive programming language, keep in mind that helloWorld is different from HelloWorld, which is different still from helloworld. Make sure that you follow all the capitalization as it appears in the text; otherwise, your programs won't work. If you write a program that seems perfect in every way but just doesn't run, check your spelling and capitalization! This is one of the most common mistakes that novice programmers make, and many a programmer will tell you tales of woe about debugging sessions running till 4 a.m. where the culprit, when eventually smoked out, was revealed to be a single misspelled or incorrectly capitalized word. The author of this book refuses comment!

Summary

Well done! You've written and published your first AS3.0 program! It wasn't so hard, was it? In fact, congratulate yourself for getting through one of the most difficult chapters in the book. I've laid the programming foundations for all the games and projects to come, and you'll find that you'll use this same format for setting up your programs over and over again in your career as a game designer.

This chapter has covered a lot of theory, and if you are new to programming, you might have found some of it a bit heavy. I sympathize with you! But you don't necessarily need to completely understand all the theory to create games. The most important thing is that you know what programming code you need to use to get the results you want. A deeper understanding will come with time, a lot of trial and error, and doing as much experimenting with your own projects as you can.

A deep dark secret that most programmers often don't like to share with the rest of the world is that a great deal of the world's software is built with a little bit of understanding and an awful lot of "copy/paste." That's all part of the learning process. Of course, you need to know exactly what bits of code you need to copy and paste, and how to change them to get the results you want, which is something only experience (and this book!) can teach you. But as time goes on, you'll soon recognize the usual suspects and be copying and pasting to your heart's content along with the best of them.

I encourage you to go back to parts of this chapter that might have been little fuzzy the first time through to try to get a solid understanding of them before continuing much further. If you don't get it all just yet, don't worry! If you managed to get the little Hello World program running and you generally understand what made it work, you're in the game!

In the next chapter, you'll use this same model to start building a simple children's interactive storybook. See you there!

Chapter 2

MAKING OBJECTS

When you read a novel, you usually start on the first page, read through each page sequentially, and finish on the last page. You can't change the order of the pages without making a mess of the story line, and you certainly can't tell the characters what they should do or change the outcome of the novel if you don't like how it ends.

The development of computers over the last few decades has completely changed that scenario. With tools such as Flash, you can now create completely interactive media. Readers or viewers are no longer just passive spectators to a story; they are active participants.

The next three chapters will cover a number of important techniques that form the basis of what you need to know to build interactive media. Although the focus will be on how you can use these techniques to make games, you can also use them as the basis for building highly interactive Flash websites.

I'll cover all the core programming and design skills that you need to know, so if you've never used Flash before or never done any programming, relax—it's all here. By the end of Chapter 4, you'll have a broad repertoire of skills you'll be able to use to build even very complex interactive environments such as point-and-click adventure games and text-based logic and puzzle games. And you'll be all set with all the skills you need to know when you start to look specifically at video game design.

Understanding Interactive Objects

AS3.0 is what's known as an object-oriented programming language (OOP). **Objects** are at the core of everything you do, but what are they? Objects are just "things" that you can control with programming code. Those objects can be graphics, animations, videos, buttons, or sounds—really anything at all. I'll be discussing objects in much more detail a little later on, but for now all you need to know is that an object is something that you want to be able to control and program.

If you've heard or read about object-oriented programming before now, you might have bumped into other words surrounding the phrase such as "advanced" or "not for beginners." Actually, nothing could be further from the truth. By learning about objects right from the beginning and understanding how to control them, doors of understanding will start to open up for you that will provide you with immense control over your programming code in a very short time.

Over the next few pages you'll create your first objects: three scenes for an interactive children's storybook. You'll then create some buttons to control those objects. In Chapter 3 you'll learn to program those buttons using event listeners, and in Chapter 4 you'll add some characters to the pages and control those characters using properties. But you can just file that away for later because you'll take just one small step at a time.

If you've used Flash, creating objects is an almost laughably simple process that you've probably already done many times without even realizing it. If you haven't used Flash very much, don't worry; I'll cover everything you need to know in detail in this chapter.

There are two ways to create objects in Flash. You can create them with AS3.0 programming code or in Flash's visual authoring environment. One of Flash's great strengths as a game development platform is that it enables you to draw and animate complex objects without having to look at a single line of code and then use those objects anywhere in your program. This is a huge time-saver, and it's also loads of fun!

In the next example, you'll draw three scenes for a children's interactive storybook and set them up as objects that you can control with code. This chapter will cover the following topics:

- Flash's vector drawing tools
- Creating symbols in the Library
- Instances and the stage
- Making buttons

In this chapter, you'll make these objects; in the next chapter, you'll program them.

Setting up the work environment

Your first job is to create the files that you'll need for this project. Like the Hello World program from Chapter 1, you need to start with an FLA and an AS file. You'll create the FLA and then use it to create a Quick Project in Flash's Project panel.

1. Find a convenient spot on your hard drive and create a project folder called InteractiveStorybook.

2. Open Flash. Select File ➤ New and choose Flash File (ActionScript 3.0) from the New Document dialog box.

3. Click the OK button.

4. Select File ➤ Save As.

5. Give your new FLA file the name interactiveStorybook.fla.

6. Find the InteractiveStorybook project folder that you created in step 1.

7. Click Save to save the file.

8. In the Project panel, click the drop-down menu. Select Quick Project. You'll see the new interactiveStorybook.fla file you just created appear as a project file.

9. In the Project panel, click the New File button, as shown in Figure 2-1.

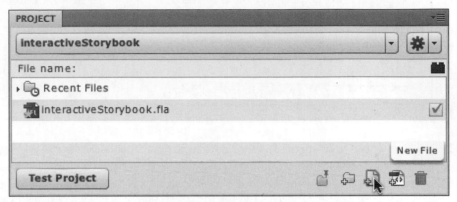

Figure 2-1. Create a new AS file in the Project panel.

10. Enter Main.as in the File field.

11. Check that ActionScript is selected as the File type. If the Create File window looks like it does in Figure 2-2, click the Create File button.

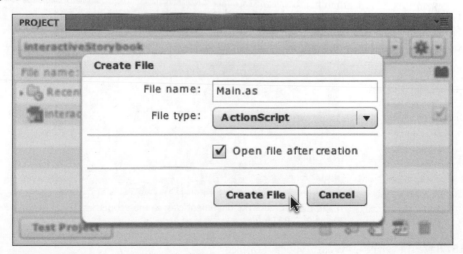

Figure 2-2. Create a new AS file called Main.as in the Project panel.

12. Flash will create and open the Main.as file.

Your Project panel should now look like Figure 2-3.

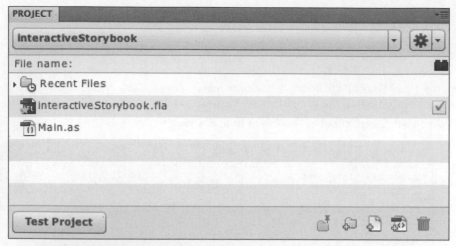

Figure 2-3. The Project panel shows the new FLA and AS files.

13. Finally, you need to create the FLA file's document class. Double-click the interactiveStorybook.fla file in the Project panel.

14. To the right of the stage you'll notice a panel called Properties. (If the Properties panel isn't open, select Window ➤ Properties.) In the Publish section, you'll see a text field called Class. Enter Main in the Class field. Your Properties panel should now look like Figure 2-4.

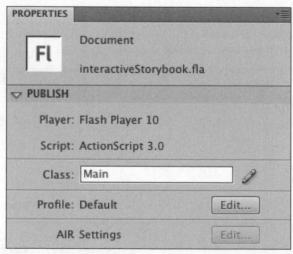

Figure 2-4. Create the document class in the Properties panel of the FLA file.

15. Save the interactiveStorybook.fla file.

Now that you've created the FLA and AS files and have set Main as the document class, you're ready to start creating the storybook.

Creating the first page

The interactive storybook will have three pages. Create the first page by following these steps:

1. Make sure that your interactiveStorybook.fla tab is open on the screen. If it's not, double-click the interactiveStorybook.fla file in the Project panel or in the tab menu near the top of the stage.

2. Select Insert ➤ New Symbol from the menu to open the Create New Symbol dialog box. Click the Advanced button to see all the extra settings available to you, as shown in Figure 2-5. (If your Create New Symbol dialog box already looks like Figure 2-5, it's already in Advanced mode.)

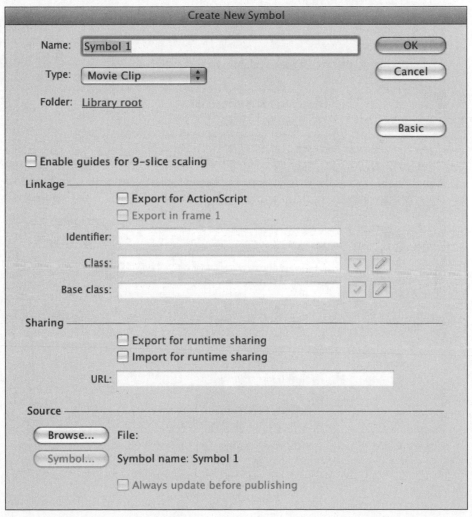

Figure 2-5. Create New Symbol dialog box

3. Enter StartPage in the Name field and make sure that Movie Clip is selected as the Type symbol. In the Linkage section, select the Export for ActionScript option. As soon as you do this, a number of other options and fields will be automatically set for you. The New Symbol dialog box should now look like Figure 2-6.

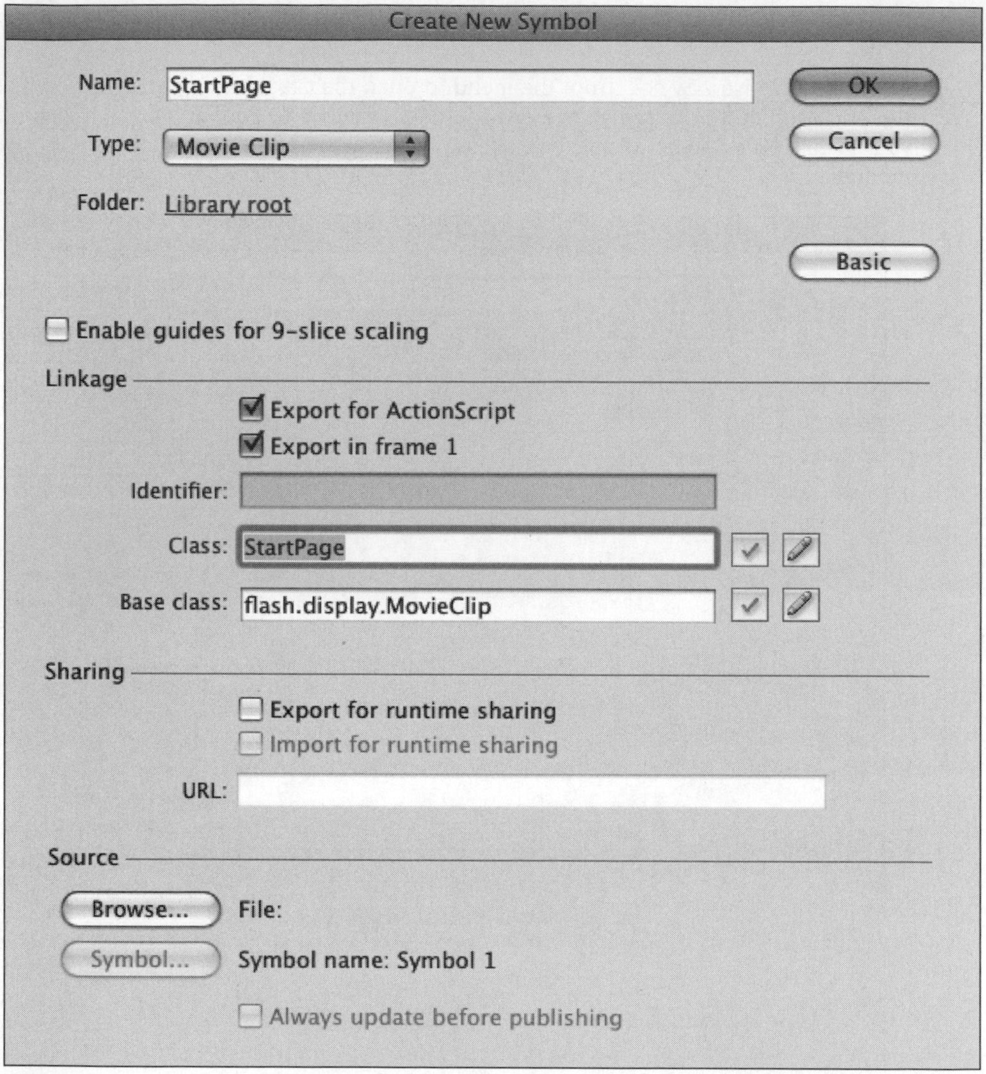

Figure 2-6. Create a new symbol called StartPage. Make sure that Export for ActionScript is selected.

4. Click the OK button. A warning dialog box will appear (see Figure 2-7), warning you that Flash couldn't find the class you've specified but will generate it for you automatically when you publish the SWF file. This is merely Flash's helpful way of saying, "Um, it doesn't look like you've got a class called StartPage yet. But don't worry, I'll create one for you!" You know you haven't created this class yet, so that's just fine. "Thanks, Flash! Such a helpful little fellow!" (You can click Don't show again. to prevent this warning from appearing the next time you create a symbol.)

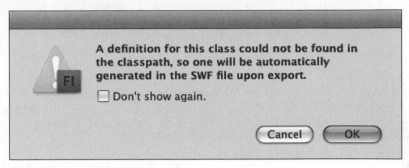

Figure 2-7. Class definition warning

5. Click the OK button to ignore this warning.

When you clicked the OK button in step 5, two things happened:

First, Flash created a new symbol in the Library called StartPage.

In the Library you can view all the symbols you create and all the **assets** (additional imported files) such as sound, images, and videos that you import into Flash. The Library panel is located in the panel on the left of the Flash workspace. (If you don't see it, select Window ➤ Library.) Your Library should now look like Figure 2-8.

Figure 2-8. Your new StartPage symbol is in the Library.

> I recommend using the Developer workspace for the projects in this book. To set up Flash's Developer workspace, select Window ➤ Workspace ➤ Developer. Flash's workspace is designed using **panels**. Each area of the workspace, including the Library or Properties, is a panel. You can rearrange, minimize, and mix and match these panels in whatever order you like. It's quite a nice feature but it's also easy to accidentally delete a panel or drag it into some strangely inaccessible part of the workspace. It can cause a lot of frustration if the panel you are using suddenly disappears and you can't figure out how to get it back. Fortunately, it's very easy to restore the workspace to its original state if this happens. If you're in the Developer workspace, click the Developer button near the top-left corner of the Flash window (next to the search box.) Select Reset 'Developer' from the option menu. All the panels in the workspace will return to their original state.

Flash also placed you in **symbol editing mode** for the StartPage symbol. If you are new to Flash, this might be a bit confusing. You created StartPage as a Movie Clip symbol. Movie Clip symbols have timelines and stages. When you enter symbol editing mode, Flash replaces the main stage and timeline with the stage and timeline of the Movie Clip symbol you selected. If there's any doubt about which stage and timeline you're working in, have a look at the top-left corner of the stage shown in Figure 2-9.

Figure 2-9. Are you working on Flash's main stage or inside a Movie Clip symbol?

If you see the name of a symbol with the Movie Clip icon next to it, you know you're in symbol editing mode and that the stage and timeline you see on the screen belong to the that symbol. If you just see Scene 1, you know you're working on Flash's main stage. (To exit symbol editing mode and return to the main stage, simply click Scene 1. To reenter symbol editing mode, you need to select the symbol again from the Library by double-clicking it.)

Drawing the first page

You'll now create a page for the characters in the storybook. This project will take you on a quick introductory tour of Flash's vector-drawing capabilities and show you how to organize graphics using layers on the timeline. Figure 2-10 shows what the finished page will look like.

Figure 2-10. A happy sunny scene for the first page of the storybook

Drawing the background

The first thing you'll do is create the sky. It's just a big blue rectangle that will completely fill the stage. Follow these steps:

1. In the Tools toolbar, select a color for the sky by clicking the Fill Color box. (If the Tools toolbar isn't visible, select Window ➤ Tools.) A color palette will open, and the mouse pointer will change to an eyedropper to allow you to choose an appropriate color for the sky. Figure 2-11 shows what this looks like. (If you have a small monitor, the Fill Color box might actually be hiding under the Properties panel. You can access it another way by selecting the Paint Bucket tool and selecting the Fill Color box from the Properties panel.)

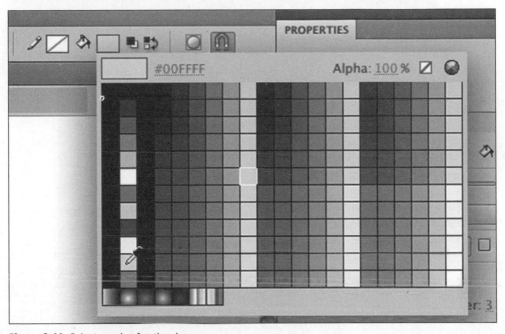

Figure 2-11. Select a color for the sky.

Next to the Fill Color box is another box with a pencil icon on the left side. This box allows you to select the **stroke color**, which refers to the color of a shape's outside border. If you select a stroke color, your rectangle will be drawn with a colored border around it. For this example, I didn't want a border for the sky, so I made sure that none was selected (indicated by the red stripe through the stroke color box). Look carefully at the top-right corner of the color palette shown in Figure 2-11, and you'll notice that you can choose this "no color" option for either the stroke or fill color by selecting the small white square with the red stripe through it.

2. Use the Rectangle tool to draw a rectangle on the stage, as shown in Figure 2-12. The size and shape of the rectangle doesn't matter for this step.

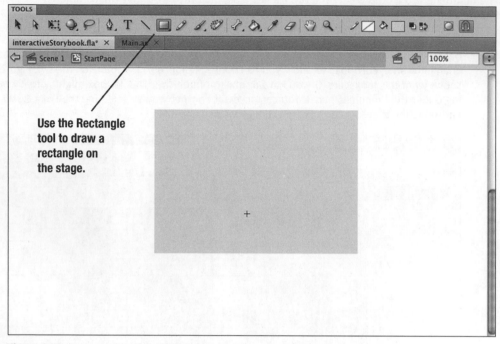

Figure 2-12. Draw a rectangle on the stage.

3. Select the rectangle by clicking it once with the Selection tool, which is the first tool (the black arrow) on the toolbar. (If you drew the rectangle with a border around it, double-click it to select both the fill and stroke completely.) You will know that the rectangle has been selected when you see a black dot pattern appear across the surface, as shown in Figure 2-13.

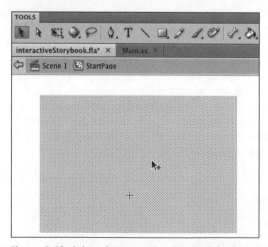

Figure 2-13. Select the rectangle with the Selection tool.

The Properties panel is **context-sensitive** (it gives you information about whatever object you've selected on the stage, and that information will change if you select another object). The Properties panel allows you to change the properties of selected objects. You want to change the height and width of the rectangle so that it matches the dimensions of the stage. You also want to align its top-left corner with the center point of the Movie Clip symbol's stage.

4. While the rectangle is still selected, use the Properties panel to change its W (width) property to 550 and its H (height) to 400. The numbers you enter here represent the size of the object in **pixels**, which are tiny dots that are the smallest possible image that can be displayed on the stage. All visual elements are made up of lots of tiny pixels, and you can see them if you look carefully. I'll discuss pixels in a bit more detail soon.

5. Change the rectangle's X (horizontal) position to 0 and the Y (vertical) position to 0. Your Properties panel should now match that shown in Figure 2-14.

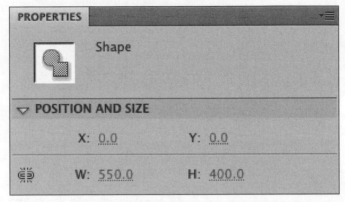

Figure 2-14. Change the size and position of the rectangle in the Properties panel.

6. As soon as you enter those numbers, the size of the rectangle will change, and the top-left hand corner will snap to the small black crosshairs in the middle of the stage. The crosshairs (also known as the **registration point**) represent position 0 for both the X and Y position (this is important to remember, and you will be returning to this soon).

7. From the Tools toolbar, select the Hand tool and use it to scroll the stage so the entire rectangle is visible, as shown in Figure 2-15. (Double-check that the rectangle's top-left corner is aligned against the bottom-right quadrant of the crosshairs. This will be very important for correctly positioning the page later.) The Hand tool doesn't move the object on the stage; it just *repositions your view of it*. The effect it has is the same as using the horizontal and vertical scrollbars on the bottom and right of the stage.

Figure 2-15. Use the Hand tool to reposition the stage so that whole rectangle is visible in your work area.

Before going any further, now is a good time to organize the drawing layers.

Organizing layers and the timeline

If you look at the bottom of the workspace you'll see the timeline (if it isn't visible, select Window ➤ Timeline.) The timeline is most commonly used for animation (I'll be discussing that function in some detail a bit later in the book), but it's also used to create drawing layers as in Photoshop or other graphic design software. Using layers allows you to create drawings or graphics on different layers, and then arrange those layers so that graphics sit above or below other graphics.

Look at the bottom of the Flash workspace, just below the stage, and you'll see something that looks much like Figure 2-16.

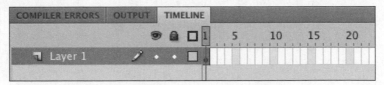

Figure 2-16. StartPage's timeline

Layer 1 is the current layer on which you've made your drawing. To the right of it, just below the number 1 and with the red line running though it, is a black dot known as a **keyframe**. Black keyframes tell you that that frame has some graphics on it. In this case, it's the blue background rectangle that you've just drawn. The red rectangle, which is highlighting frame 1, is known as the **playhead** (sometimes referred to as the **scrubber**). The playhead is used to navigate between frames.

To help you stay organized, create two more layers: one for the foreground drawings and one for the text.

1. Click the New Layer button on the bottom-left corner of the timeline to create two new layers, as shown in Figure 2-17. Notice that the keyframes of these layers are empty circles, indicating that they don't contain any graphics.

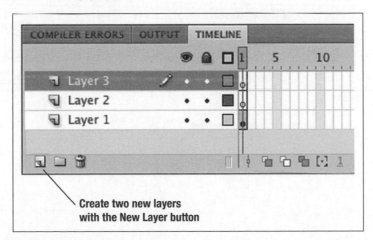

Figure 2-17. Create two new layers.

2. It's a good idea to label the layers properly so you can quickly identify them. To change the name of a layer, click the layer name with the mouse and enter the new name. Change Layer 1 to background, change Layer 2 to foreground, and change Layer 3 to characters. Figure 2-18 shows how your timeline should now look.

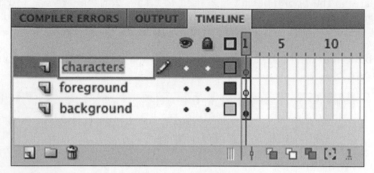

Figure 2-18. Give your new layers descriptive names.

3. You'll create the next set of drawings on the foreground layer. But before that, you should lock the background layer so that you don't accidentally click it and possibly undo all the work you've already done. To lock the background layer, click the small black circle in the column indicated by the padlock. Figure 2-19 shows what the background layer looks like when it's locked. (If you need to make any changes to the background layer later, you can unlock it by clicking its padlock icon.)

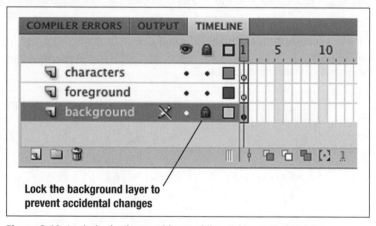

Figure 2-19. Lock the background layer while working on other layers.

4. Click the empty keyframe on the foreground layer to select it, as shown in Figure 2-20.

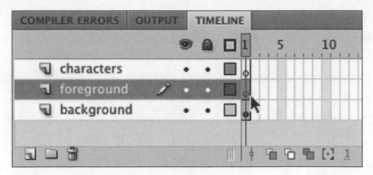

Figure 2-20. Make sure that the keyframe in the foreground layer is selected.

You're now ready to draw something on the foreground layer.

Drawing the foreground objects

Now that you've created a new layer for the foreground objects, let's draw something on it. One of the great pleasures of working with Flash is that you can create simple but effective graphics very easily using its built-in vector drawing tools. Put together a few circles and squares in the right way, and even if you think you don't have much design talent, you might still be able to come up with something fun and colorful.

Before you start, you might want to switch on one of Flash's **snapping** options. With snapping turned on, Flash will assist you in aligning objects by "snapping" them in place next to other objects. There are a number of different snapping options to choose from, but for this project, use Snap to Objects. To turn on Snap to Objects, select View ➤ Snapping ➤ Snap to Objects. You can also turn on snapping by clicking the Snap to Objects button in the toolbar (it looks like a magnet and is on the right side of the toolbar).

> *If you ever make a mistake while doing any of these drawings, simply undo your last move by selecting* Edit ➤ Undo. *If you're using OSX, hold down the* Apple *key and press* Z; *if you're using Windows, hold down* Ctrl *and press* Z. *Flash will allow you to undo up to 100 times, and you can increase this number in* Preferences *if you need to.*

Creating a hill

The first thing you'll draw on the foreground layer is a green hill.

1. On the foreground layer, draw a green rectangle at the bottom of the stage, as shown in Figure 2-21. Make sure that you create the rectangle without a border.

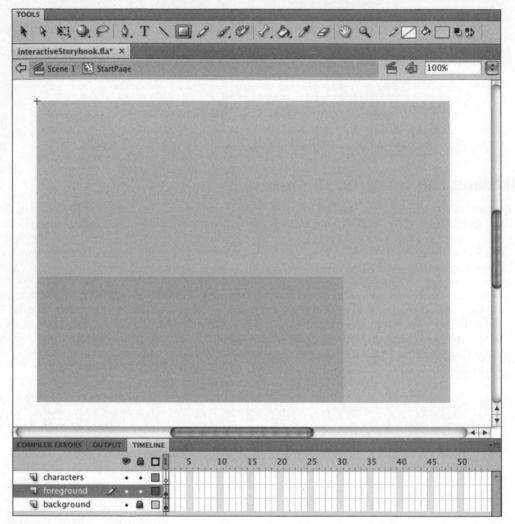

Figure 2-21. Draw a green rectangle.

2. Draw another green rectangle on top of the first one at a 90-degree angle to form an *L* shape, as shown in Figure 2-22.

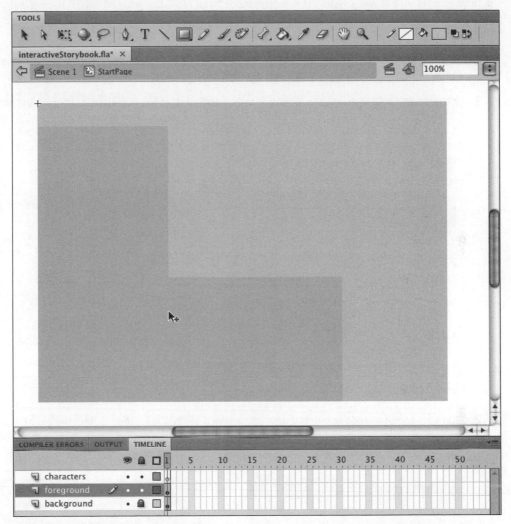

Figure 2-22. Add a second rectangle.

Flash's built-in drawing system uses **vector** lines and shapes (created by plotting points mathematically). If you overlap two vector shapes that are the same color on the same layer, they merge to become one shape. If you try selecting either of the green rectangles you created in the preceding steps with the arrow Selection tool, they will become one big shape (you can't select them individually anymore).

Flash has two drawing modes: **merge mode** and **object drawing mode**. When Flash is in object drawing mode, overlapping vector shapes don't automatically merge when they overlap; they remain as individual objects. Flash's drawing system is in merge mode by default, but you can switch to object drawing mode by clicking the Object Drawing button near the right edge of the toolbar. For now, however, stay with merge mode because you'll use it to demonstrate a new technique in the following steps.

The great thing about working with vector shapes is how malleable they are. In the next few steps, you'll use the Selection tool to bend the edge of one of the rectangles to create a curved slope.

1. In the Tools toolbar, select the Selection tool. Position it at the top-right corner of the second rectangle (the vertical section of the *L*). A small black angle icon appears next to the arrow, which indicates that you can now reposition the corner. Hold down the left mouse button and drag the corner down and to the left. When you release the mouse, the shape of the rectangle will be transformed, as shown in Figure 2-23.

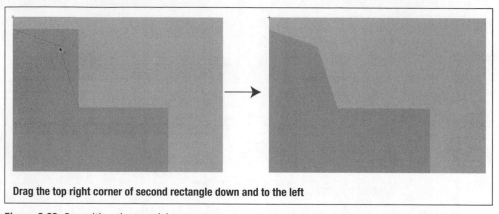

Drag the top right corner of second rectangle down and to the left

Figure 2-23. Reposition the top-right corner.

2. That's a good start for the hill, but now let's make it slightly less steep. Select the point at which the two rectangles join and drag it to the right. When you release the mouse, the slope will be less steep, as shown in Figure 2-24.

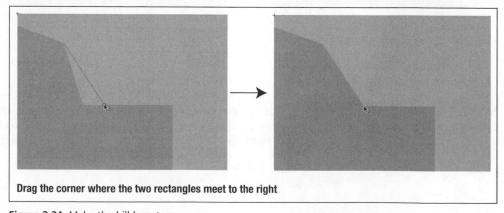

Drag the corner where the two rectangles meet to the right

Figure 2-24. Make the hill less steep.

3. The hill might look a bit prettier if the top were rounded. Position the Selection tool to intersect with the line that represents the top of the hill. You'll notice that a curved line icon appears next to the arrow. This icon indicates that you can bend the line. Hold down the left mouse button and drag the line upward to form a gentle curve. When you release the button, the top of the hill will be rounded. Figure 2-25 shows what this should look like.

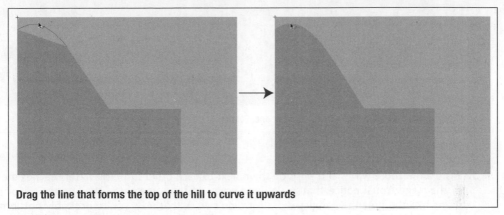

Drag the line that forms the top of the hill to curve it upwards

Figure 2-25. Make a rounded top for the hill.

I told you that drawing with Flash was fun!

Making some water

The next thing you'll do is create some water for the pond next to the grassy hill. You'll create a "wave" first, and then copy and paste it a few times to make a body of water.

1. Draw a dark blue rectangle next to the edge of the hill. Make sure that you draw it without a border. Use the Selection tool to curve the top of the blue rectangle downward. Figure 2-26 shows how.

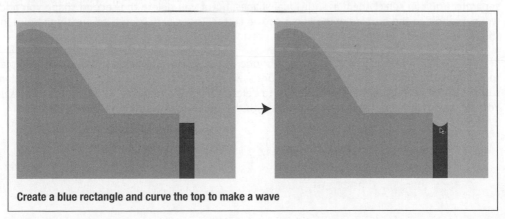

Create a blue rectangle and curve the top to make a wave

Figure 2-26. Design the first wave.

2. Click the blue rectangle to select it. Click Edit ➤ Copy and then Edit ➤ Paste to make another copy of it. Position the new copy next to the first (see Figure 2-27).

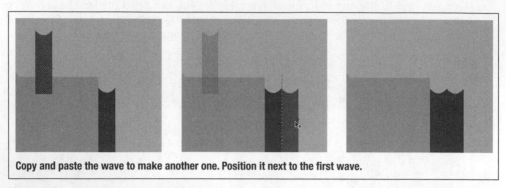

Copy and paste the wave to make another one. Position it next to the first wave.

Figure 2-27. Copy and paste a second wave.

3. Paste a few more waves and position them next to each other until the water reaches the edge of the stage. You'll notice that as you add waves of the same color, they merge to form one shape like the green rectangles did. (If it didn't work that way, you're probably not in merge mode. To toggle between merge and object mode, click the Object Drawing button near the top left of the toolbar.)

4. You'll probably find that one of the waves overlaps the stage edge slightly. If this is the case, draw a black rectangle outside the stage and position its left edge so that touches the right-most edge of the stage and completely covers the part of the wave that extends too far. Click the rectangle once with the Selection tool to select it. Next, delete the black rectangle. Not only will the rectangle disappear but the portion of the wave that it covered will also be gone. Figure 2-28 shows this process.

This figure illustrates an important feature of Flash's merge mode drawing style. If you draw two overlapping vector shapes that are the same color, they'll become part of the same shape—just as the two green rectangles did. If the shapes that overlap are different colors, they'll also merge but remain separate. You can select them as individual shapes, but if you delete the second shape you added, it will cut a hole in the bottom shape like a cookie cutter. This is very useful for punching holes in solid shapes or trimming edges, as you did in the previous steps.

This is a good demonstration of how merge mode works. However, there's another much simpler way to delete rectangular-shaped sections of your drawings. Use the Selection tool and draw a rectangular selection area around the section you want to delete. Click the Delete key, and the area will disappear. You can also remove parts of your drawings with the Eraser tool (also in the Tools toolbar).

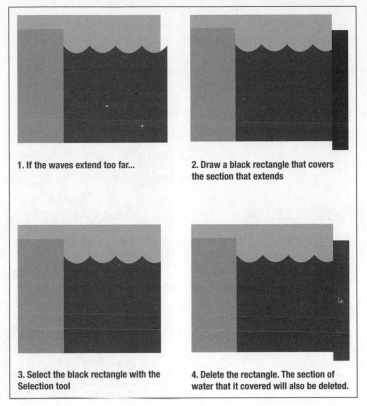

1. If the waves extend too far...

2. Draw a black rectangle that covers the section that extends

3. Select the black rectangle with the Selection tool

4. Delete the rectangle. The section of water that it covered will also be deleted.

Figure 2-28. Trim the blue water graphics.

Now let's make the water transparent. You can do this by converting it into a graphic symbol and then setting its **alpha** (transparency) property to 40%, as follows:

1. Select the water with the Selection tool.

2. Select Modify ➤ Convert to Symbol.

3. The Convert to Symbol dialog box opens. Give the symbol the name Water and change its Type to Graphic. Figure 2-29 shows an example of what this looks like.

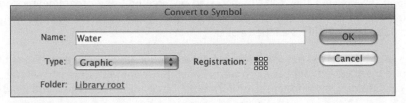

Figure 2-29. Convert the water to a graphic symbol.

4. Click the OK button. Two things happen:

- A new symbol appears in the Library called Water.
- The water shape that you selected and converted into a symbol becomes surrounded by a blue rectangle. This rectangle is called a **bounding box** and indicates that the object is a symbol.

Figure 2-30 shows what your Library and workspace might now look like.

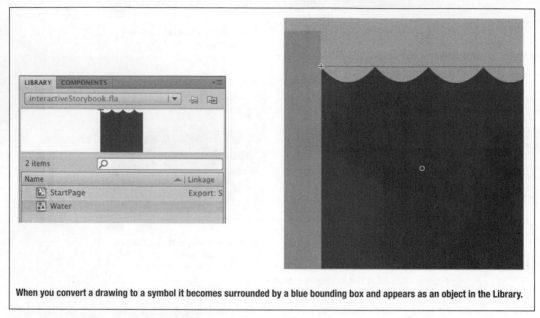

When you convert a drawing to a symbol it becomes surrounded by a blue bounding box and appears as an object in the Library.

Figure 2-30. The Water symbol in the Library

Any object on the stage that is represented by a symbol in the Library is an **instance** of that symbol. You'll be coming across the term *instance* a lot in this book, so it's worth remembering this. What you've done in these steps is "create an instance of the Water symbol on the stage."

Graphic symbols differ from Movie Clip symbols in two important ways. They take up slightly less storage space in the FLA, but they can't be accessed or targeted using programming code. If you don't think you'll want to program any of your symbols later, you can create them as graphic symbols so that your published SWF file is a little smaller.

Now that you've converted the water into a graphic symbol, it's become a unified entity that you can drag around the stage without having to worry about it merging with other shapes. Because it's a symbol, you can also drag more instances of it from the Library onto the stage if you need to.

You can change graphic symbols into Movie Clip symbols later if you need to. To do this, select the symbol in the Library. *Click the* Properties *button, which is located at the bottom of the* Library *panel and looks like a circle with an* i *in the center of it. This will open the* Symbol Properties *window. Change the symbol* Type *to* Movie Clip *in the drop-down menu. You can change any symbol to any other type using this method.*

You can also change a symbol's type by selecting the instance on the stage and changing its type from the drop-down menu in the Properties *panel.*

If you need to make changes to the actual shape of the water itself, double-click it on the stage or its icon in the Library. This will bring you into symbol editing mode, and you can make changes to the lines, colors, and shapes of the drawing. All these changes are automatically saved and will be immediately reflected in any instances of this symbol on the stage.

Now that the water is a graphic symbol, you can give it some transparency by setting its alpha property. (**Alpha** is a graphic design term that simply refers to transparency.)

1. Make sure that the Water symbol instance is still selected on the stage. You can tell that it's selected if you can see a blue bounding box surrounding it. Click it once with the Selection tool if you need to select it.

2. In the Properties panel, find the Color Effect section. It might be in its closed state, so none of its options will be visible. Click the Color Effect heading once, and it will open to reveal a drop-down menu. Select Alpha from the menu, as shown in Figure 2-31.

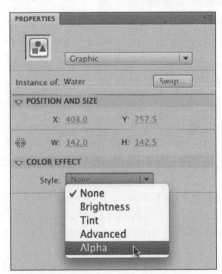

Figure 2-31. Select Alpha from the Color Effect section of the Properties panel.

3. Change the Alpha to 40%. You can do this either by moving the slider or entering 40 into the text field next to it, as shown in Figure 2-32.

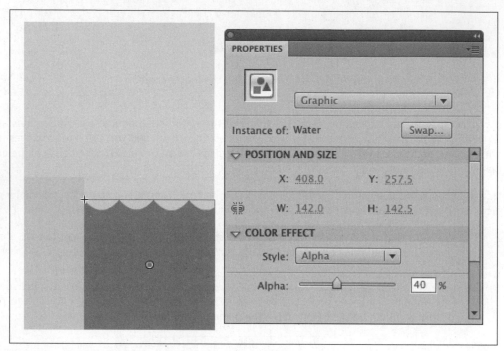

Figure 2-32. Set the water's alpha to 40%.

With the alpha at 40%, the background is visible through the water. In this example, the water will appear to be a much lighter blue color.

Grouping objects

Flash's drawing system allows you to group objects together so that you can move them around the stage as a single unit. You'll group the water and grassy hill to keep them separate from the objects that you'll add in later steps. Follow these steps:

1. Select the Water instance if it's not already selected.

2. Hold down the Shift key on the keyboard. When you hold down the Shift key, Flash allows you to select multiple objects. Select the grassy hill. Both the water and hill should now be selected.

3. Select Modify ➤ Group. As soon as you do this, a big blue bounding box surrounds both objects. They're now grouped.

Grouping objects allows you to treat multiple objects as a single unit so that you can move them around the stage together. It also prevents the shapes of other objects merging with the grouped shapes. Unlike creating a symbol, grouping objects doesn't create a new Library item. This is great if you're working on a complex design but don't want to clutter up the Library with too many extra symbols.

You can modify the shapes or instances inside a group by double-clicking the group with the Selection tool. When you do, the effect is almost identical to entering symbol editing mode. The word Group appears above the stage to show you that you're now working inside the group, and the other objects on the stage will dim. To exit this mode, double-click the outside edges of the stage, double-click another object that's not part of the group, or select the name of the symbol or scene that you're working in on the object name display bar above the stage.

If you ever need to separate the objects in the group again later, select the group and select Modify ➤ Ungroup.

Adding some clouds

Next you're going to create a Cloud graphic symbol and then drag a few instances of it onto the scene.

1. Select the Oval tool from the Tools toolbar. The Oval tool occupies the same button menu as the Rectangle tool, so if you've just used the Rectangle tool, it won't be visible. To find it, hold the left mouse button down over the Rectangle tool. A menu will open allowing you to select the Oval tool.

2. Select a white fill color.

3. Draw a few overlapping ovals in the sky to create something that looks like a cloud. Figure 2-33 shows what it might look like.

Figure 2-33. Use the Oval tool to create a cloud.

4. Click the cloud once with the Selection tool to select it.

5. Select Modify ➤ Convert to Symbol.

6. Give the new symbol the name Cloud and make sure that the Type is Graphic.

7. A Cloud graphic symbol appears in the Library. Drag five or six instances of it onto the stage, as shown in Figure 2-34. This illustrates one of the best things about using symbols: once you've made one, you can drag as many instances of it as like into your scene.

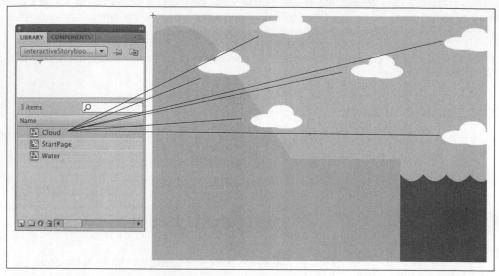

Figure 2-34. Drag instances of the Cloud symbol onto the stage.

As you can see, some of the clouds overlap the hill, which looks rather awkward. It would look more natural if the clouds were behind the hill. Ideally, you'd probably want to put these clouds on their own layer between the background and foreground layers, but, in the interest of showing you a new technique, you'll arrange the depths of objects within a single layer. Do the following:

1. Select one of the clouds that overlap the hill. (If more than one overlaps the hill, hold down the Shift key on the keyboard and select both of them.)

2. Select Modify ➤ Arrange ➤ Send Backward. The selected clouds will move behind the hill. Figure 2-35 shows how this will look.

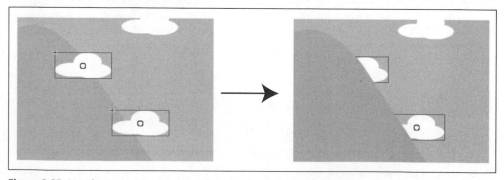

Figure 2-35. Use the Arrange menu to send the selected clouds backward.

The order in which Flash arranges the depths of visual objects on the stage is called the **stacking order**. If you select the Send Backward option, the selected objects will move back one place in the stacking order. If you have three or four objects stacked on a layer, you can use the alternative Send to Back option to move a selected object that's at or near the top of the stack all the way to the very back.

> *When you drag a symbol from the Library onto the stage, you create an instance of that object. If the symbol is a rubber stamp, the instance is like the ink impression of that stamp.*
>
> *You can also think of a symbol as a template or cookie cutter. In the same way that you can eat a bag full of cookies but not the cookie cutter that made them, you can use a symbol to make as many copies of that object as you want while still keeping the original intact. That's why even when you drag your cloud object from the Library onto the stage, the cloud still sits in the Library, floating serenely without a care in the world. And you can still use it to make as many more instances of that cloud in your storybook as you want to.*
>
> *The interesting thing about the relationship between the symbol and its instance is that whenever you make a change to the symbol, all the instances of that symbol are changed in exactly the same way. You can try this with your Cloud object. Open the Cloud symbol and make a small change to it, such as giving it a darker fill color. When you then take a look at your StartPage symbol, you'll notice that all the instance of the cloud that you used there also acquired the same darker fill color. If you had used 1000 instances of your Cloud symbol somewhere in your storybook, all of them would suddenly darken. All that from just making one small change in the symbol!*
>
> *This is an extremely powerful aspect of the relationship between symbols to instances and is an important concept to grasp before you go much further. AS3.0 programming is completely based around this same model. In AS3.0, a class is analogous to a symbol, and you can make as many instances of a single class as you need to in your programs. If you understand the relationship between symbols in the Library to instances on the stage in the visual way that you've used it with the cloud, it will give you a huge advantage to understanding the more abstract way this works in programming code. It's completely identical.*

Creating some flowers

Flash's drawing tools are not the only way to create vector graphics with Flash. Another very useful technique is to make a graphic using a **dingbat** font. Dingbat fonts are fonts that contain graphic images instead of letters or numbers. The Wingding and Webding dingbat fonts are installed on most computers as part of the operating system, but there are thousands of others that specialize in certain character sets. Many dingbat fonts are free; you just need to download and install them on your computer to use them.

Dingbat fonts are especially useful when you're just getting started with game design because they will save you the tedium of creating common graphic shapes from scratch. Lots of the little shapes that you'll need to make things like bullets, features for characters, and buttons you'll find ready-made as part of a dingbat font set. Flash allows you to convert fonts into ordinary vector graphics, so you have complete control over the final look of graphics created from dingbats.

You'll add some flowers to the hilly scene with the help of a free dingbat font called *saru's Flower Ding* (a simple web search will turn up the download link if you look for it). Of course, you can use any character from any dingbat font you choose.

1. Select the Text tool from the toolbar. The Properties panel will fill with text options. Make sure that Static Text is selected and choose an appropriate font, color, and font size. For this example, a nice big font size such as 36 points will work well.

2. Click the scene with the Text tool and type the key that corresponds to the dingbat symbol you want to use (an uppercase E produces a playful flower character with saru's Flower Ding). Figure 2-36 shows an example of what your text and the Properties panel might look like.

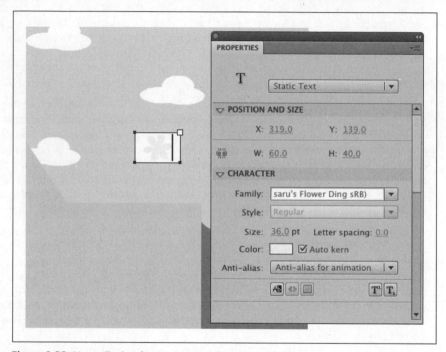

Figure 2-36. Use a dingbat font to create a flower graphic.

3. The next step is to convert the font into an ordinary vector graphic. Make sure that the text is selected and select Modify ➤ Break Apart. This transforms the font into a vector shape. It's now just like any other vector shape you could draw or transform with Flash's drawing tools.

4. While the flower shape is still selected, convert it into a graphic symbol by selecting Modify ➤ Convert to Symbol. Give the symbol the name Flower and click OK.

5. You now have a symbol called Flower in the Library. Drag a few instances of it onto the grassy hill, as shown in Figure 2-37.

Figure 2-37. Drag instances of the Flower symbol onto the hill.

The last little trick you'll look at is how to automatically align objects. Looking at the design in Figure 2-37, it might be nice if the three flowers farthest on the right were aligned in a row. I could struggle to do this by eye, but Flash's Align feature makes this easy:

1. Hold down Shift and select each of the three flowers. You'll see black circles appear in the center of the flowers, which represents the point by which they will be aligned.

2. Select Modify ➤ Align ➤ Vertical Center. The three flowers align in a neat row. Figure 2-38 shows what happens.

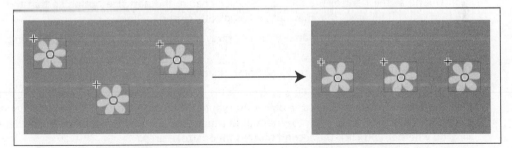

Figure 2-38. Use Flash's Align feature to align objects on the stage.

The Align menu has quite a few other nifty features that you should try out when designing graphics with Flash. You can use Distribute Widths and Distribute Heights to space objects evenly. You can use Make Same Width and Make Same Height to make two selected objects the same size. These are all big time-savers and very easy to use. Play around with them when you have the chance.

Learning a few more techniques

There are a few more basic drawing tools in the Tools toolbar that you should be familiar with. All these tools have many properties, including color, style, and stroke thickness, which can be set in the Properties panel. Here's a brief description of each:

- Line: Used to draw lines. You can curve the lines and reposition the start and endpoints with the Selection tool.

- Brush: Used like a paintbrush, it paints wide areas of color known as **fills**. You can set the brush's color, line style, and thickness (known as **stroke**) in the Properties panel. To change these properties, you need to make sure that the Object Drawing button is selected, which puts Flash in object drawing mode. The Brush tool also has a number of different modes that allow you to paint inside shapes, paint selected shapes, and paint behind shapes or fill areas. You can access these different modes from the Brush Mode menu button near the left edge of the toolbar when the Brush tool is selected.

- Pencil: Simulates drawing with a pencil. The Pencil tool will also try and interpret basic shapes such as circles, squares, and triangles (and creates them for you automatically if it thinks you're trying to draw them). Use this tool in conjunction with the Smooth and Straighten buttons on the right side of the toolbar to make selected lines more or less smooth or straight.

- PolyStar: Allows you to create polygons or stars with multiple sides. You can set this by clicking the Options button in the Tool Options section of the Properties panel.

- Rectangle Primitive: Like the Rectangle tool, but it also allows you to control the corner radius of the rectangle by dragging its bounding box handles.

- Oval Primitive: Like the Oval tool, but with the additional feature of being able to set the start and end angles of an oval, as well as its inner radius.

- Paint Bucket: Used to fill the inner areas of shapes. If you use it to fill areas that you've outlined with the Brush, Pencil or Line tool, you can do that in conjunction with the Gap Size menu button (found at the right of the toolbar.) You can change the **gap size** option so that the Paint Bucket will still fill areas that may not be completely closed by lines.

- Spray Brush: Used to simulate an airbrush or spray paint can effect. Great for splattering color everywhere!

- Ink Bottle: Used to change the style and color of stroke borders.

- Eyedropper: Used to copy the fill and stroke of one object and apply it to another object. To use it, click the fill or stroke of the object that you want to copy. Next, click the fill or stroke of the object you want to apply it to. The tool will change to a Paint Bucket or Ink Bottle, depending on whether you click the second object's fill or stroke area.

- Deco: A specialized tool that allows you to create three effects: Symmetry, Grid Fill, and Vine Fill.

- Pen: Used to create precise vector lines by adding and adjusting anchor points.

- Subselection: Especially useful for moving anchor points created with the Pen tool. It can also be used to select and move points in any vector object, such as the corners of rectangles.

- Lasso: Used to draw a selection area around an object.

Although you may use many of these tools infrequently, there are two tools that you'll find yourself using almost constantly:

- Free Transform: Use this tool to make selected objects bigger or smaller by dragging the black squares (known as **handles**) on the edges and corners of the tool's bounding box. If you want to scale the object proportionately without distorting its height or width, hold down the Shift key on the keyboard while you do this. You can rotate the object if you position the mouse pointer just beyond one of the corner handles. A circular arrow icon will appear, which means you can rotate the object by holding down the left mouse button and moving the mouse. The Free Transform tool also allows you to skew an object. If you move the mouse pointer so that it intersects with the bounding box, a double-arrow icon will appear to allow you to distort the object horizontally or vertically. Figure 2-39 illustrates these features of the Free Transform tool.

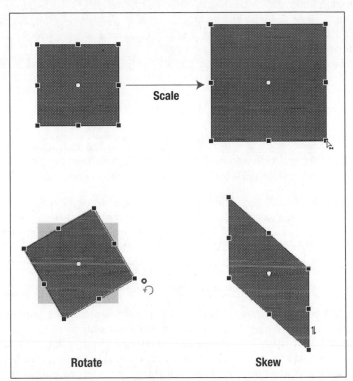

Figure 2-39. Use the Free Transform tool to scale, rotate, and skew objects.

- Zoom: When this tool is selected, you can click the stage to zoom in. You can also use it to drag a selection square around a certain area to magnify it. When the Zoom tool is selected, two additional buttons appear on the right side of the toolbar that allow you to increase or decrease the magnification. A more convenient way to do this, however, is to use keyboard shortcut keys. In OSX, hold down the Apple key and press the plus or minus key. In Windows, hold down Ctrl and press the plus or minus key. This is a good shortcut to learn because it works with most graphic design software, not just Flash. If you want to return to normal 100 percent magnification, double-click the Zoom button.

> *You can also adjust the magnification of the stage by selecting a magnification per-centage in the* Zoom *option menu at the top-right corner of the stage.*

The best way for you to learn how these tools work is just to start playing with them. Flash has the most accessible and easy-to-use vector drawing system around, and you'll soon see how much fun and quick it is to create graphics for your games. You don't need to be the world's best designer to create servicable graphics—rectangles and ovals can take you pretty far!

> *For much more detail on graphic design with Flash than I have space for in this book, you might want to pick up a copy of* Foundation Flash CS4 for Designers, *by Tom Green and David Stiller. It also includes a detailed discussion of the four more special-ized tools (*Bone, Bind, 3D Rotation, *and* 3D Translation*), which I haven't discussed here but have great potential for use in games.*

Creating a character

Let's create a cat character for the storybook. You'll create the character as a separate Movie Clip symbol and then drag it into the scene from the Library. This will give you a lot more flexibility to manipulate the character with AS3.0 code a little later in the project. Follow these steps:

1. Select Insert ➤ New Symbol. The Create New Symbol dialog box opens. Give your new symbol the name Cat. (Make sure to follow the naming convention for classes and use UpperCamelCase for Movie Clip symbol names.) Select Movie Clip from the Type drop-down menu. Select the Export for ActionScript option and click the OK button.

2. Click the OK button when the class definition warning box appears.

3. Flash opens symbol editing mode for your new Cat symbol.

Before you design your character in Flash, make a quick sketch on a piece of paper to give you a rough idea of how it might look. Remember that you'll probably need to organize different features of the cat onto different layers so that you can put certain features above or behind other features. For example, you probably want to put the cat's eyes on a layer that's above the body. Create a layer for each of these features and then use Flash's drawing tools to draw the feature on the correspond-ing layer. When you put all these individual features together, your character will appear fully formed from all these parts. Refer to the section on layers if you're still unsure about creating and using them.

4. The timeline has an option called Preview that shows you a small thumbnail image of each layer directly in a frame. This is a great way to work when designing objects on layers like this because you don't need to remember exactly which graphics you drew on which layer—you can see it directly. To turn on Preview, click the Timeline Option button at the top-right corner of the timeline and select Preview, as shown in Figure 2-40. (The Timeline Option button is very small and hard to locate, but don't give up—you'll find it eventually!)

Figure 2-40. Turn on the timeline's Preview option.

5. Try it! Use the drawing techniques you learned earlier in the chapter to create your cat character. Figure 2-41 shows how I created my cat using simple geometric shapes and the same basic
drawing techniques that were just covered.

You can create most of these shapes by using the Rectangle and Oval tools. Once you've got the
basic shape, use the Selection tool to bend the edges of rectangles and distort circles. You can
then use the Free Transform tool to scale and rotate the shapes, and the Eraser to trim away any
bits you don't want.

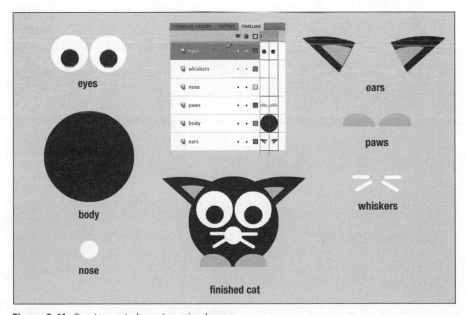

Figure 2-41. Create a cat character using layers.

> *If you need to rearrange any of your layers, hold the left mouse button down over any of the layer names and drag the layer up or down. While the mouse button is down, a black bar will indicate the new position of the layer. When you release the mouse button, the layer will snap to that position in the stack.*
>
> *You might discover that it's hard to focus on drawing a particular feature of your character with graphics from the other layers cluttering up your view. You can temporarily switch the visibility of a layer on or off by clicking the dot in the column represented by an eye icon. If you click the dot, a red X icon will appear next to the layer name, and any graphics on that layer will be temporarily hidden. Click the X again to reveal the layer.*

Now that your character has been created, let's add it to the StartPage symbol:

1. Double-click the StartPage symbol in the Library to open its editing mode.

2. Select the characters layer.

3. Drag an instance of the Cat symbol from the Library onto the stage, as shown in Figure 2-42. A black keyframe will appear in the characters layer to show you that an object has been added to that layer.

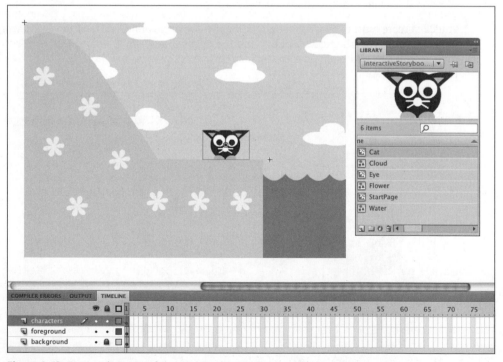

Figure 2-42. Drag an instance of the cat into the StartPage symbol.

4. If your cat object was anything like mine, it was probably too big or too small in comparison with the other objects on the stage. To scale the cat proportionately without distorting it, select the Free Transform tool and drag the corner handles while holding down the Shift key on the keyboard. Figure 2-43 shows how I scaled my cat. Reposition your cat on the stage when it's the right size.

Figure 2-43. Scale the cat instance with the Free Transform tool.

5. The last step is to give the cat an instance name. Instance names allow you to easily identify and target objects with AS3.0 code. Instance names are usually written using lowerCamelCase, so you can tell them apart from the symbol or class that they are derived from. Make sure that the cat instance is still selected, and in the Properties panel, type the name cat in the Instance name box. Figure 2-44 shows an example of this.

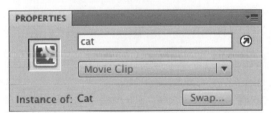

Figure 2-44. Create an instance name in the Properties panel (be sure to use lowerCamelCase).

Adding some more pages

The interactive storybook will be very short—only three pages long. Because it's nonlinear, the pages don't have to be sequential. For my storybook, I decided to give readers the choice of guiding the cat character up the hill to the left or into the pond on the right. That means you'll need to create two more Movie Clip symbols: HillPage and PondPage. Then you need to drag instances of the Cat symbol into both of these new pages. Make sure to assign the instance name cat in the Properties panel each time you do this. Each new cat instance you drag onto a scene is a new and separate object, so it needs its own name, even if the name is the same for all three.

Use the techniques covered so far in this chapter to create your two new pages. Remember to keep the top-left corner of your page aligned to the center of the stage (the black crosshairs), and be precise with the spelling and case of the name you give them in the Create New Symbol dialog box—all these things will soon become very important. Of course, you're free to design your storybook pages however you like, but Figure 2-45 shows what my three finished pages look like.

Figure 2-45. Three finished storybook pages

When you're done, your Library should contain two new symbols and look something like Figure 2-46.

Figure 2-46. Your new symbols in the Library

Have fun designing, and I'll meet you at the next section when you're done!

Using buttons

If interactive media were to pay a visit to the doctor's office for its annual checkup, the GP would probably be very surprised to hear the unnerving sounds "click, click, click" coming through the stethoscope. For at the heart of interactive media (if not most of what we know as the modern world) there lies the almighty click. But whether it's via a mouse, a touch screen, or possible future brain-wave interface, it's the lowly button that orders your books on Amazon, deletes your mail from dispossessed overseas millionaires, and obliterates entire civilizations in Spore.

And you can also use buttons to turn the pages of the children's storybook. The art of creating and programming buttons to control the display of information is such an important part of interactivity that just the basic techniques that you'll be learning over the next few pages will alone be enough to fuel the design of Flash-based websites, interactive information kiosks, and point-and-click adventure games. With nothing more than a button and a bit of imagination, a rich interactive experience is only a click away.

The first step is to actually make the buttons. Buttons are just another type of symbol, and you can create them as easily as you created your storybook pages. The only difference is that buttons have their own timeline with some special keyframes that allow you to specify how the button will look when it's in its various states, such as being pressed or when the mouse is hovering over it.

Creating a button symbol

Let's create two buttons for the storybook. You want to give the reader the option of guiding the cat either up the hill, or down into the pond. So, to keep things simple, let's call the two buttons HillButton and PondButton. You'll start with the HillButton.

1. Select Insert ➤ New Symbol from the menu to open the Create New Symbol dialog box. Enter HillButton as the button's name and select Button as the Type. Select the Export for ActionScript option, as you did when making scene symbols. (If you don't see any of these options, click the Advanced button to reveal them.) The Create New Symbol dialog box should look like Figure 2-47 when you are done.

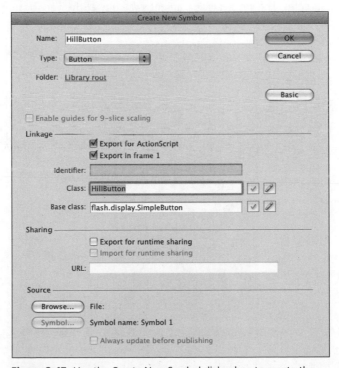

Figure 2-47. Use the Create New Symbol dialog box to create the HillButton symbol.

2. Click OK and then click OK again when the class definition warning dialog box appears.

3. Flash opens the HillButton symbol editing mode. You'll notice that the timeline looks quite a bit different from the timeline of Movie Clip symbols. Create a new layer and label your layers background and foreground. Figure 2-48 shows what your timeline should look like.

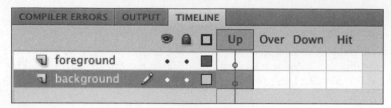

Figure 2-48. Create a background and foreground layer.

You'll create a rectangular button with a **gradient** background fill. Gradients are color fills that gradually change from one color to another. They're often used to create an illusion of shallow depth or surface texture. Do the following:

1. Select the Rectangle tool.

2. Choose a stroke color, thickness, and line style from the Properties panel. For this example, I chose a thickness of 2.0 and a Ragged line style.

3. Click the Fill box. Select the white-black linear gradient **swatch** from the color palette. (Swatches are color samples. The white-black gradient swatch is at the very bottom left of the color palette.) Figure 2-49 shows what this looks like.

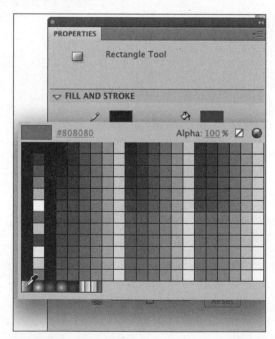

Figure 2-49. Select a gradient fill.

4. Draw a rectangle on the stage. Make sure that the rectangle is roughly centered over the crosshairs that indicate the center point of the symbol.

5. You want the button to be an appropriate size for the storybook pages. Double-click the button to completely select both the inside fill and outside stroke. (If you single-click it, only the fill will be selected.) Have a look at the Properties panel. To the left of the W label is a button that looks like a chain link. When the chain is unbroken, it means that Flash will proportionately resize the selected object if you change its height or width value. So if you change the height value, its width will automatically update to compensate and prevent the object from becoming distorted. If the chain is broken, you can set the values for height and width individually. You want to give the rectangle a specific width and height, so click the chain button to display its broken state if isn't that way already.

6. In the Properties panel, give the rectangle a width (W) of 130 and a height (H) of 40. Figure 2-50 shows how the rectangle might now look.

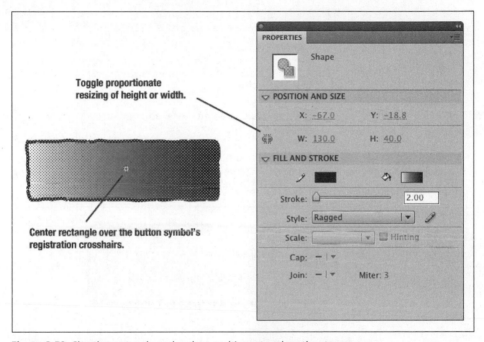

Figure 2-50. Size the rectangle and make sure it's centered on the stage.

7. You can now fine-tune the gradient fill. Select the Gradient Transform tool. (The Gradient Transform tool shares a button menu with the Free Transform tool, so hold the left mouse button down over the Free Transform tool button to reveal it.)

8. Click the rectangle's center fill with the Gradient Transform tool. Three new handles will appear, represented by icons that you can drag to change the gradient:

- A circular arrow at the top-right corner of the fill. Drag this arrow to rotate the gradient.
- A right-pointing arrow on the fill's right edge. Drag this arrow to expand the size of the gradient.
- A white dot in the center of the fill. Drag this dot to change the gradient's center point.

9. Play around with these settings until you like the way the gradient looks. My gradient looks like Figure 2-51.

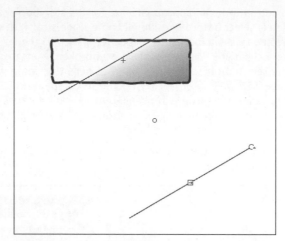

Figure 2-51. Use the Gradient Transform tool to create a subtle texture effect.

Now that the button's background has been created, let's add an arrow and some text to the foreground.

10. In the foreground layer, draw an arrow pointing to the left, as shown in Figure 2-52. You might want to lock the background layer while you do this to prevent accidentally ruining the work you did in the preceding steps.

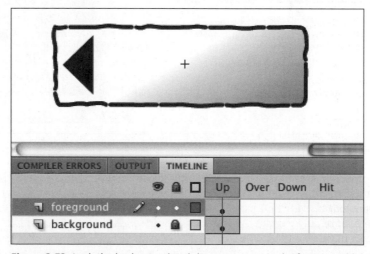

Figure 2-52. Lock the background and draw an arrow on the foreground layer.

11. Select the Text tool in the Tools toolbar. In the text Properties panel, choose an appropriate font and font size and make sure that Static Text is selected as the text type. Type the word Hill next to the arrow on the foreground layer, as shown in Figure 2-53.

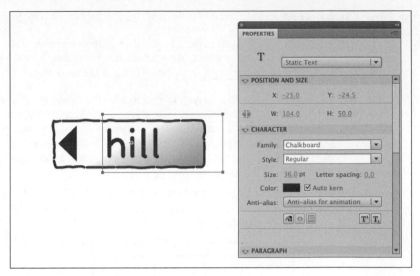

Figure 2-53. Choose a font and type some text.

You're now ready to design the button's Over and Down states.

Understanding button states

You'll notice the words Up, Over, Down and Hit in the button's timeline. They refer to what's known as the button's **state**. Each state has its own frame.

Understanding a button's state is really very simple. The Up state frame shows what the button looks like when it is not being pressed while it is still waiting for the user to click it. The Over state frame shows how the button looks when the mouse is hovering over it, just before the user clicks it. Usually button designers will create some sort of highlighting effect in the Over state, almost as if the button were say-ing, "Click me! Click me!" The Down state frame shows what the button looks like when the user actually clicks it. Designers will often create an illusion of the button being actually physically pressed down to create a sense of tactile feedback. You'll see all of these button states in use very soon.

> *The odd one out here is the Hit state frame. The Hit frame defines the area of the but-ton that is actually sensitive to the mouse. If you have a really small button, or one made up of irregular shapes or plain text, you could give the button a large rectangu-lar Hit state to make it easier for the user to click. Interestingly, whatever you draw in the Hit state doesn't display on the screen. That means that you can leave all the other states blank and just create a Hit state to make an **invisible button**. Invisible buttons have a lot of potential for certain types of point-and-click adventure games, in which you might want to give certain areas of your scene button-like sensitivity, but not have them look or behave like buttons. You won't need to use the Hit state in any of the examples in this book, but it's important to keep in mind what it's used for. If you don't define a Hit state, the button's Up state is used as the area sensitive to the mouse.*

Creating the Over state

Now that you've learned about the Up state, you can use the graphics you've already drawn and modify them just slightly to make the other states. You can do this by adding a new keyframe in the state's corresponding frame. The following steps show how to make the Over state:

1. Select the Over frame of the background layer. (If you locked the background layer in the previous steps, unlock it first.) Select Insert ➤ Timeline ➤ Keyframe. (Alternatively, you can right-click the frame and select Insert Keyframe from the option menu.) As soon as you do this, a black keyframe will appear in the Over state, and all the graphics from the previous frame, the Up state, will be copied into it. All you need to do now is make some small modifications to differentiate the Over state from the Up state.

2. Change the rectangle's inner fill color to bright yellow, which will give the user a very clear highlighting effect when the mouse hovers over the button. Figure 2-54 shows what the background layer of the Over state now looks like.

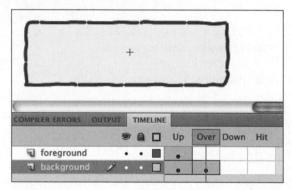

Figure 2-54. Choose a bright color for a highlighting effect in the button's Over state.

3. All that's missing is the black arrow and the text. Select the foreground layer and right-click the blank frame on the Over state. Choose Insert Keyframe from the menu. This automatically copies the contents of the keyframe from the previous frame and positions it in exactly the same place. The Over state should now look like Figure 2-55.

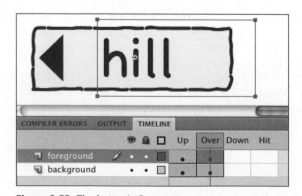

Figure 2-55. The button's Over state

The last state that you need to create is the button's Down state.

Creating the Down state

To create the button's Down state, you'll simply copy all the graphics from the Over state and move them slightly down and to the right. This is a very basic way to create the illusion that the button is being pressed down when you click it. Follow these steps to create the Down state:

1. Insert keyframes in both the background and foreground layers of the button's Down state. This will give you an exact copy of the Over state, as shown in Figure 2-56.

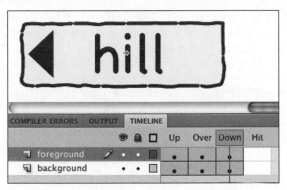

Figure 2-56. Insert keyframes in the button's Down state to copy the text and graphics from the previous frame.

2. Select all the graphics with the Selection tool. (You can do this by dragging a rectangular selection box around the graphics with the Selection tool.) Use the arrow keys on your keyboard to move them slightly down and to the right. You just need to nudge it two or three pixels in each direction. Figure 2-57 shows a slightly exaggerated example of this.

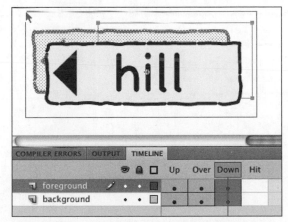

Figure 2-57. Select all the text and graphics and nudge them slightly down and to the right, creating the illusion that the button is being physically pressed.

Duplicating the button

You've now got the Hill button; all you need is a Pond button. You could always create one from scratch, but because you just need to change the text and the direction of the arrow, the easiest way to do it is to duplicate and modify the existing button.

1. Right-click the HillButton symbol in the Library. Select Duplicate in the Duplicate Symbol dialog box and give the new button the name PondButton. Remember to select Export for ActionScript and click OK.

2. Click OK when the class definition warning dialog box appears.

3. Double-click the PondButton icon in the Library. The PondButton symbol editing mode opens.

4. Change the arrow in each of the button state frames in the foreground layer so that it's pointing in the opposite direction. (The quickest way to do this is to select the arrow in the Up frame. Select Modify ➤ Transform ➤ Flip Horizontal. Move the arrow to its new position on the opposite side of the button. While it's still selected, select Edit ➤ Copy. Next, delete the arrow in both the Over and Down frames. Select Edit ➤ Paste in Place to paste the new arrow from the Up frame into the Over and Down frames. Reposition the arrow slightly in your Down frame so that it matches the slight left and down offset.)

5. Change the text in all the frames so that it reads pond.

You now have two buttons, and the Library should start to look quite satisfyingly crowded. Figure 2-58 shows what mine looks like.

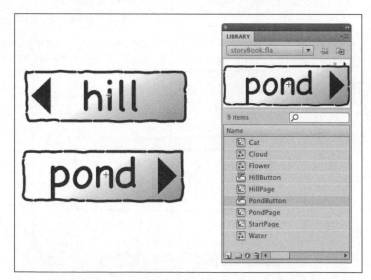

Figure 2-58. The completed navigation buttons

Organizing the Library

Depending on how organized you like to be, you might want to add some folders to your Library so that you can keep related objects together. Looking at what I created in the Library so far, it might make sense to create three folders called Pages, Buttons, and Items. Follow these steps to create the folders and organize the symbols into them.

1. Click the New Folder button near the bottom-left corner of the Library to create a new folder. Do this three times to have all the folders you need to organize your symbols.

2. Name the folders Pages, Buttons, and Items.

3. Drag the button symbols into the Buttons folder. Drag the StartPage, HillPage, and PondPage symbols into the Pages folder. Drag the remaining symbols into the Items folder.

Figure 2-59 shows what your Library might look like after it's been reorganized using folders. You can open or close folders to view or hide their content by clicking the triangle icons next to the folder names.

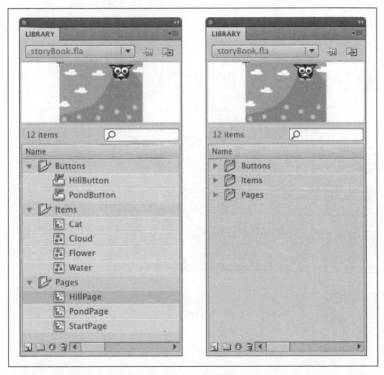

Figure 2-59. The full set of finished buttons in the Library

Adding the buttons to your scene

The final step is to add the buttons to the StartPage symbol.

1. Double-click the StartPage symbol in the Library to enter its symbol editing mode. Create a new layer on the timeline called Buttons. Drag the Buttons layer to the very top of the layer stack.

2. Drag instances of both the PondButton and HillButton symbols onto the stage. If a black keyframe appears on the Buttons layer, you added them correctly.

3. Select the instance of the HillButton symbol and assign it the name hillButton in the Instance name field of the Properties panel. Remember to use lowerCamelCase for instance names.

4. Select the instance of the PondButton symbol and give it the instance name pondButton in the Instance name field of the Properties panel. The StartPage symbol might now look something like Figure 2-60.

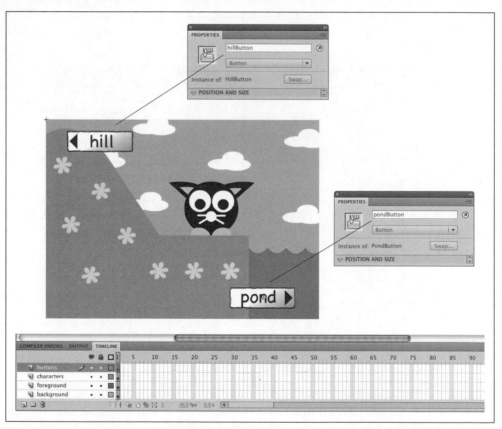

Figure 2-60. Add instance names to the HillButton and PondButton instances in the StartPage symbol.

5. Finally, save the interactiveStorybook.fla file.

You're now ready to start programming!

Summary

If you're new to Flash, I hope you enjoyed this chapter on how to draw basic objects and characters. The Flash drawing tools give you a great deal of control and are very easy to use. For designing game characters and environments, they're ideal.

I covered quite a lot of new material very quickly, so if this is your first time using vector-drawing tools, you might want to take a short break and experiment further. Create a new blank FLA file and create a few objects and characters. You'll soon become comfortable with it and, if you're like me, Flash will soon become your favorite drawing application.

In this chapter, you created objects. From a programming point of view, objects are things you can control with programming code. In the next chapter you'll bring these objects to life with a bit of simple programming magic.

Chapter 3

PROGRAMMING OBJECTS

In Chapter 2, you created button and Movie Clip objects, and this chapter shows you how to use AS3.0 programming code to start programming those objects. You'll make them do something useful!

This chapter covers some very important AS3.0 programming concepts and techniques:

- Using the addChild method to display objects from the Library on the stage
- What variables are and how to use them
- Variable types
- Dot notation
- Method calls and function definitions
- Method arguments and parameters
- Event listeners

After you finish the chapter, you'll be surprised at how easy it is to program the buttons for your interactive storybook.

But I'm a bit scared of programming!

Although I'll cover a lot of important programming theory in this chapter, the most important thing you should come away with is how the programming code you type in the ActionScript editor window changes the behavior of the objects on the stage. The theory is important, but don't agonize too much if you don't understand it all right away. If you're like me (and almost everyone else), it will take time and quite a few more practical examples before it all sinks in and starts to make sense.

Just as having a general idea of how a car's engine works is a good idea for any driver, you don't need to become a mechanical engineer if all you want to do is drive a car. You can always come back to this theory later if you have some specific questions about how some detail of the code works. If you generally understand how the code you type affects the objects on the stage and can use that code with confidence in your projects, you're more than halfway there.

Always remember that programming is a creative tool to help you express yourself, just as a paintbrush is a creative tool for an artist. It can help create the painting, but is of no use at all without the imagination of the artist—you!

Displaying the first page of the storybook

You'll work on the interactive storybook from the previous chapter. All the objects are ready to go. Your first job is to display the first page of the storybook.

To display the first page, you'll use AS3.0 to do two things:

- Use the var and new keywords to create an instance of the StartPage symbol that you can control with programming code.
- Use the addChild method to visually display that new instance on the stage.

Remember that when you set up this project you created a file called Main.as. This is the ActionScript file that will contain all the programming code for the storybook. The first thing you need to do is open this file so that you can start programming into it. Follow these steps:

1. Open the interactive storybook project from the previous chapter. If you created it as a Flash project, you should be able to select it from the drop-down menu in the Project panel near the top-left corner of the Flash workspace.

2. Double-click the Main.as file in the Project panel or select it from the tab menu above the stage if it's already open. A blank ActionScript editor window will open, allowing you to enter programming code.

You might want to see what the project looks like before you add any programming code. Click the Test Project button in the Project panel. Flash will generate a pop-up message: Exporting SWF Movie. A few moments later, you'll see a blank window with the name interactiveMovie.swf in the title bar. This is the SWF file that will be your finished product. Why is it blank? What happened to all the hard work you put into designing the buttons, the pages, and the poor little cat?

All those elements were created as symbols in the Library. When you publish a SWF file, it will display only what has been added to the FLA file's main stage. So far, the main stage of the FLA is blank. You can check this by opening interactiveStorybook.fla and clicking the Scene 1 button at the top of the stage. You'll just see a blank white stage—there's nothing there—which is what the SWF displayed.

This illustrates an important concept. Symbols in the Library can't be seen unless you create an instance of them on the main stage. The first bit of code that you'll add will do exactly that.

Let's add the lines of code to see the first page of the storybook:

3. Add the following to the Main.as file (your ActionScript editor window will look like Figure 3-1 when you're done):

```
package
{
  import flash.display.MovieClip;
  public class Main extends MovieClip
  {
    var startPage:StartPage;

    public function Main()
    {
      startPage = new StartPage;
      addChild(startPage);
    }
  }
}
```

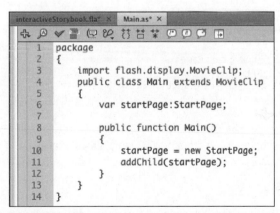

Figure 3-1. Add the code to the Main.as file in the ActionScript editor window.

4. Save the Main.as file.

5. Test the project. You should see the interactiveStorybook.swf movie displayed with the first page. You'll even be able to click the buttons, although they won't do anything just yet.

> *In this book I use the phrase "test the project" to mean publishing a SWF while working on it. There are three ways to do this:*
>
> - *Click the* Test Project *button in the* Project *panel.*
> - *Select* Control ➤ Test Movie.
> - *Use this useful Flash shortcut: in OSX, hold down the* Apple *key and press* Enter. *In Windows, hold down the* Ctrl *key and press* Enter.
>
> *All these techniques generate a SWF file in the project folder on your computer's hard drive and then run it immediately for you to see the result.*

How did that work?

The format that you've used for the program so far is exactly the same as the format you used for the Hello World program in Chapter 1. Refer to that chapter if there's anything about the basic structure of this code that you think you don't quite understand. There are three new lines of code that you haven't seen before, and I'll go into detail about how they work. I've highlighted the new code for you here:

```
package
{
  import flash.display.MovieClip;
  public class Main extends MovieClip
  {
    var startPage:StartPage;

    public function Main()
    {
      startPage = new StartPage;
      addChild(startPage);
    }
  }
}
```

The first thing the code did was to create a new variable called startPage. That's what this line does (the variable's name is highlighted):

```
var startPage:StartPage;
```

In programming terms, this directive is known as a **variable declaration.** It creates a variable called startPage that you can use in the program and control with code.

Figure 3-2 illustrates the structure of this variable declaration in detail. (Pay very close attention to the two terms in the new code: startPage and StartPage. They're actually two completely different objects, and the differences in their capitalization help to tell them apart. I'll explain how in a bit.)

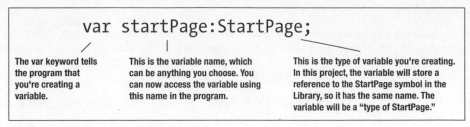

Figure 3-2. The variable declaration

Whoa, that's suddenly a lot to absorb very quickly! And what are variables, anyway? Let's take a break for a moment and find out what they are and how to use them.

Variables

You can think of **variables** as little boxes that store information. Every box has its own name and stores different kinds of information.

Figure 3-3 illustrates three imaginary variables called score, name, and enemy. Each variable name is associated with a box that contains information.

Figure 3-3. Variables are like boxes that store information.

If you need to use the information inside the box, you just need to refer to the box's name anywhere in the program. For example, if you want to find out what the current score is, use the variable name score; the program will interpret it as 38. If you want to reference the dragon Movie Clip, use the word enemy.

You can also empty the box at any time and put new information into it. It's variable!

That's all variables are: storage containers with names.

Variable types

If you're organizing lots of little boxes filled with different types of things, it's sometimes useful to know what **type** of information each box should contain. Imagine that you have a sugar container and you accidentally pour a bag of salt into it. That could be a problem when the aunties come to visit for tea! You need to know that the container you fill is the sugar container.

In AS3.0, you can tell a variable what type of information it should store. To do this, use a colon and the name of the type, like this:

> *:Sugar*

If the kitchen existed in an AS3.0 universe, you could label the containers in the cupboards like this:

> *smallBluePlasticTub:Sugar;*
> *glassJar:Salt;*

That labeling would prevent you from putting the wrong substance in the wrong container and spoiling the tea parties. Mom would be proud!

Figure 3-4 shows what the imaginary variables might look if like you assigned them types. This will prevent you from putting the wrong type of thing into the wrong container. (In AS3.0, any information made up of letters is referred to as a **string**, as in "string of letters or words.")

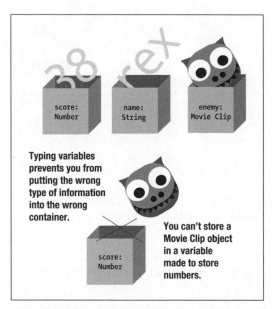

Figure 3-4. Assign types to variables so that you don't put the wrong type of information or object into the wrong container.

Creating empty boxes

Let's have a quick look at that first new line of code:

var **startPage**:StartPage;

Is it making a little more sense to you now?

The directive is creating an empty storage container called startPage that can be used to store StartPage objects.

What are StartPage objects? You made one—it's sitting in the interactiveStorybook.fla Library and is the first page of the storybook. It's the StartPage symbol.

> *When you created the StartPage symbol, you checked the* Export for ActionScript *option. This option makes the symbol accessible by code. Technically speaking, AS3.0 isn't accessing the symbol directly; it's accessing a class that it created automatically called StartPage, which is bound to the StartPage symbol. In Chapter 8, you'll be taking a detailed look at this process. For now, this is a process that is pretty much invisible to you, so you can think of the StartPage symbol and class as one and the same.*

The line of code creates an empty storage container that you can use to store an instance of the StartPage symbol. Figure 3-5 illustrates visually what you just created.

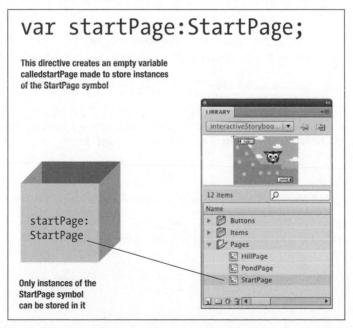

Figure 3-5. The startPage variable declaration

The startPage variable has been created, but it's empty. Let's fill it with something!

> *I could have chosen any name for this variable, such as theVeryFirstPage or star-tOfTheStory, but just to keep things organized in my own mind, I chose to give it exactly the same name as the symbol in the* Library *that I want it to refer to. One important difference between the name of the variable and the name of the type is the choice of capitalization used. The variable name is written in lowerCamelCase. The type is written in UpperCamelCase. This is the same reasoning I followed when I named the cat instance on the stage as a lowerCamelCase version of its parent Cat symbol in the* Library. *It means that I can easily tell the difference between the class and the instance just by looking at the capitalization. (This book follows the naming convention of using lowerCamelCase with variable names; class and symbol names use UpperCamelCase.)*

Creating an instance

Previous chapters looked at how instances differ from the parent symbols that they come from. The cat character on the stage is an instance of the Cat symbol in the Library. The clouds in the storybook sky are all instances of their parent Cloud symbol. It's very easy to see this relationship when you're working with Flash's graphic design tools.

You can also create instances of symbols using AS3.0 programming code. Although it's not so easy to see this visually, the result is exactly the same as dragging an instance of a symbol from the Library onto the stage.

So far, the code has created an empty variable called startPage to store an instance. The next step is to create an instance of the StartPage symbol and store it in that variable. That's what the next directive does:

```
startPage = new StartPage;
```

The job of the new keyword is to make instances. In this directive, it's used to tell the program that you're creating a new instance of the StartPage symbol. The equal sign is used to copy a reference of that instance into the startPage variable.

In simpler terms, you took the empty startPage variable and put an instance of the StartPage symbol into it. The empty container is now full and ready to be used. Figure 3-6 illustrates what happened.

Now you have an instance of the StartPage symbol that you can access with programming code. The next step is to actually display the instance on the stage so you can see it.

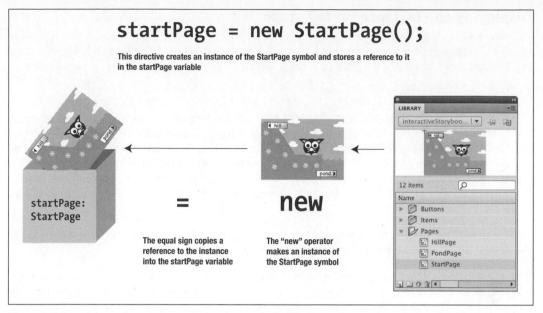

Figure 3-6. Use the new keyword to create an instance of a class or symbol and store it in a variable.

Before you go much further, you should take a closer look at exactly what the purpose of that equal sign is. In AS3.0, an equal sign is known as an **assignment operator** because it is used to assign a value from whatever is to the right of it to a variable on its left. This is very different from how an equal sign is used in mathematics, and this difference often trips up novice programmers. In math, an equal sign means "is equal to." In programming, an equal sign means "gets the value of."

Here's a really simple example. Let's say you have a variable that you want to use in a game to keep track of the player's score. Let's call it playersScore. Suppose that one player in the game gets a score of 12 points, and you want the game to remember this number so you can figure out how well the player is doing. You can use the equal sign to copy the number 12 into the playersScore variable, the same way you would write an important number into a notebook for future reference. The code might look something like this:

```
playersScore = 12;
```

AS3.0 literally interprets this as follows: "The playersScore variable gets the value of 12." Now whenever the AS3.0 program sees the playersScore variable, a little light goes on and it thinks, "Aha! That means 12!"

Displaying the instance on the stage

You now have a shiny new instance of the StartPage symbol stored as a reference in the startPage variable. This new instance exists as an object you can access with code. But it isn't visible on the stage yet. You first need to tell the program to actually display it. That's exactly what this directive does:

```
addChild(startPage);
```

addChild is one of AS3.0's built-in methods. (The first built-in method you saw in Chapter 1 was trace, which displays information in the Output panel.) addChild is a deliciously cute little method that (besides its many other talents) displays instances of Movie Clip symbols on the stage. Any information inside the parentheses of a method is known as the method's **argument**. When you use the addChild method, it assumes that you want to display the instance you provided in the parentheses on the stage. (You can also use addChild to display instances inside other objects; you'll see examples of how to do this in later chapters.)

What addChild has done in the program is take the startPage instance and add it to something called the **display list**. Any instances that are on the display list are visible on the stage.

With the first three directives that you've written in the program, you created a storage box, filled the box with an instance, and then tipped the box over to display its contents on the stage. Figure 3-7 takes you on a tour of how these three directives have worked together to display the startPage instance.

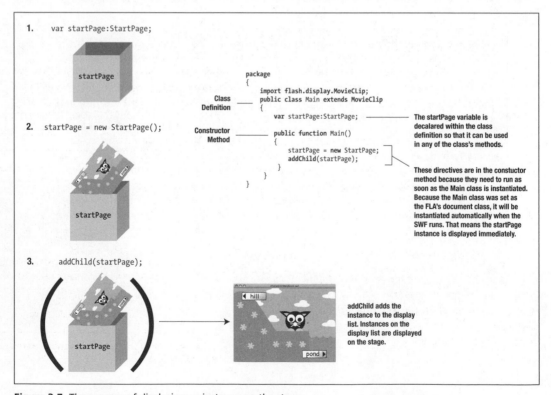

Figure 3-7. The process of displaying an instance on the stage

> *Recall from Chapter 1 that whatever code is in a class's constructor method will run immediately as soon as the class is instantiated. The Main class was assigned as the FLA's document class, so this happens as soon the SWF file runs.*

Programming buttons

The next step in the interactive storybook project is to program the buttons so that you can see the other pages in the storybook. But before I go into the specifics of how to do this, you need to take a few steps back and look at some of the underlying principles behind the code you're going to write. It's not difficult, but there will be a lot of new concepts to absorb quite quickly. You need to break them down into manageable chunks and look at them one at a time.

So grab a cup of masala chai and make yourself comfortable on the sofa. You'll take a short break from programming to have a detailed look at the following topics:

- Dot notation
- Methods
- Event listeners

These three elements will be working together in the new code you're going to write.

Using dot notation

You have two buttons in the storybook so far: hillButton and pondButton. You may recall that you gave them these names in the Instance name field of the Properties panel after you dragged instances of them into the StartPage symbol from the Library. (Refer to Figure 2-60 if you need a reminder.) These buttons still exist with those names; the only difference is that now they're contained within the startPage instance that you created in the program.

You can refer to the buttons inside the startPage instance using these names:

```
startPage.hillButton
startPage.pondButton
```

The dot is used to show that these button objects live *inside* the startPage instance. This method of naming objects and their properties hierarchically using dots is called **dot notation**. Figure 3-8 illustrates this.

The concepts behind dot notation are crucial to understanding how to program with AS3.0. Let's quickly have a look at a very simple example.

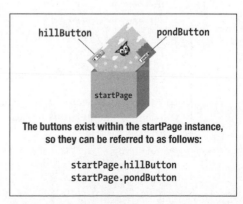

The buttons exist within the startPage instance, so they can be referred to as follows:

```
startPage.hillButton
startPage.pondButton
```

Figure 3-8. The button instances are contained within the parent instance.

My name is Rex. However, I'm not the only Rex in the world. There's another Rex: my friend's dog, which lives in a very pretty little village just outside of Bangalore, India. So there are two Rex's:

    rex

and

    rex

How can you tell the difference? Well, one of them wags his tail and barks. I'll leave it up to you to guess which one. But, apart from that, you know that they live in *different places*. I live in Canada, so my proper object name might be this:

    canada.rex

My friend's dog lives in India, so his proper object name might be this:

    india.rex

This is another basic feature of dot notation. In front of the most basic bit of information, the object's name, you need to indicate where the object lives. You can add as much or as little information about where the objects live as you need to. Because both India and Canada are on the Earth, you could go one step further:

    earth.canada.rex

and

    earth.india.rex

The objects are still the same, even though they're described a little more clearly.

You can use this general model for naming objects with dot notation:

    place.objectName

or

    biggestPlace.smallerPlace.objectName

Once you know the name of the object, you can add or modify **properties** to change it in some way, or you can invoke **methods** to allow it to run certain directives.

Invoking methods

I've written a lot about methods so far in this book, but before you go much further you should take a detailed look at exactly what they are and how they work.

Methods perform some kind of useful action in the program. They're made up of two parts:

- **Function definition**: This part is a block statement that includes directives that do the tasks you want the method to perform.
- **Method call**: This part is a word that activates the directives in the function definition.

Let's have a closer look at these two elements.

Using method calls

You've seen two method calls already in this book so far: trace and addChild.

Method calls trigger directives in the method's function definition. (You'll be looking at function definitions in a moment.) The nice thing about method calls is that you can use them without having to know how the function definition is programmed.

Many methods require some extra information to do their job. In programming terminology, this extra information is called an **argument**. Arguments in method calls are included in parentheses after the method name.

Here's an example of a trace method call:

```
trace("Wow! This is an argument!");
```

The text in quotation marks inside the parentheses is the method call's argument. You can use this trace method call to display the argument in the Output panel when the SWF runs. Here's another example:

```
addChild(startPage);
```

No surprise. You saw this one before! addChild() is the method call, and startPage is the method's argument. Any instance name supplied as the argument of the addChild method is displayed on the stage.

Some methods don't need arguments to do their job. Method calls without arguments simply use empty parentheses. Here's an example:

```
simpleMethod();
```

Even though this method call has no arguments, you still need to provide empty parentheses.

Using function definitions

With one exception, all the methods used in the book were built in to AS3.0. (The one exception is the constructor method, which is a special kind of function definition used to initialize classes.) You've been lucky because these built-in methods have been very useful and have saved you some work. However, as a programmer you can create your own methods. If there's any specific task that you need your program to perform, you can create a method that is specialized to do that job.

To create your own method, you need to define it. Here's the basic format for defining a method:

```
function methodName():void
{
  //add directives here
}
```

This is called a **function definition**. Function definitions are block statements. As discussed in Chapter 1, block statements are sections of code that are structured using opening and closing braces. The braces form a "block" of code. Any code that is inside the braces is part of that block. Programs are structured by using many of these blocks together.

Function definitions start with the keyword function, followed by the name of the method and then the parentheses. If the method call doesn't use any arguments, the parentheses are empty. If the method call uses arguments, the parentheses have to include a parameter (you'll be looking at how to use method parameters in a moment).

After the parentheses comes the **type declaration**, which is a colon followed by a word that describes the type of information the method might return to the rest of the program. You've seen types before. Remember these?

```
:Sugar
:Salt
:StartPage
```

Methods need to include types, too. However, many methods don't need to return any information to the program, so their type is irrelevant. To specify that a method doesn't return any information, you can specify a return type of void. It looks like this:

```
:void
```

Before you become overwhelmed by all this new information, spend a bit of time looking over Figure 3-9 and get comfortable with what method calls look like and how function definitions are structured.

Here's an example of a simple method, called displayText, which will display some text in the Output panel. The first thing you need to do is create the method's function definition. Here's what it looks like:

```
function displayText():void
{
  trace("This is text from the function definition");
}
```

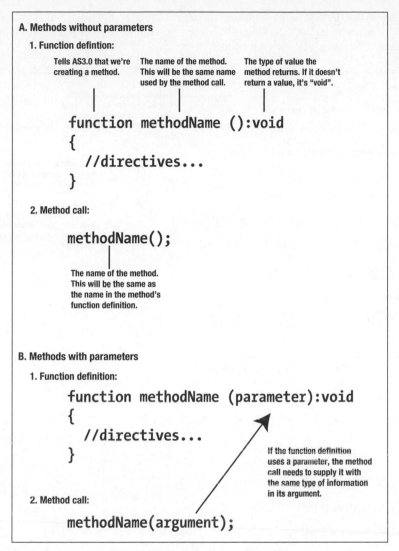

Figure 3-9. Methods: function definitions and method calls

Now that the method is defined, you can use it in the program with a method call:

```
displayText();
```

This is text from the function definition displays in the Output panel.

Figure 3-10 illustrates how to write a simple program that uses this method. If you want to take a closer look or experiment with it a bit on your own, you'll find this sample program in the Method without parameters folder in the chapter source files.

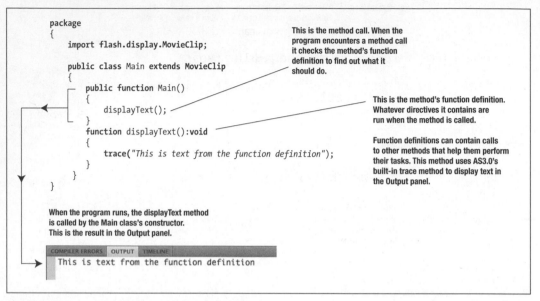

Figure 3-10. An example of a simple method in action

To use the source files in this book, do the following:

1. Make sure the Project panel is open. If it isn't, select Window ➤ Other Panels ➤ Project.

2. In the Project panel, select Open Project from the drop-down menu.

3. Find the folder that contains the source files and select it.

4. Click the Choose button.

5. All the files required for the project will be loaded into the Project panel.

6. You now need to assign an FLA file as the default document. The default document is the file that Flash uses to create the SWF file. If the project's default document has already been assigned, this will be indicated by a yellow star on the FLA file's icon. If the default document hasn't been assigned, you need to assign it manually. To do this, right-click on the FLA file and select "Make default document" from the context menu. (Sometimes this option won't appear the first time you select the file. If it doesn't, try selecting the FLA again.)

7. Once the default document has been assigned, you can click the Test Project button to see the result of the program. Double-click any of the files to open them to make changes.

Keep in mind that methods are a two-part system: you have to create a function definition to define the method and then you need a method call to use it.

Creating method arguments and parameters

The simple displayText method works pretty well, but there's a problem with it. The text it displays always stays the same. Wouldn't it be nice if you could write the method so that you could supply it with new text to display every time it's called?

Of course it would be! Here's what the new method call might look like:

```
displayText("You can write any text you like here!");
```

The method call now includes an argument. The argument is the text that you want to display.

To display this text, you need to rewrite the function definition with a parameter, which is a variable that is used to store the new information. That variable can then be used anywhere in the function definition to access the information that was sent by the method call.

It's really easy to do. Have a look:

```
function displayText(textYouWantToDisplay:String):void
{
   trace(textYouWantToDisplay);
}
```

If you use this method in a program, the Output panel displays You can write any text you like here!

The beauty of this system is that you need to write the function definition only once. You can change the text that the method displays just by changing the text in the method call's argument. For example, you can use any of these method calls, and the display in the Output panel will change to match it:

```
displayText("All this text");
displayText("can change whenever you want it to");
displayText("without changing the function definition");
```

This makes the method very versatile. Here's the key to understanding it:

1. The text in the method call's argument is sent to the function definition.
2. The function definition stores that text in a variable. The name of the variable that it stores it in is supplied in the parameter. In this case, the name of the variable is textYouWantToDisplay.

3. Whenever you use textYouWantToDisplay in the function definition, it's replaced by the text that was supplied in the method call's argument. Figure 3-11 illustrates how all this works.

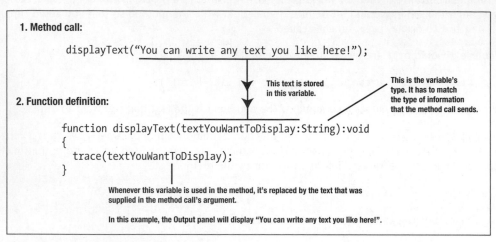

1. Method call:

displayText("You can write any text you like here!");

This text is stored in this variable.

This is the variable's type. It has to match the type of information that the method call sends.

2. Function definition:

function displayText(textYouWantToDisplay:String):void
{
    trace(textYouWantToDisplay);
}

Whenever this variable is used in the method, it's replaced by the text that was supplied in the method call's argument.

In this example, the Output panel will display "You can write any text you like here!".

Figure 3-11. Using arguments and parameters

Figure 3-12 shows how you can use this method in a program. You'll find this sample program in the folder Methods with parameters in the chapter source files.

```
package
{
    import flash.display.MovieClip;

    public class Main extends MovieClip
    {
        public function Main()
        {
            displayText("This is text from the method call");
        }
        function displayText(textYouWantToDisplay:String):void
        {
            trace(textYouWantToDisplay);
        }
    }
}
```

COMPILER ERRORS   OUTPUT   TIMELINE
This is text from the method call

Figure 3-12. Sample program illustrating how arguments and parameters work

Using multiple arguments and parameters

Methods can use more than one argument or parameter. A function definition that uses more than one parameter looks like this:

```
function methodName (parameterOne:Type, parameterTwo:Type):void
{
  //directives
}
```

The parameters are simply separated by a comma inside the parentheses.

If the function definition uses more than one parameter, the method call also needs to send it the same number of arguments. Here's what a method call with two arguments might look like:

```
methodName(argumentOne, argumentTwo);
```

All you need to do is separate the arguments with a comma. You can create methods with any number of parameters in this same way.

> At some point in your programming career you might need to use a method, but you won't know how many parameters you'll need. Suppose that you have a method that needs to track items from trips to the grocery store and you never know how many items you're going to buy. Today you might have three items, like this:
>
> ```
> methodName (itemOne, itemTwo, itemThree);
> ```
>
> Tomorrow you might have five items, like this:
>
> ```
> methodName (itemOne, itemTwo, itemThree, itemFour, itemFive);
> ```
>
> To avoid having to write two different function definitions, you can create one that stores the arguments it receives in an array. I'll be introducing arrays in Chapter 9, so you'll probably just want to file this information away for reference later. The function definition will look like this:
>
> ```
> function methodName (...itemArray):void
> {
>   //directives
> }
> ```
>
> All the arguments are stored as elements in an array called *itemArray*. The three dots in front of the parameter name indicate that the parameter is an array, not a variable. (For now, you can think of arrays as big filing cabinets that can store lots and lots of variables.)

If you're new to programming, you'll need a bit of practice using methods and looking at different examples. Don't worry! No one completely understands methods at first. Just keep this chapter at hand and experiment with some of the sample programs included in this chapter's source files. You'll see many concrete examples of methods at work in this book and you'll gradually feel comfortable using them.

Understanding events and event listeners

Events are things in a program that happen. You'll be happy to let most things that happen in your program, such as values being assigned to variables, take care of themselves without needing to be bothered with the details. But you'll want to know about some events, such as button clicks, so that you can specify certain directives to run when they occur.

AS3.0 allows you to attach **event listeners** to objects. An event listener "listens" for things that happen in the program. When an event occurs, the listener triggers instructions for what to do. You can think of an event listener as an extremely clever little dog that loves to bark. You've trained your little dog not only to bark madly at burglars but also to dial the number of the police station while doing so and then bark the address of your house to the officer on the other end of the phone. Clever little dog! And that's the kind of dog you have at your disposal with event listeners in AS3.0.

Creating event listeners is a three-step process. You need to do the following to set them up and use them in the program:

1. Import an event class from Flash's events package.

2. Add an event listener to an object using a method call to AS3.0's built-in addEventListener method. The method call includes a number of arguments, such as the kind of event to listen for and what to do when the event occurs.

3. Create an event handler, which is a specialized function definition that tells the program what to do when the event occurs. It "handles" the event. The event handler includes a special parameter that allows it to accept an event object, which provides quite a bit of information about the event that took place. You can use this information in your program.

The best way to understand how event listeners work is to see one in action. In the chapter's source files you'll find a folder called Event listener. Open the files inside as a project, following the steps described earlier in the chapter. When you test the project, click the stage with the left mouse button. You'll see You clicked on the stage displayed in the Output panel. Figure 3-13 illustrates what the program looks like and the result in the Output panel.

Now that you've seen events in action, let's look at a way to make them.

```
package
{
    import flash.display.MovieClip;
    import flash.events.MouseEvent;

    public class Main extends MovieClip
    {
        public function Main()
        {
            stage.addEventListener(MouseEvent.CLICK, onClick);
        }
        function onClick(event:MouseEvent):void
        {
            trace("You clicked on the stage");
        }
    }
}
```

Imports the MouseEvent class. You need to import one of AS3.0's event classes before you can listen for events in your program.

Registers an event that listens for mouse clicks. The event listener is attached to the stage. When the mouse is clicked, the onClick function definition is called.

The code inside this function defintion runs when the stage is clicked. The name of the function defintion matches the second parameter in the addEventListener method call.

A function defintiion that handles events is called an "event handler."

If you click on the stage, you'll see the following in the Output window:

| COMPILER ERRORS | OUTPUT | TIMELINE |

```
You clicked on the stage
```

Figure 3-13. Add an event listener to the stage to "listen" for mouse clicks.

Importing an event class

To use an event listener, first import one of AS3.0's event classes. In this book you'll be using the MouseEvent and KeyboardEvent classes most frequently, although there are many others. The import statement for the MouseEvent class looks like this:

```
import.flash.events.MouseEvent;
```

Once it's imported, you can use it to find out what the mouse is doing, such as clicking things or moving around the stage.

Adding an event listener

The next step is to add an event listener, which detects when the mouse is clicked (you used this directive in the example program in Figure 3-13):

```
stage.addEventListener(MouseEvent.CLICK, onClick);
```

Event listeners are usually added to objects. In this example, you added it to the stage object using dot notation.

Let's break this directive down into smaller pieces. The most important thing is this method call:

```
addEventListener
```

It's a method call to one of AS3.0's built-in methods. It's used to register the event so that the listener can start its job.

At its most basic, the addEventListener method call takes two parameters. In the example from Figure 3-13, the parameters look like this:

```
(MouseEvent.CLICK, onClick)
```

The first parameter is the kind of event you're listening for. In this case, you're listening for mouse clicks. The format for describing the kind of event to listen for is to use the imported event class name, followed by a dot and then the event you're interested in:

```
MouseEvent.CLICK
```

The kind of event you want to listen for is the CLICK event. As I'm sure you can guess, it listens for mouse clicks. (Events are always written in uppercase.)

> The reason events are written in uppercase is because they're actually a programming element called a **constant**. Constants are always written in uppercase, which is the naming convention they follow. (You'll see how to use constants in Chapter 9.) The CLICK constant is built in to the AS3.0 MouseEvent class.

The second parameter is the function definition that you want to call when the event occurs. The example used this one:

```
onClick
```

This is the name of the event handler. Its name must exactly match the name of the function definition that contains the directives you want to run when the mouse button is clicked.

Using the event handler

This is what the event handler looks like in the example shown in Figure 3-13:

```
function onClick(event:MouseEvent):void
{
  trace("You clicked on the stage");
}
```

It's exactly like the function definitions that you looked at earlier in the section on methods. However, there are two unique things about event handlers that distinguish them from ordinary function definitions.

The first difference is the name. By convention, the names for event handlers always begin with the word *on*. Programmers choose to give event handlers names like onClick, onMove, or onSomeKindOfEvent so that they're easy to spot among the other function definitions. You're free to give the event handler any name you like, but you'll make your life a little easier if you stick to this convention. I'll be doing so for the rest of this book.

The second difference is the function definition's parameter:

```
(event:MouseEvent)
```

Event handlers have to declare a special **event variable**, which also has to be the same type as the event that occurred, such as MouseEvent.

What is this event variable? It's actually an object that is automatically created by AS3.0 when the event takes place. Here's how it works:

Imagine clicking the stage with the mouse. As soon that happens, a CLICK event is triggered. The CLICK event is sent by AS3.0 to something called the **event dispatcher**. (You don't need to know much about the event dispatcher except that it's a bit like a little software robot hanging around your program listening for things.) As soon as it hears an event that you've told it to listen for, it takes out a notebook and scribbles down quite a bit of information about the event. For example, if you click a button, it can tell you the name of the button you clicked and where on the stage the click took place. All this information is packaged together into an event object, which is sent to the event handler (the function definition you programmed to run when the event occurs). However, the event handler has to create a variable as one of its parameters to contain the event object. Even though you may not actually need to use this event object in the function definition, AS3.0 requires that you create a variable as a parameter to contain it.

So what kind of information does this event object contain? You can find out by using trace to display its contents in the Output panel. You can change the example function definition so that it looks something like this:

```
function onClick(event:MouseEvent):void
{
  trace(event);
}
```

Now if you save the file, test the project, and then click the stage, you'll see something like this in the Output panel:

```
[MouseEvent type="click" bubbles=true cancelable=false eventPhase=2
localX=360 localY=139 stageX=360 stageY=139 relatedObject=null
ctrlKey=false altKey=false shiftKey=false buttonDown=false delta=0]
```

That's a lot of information! Some of it might actually be very useful, although certainly not for the current needs. Later in the book you'll look at how you can access this information and use it in your games.

101

You can access all this information using dot notation. All you need to do is use the name of the event object, followed by a dot, and then followed by the property of the event object that you need to access. Based on the preceding example, you could use the following code to find out the x position of where the mouse clicked the stage:

```
function onClick(event:MouseEvent):void
{
   trace(event.stageX);
}
```

If there are other objects on the stage, you can find out the name of the object that was clicked by using the target property. Using event.target will give you the name of the object you clicked:

```
function onClick(event:MouseEvent):void
{
   trace(event.target);
}
```

If you use this in the example code, it will output the following:

```
[object Stage]
```

That's the stage.

Understanding other events

This example showed you how to use the CLICK event from the MouseEvent class. The MouseEvent class contains many other events that you're sure to find some use for. Table 3-1 shows the event names and what they do.

Table 3-1. Event names

Event name	Triggers an event when . . .
CLICK	The left mouse button is pressed down and released
DOUBLE_CLICK	The left mouse button is double-clicked
MOUSE_DOWN	The left mouse button is pressed down
MOUSE_MOVE	The mouse moves
MOUSE_OUT	The mouse leaves the area of an object
MOUSE_OVER	The mouse moves over an object
MOUSE_UP	The left mouse button is released
MOUSE_WHEEL	The mouse wheel is moved
ROLL_OVER	The mouse moves over an object (or any of its subobjects)
ROLL_OUT	The mouse moves away from an object (or any of its subobjects)

Many of these events don't work with the stage object that you used in the example, but they all work with button and Movie Clip objects. Here are some examples of how you might register these events using addEventListener:

```
addEventListener.(MouseEvent.ROLL_OVER, onRollOver);
addEventListener.(MouseEvent.ROLL_OUT, onRollOut);
addEventListener.(MouseEvent.MOUSE_MOVE, onMouseMove);
```

Figure 3-14 illustrates the basic model for creating an event listener and what happens when the event occurs.

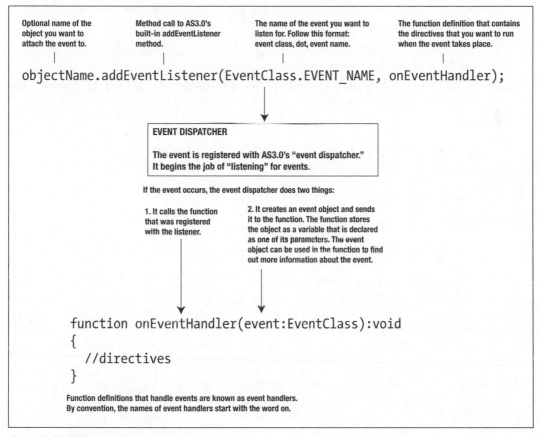

Figure 3-14. How event listeners work

As you did with methods, you'll need a bit of practice and a few more practical examples before you fully grasp how event listeners work. You'll see lots of examples of event listeners in action over the course of this book, so you'll have lots of opportunities to experiment with them and see their effects in different contexts. The nice thing about event listeners is that they all use exactly this same format. You don't have to absolutely understand every detail about how they work yet; you just need to know how to use them to get the results you want for your game.

> *In the example in this section, you attached the event listener directly to the stage object. In the interactive storybook project, you'll attach the listeners to buttons. If you use addEventListener without specifically attaching it to an object, the listener will attach itself directly to the class that it was called in. You'll see many examples of this in action when you start working with multiple classes in Chapter 8.*

Programming storybook buttons

Now that you know about dot notation, methods, and event listeners, you can use them to help you program the buttons in the storybook. Follow these steps:

1. Make sure that the interactiveStorybook project is open. Double-click the interactiveStorybook Main.as file in the project window to open it in the ActionScript editor window.

2. You need to add an import directive to load AS3.0's MouseEvent class into the program. Add the following new code in bold:

```
package
{
  import flash.display.MovieClip;
  import flash.events.MouseEvent;

  public class Main extends MovieClip
  {
    var startPage:StartPage;

    public function Main()
    {
      startPage = new StartPage();
      addChild(startPage);
    }
  }
}
```

> *From now on, follow the convention that new code to add to the program will be highlighted with bold text.*

3. Next, you need to create variables to hold references to instances of the HillPage and PondPage symbols. This is exactly the same process you followed to create the startPage instance. The only difference is that you don't need to use addChild to display them on the stage. You want to create them in AS3.0's memory so that they can be used later. (It's like keeping a jar of sugar stored in the cupboard to that it's ready to use when the aunties come.)

```
package
{
  import flash.display.MovieClip;
  import flash.events.MouseEvent;
```

```
public class Main extends MovieClip
{
  var startPage:StartPage;
  var hillPage:HillPage;
  var pondPage:PondPage;

  public function Main()
  {
    startPage = new StartPage;
    hillPage = new HillPage;
    pondPage = new PondPage;
    addChild(startPage);
  }
}
}
```

4. The next step is to use dot notation to add event listeners to the buttons in the startPage instance:

```
package
{
  import flash.display.MovieClip;
  import flash.events.MouseEvent;

  public class Main extends MovieClip
  {

  var startPage:StartPage;
  var hillPage:HillPage;
  var pondPage:PondPage;

  public function Main()
  {
      startPage = new StartPage();
      hillPage = new HillPage();
      pondPage = new PondPage();
      addChild(startPage);

      //Add event listeners
      startPage.hillButton.addEventListener(MouseEvent.CLICK,➥
        onHillButtonClick);
      startPage.pondButton.addEventListener(MouseEvent.CLICK,➥
        onPondButtonClick);
  }
  }
}
```

5. Next, you need to create event handlers that tell the program what to do when the buttons are clicked:

```
package
{
  import flash.display.MovieClip;
  import flash.events.MouseEvent;

  public class Main extends MovieClip
  {

  var startPage:StartPage;
  var hillPage:HillPage;
  var pondPage:PondPage;

  public function Main()
  {
      startPage = new StartPage();
      hillPage = new HillPage();
      pondPage = new PondPage();
      addChild(startPage);

      //Add event listeners
      startPage.hillButton.addEventListener(MouseEvent.CLICK, ➡
        onHillButtonClick);
      startPage.pondButton.addEventListener(MouseEvent.CLICK, ➡
        onPondButtonClick);
  }
    //Event handlers
    function onHillButtonClick(event:MouseEvent):void
    {
      addChild(hillPage);
      removeChild(startPage);
    }
     function onPondButtonClick(event:MouseEvent):void
    {
      addChild(pondPage);
      removeChild(startPage);
    }
  }
}
```

6. Save the Main.as file.

7. Test the project. You can now click the buttons and view the pond and hill pages. You haven't added buttons back to the start page yet, so you have to quit the SWF and run it again to get back to the start.

The folder Storybook with buttons in the chapter's source files contains the files for the project so far.

This very simple little program is a great example of how variables, dot notation, methods, and event listeners all work together.

Looking at the onHillButtonClick event handler

I've discussed the mechanics of much of these elements in quite a bit of detail, but it's worth taking a closer look at the event handlers that actually do the work of changing the storybook's pages. Here's what the onHillButtonClick event handler looks like:

```
function onHillButtonClick(event:MouseEvent):void
{
  addChild(hillPage);
  removeChild(startPage);
}
```

This event handler contains two directives: it displays the hillPage instance and then hides the startPage instance.

You've seen addChild() before. addChild(hillPage) simply displays the hillPage instance on the stage as simple as that. But when addChild adds instances to the display list, it adds them on top of other instances. That means that the startPage instance is still actually on the stage; it's just being covered up by the hillPage instance, which is completely blocking it from view.

You could leave the startPage instance there. I mean, it's doing no harm and you can't see it anyway. But it's generally not a good idea to leave things on the stage if they're not needed because the Flash Player still devotes some fraction of its precious resources to maintaining it in memory. Remember that performance is everything to a game designer. If you're not using something, don't blink; just get rid of it.

The evil twin sister of addChild() is a method called removeChild(). Its job is to remove instances from the stage so that they're no longer visible. This removes the startPage instance from the stage:

```
removeChild(startPage);
```

Oh if it were it so simple! removeChild( ) holds a dark secret. Even though it removes instances from the stage, those objects still exist as objects in the Flash Player memory. This is both a good and bad thing. It's good because if you want display the object using addChild( ) again at some later point in the program, you don't have to go to all the trouble of creating a new instance of it using the new keyword. It's bad because objects that aren't visible still consume some Flash Player resources.

If you're certain that you won't need an instance in the program again, you have to give the variable that holds a reference to that instance the value of null (a special value that means "has no value").

To give a variable a null value, use a directive that looks like this:

```
variableName = null;
```

For more information on how to completely clear an object from Flash's memory, check out the section on garbage collection in Chapter 8.

Using the onPondButtonClick event handler

Before the chapter ends, have a quick look at the onPondButtonClick event handler:

```
private function onPondButtonClick(event:MouseEvent):void
{
  addChild(pondPage);
  removeChild(startPage);
}
```

It's identical to the onHillButtonClick method, except for one of its directives:

```
addChild(pondPage);
```

Instead of displaying the hillPage instance, it displays pondPage. Pretty easy, no?

Adding back buttons

That last thing you'll do is create buttons that take you back to the startPage. There are no new techniques here, so you can think of this as a good test to see whether you've been paying attention to what has been covered so far. I'm also going to keep the details pretty brief, so if you're not entirely sure about one of the steps, refer to the section in Chapter 2 on making buttons to clarify any uncertainties. (The final program is in the chapter's source files under the Finished storybook folder if you want to take a closer look.) Follow these steps:

1. In the interactive Storybook.fla file, right-click one of the buttons in the Library and chose Duplicate from the Option menu.
2. The Duplicate Symbol dialog box opens. Give the button the name BackToStartButton.
3. Click OK.

4. Double-click the new BackToStartButton symbol in the Library to enter symbol editing mode. Modify it so that it looks similar to Figure 3-15. Remember to modify the button in all three frames: Up, Over, and Down.

Figure 3-15. Create the BackToStartButton symbol.

5. Double-click the HillPage symbol in the Library to enter symbol editing mode.

6. Create a new layer called buttons.

7. Make sure that the buttons layer is selected. Drag an instance of the BackToStartButton onto the stage and position it somewhere that seems appropriate.

8. Give the button the instance name backToStartButton in the Instance name box of the Properties panel.

9. Double-click the PondPage symbol in the Library to enter symbol editing mode. Follow steps 6 to 8 to add the new button to the PondPage symbol.

10. When you finish, the PondPage and HillPage symbols will look something like Figure 3-16.

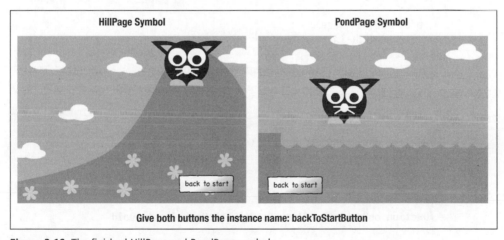

Figure 3-16. The finished HillPage and PondPage symbols

11. Open the Main.as file. Add the following new code to the program:

```
package
{
  import flash.display.MovieClip;
  import flash.events.MouseEvent;

  public class Main extends MovieClip
  {
    var startPage:StartPage;
```

```
      var hillPage:HillPage;
      var pondPage:PondPage;

      public function Main()
      {
        startPage = new StartPage();
        hillPage = new HillPage();
        pondPage = new PondPage();
        addChild(startPage);

        //Add event listeners
        startPage.hillButton.addEventListener(MouseEvent.CLICK, ➥
          onHillButtonClick);
        startPage.pondButton.addEventListener(MouseEvent.CLICK, ➥
          onPondButtonClick);
        hillPage.backToStartButton.addEventListener(MouseEvent.CLICK, ➥
          onBackButtonClick_Hill);
        pondPage.backToStartButton.addEventListener(MouseEvent.CLICK,➥
          onBackButtonClick_Pond);
      }
    //Event handlers
    function onHillButtonClick(event:MouseEvent):void
    {
      addChild(hillPage);
      removeChild(startPage);
    }
    function onPondButtonClick(event:MouseEvent):void
    {
      addChild(pondPage);
      removeChild(startPage);
    }
    function onBackButtonClick_Hill(event:MouseEvent):void
    {
      addChild(startPage);
      removeChild(hillPage);
    }
    function onBackButtonClick_Pond(event:MouseEvent):void
    {
      addChild(startPage);
      removeChild(pondPage);
    }
  }
}
```

12. Save the `Main.as` file.

13. Test the project. You should now be able to click the back to start buttons in both pages to return you to the first page of the storybook.

It should be fairly obvious by now what the new code does. You've added new event listeners to the buttons in the `pondPage` and `hillPage` instances and then wrote event handlers that displayed and removed the appropriate page.

Knowing when to use this model

As a model for creating your own interactive movies, the simple system you used here has a number of advantages:

- **It's understandable**: the relationship between the objects, event listeners, and methods is very clear. You can play with this model while gradually acquiring more confidence as a programmer. And when you're ready to try something a little more daring, you can easily adapt it.

- **Only minimal programming skill is required**: if you understand what you've written in this sample program, making a much larger interactive movie with dozens of pages and buttons is simply a question of doing more of the same. You don't need to know any more programming, and what you lack in programming skill you can easily make up for in imagination. Copy/paste will become your best friend!

- **It's easy to make changes to the program**: if you want to change what the buttons do, you just need to change the directives in the event handlers.

There is one glaring disadvantage, however. Imagine that you have hundreds of pages and hundreds of buttons. You'll have a program that is thousands and thousands of lines of code long, and managing all that could become a horrendous job.

For really big projects, you need a different strategy. You'll probably want to store information about the pages and buttons in some sort of data storage system (such as in an array, which you'll look at in Chapter 9) and then write a small handful of short-but-sweet methods that switch pages based on context. You'll have *much* less code, and it would all be self-administrating. But you'll have to actually know how to do this, and the programming skill and experience required are quite considerable. It's a worthy project and it's one that you'll have the skills to attempt by the time you get to the end of this book.

One word of advice: make sure that whatever you program, you actually understand what you're doing and why it works. A program that's 100 lines long and understandable is better than a super-efficient 10-line program that does the same thing but which you don't understand. Don't feel any pressure to write the most compact and elegant code. That will happen naturally as your skills and confidence grow . . . and they will!

Summary

This chapter covered a lot of new concepts: variables, methods, events, and (programming) buttons. These concepts are some of the most important in AS3.0, and you'll see them in use in many contexts throughout this book. Don't worry too much if it hasn't all sunk in yet; it will take time. You can think of this chapter as a reference to turn back to if you need a refresher on any of these subjects.

If you're a bit hazy on any of these new concepts, go back to the sample programs in the chapter's source files and make some small changes to them. Observing how your changes affect the output is the best way to learn.

The most important thing is this: did you actually make your buttons work? You did? Good for you; you've graduated to Chapter 4!

In Chapter 4, you'll continue to build the interactive storybook. You'll look at how to use properties to control the position and size of objects on the screen, and how to use the timeline and frames to change an object's state.

Chapter 4

CONTROLLING MOVIE CLIP OBJECTS

A large part of game design with Flash is all about learning how to control Movie Clip objects. In this chapter you'll be looking at how you can control Movie Clip objects in two important ways:

- Use the MovieClip class's built-in properties to move, rotate, and scale an object; and toggle its visibility.
- Use code to control a Movie Clip object's timeline, and learn how it can be used to create a simple state machine.

You'll also expand your repertoire of programming skills:

- Use conditional statements with the if keyword.
- Remove event listeners you no longer need.
- Use the MovieClip class's CLICK and MOUSE_OVER events.

You'll continue the storybook project from Chapter 2; by the end of this chapter, you'll have all the skills necessary to build your own completely interactive objects and worlds.

The focus of this book is on making games with the MovieClip class. If you don't need to use a timeline in any of your game objects, however, consider using the slightly leaner Sprite class instead.

Movie Clip properties

Properties are the features of an object that you can control with code. What are these features? They can be variables that are attached to objects that you create. Or they can be any of the built-in properties that are part of the MovieClip class. These built-in properties are of particular use to game designers and will be the subject of the first part of this chapter.

The MovieClip class has a huge number of properties that you can access, use, and sometimes modify. Any Movie Clip object can make use of these properties. You can have a look at these properties by opening up the AS3.0 language reference panel, which is on the left of the script window in which you've been adding all of the programming code. (The language reference window might be closed; if it is, you can open it by clicking the small arrow on the left side of the script window frame.) To find the properties that are available to the MovieClip class, navigate to flash.display ➤ MovieClip ➤ Properties. You should see something like Figure 4-1.

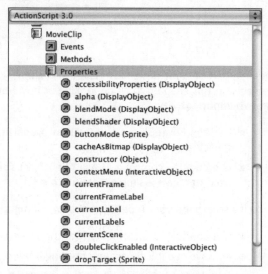

Figure 4-1. Some of the properties of the MovieClip class

Keep scrolling—that's a lot of properties! Fortunately, most of them have specialized uses that you won't use very often.

But for the kind of basic interactivity that you'll need in the storybook, as well as for most of the games in this book, there are a few properties that you'll be using very frequently. As a bonus, they're the really fun-to-use properties, too! Table 4-1 shows the "MovieClip Class Properties' Greatest Hits."

Table 4-1. MovieClip Class Properties

Property	What it represents
alpha	Refers to the transparency of an object. You can assign it any value between zero (0) and 1. Zero means that the object is completely transparent; 1 means that it's completely opaque. The values in between, such as 0.5, make the object translucent. All objects start out with a default value of 1.
height	The height of an object in pixels. If you assign it a value of 100, the object becomes 100 pixels tall. A **pixel** is an illuminated dot on the screen. One pixel is the smallest possible size that a graphic can be. However, you can assign a fractional value (a value with a decimal) if you need to, such as 7.8.
width	The width of an object in pixels.
rotation	The rotation of the object in degrees. A value from 0 to 180 represents a clockwise rotation. Values from 0 to -180 represent a counterclockwise rotation.
scaleX	The horizontal scale of an object. All objects start out with a scaleX value of 1. If you change it to 2, the object will become twice as wide (200%). A value of 0.5 will make the object 50% narrower. A value of 1.1 will make the object 10% wider. scaleX is similar to the width property, except that it deals with percentages of scale instead of fixed pixels.
scaleY	Similar to scaleX, except that it refers to the vertical scale of the object.
visible	Determines whether the display object is visible. The visible property can take two values: true or false. True/false values are known in computer programming terminology as **Boolean** values. The word *Boolean* refers to George Boole, the founder of Boolean algebra, which is the basis of computer mathematics.
x	The horizontal position of an object on the stage in pixels. The leftmost position of the stage is 0. If the stage is 550 pixels wide, and you want to position an object in the center, you'd give the x property a value of 275. To move it to a position 100 pixels from the right side, you'd give it a value of 450.
y	The vertical position of an object on the stage. This is also a value in pixels. The very top of the stage is position 0. As you work your way down, the numbers increase. This means that if the stage is 400 pixels high, and you want to position an object 100 pixels from the top, you'd give its y property a value of 100. To position it 100 pixels from the bottom of the stage, you'd give the y property a value of 300.

Several additional properties are used for transforming an object in 3D space. You won't be using them in this book, but you should know that they exist and experiment with them when you have the chance. Although their primary purpose is to be used as building blocks for creating 3D objects and spaces, you might find uses for these properties for special effects in some of your games. Table 4-2 shows 3D properties you might want to get to know.

Table 4-2. MovieClip Class's 3D Properties

3D property	What it represents
z	The depth of the object in 3D space. Higher numbers make the object appear farther away; lower numbers make it appear closer.
scaleZ	The scale (ratio of its original size) of the object in 3D space. The object is scaled from its center registration point.
rotationX	The rotation of the object around the x axis.
rotationY	The rotation of the object around the y axis.
rotationZ	The rotation of the object around the z axis.

You can have a lot of fun with these properties, and they're very easy to use. In the next few sections, you'll use them in the storybook to turn the cat object into an interactive toy.

Setting up the project files

You're welcome to continue working on the same project files from Chapter 2, but you can start working from the start files in the chapter's source if you prefer. To do that, follow these steps:

1. In Flash, select File ➤ Open.
2. Navigate to the Start Files folder in the chapter's source files.
3. Select the FLA file called interactiveStorybook_Part2.fla and click the Open button. The FLA will open in Flash's main workspace.
4. In the Project panel, click the drop-down menu. Select Quick Project. The interactiveStorybook_Part2.fla and Main.as files appear as project files.

To open any of these files in Flash's workspace, just click the file's name in the Project panel.

Going up and down

The first thing you'll do is create an **up button** and a **down button** to move the cat up and down the hill. There are a few ways to program these buttons. To demonstrate exactly how the x and y properties work, you'll start with the simplest way and then modify the program a little so that the effect is a bit more realistic.

1. Create a button called DownButton. You can either create it from scratch or duplicate one of the existing buttons in the Library. If you're creating one from scratch, remember to select Export for ActionScript when you create the button symbol and make sure that the button contains Up, Over, and Down states.

2. Create another button called UpButton, following the same steps.

3. Double-click the HillPage symbol in the Library to enter symbol editing mode.

4. Click the HillPage symbol's buttons layer once to select it.

5. Drag an instance of the DownButton onto the stage. Make sure that it is added to the buttons layer (you can confirm that this has happened if the buttons layer's first frame contains a solid black keyframe).

6. Give the button you just added the instance name downButton.

7. Drag an instance of the UpButton onto the HillPage symbol's stage. Give it the instance name upButton.

8. Select the cat object. Give it the name cat in the Instance name box in the Properties panel, as shown in Figure 4-2.

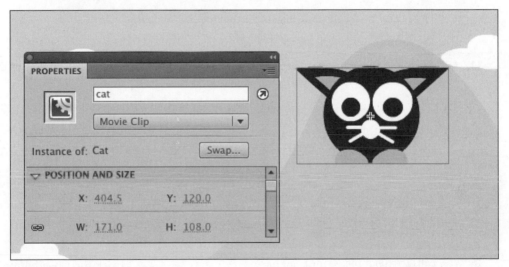

Figure 4-2. Assign the instance name.

While the cat is still selected, have a look at the Position and Size pane of the Properties panel, an example of which you can see in Figure 4-2. X: and Y: stand for the horizontal and vertical positions of the object. All these values are given in pixels. H: and W: stand for height and width.

9. Write down the number next to Y:. This is the current vertical position of the cat on the stage, and you'll need to use this number very soon in your program. My cat's Y: position is 120, but yours will almost certainly be different. Remember it!

10. When you finish, the `HillPage` symbol might look something like Figure 4-3.

Figure 4-3. The new cat, upButton, and downButton instances

11. Add or change the following code in bold to the `Main.as` file (you'll be taking a look at exactly how it works in the next section):

```
package
{
  import flash.display.MovieClip;
  import flash.events.MouseEvent;

  public class Main extends MovieClip
  {
    var startPage:StartPage;
    var hillPage:HillPage;
    var pondPage:PondPage;

    public function Main()
    {
      startPage = new StartPage();
      hillPage = new HillPage();
      pondPage = new PondPage();
      addChild(hillPage);

      //Add event listeners
      startPage.hillButton.addEventListener(MouseEvent.CLICK, ➥
        onHillButtonClick);
      startPage.pondButton.addEventListener(MouseEvent.CLICK, ➥
        onPondButtonClick);
```

```
        hillPage.backToStartButton.addEventListener(MouseEvent.CLICK, ➡
          onBackButtonClick_Hill);
        pondPage.backToStartButton.addEventListener(MouseEvent.CLICK, ➡
          onBackButtonClick_Pond);
        hillPage.upButton.addEventListener(MouseEvent.CLICK, ➡
          onUpButtonClick);
        hillPage.downButton.addEventListener(MouseEvent.CLICK, ➡
          onDownButtonClick);
      }
      //Event handlers
      function onHillButtonClick(event:MouseEvent):void
      {
        addChild(hillPage);
        removeChild(startPage);
      }
      function onPondButtonClick(event:MouseEvent):void
      {
        addChild(pondPage);
        removeChild(startPage);
      }
      function onBackButtonClick_Hill(event:MouseEvent):void
      {
        addChild(startPage);
        removeChild(hillPage);
      }
      function onBackButtonClick_Pond(event:MouseEvent):void
      {
        addChild(startPage);
        removeChild(pondPage);
      }
      function onUpButtonClick(event:MouseEvent):void
      {
        // Replace 120 with the y position of your cat
        //that you wrote down in step 7
        hillPage.cat.y = 120;
      }
      function onDownButtonClick(event:MouseEvent):void
      {
        // Replace 220 with a value that is aproximately
        //100 pixels greater than your cat's original position
        hillPage.cat.y = 220;
      }
    }
  }
```

12. Save the Main.as file.

13. Test the project.

14. Click the down button and then the up button. The cat should now be able to move up and down the hill, as shown in Figure 4-4.

Figure 4-4. Click the buttons to move the cat up and down the hill.

That's amazing, isn't it? Funny how such a simple little effect can be so satisfying to watch, especially after all the effort you've put into the storybook so far.

You should recognize much of the new code from Chapter 2. You've simply added event listeners to the two new buttons and created event handlers to run the appropriate directives. However, there is one new line of code that might stand out:

```
addChild(hillPage);
```

Previously, that line read addChild(startPage);. Why was it changed? In this part of the chapter you'll be working with the hill page. It would have been a big bother if every time you tested the program you needed to first click the hill button on the start page to get there. For testing purposes, it makes sense to display the hill page right away. Later, when the program is finished and you're happy with the way everything is working, you can change it back to the way it was.

Let's have a look at the directive in the onDownButtonClick event handler:

```
hillPage.cat.y = 220;
```

The object name of the cat is hillPage.cat. The cat object is an instance inside the hillPage object, so you need to write out its full name using dot notation. The y stands for the y property of the object. The y property represents its vertical position, in pixels, from the top of the stage. The equal sign is used to assign it a value of 220. (The value you use might be different.) The original position of the cat is 120, so when you click the button, the event handler moves the cat to the new position, creating the illusion that it has moved down the hill.

The directive that is triggered by the onUpButtonClick event handler is almost identical. Only the y value is different.

```
hillPage.cat.y = 120;
```

The number 120 (which will be different in your program) is the original position of the cat—that you noted from the Position and Size panes in the Properties panel. All you did is move the cat back to that original position when the up button is clicked.

Understanding x and y positions of objects

In Flash and AS3.0, the leftmost side of the stage has an x position number of zero. As you move to the right, the numbers increase. The rightmost side of the stage in the storybook has an x position number of 550.

The very top of the stage has a y position number of zero. As an object moves down the stage, its y position number increases. The very bottom of the stage in the storybook has a y position number of 400.

The fact that the y position number *increases* as you move down the stage is an odd quirk in Flash and AS3.0's coordinate system that might take some getting used to. Figure 4-5 illustrates how to find the x and y positions of objects on the stage.

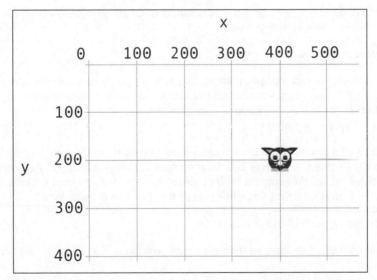

Figure 4-5. The cat in this illustration has an x position of 400 and a y position of 200.

As you can see, to move an object down the stage, you need to increase its y value.

Moving incrementally

The buttons work: they move the cat up and down the hill. But wouldn't it be nice if you could move the cat down the hill gradually? That would be a much more realistic effect and make the cat toy a little more fun to play with. Fortunately, this is very easy to do:

1. Update the directives in the onUpButtonClick and onDownButtonClick event handlers with the following new text in bold:

```
function onUpButtonClick(event:MouseEvent):void
{
   hillPage.cat.y = hillPage.cat.y - 15;
}
function onDownButtonClick(event:MouseEvent):void
{
   hillPage.cat.y = hillPage.cat.y + 15;
}
```

2. Save the Main.as file and test the project.

Now each time you click the up or down button, the cat moves 15 pixels in either direction. Much better!

But how did this work? The logic behind it is very simple once you get your head around it. Let's have a look at the onDownButtonClick directive:

```
hillPage.cat.y = hillPage.cat.y + 15;
```

This directive takes the current y position of the cat, adds 15 pixels to it, and then reassigns the new total back to the cat's current y position. Think of it this way: the cat's new position is a combination of its position before the button was clicked, plus 15 pixels. You want to move the cat down the stage, so you need to *increase* its y position.

I know, this is a bit of a brain-twister! Let's break it down a little more. The starting position of the cat in my program is 120 pixels. Whenever the program sees hillPage.cat.y, it interprets that to mean "120 pixels." You've set up the program so that every time the down button is clicked, 15 pixels are added to the cat's y position. That's what this part of the directive in bold does:

```
hillPage.cat.y = hillPage.cat.y + 15;
```

It just adds 15 to the cat's y position, so the cat's new y position is 135. So you could actually write the directive this way:

```
hillPage.cat.y = 135;
```

Pretty simple, really, isn't it?

The next time the button is clicked, exactly the same thing happens, except that hillPage.cat.y now starts with a value of 135 pixels. Fifteen pixels are added again, so the new value becomes 150. Each new button click adds another 15 pixels to the position, and the result is that the cat looks like it's gradually moving down the hill.

Tracing the output

To help you come to grips with how this is working, add a trace directive to the event handlers in the program:

1. Add the following code in bold to the onUpButtonClick and onDownButtonClick event handlers:

```
function onUpButtonClick(event:MouseEvent):void
{
  hillPage.cat.y = hillPage.cat.y - 15;
  trace(hillPage.cat.y);
}
function onDownButtonClick(event:MouseEvent):void
{
  hillPage.cat.y = hillPage.cat.y + 15;
  trace(hillPage.cat.y);
}
```

2. Save the Main.as file and test the project.

Click the down button a few times. Each time you click it, you'll see the new value of the hillPage.cat.y property displayed in the Output panel. Although your numbers will be different, the effect will be similar to what I see in my Output panel, as shown in Figure 4-6. You can see that the values increase by 15 with each click.

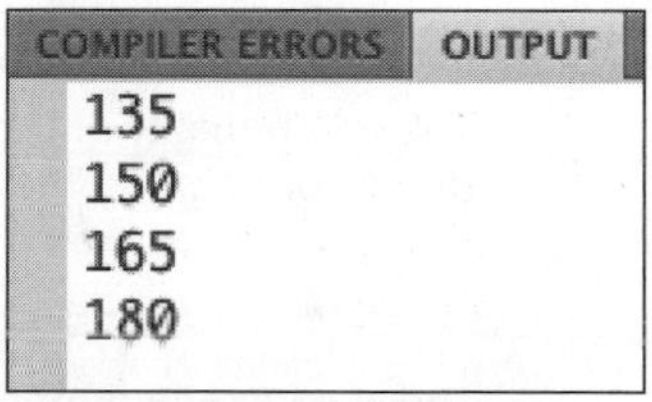

Clicking the up button produces numbers in the opposite direction as the cat moves up the stage.

Using a trace directive is a great way to help you figure out what your code is doing, and you'll be using it a lot to help test and debug the projects in this book.

COMPILER ERRORS	OUTPUT
135	
150	
165	
180	

Figure 4-6. Trace displays the value of the cat's y property each time you click the down button.

Using increment and decrement operators

There's a slightly more efficient way to write this code. Updating values incrementally, as you did before, is such a common and useful thing that AS3.0 has specialized operators that do the work for you.

> **Operators** are symbols such as =, -, + and *, which perform specialized tricks with values, such as assigning, adding, or subtracting them.

The two new operators that you'll use are called the **increment** and **decrement** operators. Update the onUpButtonClick and onDownButtonClick event handlers so that they use these operators:

1. Modify the onUpButtonClick and onDownButtonClick event handlers so that they reflect the changes shown following. (I haven't included the trace directives, and you can remove them if you want to, but leaving them in is just fine, too! It won't affect how the program runs.)

```
function onUpButtonClick(event:MouseEvent):void
{
  hillPage.cat.y -= 15;
}
function onDownButtonClick(event:MouseEvent):void
{
  hillPage.cat.y += 15;
}
```

2. Save the Main.as file and test the project.

The functionality of the program is exactly the same, but I simplified the code a bit by using the decrement operator:

```
-=
```

and the increment operator:

```
+=
```

All these operators do is assign the new value back into the property on the left of the operator sign. The -= operator subtracts the value, and the += operator adds it.

Incrementing and decrementing are a game designer's staple, so get used to using them because you'll be seeing them a lot from now on.

Limiting movement

You might have noticed that there's no limit to how high or low the cat can go on the stage. In fact, you can make the cat go all the way to the top of the stage and continue going beyond it endlessly. There is a kind of existential appeal to being able to model such an abstract concept as infinity in such a concrete way, but it doesn't help your game!

You have to limit the cat's range by using a **conditional statement** with the if keyword. The conditional statement checks to see whether the cat's y position is in an allowable range; if not, it prevents the directive in the event handler from running.

An if statement is very easy to implement. It's a block statement that you can drop anywhere in the program to check whether a certain condition is true. If the condition is true, the directives inside the block run. If they're false, they don't run.

Here's a plain English example of how an if statement works:

```
if (whatever is inside these parentheses is true)
{
   ... then run the directives inside these braces.
}
```

Let's use a real-world if statement in the methods you've just written to test it:

1. Add the following code in bold to the program (remember to replace 120 and 220 with whatever numbers you've been using):

```
function onUpButtonClick(event:MouseEvent):void
{
  if(hillPage.cat.y >= 120)
  {
    hillPage.cat.y -= 15;
  }
}
function onDownButtonClick(event:MouseEvent):void
{
  if(hillPage.cat.y <= 220)
  {
    hillPage.cat.y += 15;
  }
}
```

2. Save the Main.as file and test the project.

Try clicking the up and down buttons. The cat is now prevented from moving beyond a certain distance. Exactly the effect you want to achieve!

Let's look at how the if statement works in the onUpButtonClick event handler:

```
if(hillPage.cat.y >= 120)
{
   hillPage.cat.y -= 15;
}
```

The key to making it work is the conditional statement inside the parentheses:

if(hillPage.cat.y >= 120)

Conditional statements are used to check whether a certain condition is true or false. The preceding conditional statement is checking to see whether the y position of the cat is greater than or equal to 120. If the condition resolves as true, the directive it contains inside the curly braces is executed.

Conditional statements use **conditional operators** to do their checking for them. The conditional operator used in the if statement is the **greater-than-or-equal-to** operator. It looks like this:

```
>=
```

This operator checks whether the value on its left (the cat's y position) is greater than or equal to the value on its right. There are many conditional operators available to use with AS3.0, and Table 4-3 shows the most common ones.

Table 4-3. Conditional Operators

Symbol	Name	What it does
==	Equality operator.	Literally means "is equal to." Checks to see whether two values are equal to one another. 10 == 10 returns a value of true. 10 == 3 returns a value of false. Make sure that you don't confuse the equality operator (==) with the assignment operator (=). This is a common confusion! Remember that = means "gets the value of" and is used to assign values to variables or properties. == is used to compare values. There is a strict version of the equality operator that makes sure that the two values are of the same type before the comparison is made. This can help avoid certain kinds or errors that happen when trying to compare incompatible value types, such as trying to compare apples and oranges. The strict equality operator looks like this: === You should know that this strict version exists, but you won't be using it in this book.

Symbol	Name	What it does
!=	Inequality operator.	Literally means "is not equal to." (The ! sign represents the word *not*.) Checks to see whether two values are not equal to one another. 10 != 15 returns a value of true. 10 != 10 returns a value of false. You might be surprised at how useful the inequality operator is. In many cases, it's more useful to know if a condition isn't true instead of whether it is. You'll be using this operator a lot in your game design projects. The strict version of the inequality operator, which prevents you from comparing incompatible types of objects, looks like this: !== Again, you won't be using this strict version in the book.
<	Less-than operator.	Checks to see whether the value on the left is less than the value on the right. 10 < 15 returns a value of true. 15 < 10 returns a value of false.
>	Greater-than operator.	Checks to see whether the value on the left is greater than the value on the right. 10 > 15 returns a value of false. 15 > 10 returns a value of true.
<=	Less-than-or-equal-to operator.	Similar to the less-than operator, but it also resolves as true if the values are equal to one another, which is a very useful thing to test for in many cases. 10 <= 15 returns a value of true. 15 <= 10 returns a value of false. 10 <= 10 returns a value of true.
>=	Greater-than-or-equal-to operator.	Similar to the greater-than operator, but, like its sister operator, it also resolves as true if the values are equal to one another. 10 >= 15 returns a value of false. 15 >= 10 returns a value of true. 10 >= 10 returns a value of true.

Keep this chart nearby because you'll be using many of these operators very frequently in the projects to come.

It's not a bug, it's a feature!

There's one anomaly in the way if statements were written in the program. It's an extremely important thing to look at because, as a game designer, you'll be dealing with this sort of thing all the time. In fact, finding techniques to avoid it will be the cornerstone around much of the code you'll be writing in later chapters. If you understand the problem now, you'll be miles ahead of the curve when you get into collision detection and stage boundaries. What is it? Let's do a bit of detective work and find out.

You set up the conditional statements so that the directives execute only if the cat's y position is less than 120 or greater than 220. But is that really what is happening? It is, but it's not working in the way you might have expected. Let's use trace to make a quick test:

1. Add the following two trace directives in bold to the onUpButtonClick and onDownButtonClick event handlers:

```
function onUpButtonClick(event:MouseEvent):void
{
  if(hillPage.cat.y >= 120)
  {
    hillPage.cat.y -= 15;
    trace(hillPage.cat.y);
  }
}
function onDownButtonClick(event:MouseEvent):void
{
  if(hillPage.cat.y <= 220)
  {
    hillPage.cat.y += 15;
    trace(hillPage.cat.y);
  }
}
```

2. Save the Main.as file and test the project.

3. Click the down button a few times and have a look at the Output panel. Do you see a number greater than the maximum that you specified your cat should be allowed to go to?

4. Click the up button a few times. Does the cat's y position become less than the lowest position that you specified in the conditional statement?

When I click the down button seven times in my storybook, I get this output from the trace statement, as shown in Figure 4-7.

I set my conditional statement to limit the cat's y position to 220, but the trace clearly shows that the cat moves to a y of position of 225! What happened?

It looks like a bug, but the code is actually working exactly as it should be. Think about it carefully. Let's say I clicked the down button six times. That would give the cat a y position of 210. The next time I click the button, the conditional statement runs:

```
if (HillPage.cat.y <= 220)
```

At this stage in the program, you can interpret it to mean this:

```
if (210 <= 220)
```

COMPILER ERRORS	OUTPUT
135	
150	
165	
180	
195	
210	
225	

Figure 4-7. The cat's y position value is higher than the limit you set in the if statement.

In plain English, this statement is asking this question: is 210 less than or equal to 220? The answer is yes, of course! The directives execute and move the cat an additional 15 pixels to its new y position of 225. The code is working perfectly!

"It's not a bug; it's a feature!" This phrase has been uttered by more than a few programmers in the face of disgruntled clients who think a piece of software is buggy, even though code is working perfectly as written. Depending on the charm of the programmer, he or she might be able to convince the client that the supposed bug is actually a good thing in some way and thus save a lot of time reprogramming.

In most of your game projects, at least your first few, you'll be your own client. So you need to ask yourself whether you can accept the way the code is behaving, or whether you need to roll up your sleeves and get down to the hard work of figuring out what's wrong, why it's wrong, and what you have to do to fix it.

Let's think about the current problem a little more. Is it okay for the cat to move as far as it does? After all, pixel-perfect precision isn't really important in this project, and if you click the button again, the code continues to do its job and prevents the cat from moving any farther. You could shrug your shoulders and move on.

But what if that weren't okay? It's an interesting problem to consider. Let's see whether you can fine-tune the code a bit to prevent the cat from moving beyond the bounds you've set for it. There are few ways to solve this, but I'll discuss the most interesting solution because it will really help your future understanding of later chapters.

First, is it possible for the cat to actually reach a y position of 220? No, it isn't. Each button click moves the cat 15 pixels at a time, so if it starts out at a y position of 120, it will "jump over" 220 on its way from 210 to 225. The only way you can get it to stop at 220 is to actually force it back to that position if it happens to go over (similar to a car that accidentally drives through a red light, screeches to a halt in the middle of an intersection, and then sheepishly reverses back to the white line). That might work! Maybe you just need a traffic cop to blow a whistle at the wayward code. You can actually program a traffic cop with additional if statements pretty easily. Let's try it:

1. Add and change the following code in bold to the onUpButtonClick and onDownButtonClick event handlers. It's considerably different from the first version, so make sure to update it carefully. Replace 120 and 220 with the values you've been using in your own program.

```
function onUpButtonClick(event:MouseEvent):void
{
  hillPage.cat.y -= 15;
  if (hillPage.cat.y < 120)
  {
     hillPage.cat.y = 120;
  }
  trace(hillPage.cat.y);
}
function onDownButtonClick(event:MouseEvent):void
{
  hillPage.cat.y += 15;
  if (hillPage.cat.y > 220)
  {
```

```
        hillPage.cat.y = 220;
    }
    trace(hillPage.cat.y);
}
```

2. Save the `Main.as` file and test the project.

3. Click the up and down buttons and see what happens to the cat when it reaches the outer bounds of its range. It will stay in range and never move beyond the two values you gave it. The traffic cop is doing its job!

How does this work?

Let's imagine that the cat is at y position 210. You click the button, and the first directive executes. It assigns the cat a new y position of 225. But now you have an `if` statement that runs immediately after this one. Its job is to check to see whether the cat's y position is greater than 220. Yes, 225 is definitely over, so the conditional statement resolves as `true`, and the directive in the `if` statement runs. That directive is a really simple one:

```
    hillPage.cat.y = 220;
```

All it does is force the cat to a y position of 220. So even though the first directive produced a value of 225, the `if` statement corrected it, and that's the result you see on the stage. The cat stops at a y position of exactly 220 pixels. The traffic cop is doing its job!

The `if` statement in the `onUpButtonClick` method does exactly the same thing by checking whether the cat's y position is less than 120 and then forcing it to position 120 if it is.

Bugs? Ha! You've got a real feature now!

This might all seem a little overly technical, but these kinds of bugs-that-aren't-really-bugs-but-things-that-could-be-better will probably end up taking up the majority of your programming time as you refine how your games work. As another rule of thumb, about 30% of development time is spent getting a game to work; the other 70% is spent getting it to work well.

The other reason why this is such an important issue to deal with early on is that you'll be faced with this exact same problem when you look at collision detection and stage boundaries—except that your objects will be updating their positions 30 frames per second at speeds and in directions that you'll have no direct control over. Remember this solution because it will come to your rescue in a massive way a few chapters from now.

Making it bigger and smaller

There's so much fun you can have playing around with Movie Clip properties. The next thing you'll do is tear a page out of *Alice in Wonderland* and use the scaleX and scaleY properties to make the cat shrink and grow in size:

1. Create a button called GrowButton.

2. Create another button called ShrinkButton.

3. Double-click the HillPage symbol in the Library to enter symbol editing mode.

4. Select the buttons layer if it isn't already selected.

5. Drag an instance of the GrowButton onto the HillPage symbol's stage. Give it the instance name growButton.

6. Drag an instance of the ShrinkButton onto the HillPage symbol's stage. Give it the instance name shrinkButton. The HillPage symbol might now look something like Figure 4-8.

Figure 4-8. Add grow and shrink buttons to the HillPage symbol.

7. Add the following code to the Main.as file:

```
package
{
  import flash.display.MovieClip;
  import flash.events.MouseEvent;

  public class Main extends MovieClip
  {
```

133

```
var startPage:StartPage;
var hillPage:HillPage;
var pondPage:PondPage;

public function Main()
{
  startPage = new StartPage();
  hillPage = new HillPage();
  pondPage = new PondPage();
  addChild(hillPage);

  //Add event listeners
  startPage.hillButton.addEventListener(MouseEvent.CLICK, ➥
    onHillButtonClick);
  startPage.pondButton.addEventListener(MouseEvent.CLICK, ➥
    onPondButtonClick);
  hillPage.backToStartButton.addEventListener(MouseEvent.CLICK, ➥
    onBackButtonClick_Hill);
  pondPage.backToStartButton.addEventListener(MouseEvent.CLICK, ➥
    onBackButtonClick_Pond);
  hillPage.upButton.addEventListener(MouseEvent.CLICK, ➥
    onUpButtonClick);
  hillPage.downButton.addEventListener(MouseEvent.CLICK, ➥
    onDownButtonClick);
  hillPage.growButton.addEventListener(MouseEvent.CLICK, ➥
    onGrowButtonClick);
  hillPage.shrinkButton.addEventListener(MouseEvent.CLICK, ➥
    onShrinkButtonClick);
}
//Event handlers
function onHillButtonClick(event:MouseEvent):void
{
  addChild(hillPage);
  removeChild(startPage);
}
function onPondButtonClick(event:MouseEvent):void
{
  addChild(pondPage);
  removeChild(startPage);
}
```

```
function onBackButtonClick_Hill(event:MouseEvent):void
{
  addChild(startPage);
  removeChild(hillPage);
}
function onBackButtonClick_Pond(event:MouseEvent):void
{
  addChild(startPage);
  removeChild(pondPage);
}
function onUpButtonClick(event:MouseEvent):void
{
  hillPage.cat.y -= 15;
  if (hillPage.cat.y < 120)
  {
    hillPage.cat.y = 120;
  }
  trace(hillPage.cat.y);
}
function onDownButtonClick(event:MouseEvent):void
{
  hillPage.cat.y += 15;
  if (hillPage.cat.y > 220)
  {
    hillPage.cat.y = 220;
  }
  trace(hillPage.cat.y);
}
function onGrowButtonClick(event:MouseEvent):void
{
  hillPage.cat.scaleX += 0.1;
  hillPage.cat.scaleY += 0.1;
}
function onShrinkButtonClick(event:MouseEvent):void
{
  hillPage.cat.scaleX -= 0.1;
  hillPage.cat.scaleY -= 0.1;
}
  }
}
```

8. Save the `Main.as` file and test the project. You can now click the grow and shrink buttons to change the size of the cat, as shown in Figure 4-9.

Figure 4-9. Click the grow and shrink buttons to change the size of the cat.

*If you want the cat object to scale evenly on all sides, the graphics in the Cat symbol need to be centered over the symbol's center point. The center point of a symbol is also known as the **registration point**. It's the black crosshairs that represents an x and y position of 0. If you test the project and see that the cat is scaling in a slightly lopsided way, it means that the graphics aren't centered on the symbol's registration point.*

To center the graphics, open the Cat symbol, select the cat entirely with the Selection *tool, and drag it so that it's centered over the black crosshairs. Figure 4-10 illustrates this process.*

Figure 4-10. Center the graphics over the registration point so that the object scales evenly on all sides.

The basic functionality of the onGrowButtonClick and onShrinkButtonClick event handlers is identical to that used for the up and down buttons. But instead of using the y property, you're using the scaleX and scaleY properties to scale the cat horizontally and vertically. You need to use both these properties together to scale the cat evenly. If you use only one, say scaleX, the cat will become very fat around the middle without growing in height at all. (Try it and see!)

> *In fact, now that you know you can change two properties simultaneously, you can also try this with the x and y properties. To move the cat up and down the hill diagonally, you can change the event handlers for the* up *and* down *buttons so that they look like this:*
>
> ```
> function onUpButtonClick(event:MouseEvent):void
> {
>   hillPage.cat.y -= 15;
>   hillPage.cat.x += 10;
>   if (hillPage.cat.y < 120)
>   {
>       hillPage.cat.y = 120;
>   }
>   trace(hillPage.cat.y);
> }
> function onDownButtonClick(event:MouseEvent):void
> {
>   hillPage.cat.y += 15;
>   hillPage.cat.x -= 10;
>   if (hillPage.cat.y > 220)
>   {
>       hillPage.cat.y = 220;
>   }
>   trace(hillPage.cat.y);
> }
> ```
>
> *There is no limit on the cat's x position, but it isn't difficult to add one with another* if *statement. Can you see how it might be done? Try it!*

The scaleX and scaleY properties use values that refer to a ratio of the object's scale. That means that all objects have a value of 1 at their original size. If you want to double the size of the object, you need to give it a scaleX and scaleY value of 2. In the new code you've added, you're increasing or decreasing the cat's scale by 0.1 each time the button is clicked, and that's a change of 10% of its original size.

It's interesting to contrast the scaleX and scaleY properties with the height and width properties. They both modify the size of an object, but the height and width properties use pixel values. Let's make a few small changes to the onGrowButtonClick and onShrinkButtonClick event handlers to test it:

1. Make the following changes to the onGrowButtonClick and onShrinkButtonClick event handlers by replacing the original code with the code in bold:

```
function onGrowButtonClick(event:MouseEvent):void
{
  hillPage.cat.width += 15;
  hillPage.cat.height += 15;
}
function onShrinkButtonClick(event:MouseEvent):void
{
  hillPage.cat.width -= 15;
  hillPage.cat.height -= 15;
}
```

2. Save the Main.as file and test the project.

Click both the grow and shrink buttons a few times, and you should see something interesting happen. The cat will grow in both directions, but unless the cat's height in pixels is exactly the same as its width, you'll soon start to notice that it will begin to distort slightly. This is because the directives are adding the same number of pixels evenly for both the height and width, even though the cat's dimensions weren't even to begin with. scaleX and scaleY avoid this problem by scaling the object proportionately in all dimensions.

It's important to understand these subtle differences because sometimes using the height and width properties is preferable to using scaleX and scaleY, and vice versa.

Vanishing!

The next little trick uses the visible property to make the cat disappear. The visible property is a little different from the others you've looked at so far because it uses Boolean values. (As discussed, Boolean values are values that can be only true or false.) This allows you to use a bit of programming sleight-of-hand to make a **toggle button**. You'll be able to switch (or **toggle**) the cat's visibility on and off with only one button. But before you do that, let's get the basic visibility button up and running.

1. Create a button called VisibilityButton in the same way you created the previous buttons.

2. Open the HillPage symbol. Select the buttons layer if it isn't already selected.

3. Drag an instance of the VisibilityButton onto the HillPage symbol's stage. Give it the instance name visibilityButton. The HillPage symbol might now look something like Figure 4-11.

Figure 4-11. Add a visibility button to the HillPage symbol.

4. Add the following code in bold to the Main.as file:

```
package
{
  import flash.display.MovieClip;
  import flash.events.MouseEvent;

  public class Main extends MovieClip
  {
    var startPage:StartPage;
    var hillPage:HillPage;
    var pondPage:PondPage;

    public function Main()
    {
      startPage = new StartPage();
      hillPage = new HillPage();
      pondPage = new PondPage();
      addChild(hillPage);

      //Add event listeners
      startPage.hillButton.addEventListener(MouseEvent.CLICK, ➥
        onHillButtonClick);
      startPage.pondButton.addEventListener(MouseEvent.CLICK, ➥
        onPondButtonClick);
      hillPage.backToStartButton.addEventListener(MouseEvent.CLICK, ➥
        onBackButtonClick_Hill);
```

```
        pondPage.backToStartButton.addEventListener(MouseEvent.CLICK, ➡
          onBackButtonClick_Pond);
        hillPage.upButton.addEventListener(MouseEvent.CLICK, ➡
          onUpButtonClick);
        hillPage.downButton.addEventListener(MouseEvent.CLICK, ➡
          onDownButtonClick);
        hillPage.growButton.addEventListener(MouseEvent.CLICK, ➡
          onGrowButtonClick);
        hillPage.shrinkButton.addEventListener(MouseEvent.CLICK, ➡
          onShrinkButtonClick);
        hillPage.visibilityButton.addEventListener(MouseEvent.CLICK, ➡
          onVisibilityButtonClick);
      }
      //Event handlers
      function onHillButtonClick(event:MouseEvent):void
      {
        addChild(hillPage);
        removeChild(startPage);
      }
      function onPondButtonClick(event:MouseEvent):void
      {
        addChild(pondPage);
        removeChild(startPage);
      }
      function onBackButtonClick_Hill(event:MouseEvent):void
      {
        addChild(startPage);
        removeChild(hillPage);
      }
      function onBackButtonClick_Pond(event:MouseEvent):void
      {
        addChild(startPage);
        removeChild(pondPage);
      }
      function onUpButtonClick(event:MouseEvent):void
      {
        hillPage.cat.y -= 15;
        if (hillPage.cat.y < 120)
        {
          hillPage.cat.y = 120;
        }
        trace(hillPage.cat.y);
      }
      function onDownButtonClick(event:MouseEvent):void
      {
        hillPage.cat.y += 15;
        if (hillPage.cat.y > 220)
```

```
    {
      hillPage.cat.y = 220;
    }
    trace(hillPage.cat.y);
  }
  function onGrowButtonClick(event:MouseEvent):void
  {
    hillPage.cat.width += 15;
    hillPage.cat.height += 15;
  }
  function onShrinkButtonClick(event:MouseEvent):void
  {
    hillPage.cat.width -= 15;
    hillPage.cat.height -= 15;
  }
  function onVisibilityButtonClick(event:MouseEvent):void
  {
    hillPage.cat.visible = false;
  }
    }
  }
```

5. Save the Main.as file and test the project.

6. Click the visibility button. The cat will vanish!

The directive that accomplished this disappearing act was this line in the onVisibilityButtonClick event handler:

```
    hillPage.cat.visible = false;
```

Like the other properties you've seen, the visible property is simply attached to the object using dot notation. Unlike them, however, this is the first property you've seen that uses the false Boolean value. This directive basically means, "No, the cat is not visible." If you want to make the cat reappear later, you can assign the true value.

After you clicked the visibility button in the storybook, the little cat was not only gone, but gone for good. No amount of clicking the button could bring it back. The cat is still actually on the stage as an object you can program; you just can't see it. How can you make the cat visible again?

There are two ways. One way is to create another button and program it with exactly the same code as the visibility button, except that you give the visible property a value of true. The second way is a bit more fun: use a single button to make the cat both disappear and reappear.

If the two states that you're toggling between can be defined with true and false values, AS3.0 allows a very easy way to make a toggle button using the **not operator**, which is simply an exclamation mark, like this:

```
    !
```

It literally means "not." When used with Boolean values, it means "the opposite value of." You can put the not operator in front of any Boolean value to read it as its opposite value. Let's use the not operator in the onVisibilityButtonClick event handler to turn the visibility button into a toggle button:

1. Modify the directive in the onVisibilityButtonClick event handler so that it looks like the following:

```
function onVisibilityButtonClick(event:MouseEvent):void
{
    hillPage.cat.visible = !hillPage.cat.visible;
}
```

2. Save the Main.as file and test the project.

3. Click the visibility button a few times. You should see the cat appear and disappear each time you click it.

The value that you've given the visible property in the previous directive is this:

```
!hillPage.cat.visible;
```

It literally means "the opposite of the cat's current visibility state." If the cat's current visibility state is true, the opposite state will be false. And if it's false, the state will be read as true.

When the program first runs, the cat is (obviously) visible. Its visible property is true. When the visibility button is clicked, the program therefore reads !hillPage.cat.visible as false. The second time the button is clicked, the cat's visibility is now false, so the program reads !hillPage.cat.visible as true.

The beauty of using the not operator in this way is that you never need to know whether the cat's visibility property is true or false. The program keeps track of this for you. And you need only one button to toggle between these two states.

You can use this feature of the not operator to toggle between two states with any variables or properties that accept Boolean values. Boolean values are extremely useful in game design for keeping track of things such as whether enemies are dead or alive, whether items have been picked up or not, and whether doors are locked or unlocked. Wherever you use Boolean values, you'll probably find a clever use for the not operator, like you've used it here.

Having a look

The next thing you'll do is make a button that lets the cat look around at the bright and beautiful world around it. But before you're able to do this, you need to make sure that the cat object is set up properly so that its eyes are independent objects that you can control with code:

1. In the storyBook.fla file, double-click the Cat symbol in the Library to enter symbol editing mode.

2. Click one of the cat's eyes and delete it. (The pupil and white of the cat's eye are actually separate shapes, so you'll need to double-click the eye to select both shapes together.) You should now have a one-eyed cat, as shown in Figure 4-12.

Figure 4-12. Delete one of the cat's eyes.

3. Double-click the remaining eye to select both its shapes (the inner black pupil and outer white eyeball). Select Modify ➤ Convert to Symbol.

4. The Convert to Symbol dialog box opens. Give the symbol the name Eye.

5. The Type drop-down menu remembers the last type of symbol you created. If the last symbol you made was a button, Button will appear as the selected symbol type. Change it to Movie Clip.

6. The Convert to Symbol dialog box has an option called Registration, which determines what point of the object should be used for its center point. You want the new Eye symbol's registration point to be directly in the center of the object. Click the center square in the Registration box to set the center as the symbol's registration point. Figure 4-13 shows what it should look like.

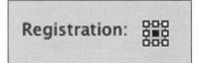

Figure 4-13. Choose the center as the Eye's registration point.

7. Check Export for ActionScript and click the OK button.

8. Click OK if the classpath warning window displays.

9. Have a look in your Library. You now have a new symbol called Eye. It will be centered directly over the registration point, as shown in Figure 4-14.

10. Double-click the Cat symbol to enter symbol editing mode.

11. Drag another instance of the Eye symbol onto the cat to replace the missing eye. You can use the keyboard's arrow keys to precisely position the eye if you're having trouble aligning it with the mouse. You can also use Flash's Align feature (found in the Modify menu) to align the eyes precisely. Refer to Chapter 2 if you need a refresher on how to do this.

Figure 4-14. The new Eye symbol

12. Select the left eye. Give it the instance name leftEye.

13. Select the right eye. Give it the instance name rightEye.

You now have a two-eyed cat that contains two independent eye instances: leftEye and rightEye. You can now control these eyes with code. Figure 4-15 shows an example of what you created.

Figure 4-15. Give the eyes instance names.

Next you need to create a Look button and add some new code to the program to make it work.

1. Create a new button called LookButton.

2. Drag an instance of the LookButton onto the buttons layer of the HillPage symbol. Give it the instance name lookButton.

3. Add or modify the following code in bold to the Main.as file:

```
package
{
  import flash.display.MovieClip;
  import flash.events.MouseEvent;

  public class Main extends MovieClip
  {
    var startPage:StartPage;
    var hillPage:HillPage;
    var pondPage:PondPage;

    public function Main()
    {
      startPage = new StartPage();
      hillPage = new HillPage();
      pondPage = new PondPage();
      addChild(hillPage);

      //Add event listeners
      startPage.hillButton.addEventListener(MouseEvent.CLICK, ➥
        onHillButtonClick);
      startPage.pondButton.addEventListener(MouseEvent.CLICK, ➥
```

```
      onPondButtonClick);
    hillPage.backToStartButton.addEventListener(MouseEvent.CLICK, ➥
      onBackButtonClick_Hill);
    pondPage.backToStartButton.addEventListener(MouseEvent.CLICK, ➥
      onBackButtonClick_Pond);
    hillPage.upButton.addEventListener(MouseEvent.CLICK, ➥
      onUpButtonClick);
    hillPage.downButton.addEventListener(MouseEvent.CLICK, ➥
      onDownButtonClick);
    hillPage.growButton.addEventListener(MouseEvent.CLICK, ➥
      onGrowButtonClick);
    hillPage.shrinkButton.addEventListener(MouseEvent.CLICK, ➥
      onShrinkButtonClick);
    hillPage.visibilityButton.addEventListener(MouseEvent.CLICK, ➥
      onVisibilityButtonClick);
    hillPage.lookButton.addEventListener(MouseEvent.CLICK, ➥
      onLookButtonClick);
}
//Event handlers
function onHillButtonClick(event:MouseEvent):void
{
  addChild(hillPage);
  removeChild(startPage);
}
function onPondButtonClick(event:MouseEvent):void
{
  addChild(pondPage);
  removeChild(startPage);
}
function onBackButtonClick_Hill(event:MouseEvent):void
{
  addChild(startPage);
  removeChild(hillPage);
}
function onBackButtonClick_Pond(event:MouseEvent):void
{
  addChild(startPage);
  removeChild(pondPage);
}
function onUpButtonClick(event:MouseEvent):void
{
  hillPage.cat.y -= 15;
  if (hillPage.cat.y < 120)
  {
    hillPage.cat.y = 120;
```

```
        }
        trace(hillPage.cat.y);
      }
      function onDownButtonClick(event:MouseEvent):void
      {
        hillPage.cat.y += 15;
        if (hillPage.cat.y > 220)
        {
          hillPage.cat.y = 220;
        }
        trace(hillPage.cat.y);
      }
      function onGrowButtonClick(event:MouseEvent):void
      {
        hillPage.cat.width += 15;
        hillPage.cat.height += 15;
      }
      function onShrinkButtonClick(event:MouseEvent):void
      {
        hillPage.cat.width -= 15;
        hillPage.cat.height -= 15;
      }
      function onVisibilityButtonClick(event:MouseEvent):void
      {
        hillPage.cat.visible = false;
      }
      function onLookButtonClick(event:MouseEvent):void
      {
        hillPage.cat.leftEye.rotation += 20;
        hillPage.cat.rightEye.rotation += 20;
      }
    }
  }
```

4. Save the Main.as file and test the project.

5. Click the look button. The cat now rolls its eyes, as shown in Figure 4-16.

Figure 4-16. Click the look button, and the cat surveys the scene.

The code hasn't done anything really new, but you haven't yet seen all these things working in combination like this before.

The code is targeting **child objects** of the cat:

```
hillPage.cat.leftEye.rotation += 20;
hillPage.cat.rightEye.rotation += 20;
```

The leftEye and rightEye are **children** (subobjects) of the cat, which itself is a child of hillPage. You can easily create very complex interactive objects simply by adding more subobjects and targeting their various properties.

The rotation property works much like the other properties that you've looked at so far:

```
hillPage.cat.leftEye.rotation += 20;
hillPage.cat.rightEye.rotation += 20;
```

The rotation property accepts values in degrees of a circle, so each object has 360 of them that you can work with. Positive values rotate the object clockwise, and negative values rotate it counterclockwise. The center of the rotation is the object's own center registration point. That was why it was important to make sure that the eye graphic was centered on the Eye symbol's registration point for the effect to look realistic.

More properties?

There are two other important properties from the table at the beginning of this chapter that you haven't yet used in the little interactive cat toy:

- **alpha**: controls the transparency of an object and accepts values from 0 (completely transparent) to 1 (completely opaque, or solid)
- **x**: controls the horizontal position of an object, and like its partner-in-crime, the y property, accepts values in pixels

The functionality of these properties is very similar to the properties you already used. So, here's a little assignment for you. How about building a pair of buttons that move the cat left and right, and another pair that gradually makes the cat disappear and reappear? I'm sure you can figure it out! Also experiment with the 3D properties z, rotationX, rotationY, rotationZ, and scaleZ.

Have fun, and I'll meet you at the next section when you're done.

Controlling Movie Clip timelines

Movie Clip properties give you a great deal of control over how objects behave, and even very basic examples like these can hold a lot of appeal if they're used in the right context. In the next section of this chapter, you'll look at how you can take your control of Movie Clip objects one step further by controlling the timeline.

You'll add another character to the storybook: a friendly frog who sits on an island in the pond. You'll set the interactive storybook up so that when the reader clicks the frog, the frog asks the cat a question.

As with anything as complex as computer programming, there are many ways to do this. The approach you'll take with this example is to use the Movie Clip object's timeline to define different states for the frog. In fact, you're going to be creating something that, in computer programming terminology, is called a **state machine**.

By **states** I refer to "states of being." If you think of something as simple as a light bulb, it has two states: on or off. Think of something a little more complex: your little sister has a whole range of states such as happy, bored, amused, frustrated, food-throwing, and so on. I'm sure you can think of many more! A state machine is a list of all these states and a mechanism for getting from one state to another.

State machines are a very complex topic in the field of computer science, and building them from code is a highly skilled art. However, one huge bonus that Flash has as a game design and programming platform is that it has an extremely usable state machine built right into it. It's called the timeline.

If you're new to Flash, the **timeline** is a long numbered strip of little boxes (called **frames**) that you can see if you click the Timeline tab just below the stage. When it's empty, it looks like Figure 4-17.

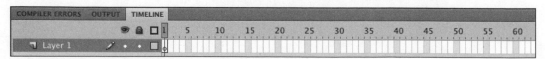

Figure 4-17. An empty timeline

The primary purpose of the timeline in Flash is as an animation tool. You can think of it as spool of film, in which each frame represents a snapshot showing an object in a slightly different position than in the previous frame. When the frames are played sequentially in quick succession, the illusion of motion is created.

The timeline is a fantastic tool for animation, but I won't delve too deeply into timeline animation in this book (it's discussed in Chapter 8, but it's a topic worthy of a book in its own right). What you'll be looking at, however, is the wonderful and unplanned side effect of the timeline as a way of storing object states.

You can think of each frame in the timeline as a little box that you can use to store some information about an object. Suppose that you want to store some of your little sister's states as information on the timeline. In one frame, you could keep her happy state, in another frame you could keep her sleeping state, and in a third you could keep her annoying state. If she were starting to annoy you too much, you could just program a button to tell the timeline to go to the frame that stores her sleeping state. Now that would be a great program!

Unfortunately, try as they might, programmers just can't seem to get as much control over the emotions of the people around them as they do over their code. But they have come up with a solution for that: to program the people from scratch in code. That's a pretty big project, and although it has been attempted many times (try a web search for "alicebot" for one example), you'll set your sights somewhat lower. You'll use the timeline to build a simple state machine for an interactive frog.

First, you need a frog Movie Clip symbol to get started:

1. In the storyBook.fla file, create a new Movie Clip symbol called Frog. (Remember to check Export for ActionScript when you do this.)

2. Design your frog however you like. If you're still getting your Flash graphic design feet wet, refer to Chapter 2 and model your frog on the design of the cat character.

   If there are graphics on the frog that you expect will change in any of your states, they need to be on separate layers. I put the frog's eyes, body, and feet on different layers to help myself stay a bit more organized, but you can keep this basic design of the frog on one layer if you want to for this project. I also designed my frog with a closed mouth because you'll be giving it an open mouth in a later state. My frog looks like Figure 4-18.

Figure 4-18. Design your frog.

So far, so good. You have a basic design you can work with. You'll create three different states for the frog:

- Sitting complacently
- Mouth open
- Speaking

Each state will be represented by a frame on the timeline. You've already got the first state, sitting complacently, on frame 1. You'll design the next state, mouth open, on frame 2.

The first job is to extend the graphics from frame 1 into frame 2. You need to do this so that the frog that you designed in frame 1 is still visible when you add new graphics to it in frame 2.

1. Highlight frame 2 in all the layers that correspond to graphics from frame 1 that you want to use in the frog's second state, as shown in Figure 4-19. To do this, hold the left mouse button down over frame 2 on the topmost layer and drag to the bottom layer.

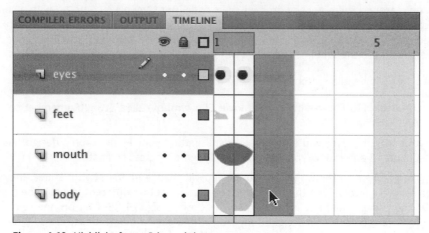

Figure 4-19. Highlight frame 2 in each layer.

The timeline examples in this chapter are illustrated using preview mode, which is helpful because it displays a thumbnail image of every graphic in each keyframe. To switch on preview mode, click the timeline's option menu button at the top-right corner of the timeline and select Preview *from the menu list items.*

2. Select Insert ➤ Timeline ➤ Frame (you can also right-click the highlighted frames and select Insert Frame from the option menu). The graphics from frame 1 will extend into frame 2. If you see something like Figure 4-20, it worked!

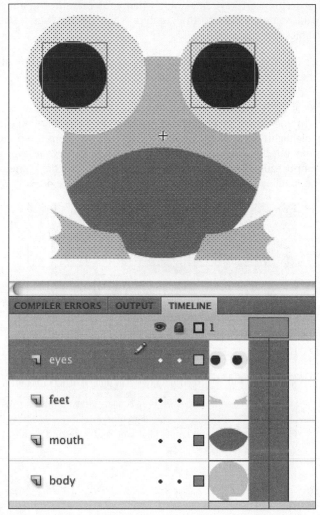

Figure 4-20. The graphics from frame 1 are extended into frame 2 with the Insert Frame command.

Great! You now have the frog graphics on frames 1 and 2.

You chose to insert *frames* on frame 2 instead of *keyframes*. (Keyframes are represented by black dots if you're working in the timeline's normal view mode and by thumbnail images of the actual graphics if you're using preview mode, as in these examples.) When you insert a frame, the graphics from the previous keyframe are extended into the frames that you've highlighted, and those frames become gray. You need to choose to insert keyframes only when you create new graphics on that frame or when you want to make some changes to the graphics from the previous frame. Keyframes define a point where the graphics change.

You'll create the frog's open mouth on frame 2, so this is exactly the kind of situation where you'll need to add a keyframe:

1. Create a new layer called mouth.

2. Click frame 2 of the mouth layer and select Insert ➤ Timeline ➤ Keyframe. (You can also right-click the highlighted frame and choose Insert Keyframe from the option menu.) Flash will insert a keyframe, but because you don't have any graphics on that layer yet, it will be represented by an empty square if it's in preview mode or an empty dot if the timeline is in normal view mode. The timeline should now look something like Figure 4-21.

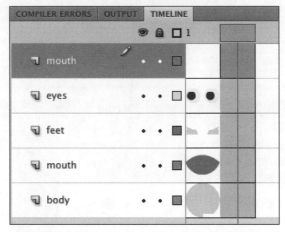

Figure 4-21. Create an empty keyframe on the second frame of the mouth layer.

3. With the new keyframe on frame 2 still selected, use Flash's drawing tools to draw an open mouth on the frog. My frog and timeline now look like Figure 4-22. (If you're working in the timeline's normal view, the keyframe in the timeline will turn solid black.)

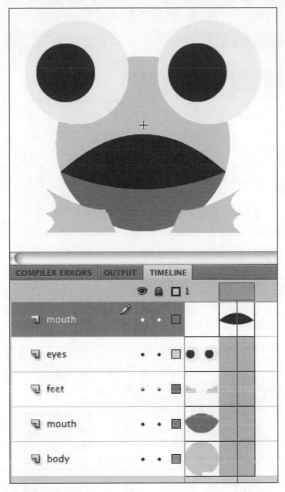

Figure 4-22. Draw an open mouth on the second frame of the mouth layer.

The frog now has two states, each represented in a separate frame. Let's add the third final state.

1. In frame 3, highlight all the frames from the layers that contain graphics that you want to extend into the third frame. Select Insert ➤ Timeline ➤ Frame. You probably want to extend all the graphics you've made so far, so the timeline might now look like Figure 4-23.

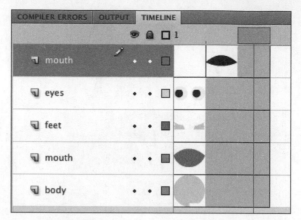

Figure 4-23. Use the Insert Frame command to extend the graphics into frame 3.

2. Create a new layer called speech bubble.

3. Click frame 3 of the speech bubble layer and select Insert ➤ Timeline ➤ Keyframe to insert an empty keyframe on this new layer, as shown in Figure 4-24.

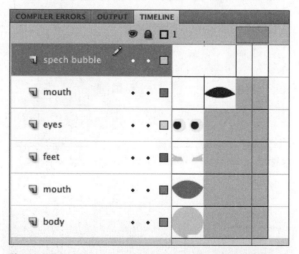

Figure 4-24. Create a new keyframe on the speech bubble layer.

4. Make sure that the new keyframe you created on the speech bubble layer is still selected. Draw a cartoon speech bubble and add some text. I'll add the words, "Hello, my friend! Can you swim?" Figure 4-25 shows what frame 3 of my frog looks like now.

Figure 4-25. Make the frog say something.

The frog now has its three states designed, and you're ready to use it in the program.

1. Double-click the PondPage symbol in the Library to enter symbol editing mode.

2. Select the characters layer.

3. Drag an instance of the Frog symbol from the Library onto the PondPage stage. Position the frog on the little island, as shown in Figure 4-26. Resize it using the Transform tool if you need to.

Figure 4-26. Add the frog to the PondPage symbol.

4. Make sure that the frog instance is selected and give it the instance name frog in the Instance name box in the Properties panel.

5. Select the cat instance, and give it the instance name cat if it doesn't already have that name. (Remember that the cats in each of the three pages are *completely separate objects*. They need to be given a new instance name inside each symbol: hillPage.cat is a different object from pondPage.cat.)

6. Open the Main.as file and add the following code in bold:

```
package
{
  import flash.display.MovieClip;
  import flash.events.MouseEvent;

  public class Main extends MovieClip
  {
    var startPage:StartPage;
    var hillPage:HillPage;
    var pondPage:PondPage;

    public function Main()
    {
      startPage = new StartPage();
      hillPage = new HillPage();
      pondPage = new PondPage();
      addChild(pondPage);

      //Add event listeners
      startPage.hillButton.addEventListener(MouseEvent.CLICK, ➥
        onHillButtonClick);
      startPage.pondButton.addEventListener(MouseEvent.CLICK, ➥
        onPondButtonClick);
      hillPage.backToStartButton.addEventListener(MouseEvent.CLICK, ➥
        onBackButtonClick_Hill);
      pondPage.backToStartButton.addEventListener(MouseEvent.CLICK, ➥
        onBackButtonClick_Pond);
      hillPage.upButton.addEventListener(MouseEvent.CLICK, ➥
        onUpButtonClick);
      hillPage.downButton.addEventListener(MouseEvent.CLICK, ➥
        onDownButtonClick);
      hillPage.growButton.addEventListener(MouseEvent.CLICK, ➥
        onGrowButtonClick);
      hillPage.shrinkButton.addEventListener(MouseEvent.CLICK, ➥
        onShrinkButtonClick);
      hillPage.visibilityButton.addEventListener(MouseEvent.CLICK, ➥
        onVisibilityButtonClick);
      hillPage.lookButton.addEventListener(MouseEvent.CLICK, ➥
        onLookButtonClick);
      pondPage.frog.stop();
      pondPage.frog.addEventListener(MouseEvent.MOUSE_OVER, ➥
        onFrogMouseOver);
```

```
  pondPage.frog.addEventListener(MouseEvent.CLICK, ➡
    onFrogClick);
}
//Event handlers
function onHillButtonClick(event:MouseEvent):void
{
  addChild(hillPage);
  removeChild(startPage);
}
function onPondButtonClick(event:MouseEvent):void
{
  addChild(pondPage);
  removeChild(startPage);
}
function onBackButtonClick_Hill(event:MouseEvent):void
{
  addChild(startPage);
  removeChild(hillPage);
}
function onBackButtonClick_Pond(event:MouseEvent):void
{
  addChild(startPage);
  removeChild(pondPage);
}
function onUpButtonClick(event:MouseEvent):void
{
  hillPage.cat.y -= 15;
  hillPage.cat.x += 10;
  if (hillPage.cat.y < 120)
  {
    hillPage.cat.y = 120;
  }
  trace(hillPage.cat.y);
}
function onDownButtonClick(event:MouseEvent):void
{
  hillPage.cat.y += 15;
  hillPage.cat.x -= 10;
  if (hillPage.cat.y > 220)
  {
    hillPage.cat.y = 220;
  }
  trace(hillPage.cat.y);
}
function onGrowButtonClick(event:MouseEvent):void
{
  hillPage.cat.width += 15;
  hillPage.cat.height += 15;
}
function onShrinkButtonClick(event:MouseEvent):void
{
```

```
    hillPage.cat.width -= 15;
    hillPage.cat.height -= 15;
  }
  function onVisibilityButtonClick(event:MouseEvent):void
  {
    hillPage.cat.visible = !hillPage.cat.visible;
  }
  function onLookButtonClick(event:MouseEvent):void
  {
    hillPage.cat.leftEye.rotation += 20;
    hillPage.cat.rightEye.rotation += 20;
  }
  function onFrogMouseOver(event:MouseEvent):void
  {
    pondPage.frog.gotoAndStop(2);
    pondPage.frog.removeEventListener(MouseEvent.MOUSE_OVER, ➥
      onFrogMouseOver);
  }
   function onFrogClick(event:MouseEvent):void
  {
    pondPage.frog.gotoAndStop(3);
    pondPage.frog.removeEventListener(MouseEvent.CLICK, onFrogClick);
  }
 }
}
```

7. Save the Main.as file and test the project. The storybook now starts at the pond page. Move the mouse over the frog; its mouth opens. If you click the frog, the speech bubble and text appear. Figure 4-27 shows what my pond page now looks like when I click the frog.

Figure 4-27. Click the frog to make it speak.

The first change that you made to the program was to display the pondPage instance right away when the storybook starts. You did that with this directive:

```
addChild(pondPage);
```

> *You made this change purely for testing purposes, so you wouldn't have to click through to the pond page from the start page to see the effect of the new code. It just saves a bit of time, and you can change it back to addChild(startPage) when the storybook is finished and you're done testing the code.*

The next line of code might come as a bit of a surprise:

```
pondPage.frog.stop();
```

stop() is a special MovieClip class method that can be used by any Movie Clip object. You may recall that earlier I described the timeline as a spool of film. The timeline was originally developed so that Movie Clip objects could play frames sequentially to create animations. By default, a Movie Clip's timeline is set to start playing all frames automatically when a Movie Clip object is on the stage. This is very helpful for objects that are animated, but not if you're using the timeline to store object states, as you're doing in this project.

The stop method stops the timeline dead in its tracks. This is exactly what you want: the frog's timeline to be stopped on frame 1. If you hadn't used the stop method here, all three frames of the frog movie clip would have flickered past in a never-ending loop on the stage.

> *If you ever want the Movie Clip objects to play a series of frames sequentially, you can use the play() method. play() is very useful if you designed one of the object's states to be a short animation that spans several frames, such as a spaceship exploding.*

The next two new lines of code add event listeners to the frog:

```
pondPage.frog.addEventListener(MouseEvent.MOUSE_OVER, onFrogMouseOver);
pondPage.frog.addEventListener(MouseEvent.CLICK, onFrogClick);
```

You're adding two separate event listeners. The first one uses the MOUSE_OVER event type, which triggers the event when the mouse moves *over* the object. The second uses the CLICK even type, just like the buttons do. You've added two event listeners instead of just one to add a little more surprise and interest to the interactive frog.

The event handlers that are triggered by the listeners contain some new directives that you haven't seen before. Let's first look at the onFrogMouseOver event handler:

```
function onFrogMouseOver(event:MouseEvent):void
    {
      pondPage.frog.gotoAndStop(2);
      pondPage.frog.removeEventListener(MouseEvent.MOUSE_OVER, ➡
        onFrogMouseOver);
    }
```

The first directive uses the MovieClip class's gotoAndStop() method:

```
pondPage.frog.gotoAndStop(2);
```

gotoAndStop is a method that is available to all Movie Clip objects. It's used to tell the object to *go to and stop* at a specific frame on the object's timeline. The number in the parentheses is the frame number that you want the timeline to go to. In this case, it's frame 2, which is the frog's open mouth state. For a children's storybook, this is a nice effect because when the reader examines the page, the frog's mouth opens when the mouse skims over it. This immediately signals that the frog is an interactive object and it tempts the reader to click it.

> Instead of using frame numbers, it's also possible to use something called **frame labels**. Frame labels are descriptive words or phrases that you can use to describe frames in your timeline.
>
> To create a frame label, create a new layer in the timeline of the FLA file called labels. The labels layer is usually at the very top of the layer stack so that you can see the label names clearly. You then insert a keyframe wherever you want to add a label, such as at a new state. In the Properties panel you'll see a pane called Label with a Name box in which you can enter the label name. The name you enter appears on the timeline at the keyframe where you assigned it, along with a tiny red flag that tells you that it's a frame label. Figure 4-28 shows an example of what a timeline with frame labels might look like.

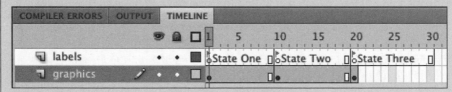

Figure 4-28. Using frame labels in the timeline

> To use the gotoAndStop() method with any frame label you create, include the name of the frame, surrounded by quotes, as part of method's argument, like this:
>
> ```
> gotoAndStop("frameLabelName");
> ```
>
> There's nothing intrinsically wrong with using frame labels. In fact, they're a really nice feature, especially if you just use them as way of reminding yourself what state each frame represents. But if you're doing a lot of coding (and as a game designer, you are!), you should avoid making your code dependent on them. Your programs will be a little more bug-proof if you use frame numbers because they're easier to manage, easier to manipulate, and can't be misspelled.

The next directive in the onFrogMouseOver event handler is this line:

```
pondPage.frog.removeEventListener(MouseEvent.MOUSE_OVER, ➥
    onFrogMouseOver);
```

What this directive does is use the removeEventListener method to *remove* the event listener that you added earlier. Yes, that's right, actually remove it. Why would you want to do that?

You want the frog to open its mouth when the mouse moves over it. But you want that to happen only once—the first time. The easiest way to prevent it from happening again is to remove the listener that called the onFrogMouseOver method as soon as the frog arrives at frame 2. Once a listener is removed, it's gone for good and will never call the event handler again.

If you left the event listener running, it would move the frog back to frame 2 *every time* the mouse moved over it. In a different context, that might have been just fine and dandy, but in this case it would mean that the frog would jump back to frame 2 even after you've reached frame 3. It would look a bit awkward. (If you like, you can see the effect of this by deleting the removeEventListener directive, saving the Main.as file, and retesting the project.)

To remove an event listener, you use exactly the same syntax and arguments as you do to add one, but use the removeEventListener method name instead. You should always make a habit of removing event listeners after you no longer need them because if you don't, they'll still be running in the background listening for events and using up precious memory and processing resources.

The onFrogClick event handler is almost identical to onFrogMouseOver, except for the specifics:

```
function onFrogClick(event:MouseEvent):void
    {
      pondPage.frog.gotoAndStop(3);
      pondPage.frog.removeEventListener(MouseEvent.CLICK, onFrogClick);
    }
}
```

The directives tell the frog to move its timeline to frame 3 and then remove the event listener that was listening for mouse clicks so that the reader can click the frog only once. Interestingly, by using the CLICK and MOUSE_OVER events, you've effectively turned the frog movie clip into a button. And, there's actually nothing stopping you from creating any of the buttons in your games like this if you want to.

Voila! The beginnings of a promising children's interactive storybook!

Using the timeline as a state machine

Using a timeline as a state machine is something that you'll find all kinds of uses for in your game projects. For example, you could have a door object that appears open on frame 1 and closed on frame 2. You could use it to store the different states of your player character in a platform game, such as "walking," "running," "jumping," and "falling." You could create an object called deckOfCards with 52 different symbols on 52 different frames, and then create a method that could shuffle the order of the frames. You could even store all your game levels on different frames of one Movie Clip object, and simply instruct it to advance by one frame each time the player reaches a new level.

Thanks to Flash's timeline, all this is very quick and easy to accomplish.

Taking it further

The storybook isn't complete, of course, and I left it that way intentionally so that you can have the fun of finishing it. There is a multitude of complex ways to combine the techniques that you've looked at in this chapter, and I'm sure many ideas occurred to you while you were working through the examples.

One of the great thrills of designing interactive media is that it frees you up from a universe that has only one possible future or one possible outcome. Nonlinear storybooks like these can be a lot of fun to design and are even more fun for the reader. Here are few suggestions on how you might want to proceed with the project.

Now that the frog has asked the cat this perplexing question, what could happen next?

You could create a yes button and no button. You could then use addChild() in the onFrogClick event handler to display them in the pondPage instance. Then you could use the x and y properties to place the buttons in the correct position on the stage, as shown in Figure 4-29.

Figure 4-29. Add a yes and no button to answer the frog's question.

You can then program those buttons to change the outcome of the story, depending on what the reader chooses. What kind of deviousness do you think the frog is up to? You could easily make this the start of a long adventure comprising 20 or 30 pages, fill it with interesting puzzles and characters, and have numerous branching outcomes. It's the very basis of a role-playing or adventure game!

Summary

Whether you know it yet or not, you now have a considerable arsenal of skills at your disposal to build very rich interactive worlds. In this and the previous chapter, you looked at the very basic techniques necessary to build these worlds—and you really don't need many more. If you understand Movie Clip properties and how to control object states using the timeline and event listeners, you have the basics that will make up rest of the projects of this book.

In Chapter 5, you'll build your first complete game, a number guessing game, which will expand your programming skills considerably. You'll learn how to analyze a player's input to create a basic artificial intelligence system, modularize your program using methods, and keep players guessing (literally!) using random numbers.

Chapter 5

DECISION MAKING

This chapter will be your first real look at designing a complete game. It's a short, simple game, but contains all the basic structural elements of game design that you'll be returning to again and again. Input and output, decision making, keeping score, figuring out whether the player has won or lost, random numbers, and giving the player a chance to play again—it's all here. You'll also be taking a much closer look at variables and if statements and you'll learn how to modularize your program by breaking down long segments of code into bite-sized methods. By the end of the chapter, you'll have all the skills necessary to build complex logic games based on this simple model.

The game you'll build is a simple number guessing game. The game asks you to guess a number between 1 and 100. If you guess too high or too low, the game tells you until you'll be able to figure out what the mystery number is by deduction.

You'll actually build this game in a few phases. You'll start with the most basic version of the game, and then gradually add more features such as limiting the number of guesses, giving the player more detailed information about the status of the game, randomizing the mystery number, and then adding an option to play the game again.

Sound like a lot? Each phase of the game is self-contained, so you can give yourself a bit of a break to absorb and experiment with the new techniques before moving on to the next phase. You'll be surprised at how easy and simple it is when you put all the pieces together.

Setting up the project files

The number guessing game, which you can now more formally inaugurate as "The Number Guessing Game," follows the same basic file and program structure that you've been using since Chapter 1. So there's really nothing new here except the details. If this seems a bit routine, give yourself a pat on the back for overcoming a considerable hurdle to getting started with AS3.0 programming!

1. Create a project folder called Number Guessing Game.

2. Open Flash. Select File ➤ New and choose Flash File (ActionScript 3.0) from the New Document dialog box.

3. Click the OK button.

4. Select File ➤ Save As.

5. Give the new FLA file the name numberGuessingGame.fla.

6. Navigate to the Number Guessing Game project folder that you created in step 1.

7. Click the Save button to save the file.

8. In the Project panel, click the drop-down menu. Select Quick Project. numberGuessingGame.fla appears as a project file.

9. In the Project panel, click the New File button, as shown in Figure 5-1.

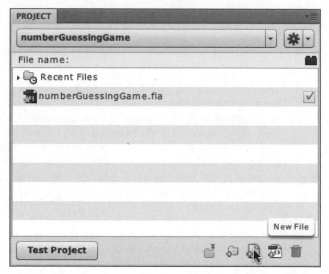

Figure 5-1. Create a new AS file in the Project panel.

10. Enter Main.as in the File field.

11. Select ActionScript from the File type drop-down menu. If your Create File window looks like Figure 5-2, click the Create File button.

Figure 5-2. Create a new AS file called Main.as in the Project panel.

12. Flash will create and open the Main.as file.

Your project panel should now look like Figure 5-3.

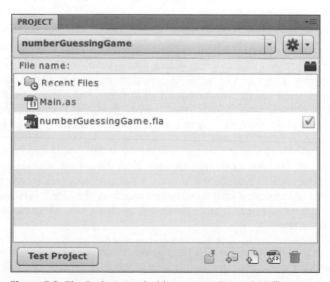

Figure 5-3. The Project panel with your new FLA and AS files

13. Finally, you need to assign the FLA file's document class. Double-click the numberGuessingGame.fla file in the Project panel.

14. In the Properties panel. Enter Main in the Class field. Your Properties panel should now look like Figure 5-4. You've now assigned the document class.

Figure 5-4. Create the document class in the Properties panel of the FLA file.

15. Save the numberGuessingGame.fla file.

You're now ready to create the number guessing game.

Designing a GUI

GUI stands for **graphical user interface**. When programmers refer to a GUI, they're talking about all the buttons, text boxes, and windows that help a user actually interact with a piece of software. GUI design is a highly specialized area of software development, and getting it right can be a tricky business. GUI designers need to not only have a lot of in-depth knowledge about the inner workings of a piece of software but also have to understand the psychology of the people using it. How people use software and how to make software easy to use is an area of software design known as **usability**.

A well-designed GUI allows users to access as much or as little of the complexity of the software as they need or want to, but also subtly teaches users how the software works while they're using it. As basic and commonsensical as a lot of this sounds, it's not an easy task by any means. The GUI design that has gone into sophisticated operating systems such as the latest versions of Windows or OS X is the result of decades of research and refinement by thousands of developers, yet no one regards either of them as perfect.

The most important thing about the GUI for a game is that it be as invisible as possible. That means that the GUI shouldn't come between the player and the experience of playing the game.

The best thing for you as a game designer is to think critically about the GUIs of games that you like, and ask why they work and how you could make something similar work in your games. There are no rules, the field is wide open for experimentation, and clever minds like the one reading this book will set the standards for the new GUIs of the future.

That said, here are two basic principles that you can consider when designing GUIs for your games:

- **Keep it simple**: Simplicity is often maddeningly difficult to achieve when you're caught up in the excitement and adrenaline rush of programming a complex game. If you don't absolutely need a button, menu option, or instruction in a game, don't use any. Try and get away with a GUI that's as lean as possible by trimming away as much of the fat as you can—your players will thank you for it. Find out the least amount of functionality or customization your game needs to still remain fun and playable, and aim for that. You can always add more complexity later if you really think it's necessary. It usually isn't. Remember that players don't want to click lots of buttons or read through complex directions; they just want to play your game.

- **Make it obvious**: If your GUI is well designed, players will know what they have to do just by a glance at the visual layout of the GUI elements. Players want immediate results and don't want to have to search for what they're looking for. If they have to click buttons, make them easy to find, make sure that their functions are self-explanatory, and ensure that that their effect is immediate. The best games are designed so players can discover the rules and how to play the game while they're playing it. If you feel you have to give players a lot of instructions on how to play the game or what to do next, there's almost certainly a problem with your GUI. And if all this seems blindingly obvious, that's just great!

One of the many advantages of Flash as a game design platform is that you can use its drawing tools to literally draw your GUI on the stage. Most other programming environments require you to create each button and text field out of code and then meticulously plot them on the screen with x and y coordinates. It's a very precise process, but it's tedious and slow. You can do that with AS3.0, too, if you really want to (and there are actually many instances in complex interactive GUI design in which that might be preferable), but there's no need to go to all that trouble when Flash's built-in drawing tools are so much fun and easy to use. For the quick little games you'll be building in this book, they're perfect.

Inputting and outputting

In the number guessing game that you'll build in this chapter, you need to process two kinds of information:

- **User input** is the number that the player enters into the program to guess the mystery number.

- **Program output** tells the player whether the guess is too high or too low, or whether the player won or lost the game.

Input and output are the two most basic elements of communication in computer programs, and all games use them to some degree. In the number guessing game, the input and output are in text form; in other games you'll be looking at, input and output take other forms. For example, the input might be in the form of moving a player character around a dungeon, and the output might be being eaten by a monster. The basic principles remain the same, however: if you understand how it works with text, the rest will be much simpler to grasp.

Adding some text fields

Text fields are boxes that display text. You create them in Flash using the Text Tool in the toolbar, and you have a choice of three types to choose from:

- **Static text** is used for text that doesn't change and is the type of text that you've been using until now in the storybook project. Use static text for instructions, button labels, or titles that you expect to remain the same throughout the program.

- **Dynamic text** is a text field that can be programmed so that the text it displays changes based on what's happening in the program. (In other words, it changes the text *dynamically*.) Dynamic text is used to display the program's output.

- **Input text** is a text field that allows the user to type in some text. The user can then enter that text into the program, usually by clicking a button. Logically enough, input text is used for the program's input.

In the number guessing game, you'll use a dynamic text field to display the game's instructions and the status of the game as it progresses. Just below the dynamic text field you'll add a large input text field to allow players to type in the number that they think might be the mystery number.

Creating dynamic text

Let's first create the dynamic text field, which is the **multiline** text field. Multiline text fields are more than one line of text high. As you develop the game in later steps, you'll use the second line of the text field to display game status information that will be useful for the player.

1. Select the Text Tool in the toolbar.

2. In the Properties panel, select Dynamic Text from the Text type drop-down menu.

3. In the Character pane of the Properties panel, choose the font family, color, style, and size that seem appropriate.

4. In the Paragraph pane, click the Align left button from the Format options. (If it's already selected, you can leave it as is.)

5. In the Behavior drop-down menu from the Paragraph pane, select Multiline no-wrap. Choosing multiline is important so that the text field knows that it needs to display text on more than one line. (Wrapping is what happens when text is automatically carried over to a new line when it reaches the right-hand margin.) The no-wrap option tells the text field not to force text from the first line onto the second line if the text from the first line is too long. You can definitely experiment with the other option, Multiline (which does wrap text onto the next line), but it sometimes has some quirky, unexpected results with long text that you don't want to be concerned with debugging in this project. You'll just keep the text wrapping off and make sure that the text field is long enough to display the maximum length of text.

6. Figure 5-5 shows what my Properties panel looks like.

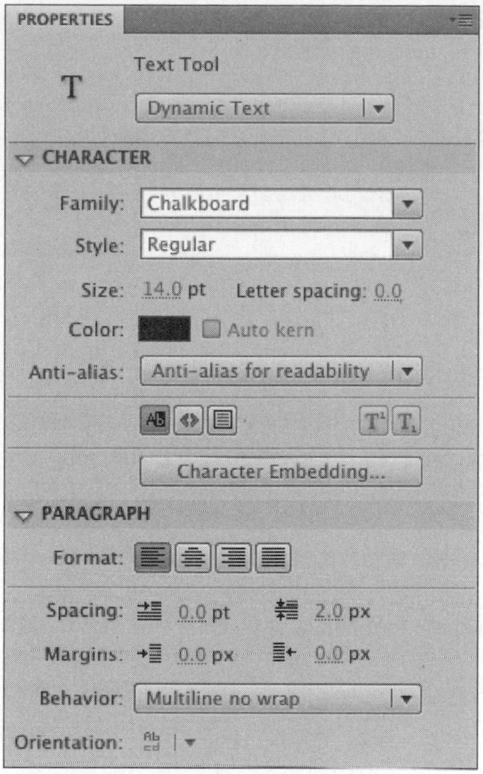

Figure 5-5. Dynamic text field properties

7. With the Text Tool still selected, click somewhere near the upper middle of the stage and draw a text field that's about 300 pixels wide and high enough to accommodate two lines of text. If you're not sure exactly how high that is, you can temporarily type in two lines of sample text to help you size it. Figure 5-6 shows you what my text field looks like.

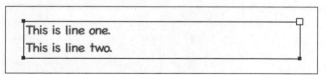

Figure 5-6. Draw a dynamic text field high enough for two lines of sample text.

8. Finally, and very importantly, you need to give the text field an instance name. Without one, you can't target it with code in the program. Make sure that the text field is still selected and enter the name output in the Instance name box at the top of the Properties panel. Don't forget this step; otherwise the game won't work.

> *The ActionScript editor window provides text object code hinting if you add _txt to the end of any text object names. If you give the dynamic text field the instance name* output_txt, *code hinting will be activated for this object, which might be helpful when you start entering your code in the editor.*

Adding input text

You'll add the input text field just below the dynamic text field you created in the previous steps:

1. Make sure that the dynamic text field you just created is not selected. (Click away from it on the empty stage if it is. If it's still selected, and you make the changes to the text field properties in the following steps, it will overwrite the properties you just set with these new properties.)

2. With the Text Tool still selected, select Input Text from the Text Tool drop-down menu in the Properties panel.

3. Choose an appropriate font family, style, color, and size from the Character pane. (Because the player will be entering no more than three numbers, and I want to try and fulfill one of my GUI design tenets to "make it obvious," I gave the input text a font size of 36 points so that it's really obvious to the player where they'll need to type, and the numbers will be nice and big when they do.)

4. You'll create the input text field so that it has a border around it. This will again help your goal to "make it obvious" by clearly indicating to the player where they have to enter the number. To add a border around a text field, you need to select the Show border around text button in the Character pane of the Properties panel. It's a little hard to find, but Figure 5-7 shows you where to look.

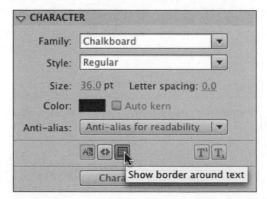

Figure 5-7. Select the Show border around text button.

5. In the Paragraph pane, make sure that that the Align left button is still selected from the Format button menu.

6. Select Single line from the Behavior drop-down menu.

7. Figure 5-8 shows what my input text Properties panel looks like.

Figure 5-8. The input text field properties

8. Just below the dynamic text field that you created on the stage, draw the input text field so that it's wide enough to accommodate a maximum of three numbers. (The game asks the player to choose a number from 1 to 100, so 100, composed of three characters, is the longest number they'll be entering.) You can add some sample text, such as three zeros, to help you find the right width. Figure 5-9 shows you what my input text field looks like with sample text.

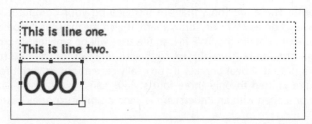

Figure 5-9. Enter some sample text to correctly size the input text field.

173

9. Finally, you need to give the input text field an instance name. Make sure that it's still selected and enter the name input in the Instance name box of the Properties panel. (Again, give this the instance name input_txt if you want to activate code hinting in the ActionScript editor window.)

The last thing that you might want to do is delete the sample text that you used to size the fields correctly, but you don't really have to do this. This sample text will be overwritten by new text that you'll create directly in the program.

> *Strangely enough, even though input text fields allow the users to input text, you can actually insert text into them with programming code, just as you can with dynamic text. You can, therefore, think of input text fields as dynamic text fields with the added bonus that text can be entered into them if you need to. You'll see how this works when you start adding the code to the program in the pages ahead.*

A little more about fonts and text fields

As you can see, there are an awful lot of other options you can add in the text Properties panel. Feel free to experiment with them. There are a few though, that are particularly important for game developers:

Anti-aliasing. The Anti-alias option is in the Character pane. When text characters curve, their edges can appear blocky and jagged, which is an effect known as **pixelation**. **Anti-aliasing** is a style of rendering text that smoothes out pixelated edges. The one big problem with anti-aliasing, however, is that it takes a considerable amount of processing power to smooth out text.

Fonts are complex vector shapes, which are plotted mathematically by the CPU on the screen by drawing lines between points. The smoother the font appears, the more vectors have to be plotted, and the harder the CPU has to work. Any power that the CPU spends plotting vectors for fonts is less power it has to make the animations, videos, and other effects in your games run smoothly. It detracts from the almighty performance, which has the final say in game development. The Flash Player has improved considerably in the text-rendering department over the years, but earlier versions of the Player were notorious for expending up to half of the available CPU power just to render text. Game developers are therefore very sensitive to this issue!

You probably won't notice this performance hit in the little games you'll be building initially, but if you have anti-aliased text on the stage and you start piling on lots of complex animations, your games will start to stutter and drag. The first thing you should do, then, is turn off text anti-aliasing. Flash provides a few different options you can use to do this:

- **Device fonts**: These are fonts that are installed on your computer, which means that Flash doesn't have to do any work to draw them. It also means that it doesn't need to include **font outlines** as extra data in the SWF file, so file sizes will be smaller. (More on font outlines soon!) Device fonts are also not anti-aliased, so they're very fast for the CPU to display. The only drawback (and a potential deal breaker if you really care about how the fonts in your games look) is that you're limited to only three font styles: _sans, _serif, and _typewriter. (All device font names are preceded with an underscore.) _sans is similar to Arial, _serif is similar to Times New

Roman, and _typewriter is similar to Courier. Because the rendering of these fonts is done by the user's computer, they'll look slightly different on different operating systems, so you won't have much control over their final appearance. Still, device fonts are fast and can save you a lot of performance if you need it.

- **Bitmap text**: This option switches off all anti-aliasing. The fonts will still look like the fonts that you chose, but they'll have pixelated edges. Sometimes it can be a good thing: text that is very small can appear blurry and hard to read with anti-aliasing on. By using bitmap text with small text, you can greatly improve readability, and it often looks more appropriate than anti-aliased text in many contexts. If used well, bitmap text can give you a performance boost and win you some style points as well.

- **Anti-alias for animation**: This option switches off anti-aliasing when text is being animated, and turns it on again when it stops moving. There might be some performance improvement with this option if the text you are using isn't too big or if it's moving around a lot. But if your text isn't moving, you won't see any performance improvement.

- **Anti-alias for readability**: Anti-aliased, all the time. It looks beautiful, but can slow your game down considerably.

- **Custom anti-alias**: This one isn't directly performance related and is more of a specialty option. Custom anti-aliasing is used to tweak the anti-aliasing properties so that fonts can look their best.

You can find all these options in the Anti-alias drop-down menu of the Character pane in the Properties panel. Definitely keep them in mind when you're building your games, and if you notice things starting to slow to a crawl, play around with some of these options.

Embedded fonts. When you select a font to use in a text field, Flash is reading from the list of fonts installed on your computer. It might look great to you on your computer, but if you view that same FLA file or the published SWF file on a computer that doesn't have that same font installed, it will look completely different. If Flash or the Flash Player can't find the font that you specified, it will try to choose what it thinks is the next best thing. The choice might be okay or it might be awful, but it will certainly be very different.

How then can you ensure that the fonts in the text fields you're using will look the same on another computer that doesn't have that same font installed? **Embedded fonts** are a solution for this. When you select the Character Embedding button in the Character pane of the Properties panel, a new window opens that allows you to select the font you want to use and embed it directly into the SWF file when you publish the Flash movie.

What Flash does is to save what's known as the font outline directly into the SWF file. The font outline is a mathematical blueprint of what the font looks like so the Flash Player can reproduce it directly in the SWF, even if the computer that the SWF file is being viewed on doesn't have that font installed. The only drawback is that the file size of the SWF increases to store this extra information. In most cases, though (and especially for games, which you want to look their best), this will be a minor consideration.

Adding a button

You've got input and you've got output. Now you just need some way of getting the text from the input text field into the program so that it can be processed. The lowly button comes to your rescue again!

1. Create a new button symbol called GuessButton.

2. Drag an instance of the GuessButton symbol onto the stage next to the input text field.

3. Make sure that the button is still selected, and give it the instance name guessButton in the Instance name box in the Properties panel.

4. The user interface for your game might now look something like Figure 5-10.

Figure 5-10. Add the Guess button to the GUI.

Building a simple guessing game

You'll build the number guessing game in three separate phases so that you can get a solid grasp of the techniques before you add more complexity. The first phase is the most basic version, but it's the most important because it contains the very heart of the game.

The game starts by asking the player to guess a number from 1 to 100. It will tell the player whether the guess is too high or too low, until eventually the correct number is found. In this version of the game, the player gets an unlimited number of guesses, but you'll fix that and add a few more interesting features in phase 2.

Setting up the Main.as file

The Main.as file is set up using exactly the same structure as the previous projects, with one striking difference. Can you spot it?

1. Copy the following into your Main.as file:

```
package
{
  import flash.display.MovieClip;
  import flash.events.MouseEvent;

  public class Main extends MovieClip
  {
    public function Main()
    {
```

```
      init();
   }
   function init():void
   {
      trace("Hello, from the init method!");
   }
  }
}
```

2. Save the Main.as file and test the program. If everything is working properly, you should see the words Hello, from the init method! displayed in the Output panel.

What's going on here? Let's have a closer look at the constructor method:

```
public function Main()
{
   init();
}
```

You might recall from Chapter 1 that the directives inside the constructor method are automatically run when the class is instantiated. You have only one directive in the constructor method:

```
init();
```

What is this? It's a **method call**. Method calls trigger a method's function definition to run its directives. The method being "called" here is the init method. This means that as soon as the constructor method runs, it immediately tells the init method to perform whatever tasks you assigned to it. The init method's function definition is declared just below the Main constructor method:

```
function init():void
{
   trace("Hello, from the init method!");
}
```

init is programmer's shorthand for *initialize*. (You could have easily called the method initialize or InitializeGame if you had wanted to, but using the short form is another one of those "old programmer's conventions" that won't harm you to get used to because it's widely used.) The init function definition is empty at the moment except for the trace directive, but all the directives that will be used to initialize the program will eventually be inside it. In the previous examples, all the directives that initialized the program were inside the constructor method. What's the point of creating another method to do this job now?

The biggest advantage is that whenever you need to *reinitialize* your program, all you have to do is call the init method again from anywhere in your program. Let's pretend that you're playing the number guessing game and hopelessly lose the first time you play. If you want to play again, it would be nice if the game would reset the number of guesses you have left to the maximum and choose a new mystery number for you to guess. If you have all the game's default settings conveniently tucked away inside an init method, you just need to call this method whenever you want to reset the game and play again. (In fact, you'll do this later in the chapter.)

The other advantage is that if you make it a habit of creating an init method for every class you create, you'll always know how to reset the objects to their default settings.

Did the spaceship you were flying in your latest galactic-shooter game get blown to smithereens? No problem; just call the spaceship class's init method with a line of code that might look like this:

```
spaceship.init();
```

Did the frog in your road-crossing game get squashed by a car? No problem; you can easily reconstitute it and place it safely back on the sidewalk by writing some code that might look like this:

```
frog.init();
```

A little later in the design of the number guessing game, you'll see how useful moving all the games initialization directives into a specialized init method can be. For now, just realize that when the program runs, it automatically calls the Main constructor method. Main, in turn, makes a method call to the init method, which runs whatever directives it contains.

Learning more about variables

The first job is to initialize some of the basic variables that you need in the game. The most important is the mystery number that the player has to guess. You'll also initialize the first message that the player receives in the output text field. Both of these values are assigned using variables. To see this in action, follow these steps:

1. Enter the following text in bold to your program. (Delete the trace method that you added to the init function definition in the preceding steps.)

```
package
{
  import flash.display.MovieClip;
  import flash.events.MouseEvent;

  public class Main extends MovieClip
  {
    var startMessage:String;
    var mysteryNumber:uint;

    public function Main()
    {
      init();
    }
    function init():void
    {
      //Initialize variables
      startMessage = "I am thinking of a number between 1 and 100";
      mysteryNumber = 50;
```

```
        //Initialize text fields
        output.text = startMessage;
        input.text = "";
    }
  }
}
```

2. Save the `Main.as` file and test the program. You should see the words I am thinking of a number between 1 and 100 appear in the output text field, and the input text field should be blank, as shown in Figure 5-11.

I am thinking of a number between 1 and 100

Guess

Figure 5-11. The text of the startMessage variable is displayed in the output text field.

The first thing you did was to declare two variables in the `Main` class. You used variables in earlier chapters, but there's something new here—the variable types (which follow the colon):

```
var startMessage:String;
var mysteryNumber:uint;
```

What are these variable types?

You might recall from the previous chapter that when you created variables to hold references to the Movie Clip objects, you declared their type to be the symbol in the Library from which they were made. A line of code such as `var pondPage:PondPage;` meant that the pondPage instance was a type of the PondPage symbol in the Library.

The previous code does something very similar. The line `var startMessage:String;` means that the startMessage variable is a type of String. The line `var mysteryNumber:uint;` means that the variable mysteryNumber is a type of uint (which stands for **unsigned integer**).

Okay, that's pretty meaningless, isn't it? Don't worry; it will become clear soon!

Let's a take a step back. When you declare a variable, you need to tell the program what type of information that variable will be holding. Will you be using the variable to store numbers or words? If you're using it to store numbers, what kind of numbers will they be? Hey, it might seem like more detail than you need, but AS3.0 wants this information to make sure that you don't start trying to mix variables that contain words with variables that contain numbers or any of the other kinds of possibly incompatible data types that variables can contain.

So what kind of variable types are there? Here are all the data types that can be used by variables in AS3.0:

- Boolean: Can take one of two values: true or false; its default value is false.

- Number: Any number, such as whole numbers (also known as **integers**) and numbers that include decimal places (also known as **floating point** numbers).

- int: An integer, which is a whole number without a decimal place. It can be positive or negative. Because the CPU doesn't have to calculate any decimal places, using it speeds up the program's performance. It's usually better to use the int type over the Number type if you know you won't need to use decimals. The default value for the int type is 0.

- uint: Stands for **unsigned integer**. uint is an integer that is only positive. This is an even leaner version of the int type, so it's the fastest of them all. Use it whenever you can for the best performance. uint has a default value of 0.

- String: Letters, words, or phrases—any text at all. You can even use the String type to store numbers, but if you do, the numbers will be interpreted as text and you won't be able to manipulate them mathematically. The default value for the String type is null, which means "no data of any kind."

- Object: A general type. The Object class in AS3.0 is the base class for all other objects. The Object class also has a default value of null.

- void: A very specialized type that is used only for methods that don't return values. It's not used for variables. It can contain only one value: undefined. The undefined value is very similar to the null value, except that it is used when the variable hasn't yet been assigned a data type, or if it contains numbers or Boolean values. All the methods so far have been declared with a data type of void.

- * (asterisk): If you want to create a variable that has no specific type or you need it to be really flexible to be able to contain different data types at different times, replace the type name with an asterisk. For example, you might use a line of code like this:

```
variableName:*;
```

This variable now can hold any type of data. One suggestion regarding the use of the asterisk is this: don't use it! Unless you have an extremely good reason why you want your variables to be able to contain more than one type of data, you're opening up your program to a potential can of worms. Forcing variables to a particular type is one of the great strengths of AS3.0 because it prevents bugs and errors that are the result of the wrong type of data being stored in the wrong type of variable. These kinds of errors can often be very difficult to debug.

> The int, unit, and void data types start with a lowercase letter; the others all start with uppercase letters.

You can file these data types away for later, but you'll be using all of them over the course of this book. From today's menu, you have two of them on the plate: startMessage is a String, and mysteryNumber is a uint type. The first thing the init method does is to assign values to these variables:

```
startMessage = "I am thinking of a number between 1 and 100";
mysteryNumber = 50;
```

The next thing that happens is that the text from the startMessage variable is copied into the output text field's special text variable:

```
output.text = startMessage;
```

output, of course, is the instance name of the dynamic text field on the stage. It's followed by a dot, and then the word text. All text field objects have this special built-in variable called text. Whatever you assign to the text variable is displayed on the stage by the text field.

You could have easily written this same line of code like this, and the result would have been identical:

```
output.text = "I am thinking of a number between 1 and 100";
```

Why did you go to all that extra trouble of creating the extra startMessage variable when you could have assigned the text directly?

First, you got some practice in creating String variables—that's not such a bad reason, is it? Second, it's sometimes useful to store all the text you'll be using in your program in variables that you can access in one spot. If you know that all the text in your program is assigned to variables in your init() method, you don't need to go hunting through your code to find it if you need to make changes to it. This isn't an important issue in small programs such as the number guessing game, but it could become a real chore in bigger programs.

Finally, you want to make sure that the input text field is completely blank so players are free to type whatever they want into it. To clear a text field of any characters, assign it a pair of empty quotation marks:

```
input.text = "";
```

Empty quotation marks are to string variables what 0 is to number variables: it just means that there's no text there yet.

Making it more obvious

The GUI is fine at the moment, but it's actually hard for the player to know that the input text field is not just a black rectangle sitting on the stage. You could add a static text field just above it with the words Please enter your guess, but let's see if you can do it by providing some visual cues. You can improve the usability of the input field in a number of ways:

- Add a blinking cursor so that players know they can type numbers into it.
- Add a gray background color to differentiate it from the surrounding white of the stage.
- Restrict the player to entering only numbers. If the player is asked to guess a number from 1 to 100, it wouldn't make sense if he or she entered something like green car, would it?

All these things are really easy to do with a few more lines of AS3.0 code:

1. Modify the init method by adding the following code:

```
function init():void
{
  //Initialize variables
```

```
        startMessage = "I am thinking of a number between 1 and 100";
        mysteryNumber = 50;

        //Initialize text fields
        output.text = startMessage;
        input.text = "";
        input.backgroundColor = 0xFFCCCCCC;
        input.restrict = "0-9";
        stage.focus = input;
    }
```

2. Save the `Main.as` file and test the program. You should now see a much more easy-to-use input text field with a gray background and a blinking cursor, as shown in Figure 5-12.

Figure 5-12. The input text field has a gray background and a blinking cursor. It prevents letters from being entered.

3. Try entering some text other than numbers. Ha! You can't do it, can you?

Text field objects belong to AS3.0's `TextField` class. You can actually create text fields out of pure code as long as you import the `TextField` class into your program, along with your other import directives, like this:

```
    import flash.text.*;
```

The `TextField` class is part of Flash's text package, which contains many useful text-related classes. To import all the classes of a given package, use an asterisk instead of a specific class name. With all classes in the text package imported, you can create a text field object and then display, size, format, and position it on the stage. All it takes are a few lines of code in your constructor or `init` method that might look something like this:

```
    var textFieldObject:TextField = new TextField();
    textFieldObject.text = "Hey guys!";
    textFieldObject.height = 30;
    textFieldObject.width = 100;
    textFieldObject.x = 230;
    textFieldObject.y = 200;
    addChild(textFieldObject);
```

Interesting! But you didn't do this in the program. Instead, you used Flash's drawing tools to create, format, and position the text fields; Flash automatically imported all the classes in the text package in the background. This is great because it means that the input and output text fields can use all the formatting options available to these classes. In fact, all the options you assigned the text fields in the text Properties panel can be accessed and changed with code. But there are also lots more that can be accessed only with code.

> *This book doesn't go into these options in any depth, but if you're curious about what's available, take a peek at the chapter "Working with Text" in Adobe's* Programming Adobe ActionScript 3.0 *manual (http://help.adobe.com/en_US/ActionScript/3.0_ProgrammingAS3/). To whet your appetite a bit, I included a few of these options in the program.*

The first thing is to make the background of the input text field a light gray color:

```
input.backgroundColor = 0xFFCCCCCC;
```

backgroundColor is a property of the TextField class. The color is represented by a hexadecimal color code, and 0xFFCCCCCC is the hexadecimal code for light gray. As long as you know the hexadecimal code, you can use any color you like. (A web search for "hexadecimal color chart" will bring up many examples of colors and their matching hexadecimal codes.)

The next line uses the restrict property to prevent the input text field from accepting any characters other than numbers:

```
input.restrict = "0-9";
```

The restrict property limits the characters you can enter to whatever letters or numbers are inside the quotes. For example, if you want to restrict the text field to only the uppercase letters A, B, and C, you can write a directive that looks like this:

```
input.restrict = "ABC";
```

You can restrict a range of numbers or letters by separating the first character in the range from the last character with a dash. Here are some examples:

- To allow only the uppercase letters from M to O, use "M-O".
- To allow all uppercase letters, use "A-Z".
- To restrict input to just lowercase letters, use "a-z".
- To allow only uppercase and lowercase letters, use "A-Za-z".

Your life as a programmer will often be improved by restricting certain types of input because if a user enters something that your program doesn't know how deal with, the whole program could stop working.

The last thing is to create the blinking cursor in the input text field. Use the following line of code:

```
stage.focus = input;
```

When an object on the stage, such as a button or a text field, has been selected by the user, it's said to have **focus**. When input text fields have focus, a blinking cursor appears, and whatever the user types is automatically entered into it. focus is a property of the built-in Stage class, which is at the root of the hierarchy for all display objects (all objects you can see on the stage). When the SWF file runs the program, an instance of the Stage class is automatically created (called, conveniently enough, stage). To assign focus to a text field, all you need to do is assign the name of the text field object to the stage.focus property, as you did here.

If you need to remove focus from a text field, you can give it a null value, such as the following:

```
stage.focus = null;
```

The GUI for the game is, of course, extremely simple, but all the important elements you'll need to get you thinking about GUIs are contained in this little example.

Making decisions

So far, the program doesn't do anything useful. Enter a number, click the button, and wow . . . nothing happens! What you need to do now is build the brains of the game so the program can figure out what number the player has entered and whether it's too high, too low, or correct.

You can do this by using an if/else block statement. if/else statements are very similar to the simple if statements that you looked at in Chapter 3, except that they provide an extra course of action if the condition being checked turns out to be false.

Here's an example of the basic kind of if statement that you looked at in the previous chapter:

```
if(this condition or variable is true)
{
  Perform this directive...
}
```

But what if the condition is not true? Obviously, the directive inside the if statement won't run. But what if you what *something else* to happen instead? That's where the addition of the keyword else comes in. Here's an example of a simple if/else statement:

```
if (this condition or variable is true)
{
  Perform this directive...
}
else
{
  Perform this directive if the condition or variable isn't true...
}
```

If the condition turns out to be false, the program will jump straight to the second directive enclosed inside the braces of the else block statement. This allows the program to make a choice between two alternatives, and at least one of them will be chosen.

You can take this system one step further and add a third or more possible choices by throwing an additional else if statement into the mix. Have a look at how this works:

```
if (this condition or variable is true)
{
  Perform this directive...
}
else if (some other condition or variable is true)
{
  Perform this directive...
}
else
{
  Perform this directive if neither is true...
}
```

This if/else statement checks each of the conditions in turn. If the first is false, it skips to the second. If the second is also false, the final directive in the else block statement is run as the default value.

This format is perfect for the number guessing game, because you need the program it to check for three possible conditions:

- If the player's guess is less than the mystery number
- If the player's guess is greater than the mystery number
- If the player correctly guesses the mystery number

To implement this decision making in the program, you need to first find a way of getting the number from the input text field on the stage into the program so that it can be processed. It is pretty easy to do:

- You need to create a new variable called currentGuess to store the number the player enters in the input text field. You'll use this new variable to convert the text from the input text field from a string to a number so an if/else statement can process it.

- You need to add an event listener to the guessButton object and then create an event handler called onGuessButtonClick that is called when the button is clicked. This is exactly the same as what you did in the previous two chapters to program the buttons.

- You need to create an if/else block statement inside the onGuessButtonClick method to check for the three conditions listed previously.

Let's get to work!

1. Add the following code to your program:

```
package
{
  import flash.display.MovieClip;
  import flash.events.MouseEvent;
```

```
public class Main extends MovieClip
{
  var startMessage:String;
  var mysteryNumber:uint;
  var currentGuess:uint;

  public function Main()
  {
    init();
  }
  function init():void
  {
    //Initialize variables
    startMessage = "I am thinking of a number between 1 and 100";
    mysteryNumber = 50;

    //Initialize text fields
    output.text = startMessage;
    input.text = "";
    input.backgroundColor = 0xFFCCCCCC;
    input.restrict = "0-9";
    stage.focus = input;

    //Add an event listener to the button
    guessButton.addEventListener(MouseEvent.CLICK,➥
      onGuessButtonClick);
  }
  function onGuessButtonClick(event:MouseEvent):void
  {
    //Assign the input from the textfield to the
    //currentGuess variable
    currentGuess = uint(input.text);

    //An if/else statement to process the input
    if (currentGuess > mysteryNumber)
    {
      output.text = "That's too high.";
    }
    else if (currentGuess < mysteryNumber)
    {
      output.text = "That's too low.";
    }
    else
    {
      output.text = "You got it!";
    }
  }
}
```

2. Save the `Main.as` file and test the program. The game will now tell you whether your guess is too high, too low, or correct (see Figure 5-13).

Figure 5-13. With an if/else statement, the game knows whether the player's guess is correct.

After you declared the `currentGuess` variable, you then added an event listener to the `guessButton` object and created a new event handler called `onGuessButtonClick` that runs when the button is clicked. It's in that event handler where all the action is, so let's a have a look at its directives in more detail.

This is the first one:

```
currentGuess = uint(input.text);
```

What's all that about? It copies the text from the input field in to the `currentGuess` variable. But that's not all; it also converts the input data from plain text into a number.

When you enter text into an input text field, that text is stored in the field's built-in text variable as a string. Strings are words or letters, and you can usually spot them because they'll be surrounded by quotes. Even if you type in numbers, those numbers are interpreted as characters in a line of text, not something that can be processed mathematically. As far as strings are concerned, "789" is just another word like "bike" or "elephant". That's bit of a problem because the game depends on the player entering numbers that can actually be understood as numbers.

What you need to do then is convert the data from the input field's text variable from a string to a number. Because the numbers from 1 to 100 are all positive and don't contain decimal values, it makes sense that they should be interpreted as data with a `uint` type.

It's very easy to convert data types in AS3.0. All you need to do is surround the data you want to convert in parentheses and then add the name of the type you want to convert it to. That's all that this bit of code in bold does:

```
currentGuess = uint(input.text);
```

It converts the string from the input field's text variable into a number of the unit type. This process of converting one type of data to another is called **casting**. You'll be encountering casting a lot over the course of the book. It's often necessary for you to cast data or objects as a certain type to encourage AS3.0's compiler to run the code correctly.

> *An alternative way of casting variables is to use the as keyword. You can write the previous line of code like this:*
>
> ```
>         currentGuess = input.text as uint;
> ```
>
> *This line is very readable, and the effect is exactly the same. It's entirely up to you which style of casting you prefer.*

Now that you have a number in the currentGuess variable, you can use the if/else statement to analyze it:

```
if (currentGuess > mysteryNumber)
{
  output.text = "That's too high.";
}
else if (currentGuess < mysteryNumber)
{
  output.text = "That's too low.";
}
else
{
  output.text = "You got it!";
}
```

The logic behind this is really simple. If the currentGuess variable is greater than the mysteryNumber, That's too high. displays in the output text field. If it's less than the mysteryNumber, That's too low. displays. If it's neither too low nor too high, there has to be only one alternative left: the number is correct. The output text field displays You got it!

Not so hard at all, is it? If you understand how this works, you might be pleased to know that writing if/else statements will be at the very heart of the logic in your game design projects. It really doesn't get much more difficult than this.

Displaying the game status

The logic works well enough, but you can't actually win or lose the game. The game gives you an endless number of guesses and even after you guess the mystery number correctly, you can keep playing forever! Again, a fascinating glimpse into the nature of eternity and the fleeting and ephemeral nature of life on earth, but not at all fun to play!

To limit the number of guesses, the program needs to know a little more about the status of the game and then what to do when the conditions for winning or losing the game have been reached. You'll solve this in two parts, beginning with displaying the game status.

To know whether the player has won or lost, the game first needs to know a few more things:

- How many guesses the player has remaining before the game finishes.
- How many guesses the player has made. This is actually optional information, but interesting to implement so you'll give it a whirl.

When a program "needs more information" about something, it usually means that you need to create more variables to capture and store that information. That's exactly what you'll do in this case: create two new variables called guessesRemaining and guessesMade. You'll also create a third variable called gameStatus that will be used to display this new information in the output text field.

1. Add the following code in bold to your program. The code that adds the new variables is pretty straightforward, but be very careful when adding the new code to the onGuessButtonClick method because there are many new things going on there that you haven't yet seen.

```
package
{
    import flash.display.MovieClip;
    import flash.events.MouseEvent;

    public class Main extends MovieClip
    {
        var startMessage:String;
        var mysteryNumber:uint;
        var currentGuess:uint;
        var guessesRemaining:uint;
        var guessesMade:uint;
        var gameStatus:String;

        public function Main()
        {
            init();
        }
        function init():void
        {
            //Initialize variables
            startMessage = "I am thinking of a number between 1 and 100";
            mysteryNumber = 50;
            guessesRemaining = 10;
            guessesMade = 0;
            gameStatus = "";

            //Initialize text fields
            output.text = startMessage;
            input.text = "";
            input.backgroundColor = 0xFFCCCCCC;
            input.restrict = "0-9";
            stage.focus = input;
```

```
  //Add an event listener to the button
  guessButton.addEventListener(MouseEvent.CLICK,➡
    onGuessButtonClick);
}
function onGuessButtonClick(event:MouseEvent):void
{
  guessesRemaining--;
  guessesMade++;
  gameStatus = "Guesses Remaining: " + guessesRemaining + ➡
    ", Guesses Made: " + guessesMade;

  //Assign the input from the textfield to
  //the currentGuess variable
  currentGuess = uint(input.text);

  //An if/else statement to process the input
  if (currentGuess > mysteryNumber)
  {
    output.text = "That's too high." + "\n"  +  gameStatus;
  }
  else if (currentGuess < mysteryNumber)
  {
    output.text = "That's too low." + "\n"  +  gameStatus;
  }
  else
  {
    output.text = "You got it!";
  }
  }
 }
}
```

2. Save the Main.as file and test the program. The output text field now tells you how many guesses you have remaining and how many you made. Figure 5-14 shows an example of what your game might look like.

Figure 5-14. The game keeps track of the number of guesses remaining and the number of guesses made.

Using postfix operators to change variable values by 1

The new code assigns the three new variables their initial values:

```
guessesRemaining = 10;
guessesMade = 0;
gameStatus = "";
```

The total number of guesses the player gets before the game ends is stored in the guessesRemaining variable. You gave it an initial value of 10, but you can, of course, change it to make the game easier or harder to play. You also want to count the number of guesses the player makes, so a guessesMade variable is created to store that information. When the game first starts, the player has obviously not made any guesses, so the guessesMade variable is set to 0. The gameStatus variable is a string that will be used to output this new information, and you'll see how it does this in a moment. It contains no text initially (it is assigned a pair of empty quotation marks).

Now take a look at the first two new directives in the onGuessButtonClick event handler:

```
guessesRemaining--;
guessesMade++;
```

When you play the game, you'll notice that Guesses Remaining in the output text field decreases by 1, and the Guesses Made increases by 1. That's all thanks to the two lines that use the extremely convenient **postfix operators**.

Remember the discussion of increment and decrement operators from the previous chapter? If you want to increase a value by 1, you can write some code that looks like this:

```
numberVariable += 1;
```

It turns out that increasing values by 1 is something programmers want their programs to do all the time. So frequently, in fact, that AS3.0 has special shorthand for it: a double plus sign, which is a special kind of operator called a postfix operator. You can use it to rewrite the previous line of code like this:

```
numberVariable++;
```

It will do exactly the same thing: add 1 to the value of the variable. You can use another postfix operator, the double-minus sign, to subtract 1 from the value of a variable in exactly the same way, like this:

```
numberVariable--;
```

Postfix operators change the value of the variable by 1 each time the directive runs. The directives in the onGuessButtonClick event handler are run each time the Guess button is clicked, which, of course, is each time the player makes a guess. Having the guessesRemaining and guessesMade variables update with each button click is therefore a perfect way to keep track of the number of guesses the player has made.

When the game starts, the guessesRemaining variable is initialized to 10. On the first click of the guess button, this directive is run:

```
guessesRemaining--;
```

It subtracts 1, making its new value 9. On the next click, the very same directive runs again, and 1 is subtracted for the second time, leaving it with a value of 8. One will be subtracted every time the button is clicked for the rest of the game.

The guessesMade variable does the same thing, but instead uses the double-plus sign to add 1 to its value. When you test the game, you can clearly see how this is working by the way the values update in the output text field.

Tying up strings

You created another new variable in the program called gameStatus. You declared this variable as a String, which means that it will be used to store text. The first time it makes its appearance is in this directive:

```
gameStatus = "Guesses Remaining: " + guessesRemaining + ➡
  ", Guesses Made: " + guessesMade;
```

For the uninitiated, this is a potentially terrifying segment of code. What on earth does it do?

The first time you make a guess in the game, you'll see the following text on the second line of the output text field:

```
Guesses Remaining: 9, Guesses Made: 1
```

This text has to come from somewhere, and it's the preceding directive that's responsible for putting it all together.

Think about it carefully: what are the values of the guessesRemaining and guessesMade variables the first time you click the Guess button? (They're 9 and 1.)

Okay then, let's imagine that you replace the variable names you used in the directive with the actual numbers they represent: 9 and 1. It will look something like this:

```
gameStatus = "Guesses Remaining: " + 9 + ", Guesses Made: " + 1;
```

Make sense, right? Great, now let's pretend that the plus signs have disappeared and everything is inside a single set of quotes:

```
gameStatus = "Guesses Remaining: 9, Guesses Made: 1";
```

Aha! Can you see how it's all fitting together now? That's exactly the text that is displayed in the output text field. Figure 5-15 shows how the entire line of text is interpreted, from the initial directive to being displayed in the output text field.

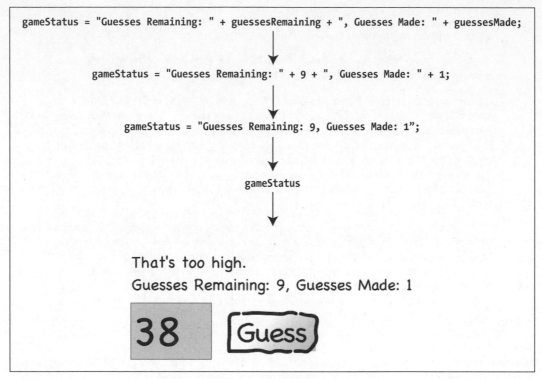

Figure 5-15. From the kitchen to the plate: string concatenation in action!

The directive uses plus signs to join all the separate elements together to make a single cohesive string of text. This is something known in computer programming as **string concatenation**, which just means "joining text together with plus signs." It's a very useful technique to use when you need to mix text that doesn't change with variables that do. Because the values of the variables change, the entire string of text updates itself accordingly. It's so simple, really, but a sort of magical thing to watch when the program runs.

When you use plus signs to concatenate strings, they don't have any mathematical meaning—they're just like stitches that are used to sew all the bits of text together into one long piece. In the program, the final result of all this stitching is copied into the gameStatus variable so you just need to use the gameStatus variable whenever you need to display this text. And that's exactly what the next bit of code does.

> *A small technical detail that you should be aware of is that the following directive actually mixes String and uint variables:*
>
> ```
> gameStatus = "Guesses Remaining: " + guessesRemaining +➡
>     ", Guesses Made: " + guessesMade;
> ```
>
> *In the program, you declared the gameStatus variable to be a String type. That means it can't contain numbers, except in the form of numeric characters (which are interpreted like letters or words). However, you declared both the guessesRemaining and guessesMade variables as uint variables (which are interpreted as numbers). Both of them are joined together with ordinary text and copied into the gameStatus string variable. Isn't the purpose of assigning variables types to prevent this sort of mixing and matching between strings and numbers? How is this possible?*
>
> *In fact, you can use number variables with strings by joining them together with plus signs, but when you do this, AS3.0 converts the values of the number variables into strings. The data type in the guessesRemaining and guessesMade variables remains unchanged as uint, but the values they contain are converted into a string when they're assigned to the gameStatus String variable. This is very useful for exactly the purpose you've put it to: to display text with numbers that are updated by the program. It's such a common requirement in programs that AS3.0 does this type conversion automatically. Thanks, Flash!*

Now that you have the gameStatus variable packed up and ready to go, you get lot of mileage out of it in the if/else statement. The new bits of code are highlighted in bold:

```
if (currentGuess > mysteryNumber)
{
  output.text  = "That's too high."  +  "\n"  +  gameStatus;
}
  else if (currentGuess < mysteryNumber)
{
  output.text  = "That's too low."  +  "\n"  +  gameStatus;
}
else
{
  output.text  =  "You got it!";
}
```

You're using string concatenation to add the contents of the gameStatus variable to the output text field. But there's something here that you haven't seen before:

```
"\n"
```

A backslash followed by the letter n is known as a **newline character**. The newline character forces whatever text that comes after it onto a "new line." That's why the game displays the game status information just below the first bit of text.

You can use the newline character in the middle of any string to break the text onto two lines or more. Here's an example:

```
"This text\nis broken in the middle."
```

It displays as follows:

```
This text
is broken in the middle.
```

In the program you added the newline character by joining it to the rest of the text using string concatenation. Here's how it looks using the example text:

```
"This text" + "\n" + "is broken in the middle."
```

The result is exactly the same, but the code is a little easier to read because it's visually very clear where the line break falls.

Hey, why use the gameStatus variable, anyway?

There's one last thing you should quickly look at, and a question that you might have had about how you've written the code in the `if/else` statement. You could have written the first two directives in the `if/else` statement to look like this:

```
if (currentGuess > mysteryNumber)
{
  output.text  = "That's too high."  +  "\n"  + ➡
  "Guesses Remaining: " + guessesRemaining + ", ➡
  Guesses Made: " + guessesMade;
}
  else if (currentGuess < mysteryNumber)
{
  output.text  = "That's too low."  +  "\n"  + ➡
  "Guesses Remaining: " + guessesRemaining + ", ➡
  Guesses Made: " + guessesMade;
}
else
{
  output.text  =  "You got it!";
}
```

Why then did you go to all the trouble of creating a special gameStatus variable if you could easily have done without it? Obviously, it's a lot of code, it makes the `if/else` statement more difficult to read, and you'd have to write it all out twice.

The other reason might be less obvious: if you have that text neatly stored in the gameStatus variable and you need to make any changes to it, you have to change it only once. Any place you use the gameStatus variable in the program is automatically updated with the new text. This might not be such a big issue in a small program like this number guessing game, but in a bigger program, being used 10 or 20 times in different places, it would be a lot of work to update.

Whenever you find yourself using a lot of the same text over and over again in any of your programs, try storing it in a variable: you'll save yourself a lot of typing and a lot of trouble in the long run.

Using uint vs. int variables

Did you try making more than the ten guesses the game said you had remaining? If you did, you would have noticed that the output text field displayed something like this: Guesses Remaining: 4294967295. Figure 5-16 shows an example.

Figure 5-16. Make too many guesses, and you'll see output like this.

At the moment. you haven't programmed the game to end when the player has run out of guesses, so the game keeps on subtracting 1 from the guessesRemaining variable even after the 10 guesses are used up. After it passes 0, it suddenly jumps to this crazy long number: 4294967295. No, your program isn't about to join a secret botnet of computers plotting to overthrow the human race; there is actually very interesting logic behind it.

You decided to declare the guessesRemaining variable as a uint type. uint variables store whole numbers that are only positive. They can never be negative. When a variable declared as a uint type does try to become less than zero, exactly the opposite thing happens: it flips to the maximum possible number, which happens to be 4294967295.

This is very important to know because sometimes you need or want to know whether a number has run into negative territory. In those cases, make sure that you declare the variable as an int type. (As mentioned before, int stands for *integer*, which is a whole number that can be positive or negative.)

To see the effect that changing the guessesRemaining variable to an int type has on your program, try it and see what happens!

1. Change the line of code near the top of your program that declares the guessesRemaining variable so that its type is set to int:

   var guessesRemaining:**int**;

2. Save the Main.as file and test the program.

3. Click the Guess button more than ten times. You should see the Guesses Remaining become negative, as shown in Figure 5-17.

Keep this in mind whenever you decide what type to declare your variables.

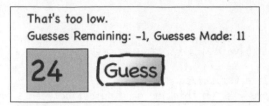

That's too low.
Guesses Remaining: -1, Guesses Made: 11

24 [Guess]

Figure 5-17. Declare variables as int if you need to use negative values.

Winning and losing

The game now has enough information about what the player is doing to figure out whether the game has been won or lost. All you need to do now is to find a way to say, "Hey, the game is over!" and tell players how well they did.

To do this, add the following to the program:

- A Boolean (true/false) variable called gameWon that is set to true if the game has been won and false if it hasn't.
- A method called checkGameOver that checks to see whether the player has enough guesses remaining to continue playing.
- A method called endGame that tells players whether they've won or lost.

An important aspect of this next bit of code is that it shows you an example of how you can use methods to help you **modularize** your code. In general terms, **modular programming** is way of breaking down complex bits of code into smaller manageable pieces, or **modules**. Modules can really be any pieces of code, such as classes or methods, which perform one specific helpful function. Have a look at the two new methods added in the following code and see if you can figure out how they're used to modularize the program.

1. Add the following code in bold text to your program:

```
package
{
  import flash.display.MovieClip;
  import flash.events.MouseEvent;

  public class Main extends MovieClip
  {
    var startMessage:String;
    var mysteryNumber:uint;
    var currentGuess:uint;
    var guessesRemaining:uint;
    var guessesMade:uint;
    var gameStatus:String;
    var gameWon:Boolean;
```

```
public function Main()
{
  init();
}
function init():void
{
   //Initialize variables
  startMessage = "I am thinking of a number between 1 and 100";
  mysteryNumber = 50;
  guessesRemaining = 10;
  guessesMade = 0;
  gameStatus = "";
  gameWon = false;

  //Initialize text fields
  output.text = startMessage;
  input.text = "";
  input.backgroundColor = 0xFFCCCCCC;
  input.restrict = "0-9";
  stage.focus = input;

  //Add an event listener to the button
  guessButton.addEventListener(MouseEvent.CLICK, ➡
    onGuessButtonClick);
}
function onGuessButtonClick(event:MouseEvent):void
{
  guessesRemaining--;
  guessesMade++;
  gameStatus = "Guesses Remaining: " + guessesRemaining + ➡
    ", Guesses Made: " + guessesMade;

 //Assign the input from the textfield to currentGuess
  currentGuess = uint(input.text);

  //An if/else statement to process the input
  if (currentGuess > mysteryNumber)
  {
    output.text = "That's too high." + "\n" + gameStatus;
    checkGameOver();
  }
  else if (currentGuess < mysteryNumber)
  {
    output.text = "That's too low." + "\n" + gameStatus;
    checkGameOver();
  }
  else
  {
```

```
            output.text = "You got it!";
            gameWon = true;
            endGame();
        }
    }
    function checkGameOver():void
    {
      if (guessesRemaining < 1)
      {
        endGame();
      }
    }
    function endGame():void
    {
      if (gameWon)
      {
        output.text = "Yes, it's " + mysteryNumber + "!" + "\n" + ➡
        "It only took you " + guessesMade + " guesses.";
      }
      else
      {
        output.text = "I'm sorry, you've run out of guesses." + "\n" + ➡
        "The correct number was " + mysteryNumber + ".";
      }
    }
  }
}
```

2. Delete the following directive from the if statement in the onGuessButtonClick event handler. This text will be replaced by the new text from the endGame method. There's actually no harm in leaving it in, but it's redundant.

```
output.text = "You got it!";
```

3. Save the Main.as file and test the program. The game prevents you from guessing more than ten times and tells you whether you've won or lost. Figure 5-18 shows what your game might now look like if you guess correctly.

Figure 5-18. The game can now be won or lost.

The game needed to figure out whether the player used up all the guesses. Before you added the new code, you could count the guesses, but the program didn't know what to do with that information. The new code solves that.

The methods help modularize the program by breaking the steps down into manageable pieces. Let's go on a little tour of how all this new code fits together.

First, you need to help the game figure out whether the player can still continue playing. You add the same directive to the first two blocks of the if/else statement in the onGuessButtonClick event handler, highlighted in bold:

```
if (currentGuess > mysteryNumber)
{
  output.text = "That's too high." + "\n" + gameStatus;
  checkGameOver();
}
else if (currentGuess < mysteryNumber)
{
  output.text = "That's too low." + "\n" + gameStatus;
  checkGameOver();
}
else
{
  output.text = "You got it!";
  gameWon = true;
  endGame();
}
```

The two new directives are method calls to the checkGameOver method. So as soon as the program reads one of these directives, it immediately jumps ahead to the checkGameOver method's function definition and runs whatever directives it contains.

This is what the checkGameOver function definition looks like:

```
function checkGameOver():void
{
  if (guessesRemaining < 1)
  {
  endGame();
  }
}
```

The method checks to see how many guesses the player has remaining. If there are still enough, nothing happens, and the game continues. But if guessesRemaining is less than 1, the game is brought to an end by calling the endGame method:

```
function endGame():void
{
  if (gameWon)
  {
    output.text = "Yes, it's " + mysteryNumber + "!" + "\n" + ➥
      "It only took you " + guessesMade + " guesses.";
  }
  else
```

```
        {
            output.text = "I'm sorry, you've run out of guesses." + "\n" + ➡
                "The correct number was " + mysteryNumber + ".";
        }
    }
```

The endGame method looks to see whether the game has been won or lost by checking whether the gameWon variable is true or false. It then displays the appropriate message. (Can you figure out how string concatenation is being used to display these messages? Compare the code with what you see in the game's output text field. I'm sure you can do it!)

> *if statements work by running their directives if the condition in the parentheses is true. With Boolean variables, there are two ways to check whether they're true or false. You can use an equality operator (a double-equal sign) and compare it with a true or false value, like this:*
>
> > `if(gameWon == true)`
>
> *If gameWon is false, this statement evaluates as false, and the directives don't run. If gameWon is true, the statement evaluates as true, and the directives run.*
>
> *You should be familiar with that way of checking for true or false conditions from the previous chapter. However, if the condition you're checking happens to be the value of a Boolean variable, it's much more convenient and often makes your code easier to read to use this shorthand:*
>
> > `if(gameWon)`
>
> *Because the value of gameWon can be only true or false, it provides exactly the same information as the first example.*
>
> *You'll be using this as the preferred way for checking the value of Boolean variables in if statements throughout the book. if(gameWon) is very close to the English phrase "If the game is won." Choose the names of your variables carefully to really help to make your programs easier to read.*

How does the program know whether the gameWon variable is true or false?

You initialized gameWon to false at the very top of the program. That means it will always be false unless you change it to true somewhere in the game. You would change it to true only if the player actually meets the conditions for winning the game. In this game, there is only one way the player can win: by guessing the correct number.

That makes things really easy because you know that if players still have enough guesses remaining, and they've guessed the correct number, they must have won the game. So all you need to do is set the gameWon variable to true and call the endGame method in the same if/else block that checks whether the player's guess is correct. Easy!

Don't believe me? Check out the code in bold that shows the section of the `onGuessButtonClick` event handler's `if/else` statement that does this:

```
if (currentGuess > mysteryNumber)
{
  output.text = "That's too high." + "\n" + gameStatus;
  checkGameOver();
}
else if (currentGuess < mysteryNumber)
{
  output.text = "That's too low." + "\n" + gameStatus;
  checkGameOver();
}
else
{
  output.text = "You got it!";
  gameWon = true;
  endGame();
}
```

Think about the logic behind what the `if/else` statement is saying. If players still have enough guesses remaining, the game will continue. If the game is still continuing, and players have guessed the right number, they must have won the game. The gameWon variable is then set to `true`, and the directives in the endGame method are run. When the endGame method runs, its conditional statement notices that gameWon is `true` and displays the message telling the player they've won.

Modular programming with methods

Can you see how the checkGameOver and endGame methods were used to help modularize the code? In truth, you could have written this program without them by adding all the conditions they check for in one extremely long `if/else` statement. But if you'd done so, you'd have to write some of the same code over twice, and it would all start to become very difficult to read and debug.

Modularizing specific tasks inside self-contained methods allows you to modify or debug those bits of code in isolation without having to change (and possibly damage) other parts of the program that are working. It also means that whenever you want to perform a certain task, you don't need to duplicate any of the code you've already written; you just have to call the method.

Using methods to modularize your code might take you a bit of practice, and you might find it a bit of a brain-twister until you've seen a few more examples and experimented with using them in your own projects. Have a look at how the game is working so far and see if you can figure out how the interrelationships between methods and method calls are working. Figure 5-19 is a map of how it all fits together.

```
function onGuessButtonClick(event:MouseEvent):void
{
  guessesRemaining--;
  guessesMade++;
  gameStatus = "Guesses Remaining: " + guessesRemaining + ", Guesses Made: " + guessesMade;
  currentGuess = uint(input.text);

  if (currentGuess > mysteryNumber)
  {
    output.text = "That's too high." + "\n" + gameStatus;
    checkGameOver();
  }
  else if (currentGuess < mysteryNumber)
  {
    output.text = "That's too low." + "\n" + gameStatus;
    checkGameOver();
  }
  else
  {
    output.text = "You got it!";
    gameWon = true;
    endGame();
  }
}
                                              function checkGameOver():void
                                              {
                                                if (guessesRemaining < 1)
                                              {
                                                  endGame();
                                              }
                                              }

          function endGame():void
          {
            if (gameWon)
            {
              output.text = "Yes, it's " + mysteryNumber + "!" + "\n" + "It only took you " + guessesMade + " guesses.";
            }
            else
            {
              output.text = "I'm sorry, you've run out of guesses." + "\n" + "The correct number was " + mysteryNumber + ".";
            }
          }
```

Figure 5-19. Use methods to modularize specific tasks.

Polishing up

In the previous chapter, I mentioned that 30% of the time it takes to program a piece of software goes into making it work, and the other 70% goes into making it work well. There's no better example of this principle at work than the number guessing game. It's playable, but there's a lot lacking that most players would complain about.

Most glaringly, try clicking the Guess button after you've won the game; the game still keeps counting your guesses! The other problem is that the only way to play the game again is by closing the SWF file and then running it again. It would be great if there were a "play again" button that you could click. And how about the mystery number? The game won't have much replay value if it's 50 every time you play. Roll up your sleeves and see if you can fix these problems!

Tackling random numbers

You'll tackle the random number problem first because you'll almost certainly find yourself needing to use random numbers in most of your game projects. AS3.0 has a built-in class called Math that includes quite a few methods that are useful for manipulating numbers. One of these is the random method, which generates a random number between 0 and 1. Here's what it looks like:

```
Math.random()
```

You can assign this random number to a variable just as you assign other values to variables, as in this example:

```
randomVariable = Math.random();
```

The fictitious randomVariable is now assigned a random number between 0 and 1, with up to 16 decimal places. So it could be anything; for example, 0.3669164208535294 or 0.5185672459021346.

What use is a random number between 0 and 1 with 16 decimal places, you ask? Well, practically none whatsoever. Fortunately, you can do a bit of tweaking to get something more useful.

First, random numbers for games usually need to be integers—whole numbers. All those decimal places have got to go! Can you imagine what a nightmare the guessing game would be to play if the mystery number were something like 33.6093155708325684? If you chop off all those decimals, you'll have something useful, such as 33, which is within the realms of most human lifetimes to be able to guess!

The Math class fortunately has a few built-in methods that can help us round decimals up or down:

- Math.round: Can be used to round numbers either up or down. For example, Math.round(3.4) returns a value of 3. Math.round(3.8) returns 4. Math.round(3.5) also returns 4.
- Math.floor: Always rounds numbers down. Math.floor(3.2) returns 3. Math.floor(3.9) also returns 3.
- Math.ceil: Always rounds numbers up. Math.ceil(3.2) returns 4, and Math.ceil(3.9) also returns 4. (ceil is short for *ceiling*. Ceilings are up; floors are down. Make sense?)

To use any of these methods along with the Math.random method, you need to use a format that looks like this:

```
Math.round(Math.random())
```

Think about what this is doing. Math.random() generates a random number between 0 and 1 with loads of decimals. So imagine that it came up with a deliciously useless number such as 0.6781340985784098. You could pretend that the preceding line of code now looks like this:

```
Math.round(0.6781340985784098)
```

How would you round that number? You'd round it up, and the result would be the following:

```
1
```

But what would happen if the random number were lower, like this?

```
Math.round(0.2459678308703125)
```

It would be rounded down to this:

```
0
```

This means that you can use the line of code, `Math.round(Math.random())`, to generate a random number that has a 50% chance of being either 0 or 1. Not yet quite what you're looking for in the game, but not entirely useless, either. There will be many instances where calculating a 50% chance of something happening will be really useful in your games, and you can use this little snippet of code to do exactly that.

> *In fact, you can use the snippet to generate random Boolean (true/false) values. Let's pretend that you have a Boolean variable called rainToday. You could initialize it with a value of false:*
>
> ```
> rainToday = false;
> ```
>
> *Oh, if only that were true! So to make it a little more realistic, you can give it a 50% chance of being either true or false. All you need to do is use the Math.round(Math. random()) code snippet in an if/else statement and compare it against a value of 1. Here's what the code might look like:*
>
> ```
> if(Math.round(Math.random()) == 1)
> {
>   rainToday = true;
> }
> else
> {
>   rainToday = false;
> }
> ```
>
> *Math.round(Math.random()) has an exactly 50% chance of generating either the number 1 or 0. If it happens to be 1, the first directive runs and rainToday becomes true. If it's 0, no rain today!*

So a random number between 0 and 1 is slightly more useful, but not exactly what you're looking for in the game. How can you get a random number between 1 and 100? Here's how:

```
Math.ceil(Math.random() * 100)
```

The asterisk is AS3.0's **multiplication operator**. * 100 means *multiplied by 100*. This line of code multiplies the random number by 100 and then uses `Math.ceil` to round it up so the lowest number it can possibly be is 1. That gives a perfect random whole number that falls within the range of 1 to 100.

Here's another way of looking at it. Let's say that the random number is 0.3378208608542148. That would mean the code will look like this:

```
Math.ceil(0.3378208608542148 * 100)
```

Multiplied by 100, the random number will then look like this:

```
Math.ceil(33.78208608542148 )
```

The decimal point is just moved two spaces to the right, giving a nice big number to work with. But you still have the problem of those infuriating decimals to deal with! Not to worry; Math.ceil comes to the rescue by rounding the whole thing up. So the result is very satisfying:

34

Perfect for the number guessing game! Figure 5-20 shows an example of this process in action.

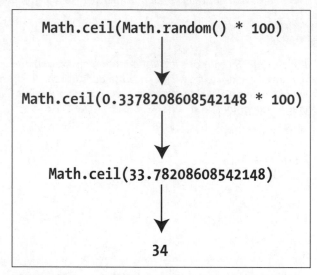

Figure 5-20. From useless to useful: using Math.random and Math.ceil to help generate random whole numbers within a specific range

You can use this same format for any range of numbers simply by changing the number that you multiply the random number by. Here are some examples:

- `Math.ceil(Math.random() * 10)` generates a random number between 1 and 10.
- `Math.ceil(Math.random() * 27)` generates a random number between 1 and 27.
- `Math.ceil(Math.random() * 5)` generates a random number between 1 and 5.

The reason why using Math.ceil starts the range of random numbers with 1 is that any number less than 1, such as 0.23, will be rounded up to 1. That saves you from having to deal with values of 0, which are often not useful for the ranges of numbers you'll be looking for in your games. If you do want 0 to be part of the range, however, use Math.round instead. Math.round(Math.random() * 100) will give you a random number between 0 and 100.

> *What if you want to generate a random number within a range of numbers that starts at something other than 1 or zero?*
>
> *Let's say you need a number between 10 and 25. That means that you have 15 possible numbers that could be chosen: 10, 11, 12 . . . up to 25. All you need to do is generate a random number between 0 and 15, and then add 10 to it push it up to within the range you need. This is what the code will look like:*
>
> Math.round(Math.random() * 15) + 10
>
> *Think about it this way. The random number is between 0 and 15. Let's say it's 8. Then you add 10 to it. You end up with 18. You've got a range of possible random numbers between 10 and 25!*

Now use what you learned about random numbers and apply it to the game:

1. Modify the init method with the new code in bold. In addition to randomizing the mysteryNumber variable, you've added a trace directive for testing purposes so that you can actually see what that number is in the Output panel. (Notice that string concatenation was used in the trace directive so that the display in the Output panel is more readable.)

```
function init():void
{
  //Initialize variables
  startMessage = "I am thinking of a number between 1 and 100";
  mysteryNumber = Math.ceil(Math.random() * 100);
  guessesRemaining = 10;
  guessesMade = 0;
  gameStatus = "";
  gameWon = false;

  //Trace the mystery number
  trace ("The mystery number: " + mysteryNumber);

  //Initialize text fields
  output.text = startMessage;
  input.text = "";
  input.backgroundColor = 0xFFCCCCCC;
  input.restrict = "0-9";
  stage.focus = input;

  //Add an event listener to the button
  guessButton.addEventListener(MouseEvent.CLICK, onGuessButtonClick);
}
```

2. Save the `Main.as` file and test the program. The mystery number is now a random number between 1 and 100. You'll also see the text The mystery number is: ?? displayed in the output window so that you can make sure everything is working as you expect it to. Figure 5-21 shows an example of what your game might now look like.

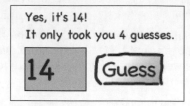

Figure 5-21. Randomizing the mystery number

Disabling the Guess button

One quirky bug in the game so far is that if the player wins the game but continues clicking the Guess button, the output text field still continues to count the guesses. If you think about how the program is working, this makes perfect sense because the button itself has no way of knowing whether or not the game is over; it just keeps on dutifully doing the jobs you assigned to it.

To fix this, you need to do three things when the game ends:

1. Remove the onGuessButtonClick event listener from the guessButton object.

2. Disable the button so that it can't be clicked.

3. Dim the Guess button so that it's obvious to the player that the button can't be clicked. This is an optional step, but anything you can do in your games to provide visual cues about how your GUI works will really be appreciated by your players.

Three very straightforward lines of code are all you need.

1. Add the following code in bold to the endGame method:

```
function endGame():void
{
  if (gameWon)
  {
      output.text = "Yes, it's " + mysteryNumber + "!" + "\n" + ➥
      "It only took you " + guessesMade + " guesses.";
  }
   else
  {
      output.text = "I'm sorry, you've run out of guesses." + "\n" + ➥
      "The correct number was " + mysteryNumber + ".";
  }
    //Disable the guess button
    guessButton.removeEventListener(MouseEvent.CLICK, ➥
      onGuessButtonClick);
    guessButton.enabled = false;
```

```
        guessButton.alpha = 0.5;
    }
```

2. Save the Main.as file and test the program. Play through the game. When it's finished, the Guess button will be dimmed, and you can't click it. Figure 5-22 shows an example.

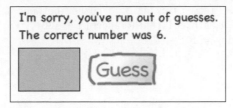

I'm sorry, you've run out of guesses.
The correct number was 6.

Guess

Figure 5-22. Disable and dim the Guess button at the end of the game.

All the new code was added inside the endGame method's function definition because its directives run only when the game is finished.

The first new directive removes the event listener from the guessButton object:

```
guessButton.removeEventListener(MouseEvent.CLICK, ➥
    onGuessButtonClick);
```

Nothing happens when the Guess button is clicked, but all the button states still work. To prevent this, you need to specifically disable the button using this line of code:

```
guessButton.enabled = false;
```

Buttons have a special property called enabled that determines whether or not they're clickable. The enabled property accepts Boolean values (the default value is true). To disable the button, simply assign its enabled property a value of false.

The last new directive dims the button on the stage. Use the button's alpha property and set it to 0.5, which makes it semitransparent:

```
guessButton.alpha = 0.5;
```

To help you keep things a bit more modular, you could actually move all these directives related to disabling buttons into their own method, perhaps called disableButtons. In such a small program as the number guessing game, however, it would probably be more trouble than it's worth. Modularize your code wherever you can, but also use your judgment about when it's appropriate or practical.

Playing again?

You've solved a bug, so let's add a feature! A Play Again button!

1. Create a new button symbol called PlayAgainButton.

2. Drag an instance of the PlayAgainButton onto the stage next to the Guess button. Give it the instance name playAgainButton.

3. Add the following code in bold to the init method. These directives will initialize the buttons for us when the game starts.

```
function init():void
{
  //Initialize variables
  startMessage = "I am thinking of a number between 1 and 100";
  mysteryNumber = Math.ceil(Math.random() * 100);
  guessesRemaining = 10;
  guessesMade = 0;
  gameStatus = "";
  gameWon = false;

  //Trace the mystery number
  trace ("The mystery number: " + mysteryNumber);

  //Initialize text fields
  output.text = startMessage;
  input.text = "";
  input.backgroundColor = 0xFFCCCCCC;
  input.restrict = "0-9";
  stage.focus = input;

  //Initialize buttons
  guessButton.enabled = true;
  guessButton.alpha = 1;
  playAgainButton.visible = false;

  //Add an event listener to the button
  guessButton.addEventListener(MouseEvent.CLICK, ➥
    onGuessButtonClick);
}
```

4. You also need to add some more code to the endGame method:

```
function endGame():void
{
  if (gameWon)
  {
     output.text = "Yes, it's " + mysteryNumber + "!" + "\n" +➥
       "It only took you " + guessesMade + " guesses.";
  }
  else
  {
     output.text = "I'm sorry, you've run out of guesses." + "\n" ➥
       + "The correct number was " + mysteryNumber + ".";
  }
  //Disable the guess button
  guessButton.removeEventListener(MouseEvent.CLICK, ➥
    onGuessButtonClick);
```

```
        guessButton.enabled = false;
        guessButton.alpha = 0.5;
        playAgainButton.visible = true;
        playAgainButton.addEventListener(MouseEvent.CLICK, ➥
          onPlayAgainButtonClick);
    }
```

5. You need an event handler for the playAgainButton. Add the following code just below the endGame method:

```
function onPlayAgainButtonClick(event:MouseEvent):void
{
  init();
  playAgainButton.removeEventListener(MouseEvent.CLICK, ➥
      onPlayAgainButtonClick);
}
```

6. Save the Main.as file and test the program. The Play Again button appears only at the end of the game and disappears when you click it (see Figure 5-23). The Guess button is also fully functional when the game starts again.

Figure 5-23. Give the player the option to play again.

In the previous section, you disabled the Guess button when the game finished. Now that you can play again, you need to make sure that it's enabled and fully visible when the game starts. You also need to make sure that the Play Again button *isn't* visible when the game starts. The three new directives in the init method accomplish this:

```
    guessButton.enabled = true;
    guessButton.alpha = 1;
    playAgainButton.visible = false;
```

You also added two new directives to the endGame method:

```
    playAgainButton.visible = true;
    playAgainButton.addEventListener(MouseEvent.CLICK, ➥
      onPlayAgainButtonClick);
```

These directives simply make the Play Again button visible and add its event listener, onPlayAgainButtonClick:

```
    function onPlayAgainButtonClick(event:MouseEvent):void
    {
```

```
        init();
        playAgainButton.removeEventListener(MouseEvent.CLICK, ➥
          onPlayAgainButtonClick);
    }
```

The first directive is a call to the `init` method, which initializes all the elements of the game to their starting values and assigns the random mystery number. Calling it again from the end of the game completely resets the game. A new mystery number is also randomly chosen. Hey, it's a new game; you can play again!

You can see in this example why it made sense to move all the initialization directives into the `init` method. Whenever you want to reset the game, all you have to do is call it from anywhere in the program.

The final directive removes the event listener from the `playAgainButton`:

```
        playAgainButton.removeEventListener(MouseEvent.CLICK, ➥
          onPlayAgainButtonClick);
```

It's a good idea to remove event listeners from objects whenever you aren't using them. If you don't, the Flash Player still runs them in the background. The Play Again button's one and only function is to reset the game, and once that job is over, it's no longer needed. So as odd as it may seem, its next duty is this somewhat paradoxical and semisuicidal directive: to remove its own event listener. You don't need it until the button makes its next appearance at the end of the game, so you might as well get rid of it. Its listener will be reassigned to it the next time the game ends.

Seeing the final code

Hey, that's amazing, the game is done! Just in case you need to double-check something, here's what the final code of the game looks like:

```
package
{
  import flash.display.MovieClip;
  import flash.events.MouseEvent;

  public class Main extends MovieClip
  {
    var startMessage:String;
    var mysteryNumber:uint;
    var currentGuess:uint;
    var guessesRemaining:uint;
    var guessesMade:uint;
    var gameStatus:String;
    var gameWon:Boolean;

    public function Main()
    {
      init();
    }
```

```
function init():void
{
  //Initialize variables
  startMessage = "I am thinking of a number between 1 and 100";
  mysteryNumber = Math.ceil(Math.random() * 100);
  guessesRemaining = 10;
  guessesMade = 0;
  gameStatus = "";
  gameWon = false;

  //Trace the mystery number
  trace("The mystery number: " + mysteryNumber);

  //Initialize text fields
  output.text = startMessage;
  input.text = "";
  input.backgroundColor = 0xFFCCCCCC;
  input.restrict = "0-9";
  stage.focus = input;

  //Initialize buttons
  guessButton.enabled = true;
  guessButton.alpha = 1;
  playAgainButton.visible = false;

  //Add an event listener to the button
  guessButton.addEventListener(MouseEvent.CLICK, ➡
    onGuessButtonClick);
}
function onGuessButtonClick(event:MouseEvent):void
{
  guessesRemaining--;
  guessesMade++;
  gameStatus = "Guesses Remaining: " + guessesRemaining + ➡
    ", Guesses Made: " + guessesMade;

  //Assign the input from the textfield
  //to the currentGuess variable
  currentGuess = uint(input.text);

  //An if/else statement to process the input
  if (currentGuess > mysteryNumber)
  {
    output.text = "That's too high." + "\n" + gameStatus;
    checkGameOver();
  }
  else if (currentGuess < mysteryNumber)
  {
    output.text = "That's too low." + "\n" + gameStatus;
```

```
            checkGameOver();
        }
        else
        {
            output.text = "You got it!";
            gameWon = true;
            endGame();
        }
    }
    function checkGameOver():void
    {
        if (guessesRemaining < 1)
        {
            endGame();
        }
    }
    function endGame():void
    {
        if (gameWon)
        {
            output.text = "Yes, it's " + mysteryNumber + "!" + "\n" +➡
            "It only took you " + guessesMade + " guesses.";
        }
        else
        {
            output.text = "I'm sorry, you've run out of guesses." + "\n" ➡
                + "The correct number was " + mysteryNumber + ".";
        }
        //Disable the guess button
        guessButton.removeEventListener(MouseEvent.CLICK, ➡
            onGuessButtonClick);
        guessButton.enabled = false;
        guessButton.alpha = 0.5;
        playAgainButton.visible = true;
        playAgainButton.addEventListener(MouseEvent.CLICK, ➡
            onPlayAgainButtonClick);
    }
    function onPlayAgainButtonClick(event:MouseEvent):void
    {
        init();
        playAgainButton.removeEventListener(MouseEvent.CLICK, ➡
            onPlayAgainButtonClick);
    }
  }
}
```

Taking it farther

This is the first complete game in this book. But is it really done?

Game design is a funny thing. Games, being as complex as they are in so many ways, are never really finished. Designers just stop working on them when they seem to play well enough, and no one complains about them. There are usually many deep layers of complexity or added functionality that *could* be added to games if the designer had enough time, patience, and imagination to do so. Patience and imagination are things game designers seem to have in endless supply. It's usually *time* that throws the spanner in the works.

There's quite a bit more that you could add to this game. Here are some ideas.

Tracking guesses

You set the game up to allow ten guesses, but some players in a hurry might not have the patience to remember what some of their previous guesses were. You can add another text field that displays all their previous guesses for them and adds the new guess when they make it.

To do this, you'll need a new text field, perhaps called guessHistory. You can create a new string variable called previousGuesses that stores all the guesses as a string of text, with each number separated by a blank space. Whenever the player makes a new guess, you can add it to the previousGuess variable and then update the guessHistory text field. Here's a sample of what the core of this code will look like:

```
previousGuesses += currentGuess + " ";
guessHistory.text = previousGuesses;
```

This line of code will work well in the onGuessButtonClick event handler. Can you see how the code in the first directive would separate each number with a blank space?

Adding a visual display

A "hangman"-style visual display of how well (or poorly!) the player is doing is an interesting enhancement. (Chapter 4 discussed how to use Movie Clip frames to create object states.) For the number guessing game, you can create a Movie Clip object with ten different states. Each state can incrementally show the player how close they are to impeding peril, like the addition of limbs to the chalk figure in game of hangman.

Once you have the hangman Movie Clip object designed, the code is very simple to implement. You're already using a variable called guessesMade that tracks the number of times the player has guessed. Each guess can be equal to a new frame in the hangman object, and you can use the guessesMade variable to advance it to the next frame. All you need to do is drop a line of code in your checkGameOver method that looks something like this:

```
hangman.gotoAndStop(guessesMade);
```

Every time the number of guesses is increased by 1, the hangman Movie Clip object advances to the frame that matches that number.

There are a few places in your game where you could add this code, but it might make the most sense to add it in the checkGameOver method, outside of the if statement.

Entering numbers with the Enter key

At the moment, you can enter numbers by clicking the Guess button. Wouldn't it be nice if you could also enter them by hitting the Enter key? Of course it would!

Capturing key presses will be discussed in detail in the next chapter, but here's a sneak peek for the adventurous among you.

It isn't too difficult, but there's one major modification you have to make to the structure of your code. If you click the Guess button or press the Enter key, you'll want the same directives to run, so the Enter key and Guess button both need to call the same method. Create a new method called gameEvents and have it contain all the directives that are currently in the onGuessButtonClick event handler. Then call the gameEvents method from both onGuessButtonClick and the new event handler you create for your Guess button.

Up for a challenge? Try this modification and see whether you can make it work. (You can find the complete final source code for this modification in the chapter's source files in a folder called Number Guessing Game–Keyboard.)

1. To capture key presses with your program, you need to import the KeyboardEvent and Keyboard classes into your program. Add the following two import directives in bold to the top of your program:

```
import flash.display.MovieClip;
import flash.events.MouseEvent;
import flash.events.KeyboardEvent;
import flash.ui.Keyboard;
```

2. Add an event listener to the stage object that listens for key presses. Add the following code in bold text to the init method:

```
function init():void
{
  //Initialize variables
  startMessage = "I am thinking of a number between 1 and 100";
  mysteryNumber = Math.ceil(Math.random() * 100);
  guessesRemaining = 10;
  guessesMade = 0;
  gameStatus = "";
  gameWon = false;

  //Trace the mystery number
  trace("The mystery number: " + mysteryNumber);

  //Initialize text fields
  output.text = startMessage;
  input.text = "";
  input.backgroundColor = 0xFFCCCCCC;
```

```
input.restrict = "0-9";
stage.focus = input;

//Initialize buttons
guessButton.enabled = true;
guessButton.alpha = 1;
playAgainButton.visible = false;

//Add an event listener to the button
guessButton.addEventListener(MouseEvent.CLICK, ➥
  onGuessButtonClick);
stage.addEventListener(KeyboardEvent.KEY_DOWN, onKeyPress);
}
```

3. Modify the onGuessButtonClick event handler to look like the following. Before you delete all the directives however, copy and paste them into a text editor for safekeeping because you'll need them again in step 4.

```
function onGuessButtonClick(event:MouseEvent):void
{
  gameEvents();
}
```

4. Add the following code. Notice that all the directives that were previously in the onGuessButtonClick event handler are now in the new gameEvents method:

```
function onKeyPress(event:KeyboardEvent):void
{
  trace(event.keyCode);
  if (event.keyCode == Keyboard.ENTER)
  {
    gameEvents();
  }
}
function gameEvents():void
{
  guessesRemaining--;
  guessesMade++;
  gameStatus = "Guesses Remaining: " + guessesRemaining + ➥
    ", Guesses Made: " + guessesMade;

  //Assign the input from the textfield to the currentGuess variable
  currentGuess = uint(input.text);

  //An if/else statement to process the input
  if (currentGuess > mysteryNumber)
  {
    output.text = "That's too high." + "\n" + gameStatus;
    checkGameOver();
  }
  else if (currentGuess < mysteryNumber)
```

```
    {
      output.text = "That's too low." + "\n" + gameStatus;
      checkGameOver();
    }
    else
    {
      output.text = "You got it!";
      gameWon = true;
      endGame();
    }
  }
}
```

5. Save the Main.as file and test the program. You should now be able to enter your guesses by pressing the Enter key on the keyboard.

Don't worry if you don't understand all the new code just yet; all will be revealed in the next chapter!

Turning the tables

A more advanced project that's fun to try is to change the game so that the computer needs to guess a number that *you're* thinking of. This will be a completely new program, but you currently have all the skills you need to make it work.

Want to give it a try? Here's a hint: to get this game working, you'll need to use a **division operator**. You've already seen the multiplication operator:

```
*
```

You used the multiplication operator to multiply the random number by 100. The division operator looks like this:

```
/
```

It's a simple forward slash. You can use it in any directive to divide two numbers:

```
100 / 2
```

This example gives a result of 50. You can then assign this calculation to variable in a directive. Here's an example:

```
computersGuess = (100 / 2);
```

Hey, can you see where you're going with this? I'm not going to spoil your fun of figuring out the rest!

Summary

The number guessing game that you looked at in this chapter is extremely important for a few reasons:

- It's the first complete and "real" game in the book. It's small in size, but it contains everything that a fully working game should have. Even though you can and will build more complex larger-scale games, this number guessing game is a model for the kinds of problems your games need to solve. If you understand the problems of game design and the solutions you found for them here, you'll be in a very strong position when you attempt something a bit more ambitious.

- You now understand input and output, variables, methods, if/else statements, button and keyboard events, and modularizing programs. These topics represent the core concepts of computer programming. You have a lot of programming power now at your disposal to build a wide variety of logic-based games.

- To keep things as simple as possible, the focus of this chapter has been on the internal logic and structure of games. There's no reason, however, why you shouldn't combine these techniques with the techniques you looked at in the previous chapter for controlling visual objects on the stage. In fact, you should definitely combine these techniques! With a bit of creativity, you'll be able to build complex puzzle and logic-based mystery adventure games that can be completely visual.

Before you continue in the book, take a short break and try to create a game of your own based on the techniques covered so far. There's no better way to learn than by trying things out in your own way, and it will give you a greater appreciation for some of the more advanced techniques you'll be looking at in the chapters ahead.

In Chapter 6, you'll take a detailed look at how to control objects on the stage with the keyboard. It will be the stepping stone you need to progress from designing *games* to designing *video games*.

Chapter 6

CONTROLLING A PLAYER CHARACTER

One of the first things your games must do is allow game players to move an object around the stage. The object can be moved with either the mouse or the keyboard. In this chapter, you'll look at techniques for controlling an object with the keyboard.

This chapter covers the following topics:

- Using the KEY_DOWN, KEY_UP, and ENTER_FRAME events
- Stopping the player character at the edges of the stage and screen wrapping
- Scrolling: vertical, horizontal, and parallax scrolling

Setting up the project files

If you've worked through the projects in the previous chapters, you should by now be very familiar with the format used to set up the project files:

1. Create a project folder called Character Control.
2. Open Flash. Select File ➤ New and choose Flash File (ActionScript 3.0) from the New Document dialog box.
3. Click the OK button.
4. Select File ➤ Save As.

5. Give the new FLA file the name characterControl.fla.

6. Find the Character Control project folder that you created in step 1.

7. Click the Save button.

8. In the Project panel, click the drop-down menu. Select Quick Project. The characterControl.fla file will appear as a project file.

9. In the Project panel, click the New File button.

10. Enter Main_Character.as in the File field. In this project, you'll start giving the Main classes unique names. With a lot of projects using the same class names, you might become confused by which Main belongs to which project. But it's not just you; sometimes the Project panel isn't sure which Main you're trying to access, either, and sometimes loads the wrong one. When you see Main as part of a class or file name, you'll know that it refers to the project's document class.

11. Select ActionScript from the File type drop-down menu and click the Create File button.

12. Flash will create and open the Main_Character.as file.

13. Double-click the numberGuessingGame.fla file to make it visible again in the workspace.

14. In the Properties panel, enter Main_Character in the Class field.

15. Save the numberGuessingGame.fla file.

And now you're ready to play!

Controlling a player character with the keyboard

One of the most basic requirements of many games is being able to control a player character with a keyboard. It's not hard to do: it's a technique that makes use of two of AS3.0's built-in classes: the KeyboardEvent class and the Keyboard class. To use them, you can simply import them into the top of your program, along with your other imported classes:

```
import flash.events.KeyboardEvent;
import flash.ui.Keyboard;
```

Like the MouseEvent class that you used in earlier chapters, the KeyboardEvent and Keyboard classes contain methods and properties that you can use to help your players interact with your games using the keyboard. And, like the MouseEvent class properties, you'll be using all these new methods and properties with your eyes closed in no time at all.

Controlling with the keyboard—the wrong way!

There are two ways to control an object with the keyboard: the right way and the wrong way. You'll actually begin by learning to do it the wrong way first.

Why would you learn the wrong way? Well, the nice thing about doing player keyboard control incorrectly is that it's very straightforward and easy to understand. And, oh yeah, it kind of works, too. But even if you never use it to control a player character in one of your games, you'll find endless other uses for it as a general technique for figuring out which keys your players are pressing on the keyboard. It's also the basis for understanding the right way to do keyboard control, which adds a few extra layers of flexibility and polish to the same underlying system. If you understand how the wrong way works first, you'll be better able to understand and appreciate the right way to do things. But don't worry, you'll take things a step at a time, and you'll be surprised by how simple the process is when you put it all together.

Creating a player character

The first job is creating a player character that you can move. To make things a little easier for myself in the game design process, I decided to try and create it with the dimensions of: 50 pixels by 50 pixels. This doesn't mean that the object will be completely square-shaped, but that those dimensions will be its maximum height and width. There are some important reasons for this that I'll discuss in detail in the next chapter, but for now, just trust me when I tell you that it will make your life as a game designer quite a bit easier a few more stations down the line.

Make sure that the player character is positioned in the exact center of the symbol editing window. Many of the techniques covered in this chapter require you to calculate what the half-width and half-height of the player object is, and the numbers will be a little more consistent if the player object is exactly centered. The following steps show you how to do this.

So let's create the player character!

1. The first job is to make a grid visible so that you can design the character in it. Select View ➤ Edit Grid.

2. The Grid dialog box opens, which allows you to modify the properties of the grid. Select Show grid. (You can also select the Snap to grid option if you want Flash to help you precisely align your shapes and objects. It's sometimes very helpful, but can also sometimes be very irritating, so I'll leave it up to you whether you want to select it.) Figure 6-1 shows an example of what my Grid dialog box looks like.

Figure 6-1. Make a grid visible to help you design your player object.

3. Click OK. You'll see a 50-by-50 pixel grid of squares appear on the stage. This grid is visible only while you work and won't be visible in the published SWF file.

4. Select Insert ➤ New Symbol. Give it the name Player and make sure that it's a Movie Clip. Select the Export for ActionScript option and click OK.

5. The symbol editing window will open. Select View ➤ Zoom In a few times so that one of the gray grid squares is large in the editing window. Draw your player character. Mine looks like Figure 6-2. Draw it within the confines of one of the grid squares so that it's contained within a 50-by-50 pixel square shape. (Refer to Chapter 2 if you need a refresher on how to design characters.) You won't be targeting any subobjects like the character's eyes in this example, so you don't need to worry about creating any of your character's features as separate Movie Clip symbols if you don't want to.

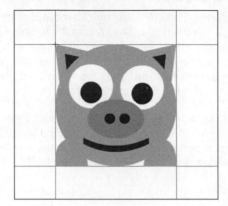

Figure 6-2. Draw your player character inside one of the grid squares.

6. Make sure that the player is centered in the middle of the editing window. Select Edit ➤ Select All to select the entire character. Figure 6-3 shows what the character looks like when it's completely selected.

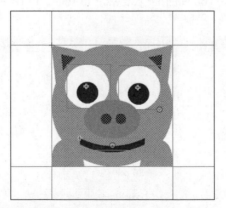

Figure 6-3. Select your character completely.

7. Now you need to center the character. You know that it's exactly 50-by-50 pixels wide, so you need to give it an x position of -25 and a y position of -25 to center it. This will place the character in the very center of the editing window. In the Position and Size pane of the Properties panel, enter -25 in the X box and -25 in the Y box. Figure 6-4 shows what your character might look like after it's centered.

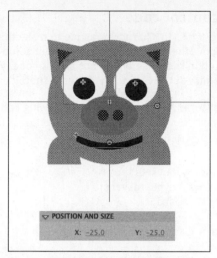

Figure 6-4. Center your character in the middle of the symbol editing window.

8. Click Scene 1 to return to the main stage, and drag an instance of the Player symbol onto the stage. In the Properties panel, give it the instance name player. Figure 6-5 shows how your main stage should now look.

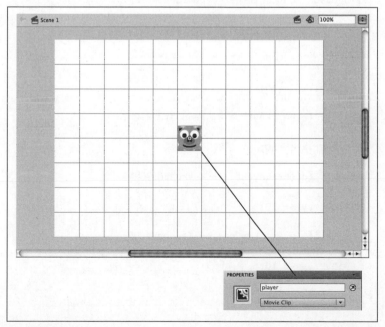

Figure 6-5. Drag an instance of the Player symbol onto the main stage, and give it the instance name player.

9. Save the characterControl.fla file.

Adding keyboard control code

Next you'll add the code to the Main_Character.as file to make the character move. You'll recognize the format you're using from other projects in the book, but some of the specifics are new. Add the new code carefully! (If you don't feel like typing out all this code, you'll find the Main_Character.as file in the chapter's source files in the Character Control subfolder.)

1. Open the Main_Character.as file and add the following code:

```
package
{

  import flash.display.MovieClip;
  import flash.events.KeyboardEvent;
  import flash.ui.Keyboard;

  public class Main_Character extends MovieClip
  {
    public function Main_Character()
    {
      init();
    }
    function init():void
    {
      stage.addEventListener(KeyboardEvent.KEY_DOWN, onKeyDown);
    }
    function onKeyDown(event:KeyboardEvent):void
    {
      if (event.keyCode == Keyboard.LEFT)
      {
        player.x -= 10;
      }
      else if (event.keyCode == Keyboard.RIGHT)
      {
        player.x += 10;
      }
      else if (event.keyCode == Keyboard.DOWN)
      {
        player.y += 10;
      }
        else if (event.keyCode == Keyboard.UP)
      {
        player.y -= 10;
      }
    }
  }
}
```

2. Save the Main_Character.as file and test the project.

3. Use the keyboard arrow keys to move the player object around the stage. It works! (If it doesn't, double-check to make sure that you assigned Main_Character as the document class and gave the player character the instance name player.)

I'm sure you noticed some obvious problems with this player character control scheme already, but before I show you the solution, let's have a quick look at how it is working. The first thing you had to do was import two new classes into the program:

```
import flash.events.KeyboardEvent;
import flash.ui.Keyboard;
```

The Keyboard class's primary job is to make it easier to figure out which keys the player of the game is pressing. The KeyboardEvent class allows you to add an event listener to the stage to listen for key presses. That's exactly what this next bit of code in bold in the init method does:

```
private function init():void
{
    stage.addEventListener(KeyboardEvent.KEY_DOWN, onKeyDown);
}
```

AS3.0 has a built-in class called Stage. When you publish a SWF file by testing the project, AS3.0 automatically generates an instance of this class called stage (with a lowercase s,) and you can use this stage object anywhere in your program. This object is very useful for attaching keyboard event listeners, and that's what you've done here.

You added an event listener to the stage object, which is triggered by the KEY_DOWN property of the KeyboardEvent class. The job of KeyboardEvent.KEY_DOWN is to listen for key presses. Whenever it "hears" the keyboard being pressed, it figures out exactly which key is pressed and assigns a **key code** to it. The key code is a number (for example, 40 or 37) that corresponds to a specific key on the keyboard. Luckily you don't need to know or remember what these key codes actually are. The Keyboard class contains convenient properties called LEFT, RIGHT, UP, and DOWN that you can use in place of the actual key code numbers.

Let's have a look how to use this in the program.

You created a method called onKeyDown, whose job is to process this event. It looks like this:

```
function onKeyDown(event:KeyboardEvent):void
    {
      if (event.keyCode == Keyboard.LEFT)
      {
        player.x -= 10;
      }
      else if (event.keyCode == Keyboard.RIGHT)
      {
        player.x += 10;
      }
      else if (event.keyCode == Keyboard.DOWN)
      {
        player.y += 10;
      }
```

```
        else if (event.keyCode == Keyboard.UP)
      {
        player.y -= 10;
      }
    }
```

> The key codes that AS3.0 uses are based on ASCII, which is a fixed standard for inter-preting numbers as characters. For example, the ASCII number 65 refers to the upper-case letter A. However, different operating systems don't map these codes to the keyboard keys in exactly the same ways. If you design and test a game using key codes on a Windows computer and then run the SWF on another operating system such as OS X, the key codes that you used might not match OS X's keyboard mapping. For this reason, it's preferable to use the Keyboard class's built-in key properties (such as LEFT and RIGHT) instead of the actual key code numbers.
>
> If you need to use a key that isn't represented by these properties, you have to use a key code number. Make sure that you test these key codes carefully on each operating sys-tem your game will run on to ensure that it's mapped to the correct keys on every one.
>
> Some keys that you might use for your game won't work while you're building and testing the game in the Flash development environment. Flash reserves some keys for shortcuts (for example, Crtl and S to save a file). So if you used any of these keys or key combinations in your game, you need to hold down Shift while testing the keys to over-ride Flash's own use of them. The keys will work fine in the published SWF.

Very simply, this is an if/else statement that figures out which key is being pressed and then moves the player object left, right, down, or up by adding or subtracting 10 pixels from its x or y positions. But there are a few new things here that might seem confusing at first glance, so I'll try to clarify this a bit.

Event listeners send a lot of information to the event handler in a special event variable. All event handlers have to include an event variable to store this information—it's just part of the deal. Event variables that contain keyboard information are typed as KeyboardEvent variables, like this:

```
event:KeyboardEvent
```

They're declared directly in the event handler, as this code in bold highlights:

```
private function onKeyDown(event:KeyboardEvent):void {
```

You can access this event variable at any time to use the information it contains. One piece of infor-mation is the key code number for the key that's being pressed. This number is stored in a property of the event variable called keyCode. You can access it like this:

```
event.keyCode
```

It contains the key code number of the key being pressed. The left arrow key is 37, the right arrow is 39, the down arrow is 40, and the up arrow is 38. You could in fact, have written the conditional statements like this and they would have worked just fine:

```
if(event.keyCode == 37)
{
  player.x -= 10;
}
else if (event.keyCode == 39)
{
  player.x += 10;
}
else if (event.keyCode == 40)
{
  player.y += 10;
}
else if (event.keyCode == 38)
{
  player.y -= 10;
}
```

And actually, if you want to write it this way, I won't stop you! But AS3.0's Keyboard class contains loads of predefined properties that already represent these numbers. So you don't have to memorize the number associated with each key on the keyboard. Instead, you just need to use the Keyboard class's easy-to-read-and-remember keyboard properties:

```
if(event.keyCode == Keyboard.LEFT)
{
  player.x -= 10;
}
else if (event.keyCode == Keyboard.RIGHT)
{
  player.x += 10;
}
else if (event.keyCode == Keyboard.DOWN)
{
  player.y += 10;
}
else if (event.keyCode == Keyboard.UP)
{
  player.y -= 10;
}
```

In fact, the Keyboard class contains a property for every key on the keyboard. If you want to have a look at the whole list, point your web browser to http://help.adobe.com/en_US/AS3LCR/Flash_10.0/?flash/ui/Keyboard.html.

Okay, so now that you know how this code is working, why is it working so badly? When you tested the program, you might have noticed a few big problems:

- The movement of the player object is jittery.

- When you press one of the arrow keys, there's a slight delay before the player object starts moving.

- You can move the player object in only one axis (x or y) at a time. You can move the player object left and right, or up and down, but not diagonally. Try pressing both the up arrow and the left arrow at the same time; it just moves the player object in the direction of whichever key you pressed last. How can you move the player object on the diagonal?

These problems are due to your computer keyboard's **key buffer**. When you press a key on the keyboard, the keyboard tells the computer that the key has been pressed down only once; it doesn't know whether the key is being *held down*. The computer's operating system has a key repeat feature built into it that resends the KEY_DOWN event at regular intervals, however. The key repeat is needed for word processors, for example, so that you can hold down a key to repeat a character on the screen. You don't have any control over how the key repeat runs, and the result with a Flash game is the jittery movement you see on the stage.

To solve this problem, you need to work around the key buffer so the keys don't directly move the object. You can use the keys to determine the object's direction and speed, but you need to find another way to actually move the object.

Controlling the keyboard—the right way!

Now that you know how AS3.0 can find out which keys you're pressing, you can use this same basic system to refine the keyboard control program.

There's a lot of new stuff here, so don't panic! I'll break everything down step by step once you have the program running to show you exactly how it works. But for now, here's a quick summary of what you need to do:

- You have to import AS3.0's Event class so that you can use its ENTER_FRAME property.

- You have to create two new variables: vx and vy. These variables will store the vertical and horizontal velocities of the object.

- You'll change the onKeyDown event handler so it no longer changes the position of the player object. Instead, it updates the vx and vy variables with the speed and direction that the object should move in.

- You have to add an event handler called onKeyUp. Its job is to detect when the arrow keys are released. When they are, it sets the player object's speed to 0.

- You'll create a new event handler called onEnterFrame that uses the vx and vy variables to actually move the player.

- Finally, you'll set the FLA file's frame rate to 30 frames per second so the player object will move smoothly.

If you entered the code from the last section in the Main_Character.as file, you could try modifying it with this new code, but it might be safer just to erase it all and start again. There are enough differences in the code to make it an almost completely new program. Let's create a new class file for this example:

1. In the Project panel, click the New File button (you'll find it in the bottom-right corner of the panel). Make sure that ActionScript is selected as the file type.

2. Enter Main_Character_Two in the File field.

3. Click the Create button.

4. The Main_Character_Two.as file opens as a blank document in a new ActionScript editor window.

5. You need to set Main_Character_Two.as as the FLA's document class. Open the characterControl. fla file and enter Main_Character_Two in the Class field.

6. Save the characterControl.fla file.

7. Open the Main_Character_Two file.

8. Add the following new code to the Main_Character_Two.as file (again, if you prefer not to type it, you'll find the finished file in the Character Control folder in this chapter's source files):

```
package
{
  import flash.display.MovieClip;
  import flash.events.KeyboardEvent;
  import flash.ui.Keyboard;
  import flash.events.Event;

  public class Main_Character_Two extends MovieClip
  {
    var vx:int;
    var vy:int;

    public function Main_Character_Two()
    {
      init();
    }
    function init():void
    {
      //Initialize variables
      vx = 0;
      vy = 0;

      //Add event listeners
      stage.addEventListener(KeyboardEvent.KEY_DOWN, onKeyDown);
      stage.addEventListener(KeyboardEvent.KEY_UP, onKeyUp);
      addEventListener(Event.ENTER_FRAME, onEnterFrame);
    }
```

```
function onKeyDown(event:KeyboardEvent):void
  {
    if (event.keyCode == Keyboard.LEFT)
    {
      vx = -5;
    }
    else if (event.keyCode == Keyboard.RIGHT)
    {
      vx = 5;
    }
      else if (event.keyCode == Keyboard.UP)
    {
      vy = -5;
    }
    else if (event.keyCode == Keyboard.DOWN)
    {
      vy = 5;
    }
  }
  function onKeyUp(event:KeyboardEvent):void
  {
    if (event.keyCode == Keyboard.LEFT || ➡
      event.keyCode == Keyboard.RIGHT)
    {
      vx = 0;
    }
    else if (event.keyCode == Keyboard.DOWN || ➡
      event.keyCode == Keyboard.UP)
    {
      vy = 0;
    }
  }
  function onEnterFrame(event:Event):void
  {
    //Move the player
    player.x += vx;
    player.y += vy;
  }
 }
}
```

9. Save the `Main_Character_Two.as` file.

10. Open the `characterControl.fla` file. You'll change the movie's frames per second to 30. The frames per second (fps) determines how many times per second the main stage is updated. The higher the fps, the smoother the movement of the player object or any other animations in the game will be. Flash's default fps is 12, but most people find that this is a little too choppy for games. A higher fps rate produces smooth movement, but consumes more CPU power. A rate of 30 fps tends to work well for games—it's smooth and doesn't affect performance too badly—so that's what you'll use. I'll discuss fps in more detail a little later in the chapter.

11. Open the FLA's properties by clicking anywhere on the main stage (except on the player object). In the Properties panel, change the FPS value to 30. Figure 6-6 shows what this looks like.

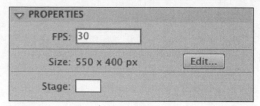

Figure 6-6. Change the movie's fps to 30 for smoother animation.

12. Save the characterControl.fla file.

13. Test the project. Use the arrow keys to move the player object around the stage. The movement is now very smooth, and you can also move the character across the stage diagonally. Just the kind of character control you're looking for!

> *When you test the movie, you might see two warnings in the* Output *panel that read something like this:* Warning 1090: Migration issue. *Earlier versions of ActionScript had two methods, called* onKeyUp *and* onKeyDown, *which were built directly into the language. They were dropped from AS3.0 when the language was overhauled, but they are exactly the same method names that you used for the methods in the program. The warnings tell you that if you want to use these methods, you need to create an event handler for them because Flash will no longer do it for you. That's exactly what you've done, so you can safely ignore these warnings. (If you don't want these sorts of warnings displayed in future, you can switch them off in the* Warnings *section of Flash's* Preferences.)*

Let's take a look at how this new program differs from the first one you wrote.

Moving with velocity

The first thing to notice are the two new integer variables, vx and vy, which store the player object's speed—how fast it's going. Actually, I need to be a little more accurate here. It's not really the *speed* of the object that you're storing, but the **velocity**. That's what the *v* stands for in the variable names: *velocity x* and *velocity y*.

Velocity is speed, but it's also direction. This is sometimes a confusing thing for beginners to grasp, so it's worth discussing in more detail. Have a look at this directive:

```
vx = -5;
```

vx refers to the velocity on the x (horizontal) axis. This actually tells you two things. First, 5 is the number of pixels that you want the player object to move each frame. You set the frame rate to 30 fps, which means that the object will move 5 pixels each frame, or 150 pixels each second. So that's the first thing: its speed.

233

Notice the negative sign:

    vx = -5;

What does it tell you? Remember that in Flash the very left edge of the stage has an x value of 0. As you move to the right, the x value increases. If you move to the left, it decreases. That means that those x values that are negative are actually *pointing to the left*. Positive values *point to the right*. This directive thus tells you the speed and direction, also known as velocity:

    5 pixels to the left.

Here's another example:

    vy = +5;

vy refers to the velocity of the object on the y (vertical) axis. The very top of the stage has a y value of 0. As you move down the stage, the values increase. This directive says the following:

    5 pixels down.

That's its velocity! Not so hard at all, is it? Figure 6-7 is a diagram of how positive and negative values can show direction.

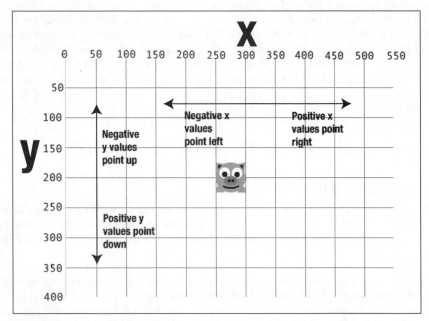

Figure 6-7. You can find the direction of movement by determining whether the x or y values are positive or negative.

If all this seems spectacularly underwhelming and blindingly obvious, good for you! It should be!

Now let's see how all this talk of velocity fits in to what's going on in the program.

> The choice of the variable names vx and vy has become a programming convention for variables that refer to horizontal and vertical velocities, so they're used in this book. Most programmers who see the variable names vx and vy immediately know what they're referring to. It's just one of those unwritten programming rules that everyone seems to follow, and no one knows why. Of course, you can give these variables any name you like, such as velocityX and velocityY (which are much more descriptive and might make your program easier to read). But, hey, conventions are sometimes a hard thing to knock, so this book sticks with vx and vy.

Using the new onKeyDown event handler

The onKeyDown event handler has changed slightly from the first program:

```
function onKeyDown(event:KeyboardEvent):void
{
  if (event.keyCode == Keyboard.LEFT)
  {
    vx = -5;
  }
  else if (event.keyCode == Keyboard.RIGHT)
  {
    vx = 5;
  }
  else if (event.keyCode == Keyboard.UP)
  {
    vy = -5;
  }
  else if (event.keyCode == Keyboard.DOWN)
  {
    vy = 5;
  }
}
```

The if/else statement is no longer changing the player object's x or y properties directly. Instead, it's simply updating the vx and vy variables with the appropriate velocity. The job of actually moving the object is delegated to the onEnterFrame event handler. More on that in a moment, but first let's take a quick look at this other new event handler: onKeyUp.

Using the onKeyUp event handler

In the first simple keyboard control program, an event handler called onKeyDown that figures out which keys are being pressed was added to the stage. The funny thing about the onKeyDown event handler is that it only knows when keys are being pressed down, not when they're released. It turns out that knowing that a key is up is just as important for games as knowing that it's down. AS3.0 therefore has a handy little property of the KeyboardEvent class called KEY_UP that can tell you this information. In the init method, you used the KEY_UP property in an event listener that you attached to the stage object in this directive:

```
stage.addEventListener(KeyboardEvent.KEY_UP, onKeyUp);
```

This listener figures out which keys are being released and sends this information to the onKeyUp event handler so that you can do something useful with it. But why would you want to know whether a key is no longer being pressed? Think about it this way: you changed the onKeyDown event handler so that when the player of the game presses one of the arrow keys, the velocity of the player object is changed by 5 pixels. That's great because when you press one of the arrow keys, you obviously want the player object to move. But what about when you stop pressing one of the arrow keys? It would make sense if the player object also stopped. However, unless you specifically tell the program this, it doesn't know what you intend, and the player object just continues moving endlessly, forever. This wasn't a problem in the simple keyboard control program in which the onKeyDown method was changing the player object's x and y properties directly, but now that you're using velocities and delegating the task of actual movement to the onEnterFrame event handler, it becomes a big problem.

The job of the onKeyUp event handler is to check whether any of the arrow keys is released and then set the player object's velocity to 0. That's what this code does:

```
function onKeyUp(event:KeyboardEvent):void
{
  if (event.keyCode == Keyboard.LEFT || ➡
    event.keyCode == Keyboard.RIGHT)
  {
    vx = 0;
  }
  else if (event.keyCode == Keyboard.DOWN || ➡
    event.keyCode == Keyboard.UP)
  {
    vy = 0;
  }
}
```

It should be pretty self explanatory, but there's one thing that will be new to you: the or operator. It looks like this:

```
||
```

It's made up of two **pipe characters**. The pipe character is a vertical line, and you'll find it somewhere on your keyboard near the brace or forward slash keys. Take a good look; it's there somewhere!

The or operator is used inside conditional statements to help you find out whether one thing *or* another thing is true.

Have a look at this line of code:

```
if (event.keyCode == Keyboard.LEFT || ➡
  event.keyCode == Keyboard.RIGHT)
```

It literally means this:

If the left arrow key is being pressed, or the right arrow key is being pressed, do the following.

Releasing either the left or right arrow key sets the horizontal velocity to 0—the player object stops moving left or right. Because both conditions have exactly the same result, it makes sense to combine them into one statement with an or operator. It very efficiently saved a few extra lines of redundant code.

Using the onEnterFrame event handler

The onEnterFrame event handler is what actually makes the player object move. It's triggered by an event listener that uses the ENTER_FRAME property of the Event class. To use it, you first have to import the Event class with this import directive in the class definition:

```
import flash.events.Event;
```

You then set up the event listener in the init method with this directive:

```
addEventListener(Event.ENTER_FRAME, onEnterFrame);
```

It follows the same format as the other two listeners, with one important difference: the listener isn't attached to the stage object. So what is it attached to? Adding an event listener without attaching to an object means that the listener is attached *directly to the actual class it's in*; in this case, the Main_Character_Two class. This won't be of much relevance now, but it will become very important when you start looking at building games using different classes in Chapter 8.

When the event listener is triggered, it calls the onEnterFrame event handler:

```
function onEnterFrame(event:Event):void
{
  //Move the player
  player.x += vx;
  player.y += vy;
}
```

What this event handler does is very simple: it takes the horizontal and vertical velocities in the vx and vy variables and assigns them to the player object's x and y properties. That makes the object move. Yay!

But wait. What is the event that calls this handler? You know that other events in the program are triggered by keys being pressed or released. KeyboardEvent.KEY_DOWN and KeyboardEvent.KEY_UP are pretty self-explanatory in that regard, but what kind of event is Event.ENTER_FRAME?

Put the kettle on and throw another log on the fire. Here's a little story that might help explain what's going on. Flash was originally designed as a tool for doing animation, which is the art of creating the illusion of motion from nonmoving objects. A lot of the concepts that Flash borrowed came from the animation industry, which you might know used celluloid film to create this illusion. Here, briefly, is how animation with film works:

Film is a long strip of celluloid (plastic) made up of a series of little squares called **frames**. Each frame contains an image, and each image in a frame is just slightly different from the image that's in the frame that comes before it. If enough of these slightly different images are flashed in front of a viewer's eyes fast enough, the individual nonmoving images will appear to be a single image that moves. This illusion of motion, which is the basis of all film, video, animation, and even game animation, is called **persistence of vision**.

To create a believable illusion of motion, these slightly different images need to be flashed in front of a viewer's eyes at least 12 times per second. (This is what was discussed earlier as fps.) Most cartoon animation is animated at 12 fps. For really fluid natural motion, you need to increase the frame rate to about 24 fps. The 24 fps rate is the frame rate used by films shown in a cinema and high-quality animated films. Video uses a frame rate of roughly 30 fps.

In this project, the fps is set to 30. This means that all the objects on the stage are updated 30 times per second. Each time Flash does one of these updates, it "enters a frame." So the program *enters a frame* 30 times per second.

In a nutshell, that is what Event.ENTER_FRAME means. Every time the program enters a new frame, the ENTER_FRAME event is triggered. So whatever directives you put inside an event handler called by an ENTER_FRAME event runs 30 times per second. It runs for the entire duration of the program or until you remove the event listener.

In the current program, these two directives are being run 30 times per second:

```
player.x += vx;
player.y += vy;
```

It makes the object appear as though it's moving. Here's how:

Let's imagine that the player object is at an x position of 100. If the player of the game presses the left arrow key, the vx variable is assigned the value -5. The next time the SWF "enters a new frame," -5 is added to the player object's x current position. The object's new position is now 95. On the next frame, -5 is added to the player object's x position again, so its new position becomes 90. If the left arrow key is released, the vx variable is assigned a value of 0. Zero is then added to the player object's x position (using the += operator), so its position remains 90 and it stops moving.

Clever, huh?

These may seem like a lot of hoops to jump through just to get the player object to move on the screen. Hang on for a bit; the advantages of this approach will be very apparent a bit later in the book when you look at natural motion using physics simulations. If you can calculate the velocity of the player first, there are all kinds of fun things you can do with it before you use it to update the position of the player. Patience, my child; all shall be revealed!

The ENTER_FRAME event is one of the most important of AS3.0's events for game designers. It's the basis for moving objects with programming code in Flash. Most of the new techniques you'll be looking at will be triggered by the ENTER_FRAME event, so you'll find that the onEnterFrame event handler will become quite a busy, bustling little place from now on—soon to be full of new friends and cheerful chitchat.

Setting screen boundaries

Now that you can move the little player character around the stage, notice that you can drive it completely off the edge and keep going on forever and ever if you want to. There are three main strategies that game designers use to prevent this from happening:

- Blocking movement at the edge of the stage.
- Screen wrapping. This is what happens when the player leaves the left side of the stage and emerges from the right.
- Scrolling. When the player object is in a very big environment, the background moves to reveal unexplored areas.

You'll have a look at each of these techniques one at a time.

Blocking movement at the stage edges

Like most programming problems, if you understand the logic behind what you're trying to accomplish, all you need to do is figure out a way of representing that logic with programming code. Here's the logic behind what is accomplished with this bit of code:

If the player object reaches the edge of the screen, push it back.

Hmm. Easier said than done? Let's see.

AS3.0 doesn't have any way of representing "the edge of the screen" as a whole, but you can access the built-in stage object. It contains stageWidth and stageHeight properties that tell you how big the stage is. Maybe you can use those properties to figure out the top, bottom, left, and right boundaries of the stage and then stop the player object from moving if you discover that its x or y positions go beyond them?

Sound promising? Give it a whirl! Follow these steps:

1. Add the following code to the onEnterFrame event handler:

```
function onEnterFrame(event:Event):void
{
  //Move the player
  player.x += vx;
  player.y += vy;

  //Stop player at stage edges
  if (player.x > stage.stageWidth)
  {
    player.x = stage.stageWidth;
  }
  else if (player.x < 0)
  {
    player.x = 0;
  }
  if (player.y < 0)
  {
    player.y = 0;
  }
  else if (player.y > stage.stageHeight)
  {
    player.y = stage.stageHeight;
  }
}
```

2. Save the `Main_Character_Two.as` file and test the project.

3. Use the arrow keys to move the player to the edges of the stage. The player will stop moving when its center point reaches the edge, as shown in Figure 6-8.

Figure 6-8. The player object stops moving when it reaches the edge of the stage.

The leftmost side and very top of the stage are always represented by a value of 0. To find out what the values of the rightmost side and bottom of the stage are, use the `stage.stageWidth` and `stage.stageHeight` properties. By default, Flash's stage dimensions are 550 by 400 pixels, which is what you're using in this project. That means that the `stage.stageWidth` property has a value of 550, and the `stage.stageHeight` property has a value of 400.

You can actually change the dimensions of the stage at any time if you decide that you want to make the game screen bigger or smaller. One advantage of using the `stage.stageWidth` and `stage.stageHeight` properties is that if you change the stage dimensions, you don't have to tediously update the code by hand with the new sizes. Using `stage.stageWidth` and `stage.stageHeight` means that they'll update automatically. But no matter the size of the stage, the top and left size of the stage will always be 0, so they remain the same.

The `if/else` statements work by checking to see whether the player object's x or y positions go beyond the values that you defined as the edges of the stage. If they do, the player object is forced back to that position, which is the very edge. Even though the player object does actually move slightly beyond the stage boundaries that you set, you don't ever see it do that; you see it only at the point at which it's been forced back. This is exactly the same situation as in Chapter 4, when you were controlling the storybook cat's y position with buttons. Same problem; same solution. Remember, I told you it would come back to haunt you at some point! But this time you're completely prepared. Problem solved!

Let's have a quick look at the first conditional statement:

```
if (player.x > stage.stageWidth)
{
  player.x = stage.stageWidth;
}
```

In plain English, this means the following:

If the player's x position is more than the stage's maximum width (which is 550), move the player back to an x position of exactly 550.

The rest of the if/else statement does exactly the same thing by checking the remaining three stage edges and then repositioning the player object if it needs to. It's a trap that the player object can't escape from! A pen for the poor little piggy, alas!

Building a better pigpen

So the code works, but can you make it work a little better? It actually looks rather awkward when half of the player object manages to squeeze past the edge before being stopped. Wouldn't it be better if you could stop the whole thing?

To do this, you need a little bit more information about the player object. You need to know the following:

- What half its width is
- What half its height is

After you know this data, you can add half of the player object's width to its x position and half its height to its y position. You can then test these new values against the stage's dimensions, which should stop the player object before it even manages to sneak as much as a trotter over the edge of the stage.

You might be catching on to the fact that whenever I talk about "getting more information," it usually means that more variables are needed to store that information. In the next new section of code, you'll create two new variables, playerHalfWidth and playerHalfHeight, directly inside the onEnterFrame event handler. This is a way of creating variables you haven't looked at before. When variables are declared directly inside a function definition, they're called **local variables**. More about that in a moment, but first let's fix up this code!

1. Make the changes and additions to the onEnterFrame event handler shown in bold text (the two if/else statements are considerably changed since the first attempt, so you might want to rewrite them from scratch instead of trying to update them):

```
function onEnterFrame(event:Event):void
{
  //Initialize local variables
  var playerHalfWidth:uint = player.width / 2;
  var playerHalfHeight:uint = player.height / 2;

  //Move the player
  player.x += vx;
  player.y += vy;

  //Stop player at stage edges
  if (player.x + playerHalfWidth > stage.stageWidth)
  {
```

```
      player.x = stage.stageWidth - playerHalfWidth;
    }
    else if (player.x - playerHalfWidth < 0)
    {
      player.x = 0 + playerHalfWidth;
    }
    if (player.y - playerHalfHeight < 0)
    {
      player.y = 0 + playerHalfHeight;
    }
    else if (player.y + playerHalfHeight > stage.stageHeight)
    {
      player.y = stage.stageHeight - playerHalfHeight;
    }
}
```

2. Save the Main_Character_Two.as file and test the project. You can now move the player object to the edges of the stage, and the entire object will be contained inside it. Figure 6-9 shows an example.

Figure 6-9. The entire player object is contained within the stage by adding half its height and width to the calculation.

The first thing is to declare and initialize the two new **local variables**:

```
var playerHalfWidth:uint = player.width / 2;
var playerHalfHeight:uint = player.height / 2;
```

These variables store a value representing half of the player object's width and height. You know that the player object is 50 pixels wide and 50 pixels high, so half that width and height is 25 and 25.

These variables are declared directly inside the onEnterFrame event handler. That's why they're referred to as **local**. They can be used only inside this event handler and nowhere else. If you try using playerHalfWidth and playerHalfHeight anywhere else in your program, the compiler will give you an error message:

> Access of undefined property...

All the variables that you used in the programs until now are known as **instance variables**. They are declared directly within the class definition (at the top of the program) and can be used anywhere in the class by any method. Local variables can be used only inside the method in which they are declared.

One thing you'll notice about playerHalfWidth and playerHalfHeight is that you declared them as uint variable types and assigned them their initial value in the same directive. So instead of writing two directives, like this:

```
var playerHalfWidth:uint;
playerHalfWidth = player.width / 2;
```

you combined them into one directive, like this:

```
var playerHalfWidth:uint = player.width/2;
```

This is a perfectly valid way to create variables, and you can create any instance variable this same way. By convention, however, instance variables separate these steps into two directives because if you make an instance of a class, you'll often want to assign a variable's value only later in the program. Don't worry if this doesn't make any sense to you now; it will a bit a later in the book when you look at more practical examples.

One advantage you have by assigning a value to playerHalfWidth and playerHalfHeight variables directly in the onEnterFrame event handler is that if the player object's width or height ever changes in the game, the values of those variables will immediately be updated. Suppose that I designed a game in which my pig character eats a magical daisy that makes him double in size. Because the onEnterFrame method is updated 30 times per second, the size change will affect any calculations involving the size of the player, such as figuring out screen boundaries or collisions with other objects.

Now that you know the player object's half-width and half-height, you can use this information to confine it more precisely within the stage's boundaries with these if/else statements:

```
if (player.x + playerHalfWidth > stage.stageWidth)
{
  player.x = stage.stageWidth - playerHalfWidth;
}
else if (player.x - playerHalfWidth < 0)
{
  player.x = 0 + playerHalfWidth;
}

if (player.y - playerHalfHeight < 0)
{
  player.y = 0 + playerHalfHeight;
}
else if (player.y + playerHalfHeight > stage.stageHeight)
```

```
    {
        player.y = stage.stageHeight - playerHalfHeight;
    }
```

The logic behind this is really simple, even though it looks like a bit of a rat's nest of code to read through. All the code does is check to see whether the left, right, top, or bottom edges of the player object are crossing the stage boundaries you set for them. It then forces the edges back if they've gone over. To find out what the edges of the player object are, all you need to do is add or subtract half the height or width of the player, depending on which edge you're checking for.

Let's take more detailed look at how this works with the first conditional statement:

```
    if (player.x + playerHalfWidth > stage.stageWidth)
    {
        player.x = stage.stageWidth - playerHalfWidth;
    }
```

This statement checks to see whether the right side of the player object is crossing the right side of the stage. You know that the stage is 550 pixels wide. Let's pretend that at some point while moving the player object around the screen, it has an x position of 530. If you add half its width, 25, to that number, you end up with 555. 555 is a position that is definitely over the stage's right boundary, so the directive inside the if statement is triggered. That directive moves the player to a position that is the same as the stage's maximum width (550) minus half of the player's width (25). That places it at a new x position of 525. And because the player object has 25 pixels of "fat" around its middle, it looks as if it has stopped exactly at the edge of the screen. Figure 6-10 illustrates how this works.

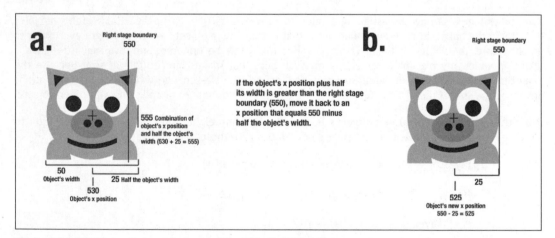

Figure 6-10. Precise screen boundaries using the object's half-width

The logic behind all the other conditional statements is exactly the same; only the values are different. See if you can figure them out!

It turns out that knowing the half-width and half-height of objects is extremely important for doing certain kinds of advanced collision detection. Remember the solution to this screen boundary problem because you'll use it to help solve a number of tricky problems throughout the course of this book.

You can find the completed version of this code in the Main_ScreenBoundaries.as file in this chapter's source files.

Screen wrapping

Screen wrapping happens when an object disappears from one side of the screen and then reemerges from the opposite side. This is quite a fun effect and very easy to implement. In fact, the logic that's used to accomplish it is almost exactly the *inverse* of the logic you used to block movement at the stage's edges. Let's try it out!

1. Change the conditional statements inside the onEnterFrame event handler to match the text in bold:

```
function onEnterFrame(event:Event):void
{
  //Initialize local variables
  var playerHalfWidth:uint = player.width / 2;
  var playerHalfHeight:uint = player.height / 2;

  //Move the player
  player.x += vx;
  player.y += vy;

  //Screen wrapping
  if (player.x - playerHalfWidth > stage.stageWidth)
  {
    player.x = 0 - playerHalfWidth;
  }
  else if (player.x + playerHalfWidth < 0)
  {
    player.x = stage.stageWidth + playerHalfWidth;
  }
  if (player.y + playerHalfHeight < 0)
  {
    player.y = stage.stageHeight + playerHalfHeight;
  }
  else if (player.y - playerHalfHeight > stage.stageHeight)
  {
    player.y = 0 - playerHalfHeight;
  }
}
```

2. Save the `Main_Character.as` file and test the project.

3. Use the arrow keys to move the `player` object past the edges of the screen. Peek-a-boo! It emerges from the opposite side.

After the detailed look at how to stop an object at the stage edges, I'm sure you can figure out what's going on in this code already. It's almost exactly the same, except for being delightfully backward! It uses the object's half-width and half-height to figure out whether the object has completely disappeared off the edge of the stage. As soon as it detects that this is the case, it positions the object on the opposite side of the stage, just beyond the visible boundary. This creates the illusion that the object is trapped on the surface of some kind of cylindrical, never-ending plane. I usually complain about these sorts of things in this book, but this time, it's a blast! Have fun with it! Screen wrapping is, of course, a staple of many Old-Skool games like Pacman and Asteroids, and now you know how to do it if you ever need to.

You can find the complete code for this screen wrapping example in the `Main_ScreenWrapping.as` file in the chapter's source files.

Scrolling

One thing that almost all 2D action and adventure games have in common is that most use an effect called **scrolling** to allow a `player` to move about in an environment that is much bigger than the confines of the stage. Like an ancient Chinese scroll being unrolled over a long wooden table, the background moves to allow the character to explore the space beyond the stage edges.

Although it's hard to pick favorites, there's probably very little to learn about game design that isn't in some way embodied in one or the other of the two greatest classic game series of all time: *Super Mario Bros.* and *The Legend of Zelda*. Pretty much anything game designers need to consider about good game design can be found in these two games, and scrolling is no exception.

Super Mario Bros. uses primarily what's known as **horizontal side-scrolling**. That's when the background moves left or right when the `player` reaches the left or right edges of the screen. The perspective in horizontal side-scrolling games is usually designed so that it looks as if you're viewing the environment from the side. *The Legend of Zelda* uses **overhead multi-axis scrolling**. In overhead scrolling, you view the environment from above, as if you were a bird flying in the sky and surveying the scene below. With multi-axis scrolling, the `player` character is free to move in any direction (up, down, left, or right), and the environment scrolls to keep up. Figure 6-11 illustrates the differences between these two related systems.

In truth, most games that use scrolling use a combination of these two systems. In this chapter, you'll look at the more complex of the two: multi-axis scrolling. Once you're comfortable with the scrolling techniques covered here, you'll be able to implement any combination of these two systems.

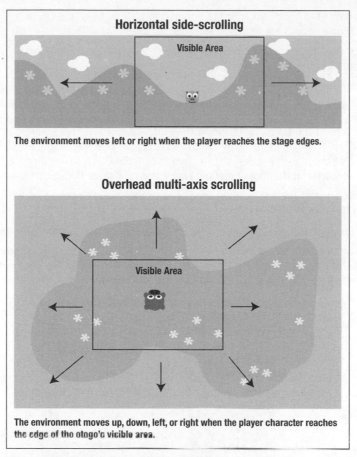

Figure 6-11. Horizontal and multi-axis scrolling

Creating an environment

The first thing you need to implement in the scrolling system is some kind of background scene that is much bigger than the stage. If you were designing a game, this would be a very big Movie Clip symbol filled with all kinds of objects that the player could interact with. In this example, you'll use a very large image.

1. Find a very large image that you think might be suitable for your scrolling system. Any picture with a width and height greater than 1000 pixels should work well for this example. I decided to give my hard-working little pig character a little holiday in space: a journey to one of Mars's moons, Phobos. Lucky for me, NASA maintains a large collection of copyright-free photos, including extremely high-resolution images of Phobos, which I was able to download. (To download your own high-resolution scenes from space, visit http://photojournal.jpl. nasa.gov/index.html. Any images labeled Full Resolution are big enough.)

247

2. Once you have your image, you need to import it into Flash. Open the characterControl.fla file if it's not already open. Select File ➤ Import ➤ Import to Library.

3. Browse for the image and click the Import to Library button when you find it. You'll then see the image sitting in the Library.

4. Create a new symbol called Background.

5. Open the Background symbol's editing window, and drag an instance of the photo you just imported from the Library onto the first frame. Position it roughly in the middle of the stage.

6. Click Scene 1 near the top-left corner of the Background symbol's editing window to return to the main stage.

7. Create a new layer in the main timeline. Name this new layer background.

8. Drag an instance of the Background symbol onto the stage. Check to make sure that it's been added on the new background layer you created in the previous step.

9. With the instance still selected, give it the instance name background in the Properties panel.

10. If you want to zoom out to see the entire image, click the zoom level menu at the top-right corner of the stage, as shown in Figure 6-12. Choose Show All to see your entire scene (100% will return the view of the stage to normal once you're done).

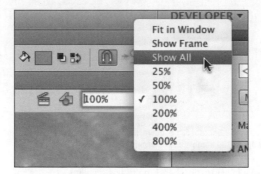

Figure 6-12. Zoom out to view your entire scene.

11. Rearrange the layers in the timeline so that the background layer is behind the layer that the player object is on. Your main stage might look something like Figure 6-13 when you're done.

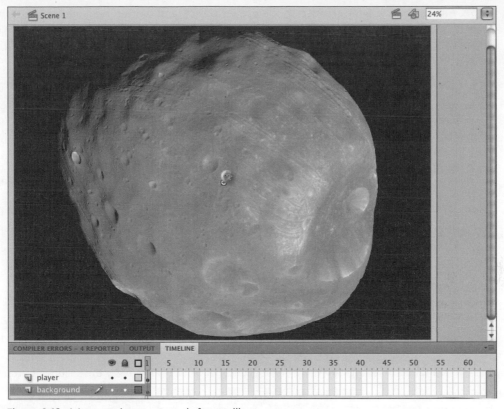

Figure 6-13. A huge environment, ready for scrolling

Fine-tuning the player character

For its journey to Phobos, I gave my pig character a space capsule to fly around in. To add a little more "realism" (if a journey to Phobos could be called that!), I'll add a **drop shadow**, which is an effect that makes an object appear as if it's casting a shadow on the objects below it. Adding a drop shadow to the space capsule makes it look as if it's hovering slightly above the surface of the moon.

Adding a drop shadow

Follow these steps to add a drop shadow to the player object:

1. Select the player object.

2. In the Properties panel there's a pane called Filters. If it isn't already open, click it to open it.

3. On the bottom of the Filters pane is the Add Filter button. It looks like a sheet of paper with the bottom-left corner turned over. Click it once and select Drop Shadow from the option menu that opens.

4. A Drop Shadow filter is added to the player object, and the settings you can use to modify it appear in the Filter pane. Play around with some of the settings until you find an effect you like. The Filter pane, and the effect that those settings have on the player object, are shown in Figure 6-14.

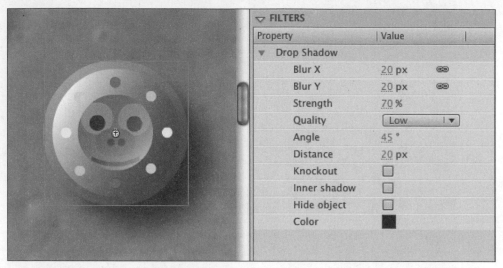

Figure 6-14. Add a drop shadow to the player object.

The Blur X and Blur Y settings are numbers in pixels that refer to how fuzzy the shadow is around the edges. More blur makes the shadow look softer.

Strength is the same as *alpha*, which is just another way of saying how more or less transparent the shadow is. A Strength setting of 100% means that the shadow is completely opaque (solid), and it becomes more transparent as the percentage falls toward zero. One of the most CPU-intensive tasks that the Flash Player does is to calculate areas of alpha transparency, so you can give your games a performance boost by avoiding transparent objects, transparent colors, or effects that use transparency. Of course, they look beautiful, so if you can get away with using some and your game doesn't slow down, go for it!

The Quality setting is quite important for games or any moving objects that will be using drop shadows. Filter effects such as drop shadows make the Flash Player work quite a bit harder to draw the effect on the screen, so you need to use them judiciously and do enough testing with your objects to make sure that they don't affect performance. For games, you'll probably always want to use the Low setting because the Flash Player does fewer calculations. In a game with fast-moving objects, no one will notice the difference, anyway.

Angle is the direction from which the imaginary light that is casting the shadow is coming from. Distance refers to the space between the object that is casting the shadow and the object below it, and this is what gives objects with drop shadows the illusion that they're occupying a shallow 3D space. The Knockout, Inner shadow, and Hide object options are a little more specialized. Play around with them to see what they do; you might find a use for them some day.

You can actually add drop shadows, or any of the other filters, to your objects by using programming code. To do this, you need to import all the filters from Flash's filters *package using this* import *directive:*

```
import flash.filters.*;
```

The asterisk means "all the filters." It's then a matter of a few more lines of code to create a filter object and assign it to a Sprite *or* MovieClip *object. Although this is a fairly advanced topic at this stage in your learning, you might someday need to add a filter to some of your objects dynamically. For detailed instructions on how to do this, visit Adobe's online AS3.0 documentation at* http://help.adobe.com/en_ US/ActionScript/3.0_ProgrammingAS3/. *You'll find the details in the chapter called "Filtering display objects." Chapter 10 of this book describes how to use these techniques to create dynamic filters.*

Scrolling basics

The key to scrolling is understanding that it's not the player object that moves; it's the background object. The new background object will become the new center of attention in the following code.

1. Change the onEnterFrame event handler to look like the following—the bold text indicates the new code. (You'll find the complete code in the Basic Scrolling folder of the chapter's source files. This example code is in the Main_Scrolling_One.as file.)

```
function onEnterFrame(event:Event):void
{
  //Initialize local variables
  var playerHalfWidth:uint = player.width / 2;
  var playerHalfHeight:uint = player.height / 2;
  var backgroundHalfWidth:uint = background.width / 2;
  var backgroundHalfHeight:uint = background.height / 2;

  //Move the background
  background.x += -vx;
  background.y += -vy;

  //Stop background at stage edges
  if (background.x + backgroundHalfWidth < stage.stageWidth)
  {
    background.x = stage.stageWidth - backgroundHalfWidth;
  }
  else if (background.x - backgroundHalfWidth > 0)
  {
    background.x = 0 + backgroundHalfWidth;
  }
  if (background.y - backgroundHalfHeight > 0)
  {
    background.y = 0 + backgroundHalfHeight;
  }
```

```
        else if (background.y + backgroundHalfHeight < stage.stageHeight)
    {
        background.y = stage.stageHeight - backgroundHalfHeight;
    }
}
```

2. Save the Main_Character.as file and test the project. Press the arrow keys and watch your player character explore Phobos!

All you did is reverse a bit of the logic you were using to move the player object. When you press the arrow keys, they move the background object in the direction *opposite* to the one you want the player to move in. That's why you should add a minus sign to the vx and vy variables with these two lines:

```
background.x += -vx;
background.y += -vy;
```

This creates the illusion that the player object is moving, when it's actually the background object that's moving in the opposite direction. Oh, the wily ways of the video game programmer!

The conditional statements stop the background object from moving when its edges reach the stage edges:

```
if (background.x + backgroundHalfWidth < stage.stageWidth)
{
  background.x = stage.stageWidth - backgroundHalfWidth;
}
else if (background.x - backgroundHalfWidth > 0)
{
  background.x = 0 + backgroundHalfWidth;
}
if (background.y - backgroundHalfHeight > 0)
{
  background.y = 0 + backgroundHalfHeight;
}
  else if (background.y + backgroundHalfHeight < stage.stageHeight)
{
  background.y = stage.stageHeight - backgroundHalfHeight;
}
```

I'll leave the mental gymnastics up to you to figure out why it works the way it does, but it's simply one more permutation of exactly the same logic that you used to stop the player at the stage edges.

Better scrolling

This simple scrolling system can actually take you quite far, but there are a few problems that some fine-tuning can help solve:

- When the scrollable area reaches its limit, the player object is prevented from moving all the way to the stage's edge. Try holding down the right arrow key and see how far you get. At some point, the background will stop moving, but the player won't be able to travel all the way to stage's right side. This seems to be an artificial constraint that would be a frustrating limitation for the player in many action or adventure games. Figure 6-15 illustrates this problem.

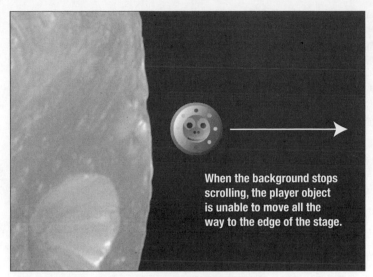

When the background stops scrolling, the player object is unable to move all the way to the edge of the stage.

Figure 6-15. When the background has reached the limit of its scrollable area, the player can't travel all the way to the stage's edge.

■ The other potential problem is that the scrolling background *always* scrolls. For many games, it might make more sense if the background scrolls only when the player object is *approaching* the edge of the stage. Otherwise, the player object should explore freely without the background moving.

Here's how to solve these problems. You can set up a system that figures out whether the player object should move or the background object should move, depending on where each is. If the background object has reached the limit of its movement, the player object should be free to travel to the edge of the stage. Also, if the player is not near any of the stage's edges, it should be free to move around without the background object moving.

The trick of making this work is to set up an imaginary **inner boundary**, which is a rectangular area inside the real stage that's exactly half the stage's height and width. The player object will be free to move around within the inner boundaries, and when it reaches the edge, it will stop moving, and the background will start to scroll. When the background reaches its scroll limit, the inner boundary that's been blocking the player from going farther will extend to the limits of the real stage to allow the player to move right to the edge.

The inner boundary that you'll create isn't a real object in the way that player and background are objects. Instead, it's just four numbers that define the top, bottom, left, and right of these boundaries. In fact, the logic behind finding these numbers is exactly the same as the logic you used to set the real stage boundaries; you just cut them down to half the size.

You'll build this code in two stages so that you can see how it's working. (For the complete final working version of this code, see the Main_Scrolling_Two.as file in this chapter's source files.)

253

1. Update the `Main_Character.as` file with the following bold text:

```
package
{
  import flash.display.MovieClip;
  import flash.events.KeyboardEvent;
  import flash.ui.Keyboard;
  import flash.events.Event;

  public class Main_Scrolling_Two extends MovieClip
  {
    var vx:int;
    var vy:int;
    var rightInnerBoundary:uint;
    var leftInnerBoundary:uint;
    var topInnerBoundary:uint;
    var bottomInnerBoundary:uint;

    function Main_Scrolling_Two()
    {
      init();
    }
    function init():void
    {
      //initialize variables
      vx = 0;
      vy = 0;
      rightInnerBoundary = (stage.stageWidth / 2)➡
        + (stage.stageWidth / 4);
      leftInnerBoundary = (stage.stageWidth / 2) ➡
        - (stage.stageWidth / 4);
      topInnerBoundary = (stage.stageHeight / 2) ➡
        - (stage.stageHeight / 4);
      bottomInnerBoundary = (stage.stageHeight / 2) ➡
        + (stage.stageHeight / 4);

      //Add event listeners
      stage.addEventListener(KeyboardEvent.KEY_DOWN, onKeyDown);
      stage.addEventListener(KeyboardEvent.KEY_UP, onKeyUp);
      addEventListener(Event.ENTER_FRAME, onEnterFrame);
    }
    function onKeyDown(event:KeyboardEvent):void
    {
      if (event.keyCode == Keyboard.LEFT)
      {
        vx = -5;
      }
      else if (event.keyCode == Keyboard.RIGHT)
      {
        vx = 5;
```

```
  }
  else if (event.keyCode == Keyboard.UP)
  {
    vy = -5;
  }
    else if (event.keyCode == Keyboard.DOWN)
  {
    vy = 5;
  }
}
function onKeyUp(event:KeyboardEvent):void
{
  if (event.keyCode == Keyboard.LEFT ||➡
    event.keyCode == Keyboard.RIGHT)
  {
    vx = 0;
  }
  else if (event.keyCode == Keyboard.DOWN ||➡
    event.keyCode == Keyboard.UP)
  {
    vy = 0;
  }
}
function onEnterFrame(event:Event):void
{
  //Initialize local variables
  var playerHalfWidth:uint = player.width / 2;
  var playerHalfHeight:uint = player.height / 2;
  var backgroundHalfWidth:uint = background.width / 2;
  var backgroundHalfHeight:uint = background.height / 2;

  //Move the player
  player.x += vx;
  player.y += vy;

  //Stop player at inner boundary edges
  if (player.x - playerHalfWidth < leftInnerBoundary)
  {
    player.x = leftInnerBoundary + playerHalfWidth;
    background.x -= vx;
  }
  else if (player.x + playerHalfWidth > rightInnerBoundary)
  {
    player.x = rightInnerBoundary - playerHalfWidth;
    background.x -= vx;
  }
  if (player.y - playerHalfHeight < topInnerBoundary)
  {
    player.y = topInnerBoundary + playerHalfHeight;
```

```
      background.y -= vy;
    }
    else if (player.y + playerHalfHeight > bottomInnerBoundary)
    {
      player.y = bottomInnerBoundary - playerHalfHeight;
      background.y -= vy;
    }

    //Stop background at stage edges
    if (background.x + backgroundHalfWidth < stage.stageWidth)
    {
      background.x = stage.stageWidth - backgroundHalfWidth;
    }
    else if (background.x - backgroundHalfWidth > 0)
    {
      background.x = 0 + backgroundHalfWidth;
    }
    if (background.y - backgroundHalfHeight > 0)
    {
      background.y = 0 + backgroundHalfHeight;
    }
    else if (background.y + backgroundHalfHeight < stage.stageHeight)
    {
      background.y = stage.stageHeight - backgroundHalfHeight;
    }
  }
 }
}
```

2. Save the Main_Character.as file. You can now move the player object freely within the inner boundaries of the stage. When it reaches the edge of the inner boundary, the background object starts scrolling. Figure 6-16 illustrates this.

The first thing the code did was to define the inner boundary with these four new variables:

```
rightInnerBoundary = (stage.stageWidth / 2) ➡
  + (stage.stageWidth / 4);
leftInnerBoundary = (stage.stageWidth / 2) ➡
  - (stage.stageWidth / 4);
topInnerBoundary = (stage.stageHeight / 2) ➡
  - (stage.stageHeight / 4);
bottomInnerBoundary = (stage.stageHeight / 2) ➡
  + (stage.stageHeight / 4);
```

Can you figure out how the boundaries were calculated? (Try it, it's not that hard!) What you end up with is an inner area that's half the size of the stage.

All these variables were defined as instance variables, as part of the class definition, and they're available throughout the entire class. The reason why is that in the next bit of code, you'll temporarily recalculate these boundaries under certain conditions. If you had defined these variables directly in the onEnterFrame method as local variables, they would have been reset to their initial values 30 times per second, which would have immediately overwritten their recalculated values.

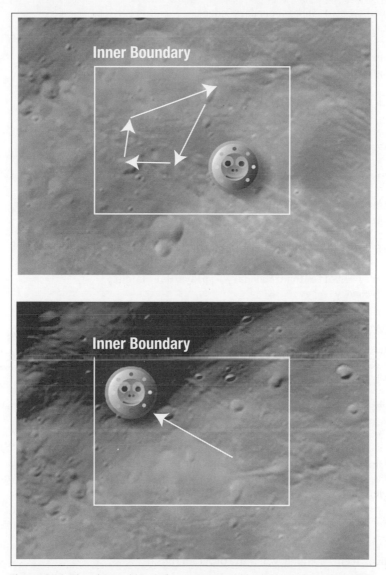

Figure 6-16. The player object is free to move within the inner boundary. When it reaches one of the edges, the player object stops moving and the background scrolls.

The following is the new code that really makes this whole system work:

```
//Move the player
player.x += vx;
player.y += vy;

//Stop player at inner boundary edges
if (player.x - playerHalfWidth < leftInnerBoundary)
{
  player.x = leftInnerBoundary + playerHalfWidth;
  background.x -= vx;
}
else if (player.x + playerHalfWidth > rightInnerBoundary)
{
  player.x = rightInnerBoundary - playerHalfWidth;
  background.x -= vx;
}
if (player.y - playerHalfHeight < topInnerBoundary)
{
  player.y = topInnerBoundary + playerHalfHeight;
  background.y -= vy;
}
else if (player.y + playerHalfHeight > bottomInnerBoundary)
{
  player.y = bottomInnerBoundary - playerHalfHeight;
  background.y -= vy;
}
```

You can see that you're back to moving the player again. But it is allowed to move only while it's within the inner boundaries. Let's have a look at how the first if statement works:

```
if (player.x - playerHalfWidth < leftInnerBoundary)
{
  player.x = leftInnerBoundary + playerHalfWidth;
  background.x -= vx;
}
```

The conditional statement checks to see whether the left edge of the player is less than the left inner boundary. If it is, the player is forced back to that edge. This is exactly the same logic you used to stop the player object at the edges of the stage. But the next line is interesting:

```
background.x -= vx;
```

The background starts moving! And that's really all there is to it. The code is quite simple, but the effect it produces seems complex when the program runs.

Even better scrolling

You still have one more problem to solve. The `player` object still can't move all the way to the edges of the stage when the scrolling background has reached its limit. To do this, you need to temporarily extend the boundaries and then move them back if the `player` returns to the center of the stage again. A few lines of very simple code in the right place are all you need to achieve this.

1. Add the following lines in bold to the onEnterFrame event handler:

```
function onEnterFrame(event:Event):void
{
  //Initialize local variables
  var playerHalfWidth:uint = player.width / 2;
  var playerHalfHeight:uint = player.height / 2;
  var backgroundHalfWidth:uint = background.width / 2;
  var backgroundHalfHeight:uint = background.height / 2;

  //Move the player
  player.x += vx;
  player.y += vy;

  //Stop player at inner boundary edges
  if (player.x - playerHalfWidth < leftInnerBoundary)
  {
    player.x = leftInnerBoundary + playerHalfWidth;
    rightInnerBoundary = (stage.stageWidth / 2)➡
      + (stage.stageWidth / 4);
    background.x -= vx;
  }
  else if (player.x + playerHalfWidth > rightInnerBoundary)
  {
    player.x = rightInnerBoundary - playerHalfWidth;
    leftInnerBoundary = (stage.stageWidth / 2)➡
      - (stage.stageWidth / 4);
    background.x -= vx;
  }
  if (player.y - playerHalfHeight < topInnerBoundary)
  {
    player.y = topInnerBoundary + playerHalfHeight;
    bottomInnerBoundary = (stage.stageHeight / 2)➡
      + (stage.stageHeight / 4);
    background.y -= vy;
  }
  else if (player.y + playerHalfHeight > bottomInnerBoundary)
  {
    player.y = bottomInnerBoundary - playerHalfHeight;
    topInnerBoundary = (stage.stageHeight / 2) ➡
      - (stage.stageHeight / 4);
    background.y -= vy;
  }
```

```
    //Stop background at stage edges
    if (background.x + backgroundHalfWidth < stage.stageWidth)
    {
      background.x = stage.stageWidth - backgroundHalfWidth;
      rightInnerBoundary = stage.stageWidth;
    }
    else if (background.x - backgroundHalfWidth > 0)
    {
      background.x = 0 + backgroundHalfWidth;
      leftInnerBoundary = 0;
    }
    if (background.y - backgroundHalfHeight > 0)
    {
      background.y = 0 + backgroundHalfHeight;
      topInnerBoundary = 0;
    }
    else if (background.y + backgroundHalfHeight < stage.stageHeight)
    {
      background.y = stage.stageHeight - backgroundHalfHeight;
      bottomInnerBoundary = stage.stageHeight;
    }
}
```

2. Save the Main_Character.as file and test the project. The player object can now explore the entire area, right up to the stage edges.

This code works by extending the inner boundaries to the stage edges when the background object has reached the limit of its movement. Let's look at how this works with the first if statement in the code (the new code is highlighted in bold):

```
if (background.x + backgroundHalfWidth < stage.stageWidth)
{
  background.x=stage.stageWidth-backgroundHalfWidth;
  rightInnerBoundary = stage.stageWidth;
}
```

If you press the right arrow, the background object moves until the conditional statement detects that it has reached its limit. When that happens, it stops the background object from moving and then gives the rightInnerBoundary variable a new value that is equivalent to the maximum width of the stage. That allows the player object to move all the way to the stage edge. Figure 6-17 illustrates how this works.

Problem solved! But you just created another one. How can you move the boundary back to its original position if the player moves back to the center of the stage?

Think about it this way. Imagine that the player object has traveled to the rightmost edge of the stage, as shown in Figure 6-17. When it travels back to the center of the stage, you don't have to start moving the background object again until the player object has reached the inner-left boundary. If it does, you know that you can safely reset the inner-right boundary to its original position. That's what this new line of code in bold does:

```
    if (player.x - playerHalfWidth < leftInnerBoundary)
    {
      player.x = leftInnerBoundary + playerHalfWidth;
      rightInnerBoundary = (stage.stageWidth / 2)➥
        + (stage.stageWidth / 4);
      background.x -= vx;
    }
```

Figure 6-18 illustrates what is happening.

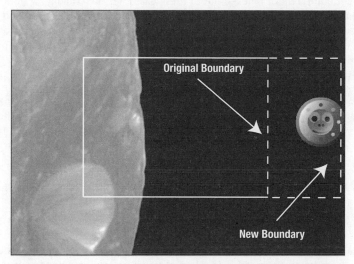

Figure 6-17. When the background object stops moving, the boundary is extended to allow the player object to travel to the edge of the stage.

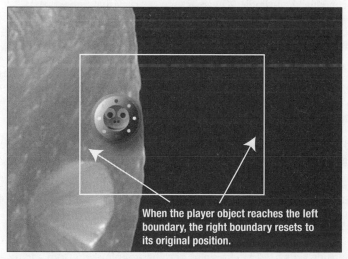

Figure 6-18. The inner right boundary resets to its original position when the player object reaches the inner-left boundary.

The other bits of new code that you added in this section follow exactly the same logic for each of the three other boundaries.

You can find the entire working example of this code in the `Main_Scrolling_Two.as` file in the Scrolling Background folder in the chapter's source files.

Taking it further

You'll be able to get quite a bit of mileage out of these examples of scrolling for your games. Any type of scrolling system you can dream up will use these same techniques in some kind of combination. You've actually tackled the most difficult type of scrolling, combined vertical and horizontal scrolling, so if you need to make a game that requires only horizontal scrolling, it should be a piece of cake. The techniques are exactly the same; you just need half the amount of code because you'll check boundaries only on the x axis.

This is not the last word on scrolling; it's really just the beginning. Have a look at some of your favorite games and study very carefully how they've implemented scrolling. You'll notice that many of them modify how and when scrolling takes place in very subtle ways. The core of all this, however, is based on the examples you looked at in this chapter.

Parallax scrolling

There's one additional scrolling technique that you'll look at very briefly here because it's very widely used and extremely effective: **parallax scrolling**.

Parallax is a visual effect in which the position of an object appears to change depending on the point of view from which it's being observed. The effect of parallax scrolling in games is used to create the illusion of shallow depth. It's a simple 3D effect in which distant background objects move at a slower rate than closer foreground objects, creating the illusion that slower-moving objects are farther away. Parallax scrolling can give even simple 2D games very strong visual impact.

It's very to easy to do. So easy, in fact, that I won't spoil the fun you'll have by figuring it out on your own. But let me at least give you a few hints about how to make parallax scrolling work.

First, you need at least two background objects (they might have the instance names `foreground` and `background`). The background object is the one farther in the distance. Figure 6-19 shows what this might look like in a horizontal scrolling game, in which the hilly meadow is the `foreground` object, and the sky scene is the background object.

Now all you need to do is move the background object at a slower rate than the `foreground` object. The directives might look like this:

```
foreground.x += -vx;
foreground.y += -vy;
background.x += -vx / 2;
background.y += -vy / 2;
```

Try it! It's a mesmerizing effect. And there's also nothing stopping you from adding a third element as a distant background object moving at an even slower rate.

Figure 6-19. To implement parallax scrolling, create two separate objects to represent your background scene.

Summary

So, is that it? No way! This chapter gave a taste of setting up a player control scheme, but there's so much more refinement that can be done. Later in the book, you'll learn how to modify these models to incorporate acceleration, friction, and gravity into the player object's movements. You'll also be looking at a player control scheme to allow the game to be played with a mouse instead of the keyboard.

In this chapter, you solved some extremely important problems central to game design that you'll see popping up again and again in different contexts in the chapters that follow. Experiment a bit with some of these techniques on your own, and I'll meet you in Chapter 7 when you're ready. I'll show you how to create an environment that your objects can interact with using collision detection.

Chapter 7

BUMPING INTO THINGS

Welcome to a fun chapter! Over the next few pages, you'll be building an interactive playground of clever little game design techniques that you can use to build completely interactive two-dimensional environments, better known as action and adventure games! A whole grab bag of things from collision detection, building walls, and picking up and dropping objects—they're all here. With a little imagination, you'll able to use these very simple techniques to produce a richly varied number of different kinds of games. Hey, congratulate yourself: you've come a long way since page 1! All your hard work is about to pay off.

At the end of the chapter, I'll introduce the Collision class, which is a custom class designed just for this book. It contains some specialized methods for handling complex collisions between objects that you can use with any of your game projects.

Setting up the project files

By this stage in the book, you've probably become quite adept at setting up project files. The examples in this chapter use the keyboard control model that you looked at in the previous chapter as a starting point. If you want to follow along with these examples, I created ready-to-go setup files for you in the chapter's source files that you can open as a project and use as a basis for these examples.

Here's how to set these files up as a project:

1. Open the chapter's source files and find the file called `interactivePlayground.fla`. Open it in Flash.

2. In the Project panel, select Quick Project from the drop-down menu.

3. interactivePlayground will be opened as a project. A check mark next to interactivePlayground.fla indicates that it's the default document (it's the FLA file that will be used to generate the SWF). You'll also notice that all the other files in the folder open as part of the project.

Take a moment to become familiar with the way `interactivePlayground.fla` is set up. It has a character on the main stage with the instance name player. The document class is set as Main_Playground. Figure 7-1 illustrates this. You'll also find some ready-made symbols in the Library that you can use with the examples in this chapter if you don't feel like making your own.

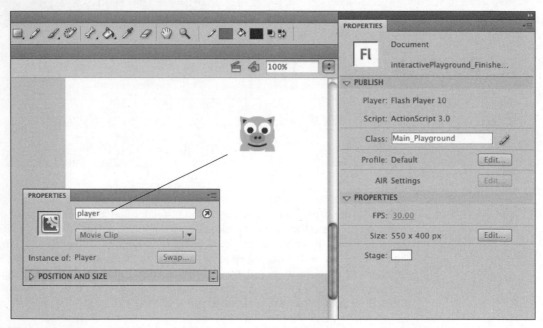

Figure 7-1. The character's instance name is player, and the document class is Main_Playground.

4. Double-click the Main_Playground file in the Project panel to open it. It looks like this:

```
package
{

    import flash.display.MovieClip;
    import flash.events.KeyboardEvent;
    import flash.ui.Keyboard;
    import flash.events.Event;

    public class Main_Playground extends MovieClip
    {
```

```
var vx:int;
var vy:int;

public function Main_Playground()
{
  init();
}
function init():void
{
  //Initialize variables
  vx = 0;
  vy = 0;

  //Add event listeners
  stage.addEventListener(KeyboardEvent.KEY_DOWN, onKeyDown);
  stage.addEventListener(KeyboardEvent.KEY_UP, onKeyUp);
  addEventListener(Event.ENTER_FRAME, onEnterFrame);
}

function onKeyDown(event:KeyboardEvent):void
{
  if (event.keyCode == Keyboard.LEFT)
  {
    vx = -5;
  }
  else if (event.keyCode == Keyboard.RIGHT)
  {
    vx = 5;
  }
  else if (event.keyCode == Keyboard.UP)
  {
    vy = -5;
  }
  else if (event.keyCode == Keyboard.DOWN)
  {
    vy = 5;
  }
}
function onKeyUp(event:KeyboardEvent):void
{
  if (event.keyCode == Keyboard.LEFT || ➥
    event.keyCode == Keyboard.RIGHT)
  {
    vx = 0;
  }
  else if (event.keyCode == Keyboard.DOWN || ➥
    event.keyCode == Keyboard.UP)
  {
    vy = 0;
```

```
            }
        }
        function onEnterFrame(event:Event):void
        {
            //Move the player
            player.x += vx;
            player.y += vy;
        }
    }
}
```

These are the files you'll be using as the start point.

> *The chapter's source files contain files called Main_Playground_2, Main_Playground_3, Main_Playground_4, and so on all the way up to Main_Playground_9. Each of these files contains the completed code for every example that you'll be looking at. If you don't feel like typing in the code manually, you can change the interactivePlayground.fla document class to match the name of one of these files. The effect will be the same as if you had typed in the code.*

Ouch!

What makes most computer games fun to play is that they are, in their essence, a simplified simulation of the real world. Like the real world, they contain objects that you can interact with in some way. These objects might be walls that block your movement, friends who help you, or enemies who harm you.

To create these sorts of interactive objects, you first need a way of finding out whether one object is touching another object. In computer game programming, this is called **collision detection**. Collision detection is just game programming jargon for "what happens when things bump into one another." AS3.0 has a very simple way of detecting collisions between objects: the hitTestObject method.

Using hitTestObject

The hitTestObject method can be used to check whether any two objects have bumped into one another. Let's say that you have a Movie Clip object called car that the player can control. You also have a Movie Clip object called wall. In your game, if the player's car hits the wall, it should crash.

In plain English, you would want to write some computer code that looks something like this:

```
if (the car hits the wall)
{
    the car must crash;
}
```

You can translate it into ActionScript like this:

```
if(car.hitTestObject(wall))
{
  car.gotoAndStop(CRASH);
}
```

The hitTestObject method is attached to the end of the car object with dot notation. It has an argument, (wall), which contains the name of the object that you want to check for a collision. Figure 7-2 shows how this all fits together.

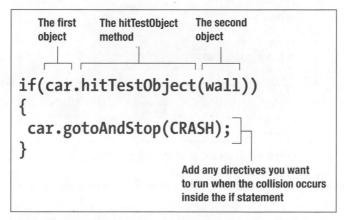

Figure 7-2. Use the hitTestObject method inside a conditional statement to check for a collision between two objects.

Usually you use the hitTestObject method inside the conditional statement of an if statement. If the objects are touching, the method returns a Boolean value of true, and the directives inside the if statement run. If it returns a value of false (if the objects are not touching), the directives inside the if statement don't run.

It's amazing what kind of power the hitTestObject method can give you. In the examples in the following pages, you'll be looking at how you can use it to do the following:

- Change text in a dynamic text field
- Trigger a change of state
- Reduce a health meter
- Update a score
- Pick up and drop an object
- Create an environmental boundary (using hitTestPoint)
- Block an object's movement

With a little imagination, you'll be able to use these techniques to produce a richly varied number of different kinds of games.

269

Changing a dynamic text field

In the following example, you'll use hitTestObject to change the text of a dynamic text field.

1. You already have a player object that you can move around the screen. Create another object that your player object can interact with and give it the instance name enemy. I created an owl character, which you can see in Figure 7-3.

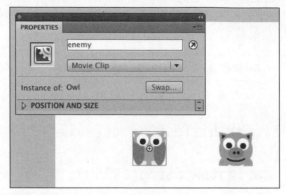

Figure 7-3. Create an object called enemy.

2. Create a dynamic text field and give it the instance name messageDisplay. Figure 7-4 shows an example.

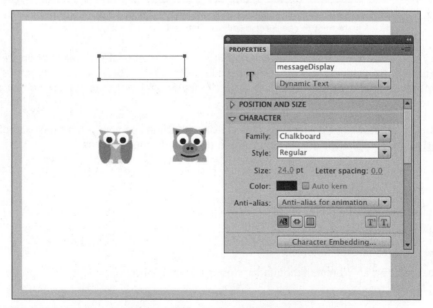

Figure 7-4. Create a dynamic text field called messageDisplay.

3. Save the interactivePlayground.fla file.

4. In the `Main_Playground.as` file, add the following code in bold to the `onEnterFrame` event handler:

```
function onEnterFrame(event:Event):void
{
  //Move the player
  player.x += vx;
  player.y += vy;

  //Collision detection
  if (player.hitTestObject(enemy))
  {
    messageDisplay.text = "Ouch!!";
  }
  else
  {
    messageDisplay.text = "No collision...";
  }
}
```

5. Save the `Main_Playground.as` file and test the project.

6. You'll see the words No collision displayed in the dynamic text field. Use the arrow keys to move the `player` object into the `enemy` object, and the text field will display Ouch!! Figure 7-5 shows what this looks like.

Not bad for a few simple lines of code, huh? If you move the `player` object away from the enemy, the text field displays No collision again. (You'll find the complete code for this example in the chapter's source files in `Main_Playground_2.as`.)

It gets even better.

Figure 7-5. The text changes when the two objects touch.

Triggering a change of state

You can put any directives you like inside the `if` statement that checks for a collision. In this example, you'll use a `gotoAndStop` method to change the state of the enemy object.

You might recall from Chapter 3 that you can give Movie Clip objects new states by changing something about how they look on another frame. The first thing you need to do is modify the enemy Movie Clip symbol. Mine is called `Owl`, but yours might be called something else.

1. Double-click the enemy object in the Library to enter symbol editing mode.

2. Add frames or keyframes wherever necessary to extend the graphics from frame 1 into frame 2.

3. Make some changes to the graphics in frame 2. You can see the changes I made to my owl in Figure 7-6. I changed it so the owl appears to flap its wings.

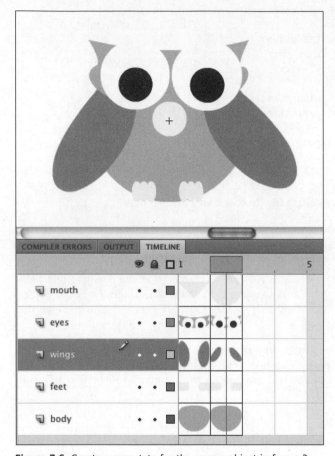

Figure 7-6. Create a new state for the enemy object in frame 2.

4. Save the `interactivePlayground.fla` file.

5. Open the `Main_Playground.as` file.

6. Now that you added a new frame to the enemy object, you need to prevent it from looping back and forth between frames 1 and 2. Add the following directive in bold to the init method:

```
function init():void
{
  //initialize variables
  vx = 0;
  vy = 0;

  //initialize objects
  enemy.stop();
```

```
                //Add event listeners
                stage.addEventListener(KeyboardEvent.KEY_DOWN, onKeyDown);
                stage.addEventListener(KeyboardEvent.KEY_UP, onKeyUp);
                addEventListener(Event.ENTER_FRAME, onEnterFrame);
        }
```

7. Add the following code in bold to the onEnterFrame method:

```
        function onEnterFrame(event:Event):void
        {
          //Move the player
          player.x += vx;
          player.y += vy;

          //Collision detection
          if (player.hitTestObject(enemy))
          {
            messageDisplay.text = "Ouch!!";
            enemy.gotoAndStop(2);
          }
          else
          {
            messageDisplay.text = "No collision...";
            enemy.gotoAndStop(1);
          }
        }
```

8. Save the Main_Playground.as file and test the project. Now when the player object collides with the enemy object, you might see something like Figure 7-7. The owl ruffles its feathers and looks perturbed.

Oh, what a pesky little pig! Maybe you can find some way for the owl to get him back in the next section. (The Main_Playground_3.as file contains the completed code for this section.)

Figure 7-7. The enemy object stops at frame 2 when it collides with the player object.

Reducing a health meter

Many games use a **health meter** to determine when the game is over. When the player bumps into bad things such as enemies, the health meter gradually shrinks in size. When the health meter disappears, the game ends.

Implementing a health meter is very easy. It makes clever use of the Movie Clip class's width property. Let's create a health meter for the player object.

1. Create a new Movie Clip symbol called Health.

2. The Health symbol's editing window will open.

3. Select the Rectangle drawing tool from the toolbar and choose a stroke and fill color. The stroke color is the color of the rectangle's outline, and the fill color is the inside color. Just below the color options is a slider labeled Stroke, which refers to the thickness of the rectangle's outside line. You can either move the slider to change its thickness or type in a value in pixels. For this example, you'll see the effect more clearly if the stroke is a little thicker than average, so I gave mine a value of 3 pixels. Figure 7-8 shows an example.

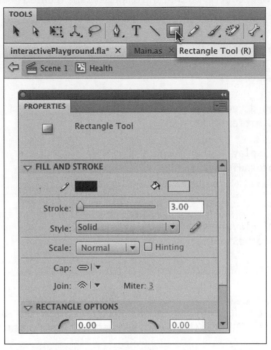

Figure 7-8. Select the Rectangle tool and choose a fill and stroke color.

4. Draw a long rectangle on the stage. In the next few steps, you'll convert the fill area into its own symbol. It's the width property of this subobject that you'll target with the code.

5. Use the Selection tool to select the fill area of the rectangle by clicking it once. You can tell that it's been selected properly if the inner fill area has a dot pattern across it and the outside stroke remains unchanged, as shown in Figure 7-9.

Figure 7-9. Click the inner fill once to select it.

6. Select Modify ➤ Convert to Symbol.

7. Give the new symbol the name Meter.

8. Just below the Name box you'll see a grid of six squares labeled Registration. This grid determines where the center point of the new symbol will be. You want the graphics for the Meter symbol to fall to the right of the center point. Click the leftmost square in the middle row, as shown in Figure 7-10. This sets the left middle of the object as its center.

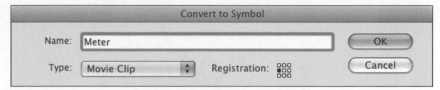

Figure 7-10. Set the new symbol's registration point.

9. Click the OK button.

10. The rectangle's fill area is now selected as a separate object. It's actually become an instance of the new Meter symbol that's sitting in the Library. You turned the rectangle's fill area into an object that you can control with code.

11. The next thing you need to do is to give the new meter object an instance name. Give it the name meter in the Instance name field of the Properties panel.

12. To make the effect appear a little neater, you'll move the meter object onto a layer below the black outline. Create a new layer in the Health symbol's timeline.

13. Click the meter object once to select it.

14. Select Edit ➤ Cut.

15. Select frame 1 of the new layer.

16. Select Edit ➤ Paste in Place. The meter object will be pasted into the new layer in exactly the same position that it was cut from.

17. Move the new layer with the meter object so that it's under the layer containing the black outline. Figure 7-11 shows what your Health symbol should now look like.

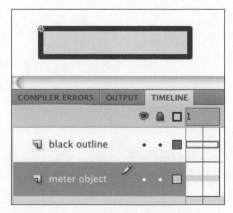

Figure 7-11. The finished Health symbol

18. Drag an instance of the `Health` symbol onto the main stage.

19. Give it the instance name `health`. Figure 7-12 shows what the stage should now look like.

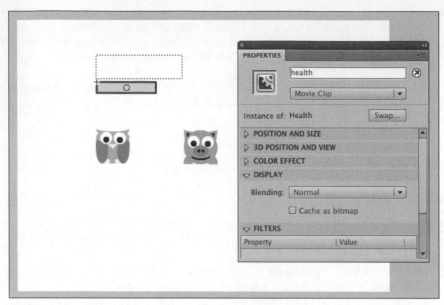

Figure 7-12. Add a new object called health to the main stage.

If you open the `Meter` symbol's editing window, you'll see that the rectangle's blue fill area is exactly to the right of the symbol's center point. As Figure 7-13 shows, there should be nothing to the left of the crosshairs that define the center of the symbol. This will be very important for the health meter because you'll be using the object's `width` property to reduce the size of the meter. Flash does this by squeezing together the graphics on the left and right of the object's center point. Because the `meter` object has graphics only on the right, it will look like it's gradually disappearing to nothing instead of being squeezed from both sides. You'll see this effect at work soon enough.

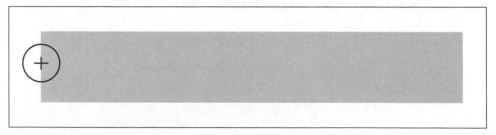

Figure 7-13. The graphics for the meter object should extend from the right of the center crosshairs.

You now have an object called `health`, which contains a subobject called `meter`. You can access the `meter` object with dot notation like this:

```
health.meter
```

Now all you need to do is program the health meter. As a bonus, the words Game Over! display in the messageDisplay text field when its width is reduced to zero.

1. Modify the onEnterFrame method so that it looks like the following. The bold text indicates the new code, but notice that the two directives that displayed the words No collision and Ouch!! have been removed. It was done to simplify the code a little so you won't have a conflict with the Game Over! message.

```
function onEnterFrame(event:Event):void
{
  //Move the player
  player.x += vx;
  player.y += vy;

  //Collision detection
  if (player.hitTestObject(enemy))
  {
    enemy.gotoAndStop(2);
    health.meter.width--;
  }
  else
  {
    enemy.gotoAndStop(1);
  }

  //Check for end of game
  if(health.meter.width < 1)
  {
    messageDisplay.text = "Game Over!";
  }
}
```

2. Save the Main_Playground.as file and test the project. When the player touches the enemy, the health meter decreases. When it disappears, the words Game Over! are displayed. Figure 7-14 shows an example of what you'll see.

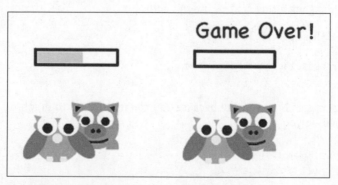

Figure 7-14. Using a health meter to end the game

Not bad for three lines of code!

The width of the `meter` object is decreased by 1 each frame, so if its width is 50 pixels, it will take 50 frames for the meter to reach zero. If you made a really long meter, it might take a bit of time before it runs out. You can easily speed up or slow down the rate at which the meter decreases by changing this line:

```
health.meter.width--;
```

For example, if you change the line like this, it reduces the meter by 2 pixels each frame:

```
health.meter.width -= 2;
```

This doubles the speed by which the health meter is reduced. (The complete code is available in the `Main_Playground_4.as` file in the chapter's source files.)

Using scaleX to scale the meter based on a percentage

You can also use the `scaleX` property to change the meter's size. `scaleX` changes the size of an object based on its ratio. You can use it to change the width of the meter based on a percentage instead of a fixed pixel amount. This is often preferable because it means the meter is reduced at the same rate, no matter how long or short it is.

A scaleX value of 1 means the object is full size. You can reduce a meter by 1% by subtracting 0.01 from the scaleX property each frame.

To duplicate the effect of this example using scaleX, you first need to add an additional `if` statement to make sure that the `scaleX` value is above zero. Without this check, the meter continues to scale negatively beyond the left border, which would not look very good. Here's the code to use:

```
if(health.meter.scaleX > 0)
{
   health.meter.scaleX -= 0.02;
}
```

A value of `0.02` reduces the meter by 2% each frame, so the meter will reach 0 in 50 frames. To check for the end of the game using scaleX, use this code:

```
if (health.meter.scaleX <= 0)
{
   messageDisplay.text="Game Over!";
}
```

Scaling by percentages is very useful because you can use meters to graph other data that might be using percentages in your game.

Updating a score

Most games keep track of whether a player has won or lost by updating a score, based on how well the player is performing. The following example shows you how to update a score and end the game when a certain score has been reached.

You'll write this code in three parts. The first part gets the basic system running, but you'll immediately see a problem with it that will illustrate a valuable concept to keep in mind when dealing with collision detection. You'll solve the problem in the second part.

1. You first need to create a new uint variable call score to store the player's score. Update the Main_Playground class definition and the init method with the following new code in bold:

```
public class Main_Playground extends MovieClip
{
  var vx:int;
  var vy:int;
  var score:uint;

  public function Main_Playground()
  {
    init();
  }
  function init():void
  {
    //initialize variables
    vx = 0;
    vy = 0;
    score = 0;

    //initialize objects
    enemy.stop();

    //Add event listeners
    stage.addEventListener(KeyboardEvent.KEY_DOWN, onKeyDown);
    stage.addEventListener(KeyboardEvent.KEY_UP, onKeyUp);
    addEventListener(Event.ENTER_FRAME, onEnterFrame);
  }
```

2. Add the following new code to the onEnterFrame method:

```
function onEnterFrame(event:Event):void
{
  //Move the player
  player.x += vx;
  player.y += vy;

  //Collision detection
  if (player.hitTestObject(enemy))
  {
    enemy.gotoAndStop(2);
```

```
      health.meter.width--;
      score++;
      messageDisplay.text = String(score);
    }
    else
    {
      enemy.gotoAndStop(1);
    }

    //Check for end of game
    if (health.meter.width < 1)
    {
      messageDisplay.text="Game Over!";
    }
  }
```

3. Save the Main_Playground.as file and test the project. When the player touches the enemy, you'll see the score increase in the messageDisplay text field. Hey, what's that!? It works, but probably not the way you expected it to! Figure 7-15 shows what happens when the two objects collide.

Figure 7-15. The score increases when the two objects touch.

The score is increased, but it's increased by one 30 times every second! If you think about it, the code did exactly what you asked it to.

When the two objects collide, the following directives run:

```
score++;
messageDisplay.text = String(score);
```

The score is increased by 1 and then displayed as a string in the messageDisplay text field. But remember that this is all happening *inside* the onEnterFrame event handler, which is updated 30 times per second. That means that every time it updates, it increases the score by 1 if the objects are touching. And so you end up with this dizzying rush of flashing numbers until the two objects are separated again.

Sometimes this might be the way you want your games to keep score, but let's try and refine it a little more in this example.

How about this: Let's try and set the program up so that the score is increased only on the first occasion that the two objects collide. Even though the two objects might be touching for an entire 6 seconds, for example, the score should be updated by only 1, not 180. Sound a bit better?

Let's take it a step farther. If the two objects are separated and then touch again, the score should register this new collision, and update by 1 again, giving you a total of 2. This seems like a much more logical way for the score system to work.

To put this in place, you need to use a new Boolean variable. In the program, you'll give it the following name:

```
collisionHasOccurred
```

You'll initialize it to false when the program starts and then set it to true when a collision takes place. That should work. Try it out!

1. Add the code in bold to the Main class definition and init method:

```
public class Main_Playground extends MovieClip
{
  var vx:int;
  var vy:int;
  var score:uint;
  var collisionHasOccurred:Boolean;

  public function Main_Playground()
  {
    init();
  }
  function init():void
  {
    //initialize variables
    vx = 0;
    vy = 0;
    score = 0;
    collisionHasOccurred = false;

    //initialize objects
    enemy.stop();

    //Add event listeners
    stage.addEventListener(KeyboardEvent.KEY_DOWN, onKeyDown);
    stage.addEventListener(KeyboardEvent.KEY_UP, onKeyUp);
    addEventListener(Event.ENTER_FRAME, onEnterFrame);
  }
}
```

2. Modify the onEnterFrame event handler so that it looks like the following (the new code makes use of the not operator, which is an exclamation mark):

```
!
```

You haven't used the not operator before, so look for it in the code and be careful to add it—it's easy to miss. I'll explain the use of the not operator in detail ahead.

```
function onEnterFrame(event:Event):void
{
  //Move the player
  player.x += vx;
  player.y += vy;

  //Collision detection
  if (player.hitTestObject(enemy))
  {
    enemy.gotoAndStop(2);
    health.meter.width--;
```

```
    if(! collisionHasOccurred)
    {
      score++;
      messageDisplay.text = String(score);
      collisionHasOccurred = true;
    }
  }
  else
  {
    enemy.gotoAndStop(1);
    collisionHasOccurred = false;
  }


  //Check for end of game
  if (health.meter.width < 1)
  {
    messageDisplay.text="Game Over!";
  }
}
```

Figure 7-16. The score now updates only once every collision.

3. Save the Main_Playground.as file and test the project. The score now only updates by 1 each time the objects collide. That's much more manageable! Figure 7-16 shows an example of what you should see after the second collision.

Let's take a quick stroll through the logic of what's going on here. First, the new collisionHasOccurred variable was initialized to false in the init function definition:

```
collisionHasOccurred = false;
```

This might be stating the obvious, but it's crucially important to keep in mind for the next bit of code to make any sense. This is the new code inside the if/else statement in the onEnterFrame event handler:

```
if (player.hitTestObject(enemy))
{
  enemy.gotoAndStop(2);
  health.meter.width--;
  if(! collisionHasOccurred)
  {
    score++;
    messageDisplay.text = String(score);
    collisionHasOccurred = true;
  }
}
else
{
  enemy.gotoAndStop(1);
  collisionHasOccurred = false;
}
```

What you did was to create a new if statement *inside* the first if statement. This is called a **nested if statement**. Nested if statements allow you to fine-tune the logic a bit to check for subconditions after the first condition has passed as true. (It's called a nested if statement because it's cozily tucked inside the first one, like an egg in a nest. If you turn this page on its side and look at the code horizontally, I'm sure you can imagine a crow or magpie making a perfectly comfortable nest in the indentation created by the second if statement.)

What you want the new if statement to check for is whether the collision between the objects *hasn't occurred*. That's right, you didn't misread the previous sentence; you want to check to see whether the collision *has not* happened. That's what this line is doing:

```
if(! collisionHasOccurred)
```

It checks to see if the collisionHasOccurred variable is false. Usually, conditional statements check to see whether certain conditions or variables are true, but not this time. Instead, you used the not operator to check for a false condition. The not operator is an exclamation mark:

```
!
```

When it's used in a conditional statement in front of a Boolean variable, it allows the directives inside the if statement to run if the Boolean value is false.

So, is it false? You initialized collisionHasOccurred to false when the program started, so the first time the collision occurs, it is false, and all the directives inside the if statement run:

```
score++;
messageDisplay.text = String(score);
collisionHasOccurred = true;
```

This updates the score and the dynamic text field, but it also does something very important: it sets the collisionHasOccurred variable to true.

Why is that so important? Because exactly 1/30th of a second later, this same if statement will be called upon a *second time* if the objects are still touching:

```
if(! collisionHasOccurred)
{
  score++;
  messageDisplay.text = String(score);
  collisionHasOccurred = true;
}
```

But hey, wait a minute! The collisionHasOccurred variable was set to true the first time it ran, and the conditional statement will let it pass if it's false. That means none of the directives runs, and the score and the text field are only updated once.

Perfect—just what you wanted!

But there's another problem. You want the score to update *again* if the objects happen to collide a second time at some future point in the game. This won't happen if collisionHasOccurred is still set to true. You have to find some way to reset it back to false so you can update the score again.

This is very simple; you just need to set it to `false` when the objects are *not colliding*. And actually, you're already checking for that in the code, remember? It's the second part of the if/else statement that tells the enemy object to return to frame 1. All you need to do is drop a line of code in that same spot, which the code in bold shows:

```
if (player.hitTestObject(enemy))
  {
    enemy.gotoAndStop(2);
    health.meter.width--;
    if(! collisionHasOccurred)
    {
      score++;
      messageDisplay.text = String(score);
      collisionHasOccurred = true;
    }
  }
else
  {
    enemy.gotoAndStop(1);
    collisionHasOccurred = false;
  }
```

Yes, I know, what you're thinking. If you're new to programming, this logic can seem a little on the mind-bending side! This is the most complex use of logical operators and if statements you've seen so far. Don't feel too discouraged if you don't understand it right away or don't think you'll be able to write similarly complex code yourself any time soon. Look it over a few times, think about it while lying in bed at night, come back to it in a few days, and try it with some of your own games. It will gradually start to make sense—trust me! Seeing how others have solved problems and then trying out those solutions in your own games is an extremely important part of learning how to program.

I made one more promise at the beginning of this section, which is that the score will also help you figure out if the player has won the game.

1. Add the following code in bold to the bottom of the onEnterFrame method:

```
function onEnterFrame(event:Event):void
{
  //Move the player
  player.x += vx;
  player.y += vy;

  //Collision detection
  if (player.hitTestObject(enemy))
  {
    enemy.gotoAndStop(2);
    health.meter.width--;
    if (! collisionHasOccurred)
    {
      score++;
      messageDisplay.text = String(score);
      collisionHasOccurred = true;
```

```
        }
    }
    else
    {
      enemy.gotoAndStop(1);
      collisionHasOccurred = false;
    }

    //Check for end of game
    if (health.meter.width < 1)
    {
      messageDisplay.text = "Game Over!";
    }
    if (score >= 5)
    {
      messageDisplay.text = "You won!";
    }
  }
}
```

Figure 7-17. You can win the game if you touch the enemy five times before the health meter runs out.

2. Save the `Main_Playground.as` file and test the project. If the player object is able to touch the enemy five times before the health meter runs out, the words You won! display, as shown in Figure 7-17.

In effect you've turned this into a little minigame. Can you touch the owl five times before the health meter runs out?

Yes, I know, it's not a *real* game, more of an accidental game, but I'm sure you can see where you can take it with only a little further refinement.

Of course, this game has some problems. With a little more playing, you can actually cheat and "win" even if the health meter runs out. Can you think of a way to make what you've built a little more cheat-proof? (Hint: you'll need another variable and another `if/else` statement!) You'll encounter these sorts of bugs-that-might-be-features-but-are-really-bugs in your games all the time, so now's a good time for a real-world challenge to sharpen your debugging skills. (The `Main_Playground_5.as` file contains the complete code for this example.)

Picking up and dropping objects

It's time for the pig and owl to put aside their differences and make peace! In the next example, you'll see how you can make the pig pick up an apple and carry it to the owl. This is very easy to implement using the techniques discussed so far in this chapter and it reintroduces a method you haven't seen since Chapter 3, the cute-as-a-button method named addChild.

1. You first need an object that the player can carry. Create a new symbol called Apple and design a simple graphic of an apple. For this technique to be clearly visible, you might want to make it smaller (half the size or smaller than the player object).

2. Drag an instance of the Apple symbol onto the stage, and give it the instance name apple, as shown in Figure 7-18.

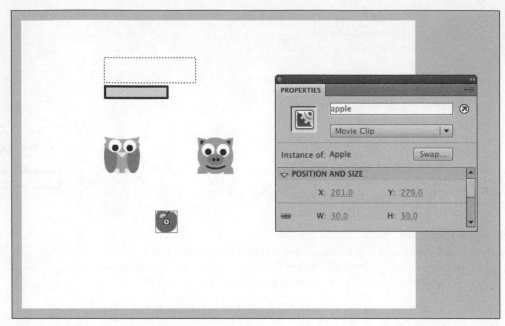

Figure 7-18. Add a new apple object to the main stage.

3. You need a new Boolean variable called playerHasApple that will tell the program whether the player is carrying the apple. You'll initialize it to false at the start of the program so that you can set it to true when the player picks it up later. Modify the Main class definition and the init method with the following code shown in bold:

```
public class Main_Playground_6 extends MovieClip
{
  var vx:int;
  var vy:int;
  var score:uint;
  var collisionHasOccurred:Boolean;
  var playerHasApple:Boolean;

  public function Main_Playground_6()
  {
    init();
  }
  function init():void
  {
    //initialize variables
    vx = 0;
    vy = 0;
    score = 0;
    collisionHasOccurred = false;
```

```
    playerHasApple = false;

    //initialize objects
    enemy.stop();

    //Add event listeners
    stage.addEventListener(KeyboardEvent.KEY_DOWN, onKeyDown);
    stage.addEventListener(KeyboardEvent.KEY_UP, onKeyUp);
    addEventListener(Event.ENTER_FRAME, onEnterFrame);
}
```

4. You might be forgiven for thinking that the onEnterFrame event handler is now the star of the show as far as making fun things happen in your games. After all, most of the new techniques shown in the last 40-odd pages involved placing directives in it. But don't forget that you have a few other just-as-useful-if-somewhat-neglected methods waiting to do the bidding if you can find some work for them. This time, it's the turn of the onKeyDown event handler to shine in the spotlight. Add the new code in bold to the onKeyDown event handler:

```
function onKeyDown(event:KeyboardEvent):void
{
  if (event.keyCode == Keyboard.LEFT)
  {
    vx = -5;
  }
  else if (event.keyCode == Keyboard.RIGHT)
  {
    vx = 5;
  }
  else if (event.keyCode == Keyboard.UP)
  {
    vy = -5;
  }
  else if (event.keyCode == Keyboard.DOWN)
  {
    vy = 5;
  }
  if (event.keyCode == Keyboard.SPACE && player.hitTestObject(apple))
  {
    if (! playerHasApple)
    {
      player.addChild(apple);
      apple.x = 0;
      apple.y = 0;
      playerHasApple = true;
    }
    else
    {
      stage.addChild(apple);
      apple.x = player.x;
      apple.y = player.y;
```

```
          playerHasApple = false;
          if (enemy.hitTestObject(apple))
          {
            messageDisplay.text = "Thanks!!";
          }
        }
      }
    }
}
```

5. Save the Main_Playground.as file and test the project.

6. Use the arrow keys to move the player object so that it's touching the apple object. Press the spacebar on the keyboard. The player object picks up the apple. Now move the player object so that it's touching the enemy object. Press the spacebar again; the player drops the apple and the dynamic text field displays the word Thanks!! If you move the player away from the apple, it stays where it is. Figure 7-19 shows what this looks like. You can pick up and drop the apple as many times as you want to, anywhere on the stage. For the purpose of this example, you haven't disabled the health meter, but that's easy to do if you want to.

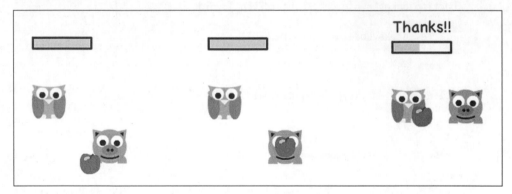

Figure 7-19. Friends at last! Use the spacebar to pick up the apple and carry it to the owl.

There are no new techniques here, but you've never seen all of these elements used together in this combination before. Let's take a tour of this code and how it works. First, initialize the playerHasApple variable to false in the init method:

```
playerHasApple = false;
```

I'm sure you can see the logic of this. Obviously, the player doesn't have the apple when the program first starts, so it should be set to false.

Next comes the new if statement inside the onKeyDown event handler:

```
if (event.keyCode == Keyboard.SPACE && player.hitTestObject(apple))
{
  if (! playerHasApple)
  {
    player.addChild(apple);
    apple.x = 0;
    apple.y = 0;
```

```
      playerHasApple = true;
    }
    else
    {
      stage.addChild(apple);
      apple.x = player.x;
      apple.y = player.y;
      playerHasApple = false;
      if (enemy.hitTestObject(apple))
      {
        messageDisplay.text = "Thanks!!";
      }
    }
  }
}
```

To understand how this works, think about what conditions need to be met before the player object can either pick up or drop the apple:

- The game player needs to press the spacebar. You can check for this condition with a conditional statement that looks like this: (event.keyCode == Keyboard.SPACE).

- The player object needs to be touching the apple. You can check for this condition using a conditional statement that looks like this: (player.hitTestObject(apple)).

If those two things happen at the same time, you know that the player is either trying to pick up or drop the apple. But the key is that *both conditions need to be true at exactly the same time*. Why? Well, obviously it wouldn't make sense if the player object could pick up the apple if it weren't touching it, and the game also needs to know that the player *wants* to pick up the object. In this example, you tell the game that you want to pick up or drop the apple by pressing the spacebar.

To check whether two conditions are true at the same time, you can combine them into a single conditional statement using the and operator. You looked at the and operator briefly in Chapter 4, but you haven't really seen it in action until now. The and operator is a double *ampersand* that looks like this:

```
&&
```

It's used in the first new if statement in this line of code:

```
if (event.keyCode == Keyboard.SPACE && player.hitTestObject(apple)) {
```

Great! In one line of code, you can check whether both the conditions for picking up or dropping objects have been met. But which one is it? Picking up or dropping?

That's pretty easy to figure out. If those two conditions are true, and the player doesn't already have the apple, you know that the apple needs to be picked up. If the player already has the apple, you know the apple should be dropped. All it requires is an additional nested if/else statement that checks whether the playerHasApple variable is false. Here's a simplified version of this logic:

```
if(! playerHasApple)
{
  Pick the apple up...
}
```

```
else
{
  Drop the apple...
}
```

Keep that in mind because this is what the actual code looks like:

```
if (! playerHasApple)
{
  player.addChild(apple);
  apple.x = 0;
  apple.y = 0;
  playerHasApple = true;
}
else
{
  stage.addChild(apple);
  apple.x = player.x;
  apple.y = player.y;
  playerHasApple = false;
  if (enemy.hitTestObject(apple))
  {
    messageDisplay.text = "Thanks!!";
  }
}
```

Is that making a little more sense now?

But how is the code actually picking up and dropping the object? First, let's look at the directives that pick up the apple:

```
player.addChild(apple);
apple.x = 0;
apple.y = 0;
playerHasApple = true;
```

You used the addChild method to make the apple a **child object** of the player object. So like a baby duckling, wherever the player goes, the apple is sure to follow.

You then set the x and y position of the apple to 0. Because the apple is now a child of the player object, it uses the player object's coordinate system. An x and y position of 0 positions it in the very center of the player object. For your purposes, this happens to be very conveniently on the tip of the pig's nose.

The last thing is to set the playerHasApple variable to true, which prevents the program from trying to pick the apple up again if the player object already has it. The directives that drop the apple are just as straightforward:

```
stage.addChild(apple);
apple.x = player.x;
apple.y = player.y;
playerHasApple = false;
if (enemy.hitTestObject(apple))
{
  messageDisplay.text = "Thanks!!";
}
```

You first use the addChild method to make the apple object a child of the stage object, which frees it from bondage to the pig. Remember that the stage object is the parent object of *all* objects on the stage, including the player and enemy objects. Objects that are children of the stage are at the top of the food chain and are footloose and fancy free. The apple object now no longer has to mindlessly follow the player object around and can get into any of its own trouble that it wants to.

The next thing was to give the apple object the same x and y positions as the player object. This fixes it on the stage at its current position, which looks like it's being "dropped." The playerHasApple variable was set to false, which allows the player to pick the apple up again later.

The last thing you did was actually a bit of a bonus. You added the following nested if statement:

```
if (enemy.hitTestObject(apple))
{
  messageDisplay.text = "Thanks!!";
}
```

It checks to see whether the enemy object is touching the apple object. If it is, Thanks!! is displayed in the dynamic text field. Awww . . . friends at last! (You can find the complete code for this example in the Main_Playground_6.as file.)

Learning the bad news about hitTestObject

First, let me just say that I *love* the hitTestObject method! You can see from these examples what incredible power it can give you with just a few lines of code, a little imagination, and a bit of simple logic. I'm sure your head must be swimming with ideas for games already. If you have any doubts, let me just confirm to you right now: yes, you have all the skills you need already to start making them! I won't stop you; go ahead, take a break from this chapter and start building them if you feel inspired. A whole universe of possibilities exists!

But before you do go any further, take a closer look at just what makes hitTestObject tick. This must be said, dear reader: hitTestObject holds a deep, dark secret that will cripple your games if you don't understand it.

Detecting collisions with the bounding box

How does Flash actually know that two objects are touching? All display objects (objects you can see on the stage) are surrounded by imaginary rectangular boxes called bounding boxes. The **bounding box** defines the area of the object that hitTestObject checks for a collision. The bounding box is usually invisible, but you can see it when you select an object on the stage by clicking it once, as shown in Figure 7-20.

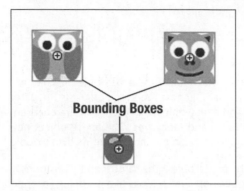

Figure 7-20. Examples of bounding boxes

A collision is detected whenever any portion of the bounding box intersects with any portion of another object's bounding box. Figure 7-21 shows some examples.

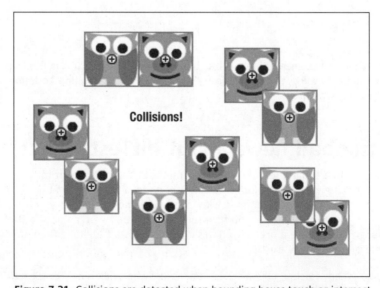

Figure 7-21. Collisions are detected when bounding boxes touch or intersect.

This is all fine if the objects are square-ish or rectangular, but what if they're not? Remember the cat from Chapters 2, 3, and 4? It heard about all the apples you were giving away and wanted to get in on the action. Funny thing about this cat, though—it has terribly long ears.

292

Take a look at Figure 7-22 as the cat approaches the apple. The cat's ears are so long that they push the edges of the bounding box well past something that defines the main part of the cat object. Yet hitTestObject, which uses these bounding boxes, regards it as a collision. The cat will get away scot free with the apple, although it appears to be nowhere close to it. The pig and the owl would desperately complain, and if you tried to get away with using this collision detection in a game, your players would think something was seriously flawed—and they'd be right.

Figure 7-22. hitTestObject registers this as a collision. Even though the objects are nowhere near one another, their bounding boxes intersect.

To be fair, this is not a problem with hitTestObject; its job is to check for collisions between the bounding boxes of two objects. If it's not working for you, you need to decide whether you want to modify the structure of your game and objects so that it starts working or find another way of doing collision detection.

You'll be looking at a few other ways to do collision detection in this book, but before you give up hope on hitTestObject, let's look at some of the advantages it has over more-complex methods and how you can make it work in your games.

Two great things about hitTestObject make it the favored first choice for doing collision detection: it is easy to implement and puts very little strain on the CPU or Flash Player. In game design, in which performance considerations can dictate many design decisions, this last reason alone is enough to spur you on to see how much mileage you can wring out of the humble hitTestObject.

So, here goes. How can you use hitTestObject and still make it work reasonably well for irregularly shaped objects?

Let's take a look at a few solutions.

Learning to live with it

The first solution, which is not really a solution at all, is to design your game according to the constraints that hitTestObject imposes on you. Limitations can be an enormous strength (in the same way that writing poetry according to the rules of a sonnet can be a strength). They can help you focus and streamline your design—just ask Shakespeare!

If you know that hitTestObject works best with square or rectangular objects, design your objects accordingly.

Have a look at the owl and pig characters that you used in this chapter. They're both square shaped, but you wouldn't know that unless you actually saw a square outline traced around them. They've been designed so that most of the edges and corners meet the edges of the grid square in which they were designed. This means that there are very few places in which the shape of the character doesn't fill the bounding box, so the shapes of the objects almost always overlap when a collision occurs.

However, there are a few spots on both of these objects where a collision will be detected even if the shapes don't overlap. Figure 7-23 shows an example.

Figure 7-23. The bounding boxes overlap, even if the shapes don't.

Isn't this the fatal Achilles heel in the whole system? Not if the objects are moving fast enough, and in most games they will be. The empty gap between the edge of the bounding box and the owl's wing isn't more than about 5 pixels at its maximum. Remember that the player object in these examples is moving at the rate of 5 pixels every 1/30 of a second. That's really fast. It's so fast, and the gap is so small, that no one playing the game would ever notice that the collision wasn't accurate.

Of course, if the objects were moving slower, you'd have a problem. But the point of this section is this: design your game so that it's *not* a problem. Make your objects short and stout, and make them move reasonably quickly. If you can do that, hitTestObject will be all you'll ever need.

Have a look some of your favorite 2D games. Isn't it funny that all the characters and objects seem to be sort of plump and square-ish? You got it, baby! They're dealing with exactly the same constraints you're dealing with here. Welcome to the video game designer's club!

Creating subobjects

The simplest way to improve collision detection using hitTestObject is to create subobjects inside the main object and use them to check for a collision.

Let's stick with the problem of the long-eared cat and the apple for a moment. You could greatly improve the collision detection between them if you created a smaller rectangular object inside the cat object that defined the collision area. You could give this subobject the instance name collisionArea. You could then access it with dot notation like this:

    cat.collisionArea

If you used it with hitTestObject in an if statement, it might look something like this:

```
if(cat.collisionArea.hitTestObject(apple))
{
 Collision directives...
}
```

Of course, you have to set the alpha of the collisionArea subobject to 0 so it is completely transparent. (To make an object completely transparent, select it, and then give it an alpha value of 0 in the Color Effect pane of the Properties panel. Alpha is one of the options in the Style menu.)

Figure 7-24 shows how using a subobject can greatly improve the collision detection between the cat and the apple. In the figure, a. shows what this would look like if the collisionArea subobject were visible, and b. shows how it would probably be used, completely transparently, in a real project.

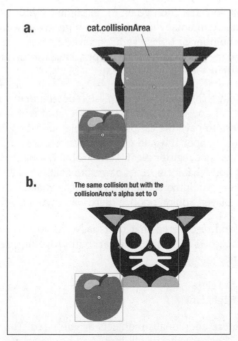

Figure 7-24. Use subobjects to improve collision detection.

That's much better, isn't it? Some of you might still see a problem, however, which is now almost the opposite of the problem you were facing before. `hitTestObject` now *won't register a collision* if the apple is touching an area of the cat that isn't covered by the `collisionArea` subobject. Figure 7-25 shows some examples.

But is this really a problem? In many games, it isn't. In fast-moving games, it can actually look *more* natural to have a slight overlap between two objects before a collision is registered than if the collision detection were too precise. Here's why:

- A slight overlap occurring between two objects gives a 2D game a very subtle feeling of shallow depth that will seem very natural to players. The human mind instinctively tries to impose depth onto flat surfaces, so overlapping objects will be thought to be occupying slightly different planes.

Figure 7-25. Even though the apple is touching the cat, neither registers as a collision because the apple's bounding box is not intersecting with the collision-Area subobject.

- When players play a game, the mind creates a kind of texture for the game that is almost tactile. When people talk about the "feel" of a game or a player control scheme, this is what they mean. Overly precise collision detection can make the texture of the game feel harsh and rough to the player. A little leniency in collision detection can give your game a softer, spongier feel to it that might be more enjoyable to play.

Take a good look at the collision detection going on in some of your favorite 2D games, and you'll notice that you can often touch an enemy just slightly and get away with it without a collision being registered. I can't count the number of times I've been saved by this "fuzzy" collision detection when jumping over barrels in *Donkey Kong* or evading Koopa shells in *Super Mario Bros.*, and it never seemed like there was something wrong with the game.

This boils down to very carefully thinking about the collision detection in your game and deciding which kinds of collisions are important and which aren't. Let's have another look at the cat and apple problem. Would it really make sense to have the cat pick the apple up if the apple were touching its ears? It definitely wouldn't, and if it did happen it would certainly look wrong. Is it okay for the apple to overlap with the cat's stomach a bit and not register a collision? Probably—because as soon as the cat touches the apple with the part of its body that includes its paws, the collision will occur. This would make sense to the player. The slight overlap would be accounted for as the shallow depth discussed previously (or maybe the cat's fur), and the player wouldn't notice there was anything wrong with it.

However, if you tested this and discovered that it actually did look really awkward, you could start adding more rectangular subobjects in areas of the cat to improve or fine-tune the collision accuracy. You could name them like this:

```
cat.collisionArea_LeftEar
cat.collisionArea_RightEar
```

You could add as many of these additional subobjects as you need. The only drawback is that you'll have to write more code to check for these collisions. And if you have a huge number of them, they might start to slow down your game. Still, it's a great solution, and there are very few collision detection problems you won't be able to solve by doing this judiciously.

All this is an art, not a science, and if you get the balance right you'll have an amazingly comfortable and natural collision-detection system. Hooray for hitTestObject!

Using hitTestPoint

Another method you can use for collision detection, hitTestPoint, allows you to see whether a single point is touching the shape of another object. This time, I mean *its actual shape*, not just its bounding box.

The best way to see how hitTestPoint works is by trying it out in a practical example. In the next few steps, you'll design a hilly background for the characters and use hitTestPoint to prevent the player object from moving off of it.

1. In the interactivePlayground.fla file, create a new layer in the timeline called background. Position it in the layer stack so that it's below the layer on which you've designed your other objects.

2. Use Flash's drawing tools to draw a curved hill behind your player, enemy and apple objects. Mine looks like Figure 7-26 (the daisies are optional!).

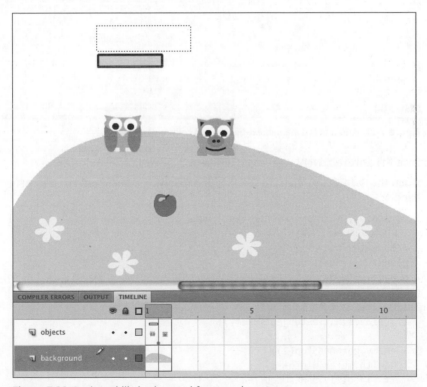

Figure 7-26. Design a hilly background for your characters.

3. Convert the hill into a symbol. Select the graphic with the Selection Tool and then select Modify ➤ Convert to Symbol. Give the new symbol the class name Hill.

4. Give the new hill object the instance name hill in the Instance name box of the Properties panel.

5. You'll add a new dynamic text field to test how hitTestPoint is working. Create a new dynamic text field in the upper part of the stage and give it the instance name collisionDisplay. Figure 7-27 shows how I set mine up.

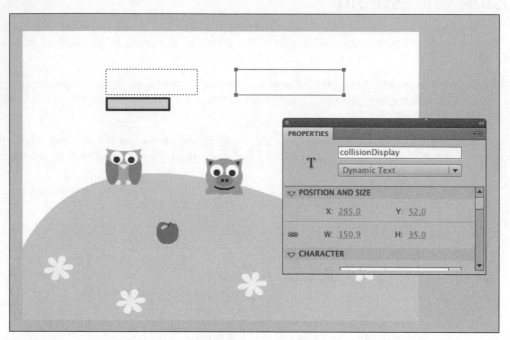

Figure 7-27. Add a new dynamic text field called collisionDisplay.

6. Save the interactivePlayground.fla file.

7. Open the Main_Playground.as file. Add the following code in bold to the onEnterFrame event handler:

```
function onEnterFrame(event:Event):void
{
  //Move the player
  player.x += vx;
  player.y += vy;

  //Collision detection
  if (player.hitTestObject(enemy))
  {
    enemy.gotoAndStop(2);
    health.meter.width--;
    if (! collisionHasOccurred)
    {
```

```
      score++;
      messageDisplay.text = String(score);
      collisionHasOccurred = true;
    }
  }
  else
  {
    enemy.gotoAndStop(1);
    collisionHasOccurred = false;
  }

  //Check for end of game
  if (health.meter.width < 1)
  {
    messageDisplay.text = "Game Over!";
  }
  if (score >= 5)
  {
    messageDisplay.text = "You won!";
  }

  //hitTestPoint example
  if (hill.hitTestPoint(player.x, player.y, true))
  {
    collisionDisplay.text = "On the hill...";
  }
  else
  {
    collisionDisplay.text = "Not on the hill...";
  }
}
```

8. Save the `Main_Playground.as` file and test the project. The dynamic text field tells you whether the player is on or off the hill. But look closely. Can you tell at which point the program detects that the player is on the hill? It's actually using the absolute middle point of the player object. When the center point of the player object is touching any part of the surface area of the hill object, the collision is detected. Figure 7-28 illustrates this a little more clearly.

This is pretty amazing. Absolutely precise collision detection without bounding boxes! Just like `hitTestObject`, you attach `hitTestPoint` to any object that you want to check for a collision using dot notation. That first object is the one whose shape you want to use in the collision. You used `hill` in the previous code:

```
if (hill.hitTestPoint(player.x, player.y, true))
```

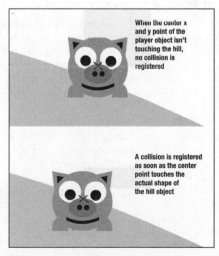

When the center x and y point of the player object isn't touching the hill, no collision is registered

A collision is registered as soon as the center point touches the actual shape of the hill object

Figure 7-28. Use hitTestPoint to check whether a single point in an object is touching the actual shape of another object.

But what about all that stuff in the argument?

```
player.x, player.y, true
```

These values define the point that you want to use to check for a collision. You can find any single point by giving two values: an x position and a y position. In this example, you used the center point of the player object as the point you want to use in the collision. The third argument, true, just means "yes, you want to check for a collision using a point and a shape." (The last argument is called the **shapeflag** in the AS3.0 documentation. If you set the shapeflag to false, hitTestPoint will just go back to checking for a collision with the objects' bounding boxes, just as hitTestObject does.) Figure 7-29 illustrates how all the elements of collision detection using hitTestPoint fit together.

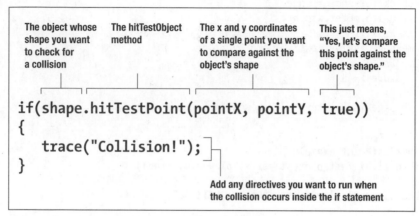

Figure 7-29. How hitTestPoint works

So what is hitTestPoint useful for? Let's go back to the cat with the long ears. Suppose that you designed a game in which it's absolutely crucial to know whether something is touching the tips of the cat's ears. All you need to do is figure out the x and y coordinates of the points that define those ear tips, and then use them in a conditional statement using hitTestPoint.

For example, you know that the tips of the cat's ears are at the very left and right side of the cat object, and about 3 pixels from the top. First, you need to define these points, and even though you could do this directly in the arguments of the hitTestPoint method, it will make the code a little more readable if you define them as variables first. You can use some code that looks like this:

```
var leftTipX:int = cat.x - cat.width / 2;
var leftTipY:int = cat.y + cat.height / 2 + 3;
var rightTipX:int = cat.x + cat.width / 2;
var leftTipY:int = cat.y + cat.height / 2 + 3;
```

Figure 7-30 illustrates these positions.

Now all you need to do is use these points to write two if statements using hitTestPoint (you need one for each ear tip):

```
if(apple.hitTestPoint(leftTipX, leftTipY, true))
{
    collision directives...
```

```
    }
    if(apple.hitTestPoint(rightTipX, rightTipY, true))
    {
        collision directives...
    }
```

If the shape of the apple object now comes into contact with either of these points, a collision is detected. I'm sure you can see how you could use this alongside hitTestObject to really fine-tune your collision-detection system.

Figure 7-30. Calculate the points that you want to use in the collision.

Using hitTestPoint to create an environmental boundary

Let me show you a neat little trick using hitTestPoint that you'll almost certainly find useful in some of your games. Have a look at the scene that you built in interactivePlayground.fla. You can make the player object move all over the stage. However, if this were a realistic scenario, the pig should not be able to move off the hill into the sky. (I could make a little comment here about "when pigs fly," but good taste got the better of me this time!) Wouldn't it be nice if you could just confine its range of movement to the area of the hill? You can, with a little help from hitTestPoint.

1. Make sure that your player object is within the area of the hill object. If its center x and y position is not on the hill, you won't be able to move it when you test the project.

2. Add the following code to the onEnterFrame event handler (note that the if/else statement from the previous example was removed to make sure that the effect of this new code is as clear as possible):

```
function onEnterFrame(event:Event):void
{
    //Move the player
    player.x += vx;
    player.y += vy;

    //Collision detection
    if (player.hitTestObject(enemy))
    {
        enemy.gotoAndStop(2);
        health.meter.width--;
```

```
    if (! collisionHasOccurred)
    {
      score++;
      messageDisplay.text=String(score);
      collisionHasOccurred=true;
    }
  }
  else
  {
    enemy.gotoAndStop(1);
    collisionHasOccurred=false;
  }

  //Check for end of game
  if (health.meter.width<1)
  {
    messageDisplay.text="Game Over!";
  }
  if (score>=5)
  {
    messageDisplay.text="You won!";
  }
  if (! hill.hitTestPoint(player.x, player.y, true))
  {
    player.x -= vx;
    player.y -= vy;
  }
}
```

3. Save the Main_Playground.as file and test the project. Try and move the player object off the hill. You can't do it, can you? As soon as its center point attempts to leave the area of the hill, its movement is blocked. Figure 7-31 shows what you'll see.

Figure 7-31. The player's movement is blocked when its center x and y point attempts to leave the hill.

The first thing that this bit of code did was to figure out if the player object is *not* on the hill:

```
if (! hill.hitTestPoint(player.x,player.y, true))
```

Notice the use of the not (!) operator. It can help you figure out whether a collision *is not occurring*, which is often just as important as knowing whether one *is occurring*.

The real magic lies in these two directives:

```
player.x -= vx;
player.y -= vy;
```

They don't look like much, so what are they doing? It's very simple. They're subtracting the x and y velocity from player object's current position. That forces the player object back to the position it was *before* the collision was detected. This effectively blocks the player object from moving.

The logic behind this is exactly the same as the logic you used to prevent the player object from moving beyond the stage boundaries. Remember that if the code detects that the player object has moved farther than the edges of the stage, it pushes the object back so it's right at the stage edge.

The previous code does exactly the same thing, with one crucial difference: you know where the boundaries of the stage are, but you don't know where the boundaries of the hill object are. However there are two important things that you *do* know:

- hitTestPoint (with a not operator) can tell you when the player is no longer touching the hill object. (This is the equivalent of figuring out whether the player has moved beyond the edge of the stage.)
- All these directives are running within the onEnterFrame event handler, which means they run each time the Flash Player "enters a new frame," 30 times per second. You know that if hitTestPoint tells you that the player is no longer touching the hill object, the player must have been touching it *in the previous frame*. This means that all you have to do is to move the player object *back to where it was in the previous frame* to prevent it from moving forward. You don't know where the player was, but (thanks to the vx and vy variables) you know exactly how fast it was moving. If you subtract the vx and vy values from the player's current x and y position, it will be back in the spot it was in before it left the hill. Neat trick, huh?

Let's make a small improvement to this example by allowing the player object to move a little farther up the hill before its movement is blocked. You'll define the bottom-center point of the player object as the point you'll use in the collision. Figure 7-32 shows where this point is.

The x position hasn't changed; only the y position has. You can define the new y coordinate with this simple calculation:

```
player.y + player.height / 2
```

Figure 7-32. Define the bottom center point of the player object.

All you need to do is update the code with this new position:

1. Add the following code in bold text to the `if` statement you just wrote:

```
if (! hill.hitTestPoint(player.x, player.y + player.height / 2, true))
{
  player.x -= vx;
  player.y -= vy;
}
```

2. Save the `Main_Playground.as` file and test the project. You'll now be able to move the `player` object up to the very top of the hill, as shown in Figure 7-33.

This is an illustration of an approach you can use for shape-based collision detection, but it will almost certainly require a bit more fine-tuning before you use it in any of your games. Each game you work on will present its own set of problems, but I outlined the starting points to solving many of them in these simple examples. (You can find the complete code for this section in the `Main_Playground_7.as` file.)

Figure 7-33. The player object is now free to move all the way to the top of the hill.

The one flaw in this technique is that it's not pixel-perfect. You don't have a way to figure out exactly where the boundary of the hill lies. You only know that it's somewhere within the range of 5 pixels that's defined by the player object's velocity. If you need greater precision, you'll have to investigate some more-advanced techniques that are just outside the scope of this book. For the adventurous among you, here are some strategies you can try.

*You can use a for loop and some **vector math** to test each point along the player's trajectory to find the edge of the shape and move the player to that spot. This technique is called **multisampling**.*

A simpler way is to use a while loop to push the player object back by one pixel until it's touching the hill. The basic code for using a while loop in the context of the present example looks like this:

```
while (! hill.hitTestPoint(player.x, player.y, true))
{
  player.y++;
}
```

This will work if the player is moving in one direction: up. You can make it work for all directions if you combine it with some of the techniques you'll be looking at toward the end of this chapter. (I'll cover for and while loops in detail in the chapters ahead. Come back to this section of the chapter when you think you are ready for the challenge.)

Creating objects that block movement

You can use the same technique of reversing an object's velocity to create an object that blocks the movement of other objects. Here's how:

1. Create a new symbol called Wall.

2. In the Wall symbol's editing window, use Flash's drawing tools to design a 50-by-50 pixel square stone block.

3. Drag an instance of the Wall symbol onto the main stage and give it the instance name wall. The stage in my interactivePlayground.fla file now looks like Figure 7-34.

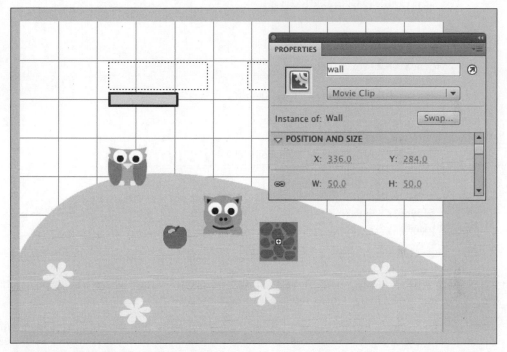

Figure 7-34. Add a wall object to the scene.

4. Add the following code in bold text to the bottom of the onEnterFrame event handler. (The complete code is in the Main_Playground_8.as file in the chapter's source files.)

```
function onEnterFrame(event:Event):void
{
  //Move the player
  player.x += vx;
  player.y += vy;

  //Collision detection
  if (player.hitTestObject(enemy))
  {
    enemy.gotoAndStop(2);
```

```
          health.meter.width--;
          if (! collisionHasOccurred)
          {
            score++;
            messageDisplay.text = String(score);
            collisionHasOccurred = true;
          }
        }
        else
        {
          enemy.gotoAndStop(1);
          collisionHasOccurred = false;
        }


        //Check for end of game
        if (health.meter.width < 1)
        {
          messageDisplay.text = "Game Over!";
        }
        if (score >= 5)
        {
          messageDisplay.text = "You won!";
        }
        if (player.hitTestObject(wall))
        {
          player.x -= vx;
          player.y -= vy;
        }
      }
```

5. Save the `Main_Playground.as` file and test the project. Try to move the player object through the wall. You can't; it blocks you in each direction.

The logic behind this is exactly the same as the logic you used to prevent the player object moving off the hill. But you might have noticed something important: it works, but it doesn't work well. The reason it doesn't work well is extremely important to understand.

Move the player object to each side of the wall object and look carefully at how close the two objects come to one another. There's probably either a small gap or a large gap. If you're really lucky, they might meet almost exactly. None of the gaps will be consistent. Figure 7-35 shows an example of how this looks in my program.

Figure 7-35. The wall pushes the player back to inconsistent positions.

Here's why it doesn't work well. Let's say that the right edge of the player object is at an x position of 97, and the left edge of the wall is at an x position of 100. You know that the player object moves 5 pixels each frame. If you press the right arrow, 5 pixels will be added to the player object's position and it will attempt to move to an x position of 102. However, it won't get that far because hitTestObject will detect a collision and push the player object back 5 pixels. That leaves the player object back where it started, with its right edge at an x position of 97 and a gap of 3 pixels between the player object and the wall.

You can see then from this example that you don't really want to push the player back 5 pixels; you want to push it back only 2 pixels, which is the depth with which it is penetrating the wall. You could easily do that, except that you never know what the depth of the penetration will be. If the player object started from an x position of 96, the depth would be 1 pixel; if it started from an x position of 99, the depth would be 4 pixels.

The problem is that you have no way of knowing by how many pixels the objects will overlap, and hitTestObject has no way of telling you that. There is actually a very precise, bulletproof way to figure it out, but to do this you need to ditch hitTestObject and say hello to axis-based collision detection.

Working with axis-based collision detection

Axis-based collision detection not only tells you whether two objects are touching but also by exactly how much they're overlapping. If you know what the overlap is, you can separate them with knife-edge precision. Axis-based collision detection works in the following way:

First, it finds out how far apart two objects are. Next, it finds out the half-widths (and half-heights) of those objects. If the combined total of half-widths (or half-heights) is more than the distance between them, the two objects must be colliding. You can work out exactly by how much the two objects are overlapping by subtracting their distance from their combined total widths or heights. Figure 7-36 illustrates how this works.

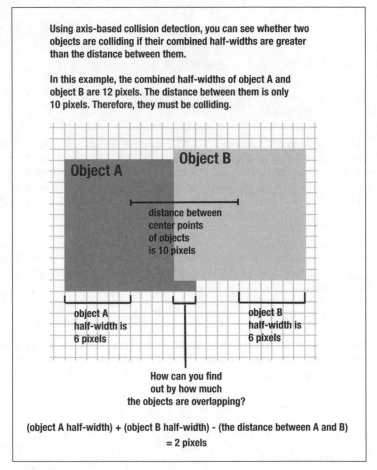

Using axis-based collision detection, you can see whether two objects are colliding if their combined half-widths are greater than the distance between them.

In this example, the combined half-widths of object A and object B are 12 pixels. The distance between them is only 10 pixels. Therefore, they must be colliding.

Object A

Object B

distance between center points of objects is 10 pixels

object A half-width is 6 pixels

object B half-width is 6 pixels

How can you find out by how much the objects are overlapping?

(object A half-width) + (object B half-width) - (the distance between A and B)
= 2 pixels

Figure 7-36. Axis-based collision detection

When you know by how much the objects are overlapping, you can then force them apart by the same amount.

Programming with the Collision class

If you understand this basic concept, all you need to do is figure out how to represent this logic in code. You'll do that in a moment, but you'll be doing it very differently to any of the other code you've added to the program so far in this book. You'll actually use this code as part of a completely separate class. The class is called Collision, and you'll find it in the chapter's source files.

Up until now, all the programming that you've done has been inside a class called Main. That's been great for learning purposes and the short programs you've been building, but as your games increase in complexity you'll find that it's vastly more efficient to break components of your games up into separate classes. How to do this will comprise much of the substance of the rest of the book, so don't panic if this seems daunting at the moment! You'll take everything in small, manageable steps.

The reason why you should put all this new axis-based collision code into a new class is because it will be so useful that you'll almost certainly want to use it in all your games from now on. Instead of having to write it over and over again each time you design a new game, if it's in its own class you can write the code once and then use the class in any game that might need it. That's one of the great things about using classes; you can easily reuse code you've written for other projects.

Using static methods

Inside the new Collision class is a method called block that blocks the player object's movement. Unlike any of the methods created in previous chapters, the block method is a special kind of method called a **static method**.

Static methods are usually designed to perform a general task that can be of use at many different times and in many different contexts in your program. Maybe you'll find that in your game you don't only want walls to block the player's movement you also want trees, locked doors, or even enemies. Instead of writing separate (and almost identical) methods to do this for each object, it's much better to write a single general method that all these objects can use if they want to. Static methods allow you to do just that.

To use a static method in your program, simply give the name of the class that the method belongs to, followed by a dot, and then the method name. Here's an example:

```
ClassName.methodName();
```

You've seen static methods before; you just weren't aware that it's what they were called. In Chapter 5, you used one of AS3.0's special built-in methods:

```
Math.random()
```

Look familiar? Yes, it's a static method! random is a method that is part of AS3.0's Math class. It does the specialized job of giving you a random number between 0 and 1, and you can use it anywhere in the program inside any other class. Static methods used like this are often called **utilities**. They do a useful little job for you in your program, and you don't need to worry about how they work as long as they provide the result you need.

You can use the block method inside the Collision class, anywhere in the program, like this:

```
Collision.block();
```

You just need to make sure that the Collision.as file is in the same folder as the class that's using it. You'll soon see how easy it is to use.

Using the method parameters

The block method is different in one other way from the methods you've written so far: it uses **parameters**, which are extra bits of information that a method uses to help it do its job. Parameters were discussed in Chapter 3, but let's review them again briefly before you continue.

Let's look at a concrete example of how to use parameters. Imagine that you want to write a method that has the task of displaying the names of fruit. Let's call the method fruitDisplay. You want to be able to give it the names of any fruit, and the method should then accept those names and display them in the output window.

The method doesn't know what the names of the fruit will be; you could send it any fruit imaginable. All it knows is that you'll be giving it two names. You could write some code that looks something like this:

```
fruitDisplay("apple", "orange");
```

The names of the fruit are provided inside the parentheses that follow the name of the method, which is known as the **argument**. You supplied the names of the fruit as strings (words surrounded by quotes), and separated them with a comma. Now it's the job of the method's function definition to do something useful with this information.

Here's what the fruitDisplay method's function definition looks like:

```
function fruitDisplay(parameterOne:String, parameterTwo:String):void
{
  trace(parameterOne, parameterTwo);
}
```

If you run this code in the program, the display in the Output panel is the following:

```
apple orange
```

You can change the method call at any time in the program to display different fruit. For example, you might decide that you're tired of apples and oranges, and write this line of code a little later in the program:

```
fruitDisplay("mango", "banana");
```

The Output panel then displays the following:

```
mango banana
```

You didn't change the method in any way; all you did was change the arguments in the method call. When the arguments are sent to the method's function definition, they're copied into the parameters, which are highlighted here:

```
function fruitDisplay(parameterOne:String, parameterTwo:String):void
{
  trace(parameterOne, parameterTwo);
}
```

The parameters are just local variables that can be used anywhere in the function definition. Because you're expecting them to accept string values, you've set their variable type as String the same way you would for any other variables.

The values of the two parameters contain whatever values are passed to them in the method call. That means that whenever the method uses the variable names parameterOne and parameterTwo, it will replace them with the values apple and orange or mango and banana—or whatever else you choose to send it.

The beauty of this system is that you can reuse the method for many different related tasks, without having to know the specific values of the variables it will be dealing with.

Here's another example. Let's create a method that adds three numbers and displays the result. Here's what it might look like:

```
function add(one:int, two:int, three:int):void
{
   trace(one + two + three);
}
```

You can then use this method with a method call that might look like this:

```
add(4,10,6);
```

It displays this in the Output panel:

```
20
```

Any three numbers you supply will give you a different result. I'm sure you can start to see how useful this can be.

You'll use the Collision.block method in the same way. In the interactive playground that you created in this chapter, you want to stop the player object from walking through the wall object. You can write the method call so that it looks like this:

```
Collision.block(player, wall);
```

It might work for this program, but what if you've got another game where you want to prevent a mouse from crossing a stream? Without changing anything in the method's function definition, you can just use this line of code:

```
Collision.block(mouse, stream);
```

The method is written in general way so that it doesn't need to know know specifically which objects it will be asked to block, just that they'll be two objects of some sort. It means you can reuse exactly the same code anywhere in any context.

Using the Collision.block method

Using the new method is simplicity in itself:

1. Open the `Main_Playground.as` file. Enter the new code in bold at the bottom of the onEnterFrame event handler. (You'll find this code in the source files as `Main_Playground_9.as`.)

```
function onEnterFrame(event:Event):void
{
  //Move the player
  player.x += vx;
  player.y += vy;

  //Collision detection
  if (player.hitTestObject(enemy))
  {
    enemy.gotoAndStop(2);
    health.meter.width--;
    if (! collisionHasOccurred)
    {
      score++;
      messageDisplay.text = String(score);
      collisionHasOccurred = true;
    }
  }
  else
  {
    enemy.gotoAndStop(1);
    collisionHasOccurred = false;
  }

  //Check for end of game
  if (health.meter.width < 1)
  {
    messageDisplay.text = "Game Over!";
  }
  if (score >= 5)
  {
    messageDisplay.text = "You won!";
  }
  //Prevent player from moving through the wall
  Collision.block(player, wall);
}
```

2. Save the `Main_Playground.as` file and test the project. Try moving the `player` object through the wall. The wall blocks its movement, and there's no gap between the objects. Figure 7-37 shows an example.

Figure 7-37. Axis-based collision detections allow for knife-edge precision.

Pushing objects

Surprise! I have one more little trick up my sleeve. Do the following:

1. Change the `Collision.block` method call in the `Main_Playground.as` file so it looks as it does here (the only difference is that the order of the object names has been reversed):

   `Collision.block(`**`wall, player`**`);`

2. Save the `Main_Playground.as` file and test the project. Move the `player` object to the wall. You can push the wall around the stage!

How is this possible? By changing the order of the arguments, the effect of the code is on the `wall` object, not the `player` object. The only difference is that because the `player` object is moving, the `wall` object has to continuously reposition itself in front of the direction the `player` object is traveling in to prevent the two objects from overlapping. (You can find this complete code in the file `Main_Playground_9.as`.)

Taking a closer look at the Collision.block method

If you are just happy that the new code works and aren't really too worried about the fine details, feel free to skip to the next chapter. The main thing is that you have a great little tool you can use in any of your games. If you now have a general idea of how axis-based collision detection works, why you might need to use it, and how to use a static method with parameters in a custom class, that's all you need to know. Like `Math.random`, it's a utility that you can use whenever you want to, and you don't need to know how it works.

But if you are a code junkie, read on! Flip back a few pages to Figure 7-36 and try to become familiar with the problem you need to solve. If you understand the problem and the logic used to solve it, all the new code does is to turn that logic into AS3.0 code. In fact, the problem you face is exactly the same as the problem you faced in Chapter 6 when you were figuring out screen boundaries. The only difference is that the calculations that you need to make to figure out how far these boundaries have been breached are a little more complex.

Let's walk the through the Collision class and have a look at what's new and how it works:

1. Double-click the Collision.as file in the Project panel to open it.
2. You'll notice quite a lot of code there that you won't understand (you'll look at most of it in later chapters). All you're interested in now is the block function definition, which is the first function definition in the class. Here's what the Collision class and the block function definition look like:

```
package
{
  import flash.display.MovieClip;
  import flash.geom.Point;

  public class Collision
  {
    public function Collision()
    {
    }
    static public function block(objectA:MovieClip,➡
      objectB:MovieClip):void
    {
      var objectA_Halfwidth:Number = objectA.width / 2;
      var objectA_Halfheight:Number = objectA.height / 2;
      var objectB_Halfwidth:Number = objectB.width / 2;
      var objectB_Halfheight:Number = objectB.height / 2;
      var dx:Number = objectB.x - objectA.x;
      var ox:Number = objectB_Halfwidth + ➡
        objectA_Halfwidth - Math.abs(dx);
      if (ox > 0)
      {
        var dy:Number = objectA.y - objectB.y;
        var oy:Number = objectB_Halfheight + ➡
          objectA_Halfheight - Math.abs(dy);
        if (oy > 0)
        {
          if (ox < oy)
          {
            if (dx < 0)
            {
              //Collision on Right
              oy = 0;
            }
          }
```

```
            else
            {
              //Collision on Left
              ox *= -1;
              oy = 0;
            }
          }
          else
          {
            if (dy < 0)
            {
              //Collision on Top
              ox = 0;
              oy *= -1;
            }
            else
            {
              //Collision on Bottom
              ox = 0;
            }
          }

          //Use the calculated x and y overlaps to
          //Move objectA out of the collision

          objectA.x += ox;
          objectA.y += oy;
        }
      }
    }
    //Other collision functions here..
  }
}
```

This is the most complex code that you've come across in the book so far, but I'll break it apart and you'll look at one little piece at a time. The first odd thing is the Collision class's constructor method:

```
public function Collision()
{
}
```

Remember that a class *has* to have a constructor method, and the constructor method name always has to be the same name as the class name. Any directives inside the constructor method run immediately when the class is instantiated.

This constructor method is completely empty, which might seem strange. But the reason is that you won't create an instance of the Collision class and you have no initialization directives that you want to run. It's perfectly fine to have a constructor method that's empty like this. In fact, you can even leave out the entire constructor method if you want to, although it's generally considered bad programming form to do so. (If you do leave it out, AS3.0 will add it automatically when it compiles the program.)

Next is the block function definition:

```
static public function block(objectA:MovieClip, objectB:MovieClip):void
```

The static keyword means that you can use this method directly in any other class, in the format Collision.block, without having to make an instance of the class first. (If that's not too clear right now, it will make a little more sense later in the book when you work more closely with instances of classes.) For now, just know that it makes it very easy to use this method anywhere in the program.

The other important things about this function definition are its parameters:

```
(objectA:MovieClip, objectB:MovieClip)
```

These are local variables that are defined with the type "MovieClip". In the Main_Playground.as file, you used this line of code to call the method:

```
Collision.block(player, wall);
```

Both player and wall are MovieClip objects, so it makes sense that objectA and objectB should be typed as MovieClip objects, too. When the method is called, a reference to the player object is copied into the objectA variable, and a reference to the wall object is copied into the objectB variable. Whenever you see objectA and objectB in the body of the method, you can replace them with player and wall in your mind if that helps you better understand how the code is working.

To allow the player to push the wall, the order of the objects in the method call is reversed like this:

```
Collision.block(wall, player);
```

The wall object was referenced by the objectA variable. The roles were reversed, and the wall object was forced to reposition itself to avoid overlapping with the moving player object, creating the pushing effect.

The first few lines of code inside the block function definition initialize the method's local variables:

```
var objectA_Halfwidth:Number = objectA.width / 2;
var objectA_Halfheight:Number = objectA.height / 2;
var objectB_Halfwidth:Number = objectB.width / 2;
var objectB_Halfheight:Number = objectB.height / 2;
var dx:Number = objectB.x - objectA.x;
var ox:Number = objectB_Halfwidth + objectA_Halfwidth - Math.abs(dx);
```

If you're this far into the book, you're pretty much an expert on half-widths and half-heights! But the last two lines deserve a good look. Let's start with this one:

```
var dx = objectB.x - objectA.x;
```

Remember that for this collision detection system to work, you need to find out two things:

- The distance between the objects
- The amount that they're overlapping

The previous line tells how far apart they are and copies that information into a variable called dx. Technically, the *d* in dx stands for *delta*, but I'll let you off the hook and allow you to think it stands for *distance*, which is a much more concrete concept to grasp. So dx is the distance between the two objects on the x axis.

To find out the distance between the two objects, all you need to do is subtract the x position of objectA from the x position of objectB. Sounds too easy to be true? Figure 7-38 explains how this works.

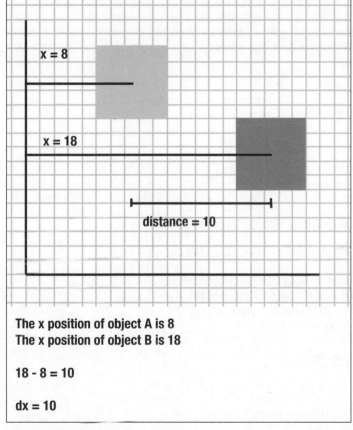

Figure 7-38. Subtract objectA's position from objectB's position to find the distance between them.

The dy variable that's used to figure out the distance between the objects on the y axis is used a little later in the code.

Now that you know the distance between the objects and their combined total half-widths, you can find out whether the objects are overlapping on the x axis with this line of code:

```
var ox:Number = objectB_Halfwidth + objectA_Halfwidth - Math.abs(dx);
```

This is the formula for figuring out whether there's any overlap. Refer to Figure 7-36 for an illustration of how this works. The variable name ox is shorthand for "overlap on the x axis."

One new thing in this directive is this:

```
Math.abs(dx)
```

Math.abs is one of AS3.0's built-in methods. (And, yes, it's a static method!) Its job is to find out what the **absolute value** of a number is. Absolute values can only be positive; negative numbers that are forced to be absolute have their sign dropped. Let's imagine that you use Math.abs in a line of code that looks like this:

```
Math.abs(-27);
```

It would return this:

```
27
```

Why is this useful for you? If objectB has a lower x position value than objectA, the value of dx will be negative. The negative value would overly complicate the code because you'd need an additional if statement to check for it. It's simpler for you just to deal with positive values.

The next bit of code is a long nested if/else statement:

```
if (ox > 0)
{
  var dy:Number = objectA.y - objectB.y;
  var oy:Number = objectB_Halfheight + ➥
    objectA_Halfheight - Math.abs(dy);
  if (oy > 0)
  {
    if (ox < oy)
    {
      if (dx < 0)
      {
        //Collision on right
        ox *= -1;
        oy = 0;
      }
```

```
        else
        {
          //Collision on left
          oy = 0;
        }
      }
      else
      {
        if (dy < 0)
        {
          //Collision on Top
          ox = 0;
          oy *= -1;
        }
        else
        {
          //Collision on Bottom
          ox = 0;
        }
      }

      //Use the calculated x and y overlaps to
      //Move objectA out of the collision

      objectA.x -= ox;
      objectA.y += oy;
    }
```

Briefly, this is what's happening:

1. The code first checks to see whether there's an overlap on the x axis.

2. If there is, it checks for an overlap on the y axis.

3. If there's an overlap on both axes, a collision must be occurring.

That's the key to how this system works.

If you know a collision is occurring, the next step is to find out *where* the collision is happening. If, for example, the player is colliding with the wall, you need to know whether the collision is happening on the top, bottom, left, or right side of the wall. If the overlap is happening on the left side of the wall, you need to *subtract* the amount of overlap from the player's x position to push it back toward the left. If the overlap is happening on the right side of the wall, you need to *add* the amount of overlap to the player's x position to push it to the right. If a collision is occurring on the top or bottom, you need to do the same kind of repositioning. All this depends on knowing the direction of the collision.

To figure this out, the code compares the dx and dy variables against zero to find out whether the overlap is happening on the top, bottom, left, or right. Figure 7-39 is a line-by-line explanation.

Figure 7-39. Axis-based collision detection

This code repositions the object with deadly accuracy and it also works for 3D objects. All you need to do is one further check on the z axis, and apply the same logic. I don't discuss 3D in this book, but if you do go on to build any 3D games in AS3.0 in future, you have all the makings of a 3D collision system right here. Axis-based collision is the keystone to understanding advanced collision detection in games.

Detecting bitmap collisions

As a final word, you should be aware of one other collision-detection system that's not discussed in the book: **bitmap collision detection**. Bitmap collision detection allows you to detect a collision between two objects based on their exact shapes.

Using it requires a relatively advanced understanding of AS3.0, which is a bit beyond the scope of this introductory book. It's also very processor-intensive, so it can really slow your games down if it's not used judiciously. And even though precise shape versus shape collision detection sounds great in theory, in practice you'll find that are actually few collision-detection scenarios that can't be adequately handled with careful application of the techniques covered in this chapter and refined in the rest of the book.

Still, there are some cases in which bitmap collision detection is essential. Imagine a game like *Worms*, in which you can use a variety of weapons to destroy irregularly shaped patches of an opponent's environment. Bounding boxes won't help you there; you need some way of changing individual pixels. Or imagine a game in which you need to navigate a spaceship through an underground lunar cave full of irregularly shaped jagged rocks. Bitmap collision detection is perfect for those kinds of situations.

When you're ready for another challenge, a web search will turn up quite a bit of information of how to do bitmap collision detection with AS3.0. Keith Peters's excellent book, *AdvancED ActionScript 3.0 Animation* (friends of ED, 2009), devotes part of a chapter to this subject.

Summary

Collision detection is quite a big subject in game design, and hopefully the introductory taste you've had of it here is enough whet your appetite for what's to come.

But before you jump ahead to the next chapter you might want to take short break to make a game. Hey, don't be scared; you can do it! And that's what this book is all about, after all. If you combine the collision-detection techniques from this chapter with the player-control techniques from the last one (along with the logical analysis you looked at in the number guessing game), you have all the tools you need to make some pretty sophisticated games.

In the next chapter, you'll combine all your new skills and learn a few fun new ones to create a game called *Dungeon Maze Adventure*. And unlike any of the previous games in this book, it will be programmed in a completely object-oriented way. What do I mean by that? Turn the page to find out!

Chapter 8

OBJECT-ORIENTED GAME DESIGN

In this book, I've described AS3.0 as an **object-oriented programming language**, which means that *objects* are at the very center of the programming universe. If that still sounds hopelessly vague, don't worry; by the end of this chapter, you'll know exactly what this means and the power it can give you as a game designer.

Up until this point in the book, all the programming has been done inside one class: Main. You set the FLA's document class in the Class field of the movie's Properties panel. This means that the Main class runs automatically when the SWF file runs. This style of programming is known as **procedural programming**. Procedural programs are composed using methods to build the program modularly. Each method does a specific job or solves a specific problem, and the program is built by all these methods working together. The number guessing game from Chapter 5 is a classic example of a procedural program.

Procedural programming is quick, convenient, and a great way to write programs and small games. In many cases, a procedural solution is a better solution to a programming problem than an object-oriented solution. The only problem is that sooner or later the complexity of your games will increase, so trying to cram them all into one class file, or even a few related ActionScript files, becomes really impractical. That's the point at which taking a look at the object-oriented way of doing things will make a lot of sense.

In Chapter 7, you looked at how to use a static method in an external class called Collision. This was helpful because you could keep the rather complex collision code from getting tangled up with the main part of the program. It made your program much easier to read, but you could still use the collision code whenever you wanted to with just one simple directive.

In this chapter, you'll go one step farther: all the important objects in the game will be programmed in their own classes. You'll also see how to use a special manager class to coordinate the behavior of these objects.

Introducing object-oriented programming

Before you get to the case study at the heart of this chapter, you'll take a quick break from programming to look at some basic object-oriented programming techniques and concepts:

- Binding classes to symbols
- Using properties and methods
- Using private properties and encapsulation
- Communicating between classes using getters and setters

There are some new concepts to grasp in the pages ahead, but you'll soon see how easy it all is to put into practice.

Binding classes to symbols

It's possible to create a symbol in the Library and then **bind** it to a class. The class is a self-contained file that contains the programming code to control all instances of that symbol.

Here's how it's done. Remember that when you create a new symbol, the Create New Symbol dialog box allows you to select Export for ActionScript as an option in the Linkage section. The Class field allows you to provide the name of the class that you want to link to that symbol. It automatically supplies the symbol name as the class name.

What this means is that whenever you use an instance of the symbol in your game, the class file that you supplied in the Class field is automatically loaded and attached to the object. Figure 8-1 shows an example. If your symbol is called Giraffe and you also used the class name Giraffe, Flash will look for a class file called Giraffe.as and attach whatever programming code it contains to any giraffe objects on the stage.

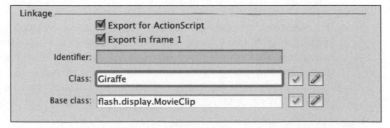

Figure 8-1. Flash looks for a file called Giraffe.as if you specify Giraffe as the class name.

To create the class, simply create a new ActionScript file with the name Giraffe.as. (Flash automatically and invisibly creates a file like this in the background if you don't create one yourself.)

Using properties and methods

Let's take a look at what this imaginary Giraffe class might look like (you'll notice a few new things in this class that you haven't yet seen before, including the keyword private; I'll discuss them shortly):

```
package
{
  import flash.display.MovieClip;

  public class Giraffe extends MovieClip
  {
     //Properties
    private var _hungry:Boolean;
    private var _favoriteActivity:String;

    public function Giraffe()
    {
      _hungry = true;
      _favoriteActivity = "eating";
    }
    //Methods
    private function eatLeaves():void
    {
       //... directives
    }
    private function wanderAimlessly():void
    {
       //... directives
    }
  }
}
```

A class is essentially a description of an object. I'm sure you can get a pretty good idea of what the life of the poor giraffe is like by looking at the preceding class! A class describes an object in two ways:

- **Properties**: The "things that it is"
- **Methods**: The "things that it does"

Properties is just another name for *variables* such as these:

```
_hungry
_favoriteActivity
```

Yes, they're just plain old variables—as simple as that! (I'll explain the underscore in front of their names in a moment.) Properties also refer to all the built-in Movie Clip properties (such as x, y, rotation, and visible) that you've been using all along.

Methods? Of course you know what methods are by now! Here are the giraffe's methods:

```
eatLeaves
wanderAimlessly
```

By using properties and methods together, you can create a **model** of an object. If you understand that, that's what 50% of what object-oriented programming is all about. The other 50% is coming up next.

Private properties and methods

In the previous code the properties and methods were declared as private:

```
private var _hungry:Boolean;
private var _favoriteActivity:String;

private function eatLeaves():void
{
  //... directives
}
private function wanderAimlessly():void
{
  //... directives
}
```

Private means that those properties and methods can be used only within the class they're defined. They can be used in the Giraffe class and nowhere else. No other class (an Elephant class, for example) can stick its nose into the giraffe's business and find out whether or not it was hungry or what its favorite activity is. Those matters are entirely private.

> *If you don't use the* private *keyword when you declare a property or method, AS3.0 assumes that they're public. Public properties can be accessed freely by any other classes. You can use the* public *keyword to make this explicit in your code if you need to.*

Why should you declare a property as private? Imagine that your house is a class, and your oven is one of the class's properties. Your oven is having trouble switching on, so you call a repairman to take a look at it. But you're really busy and can't be home when the repairman comes, so you leave the door unlocked and trust that all will be well. Best-case scenario: you come home to find that your oven works, but a vase is lying broken on the floor, an empty pizza box is on the sofa, and a bill arrives at the end of the month for all kinds of pay-per-view movies you know you never watched. Worst-case scenario: you come home to find your house a smoldering ruin and all the other houses in the neighborhood up in flames. If only you could have been there to tell the repairman (who was standing ready with his 10,000-volt charge-jumper), "It's a gas stove, not electric!"

In a very small game with only a few classes, you could probably get away with directly accessing another class's public properties and methods. In a larger game, however, you'd be opening yourself up to a potential debugging nightmare scenario. So, except for a few exceptions that you'll be looking at soon, keep all your class's properties and methods private. It might not be entirely obvious to you this early in your programming career, but (like wearing seatbelts in car) the weight of programming experience says it's a good idea. When things do go wrong, they go very, very wrong, and you'll be glad you did it.

> *Using private properties to lock down a class in this way is an aspect of object-oriented programming called* **encapsulation**. *Encapsulation means that your class is completely sealed off from tampering by other classes and is as self-contained as possible. If other classes want to access or modify any properties in an encapsulated class, they have to follow very strict rules about doing so.*

Using an underscore character to highlight private properties

Both of the `Giraffe` class's private properties begin with an underscore character:

```
_hungry
_favoriteActivity
```

This is a naming convention that is entirely optional, but one that you'll be using in this book. Preceding the names of private variables with underscore characters helps you tell at a glance which properties are private, which makes your code more readable.

> *When you start using getters and setters (more on them soon!), the underscore also helps you distinguish between the private property and publicly accessible getter and setter methods. By keeping the names exactly the same, with the exception of dropping the underscore, you can create getter and setter methods that logically share the same names as the private properties that they access or modify.*

Communicating between classes using getters and setters

Classes often need to communicate with one another. But if all their methods and properties are private, how can they do this? The trick is to create special public methods called **getters** and **setters**, which carefully negotiate communication between classes.

Using getters

Let's create a scenario in which you have a bank full of money and a bank client who wants to access that money. Let's start with an imaginary class called Bank:

```
public class Bank
{
  public var clientHasMoneyInAccount = false;
  public static var giveMoneyToClient = false;
}
```

Wow, I hope that's not my bank! Now let's create an imaginary client who wants to access as much of that many as she can:

```
public class Client
{
  public var needsToPayBills = true;
  public var hasMoney = false;

  public function Client()
  {
    Bank.giveMoneyToClient = true;
  }
}
```

The client has just robbed the bank! What? You missed it? Look again:

```
Bank.giveMoneyToClient = true;
```

Even though the client had no money in her account, and the bank was instructed not to give her any, there was nothing stopping her from taking as much as she wanted with this one simple directive. Figure 8-2 illustrates how this works.

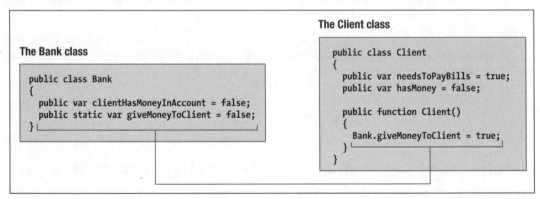

Figure 8-2. Because the bank's giveMoneyToClient variable is public, the client can change it to true on a whim, and the bank has no way of stopping it.

You want to avoid objects directly accessing the properties of other objects because you could accidentally write some code that could destroy the economy of your video game world. Even though it's a little more effort, there is a much safer way to write the code for these two objects.

Let's try again, starting with the Client class:

```
public class Client
{
  private var _needsToPayBills = true;
  private var _hasMoney = false;
  public function Client()
  {
```

```
    _hasMoney = Bank.giveMoneyToClient;
  }
}
```

The properties are now private. But this directive is the most important change:

        _hasMoney = Bank.giveMoneyToClient;

It's no longer directly changing one of the bank's properties. Instead, it's accessing a get method in the Bank class called giveMoneyToClient. It doesn't make any presumptions about whether the response from the bank will be true or false; it simply requests this information from the bank. Whatever it finds will be referenced in the client's _hasMoney property. It will be true if the client has money and false if there's no money.

This is what the new Bank class looks like, featuring the giveMoneyToClient's get method:

```
public class Bank
{
  private var _clientHasMoneyInAccount = false;

  public static function get giveMoneyToClient():Boolean
  {
    if(_clientHasMoneyInAccount)
    {
    return true;
    }
    else
    {
    return false;
    }
  }
}
```

As soon as the Client requests information from the giveMoneyToClient get method, the method first runs an if statement to check which value should be returned: true or false. (Using an if statement is optional, but this sort of checking makes using get methods particularly useful). The if statement checks whether the client has any money in her account, and returns the appropriate value.

Figure 8-3 illustrates the new improved relationship between the Bank and the Client.

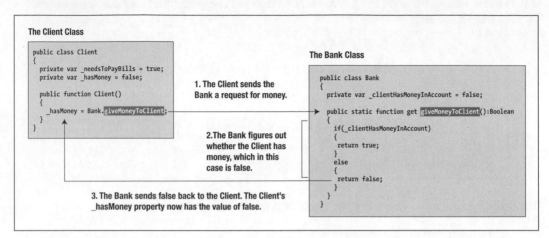

Figure 8-3. Using a getter allows the Bank to check the request and send back only the correct information.

get methods look and behave like variables, but they can be programmed with conditions attached. They look like ordinary function definitions, but include the keyword get after the keyword function. Here's a general format for using them:

```
public function get methodName():ReturnType
{
    return someValue;
}
```

They can include any code but always return a single value (they send some information back to whatever object was requesting it).

Although the other methods and properties in the class are private, get methods are always defined as public so that other classes can access them.

The keyword return is used to send the value back. This sends true back to the Client class:

```
return true;
```

This sends false back to the Client class:

```
return false;
```

In the previous example, _clientHasMoneyInAccount is false, so the get method returns false. The poor client's _hasMoney property then also gets a value of false. true and false are Boolean values, so you need to include this information as part of the function definition:

```
function get giveMoneyToClient():Boolean
```

The result of all this is bad for the client, but great for the bank, and actually reflects the reality of the situation. Using the get method prevented the client from directly changing one of the bank's properties and the bank from being robbed. It's this kind of careful programming that that will save your games from strange bugs that might be extremely difficult to trace or track down.

> As you might have guessed, get methods are affectionately known as **getters**.

Using setters

Getters have partners in crime called **setters**. Setters use the set keyword and are used by an object to receive information from another object.

Hooray! The client just a received a check in the mail for a Flash game she designed! Let's have a look at how you could use a setter to help the impoverished client put this money into the bank:

```
public class Client
{
  private var _checkValue = 100;
  public function Client()
  {
    Bank.deposit = _checkValue;
  }
}
```

Here's what the Bank class looks like, featuring a setter called deposit:

```
public class Bank
{
  private var _clientAccountValue = 0;

  public static function set deposit(money:int):void
  {
    if(money > 0)
    {
     _clientAccountValue += money;
    }
  }
}
```

In this example, the client is sending the bank's deposit setter the value of its _checkValue (which is 100). The setter first checks to make sure that it's actually being sent a value that would be appropriate to deposit. (Hey, these clients are sneaky, it has to check everything!) If it seems okay, the value is deposited into the bank's _clientAccountValue property. Like getters, setters are also defined as public.

Figure 8-4 illustrates this relationship.

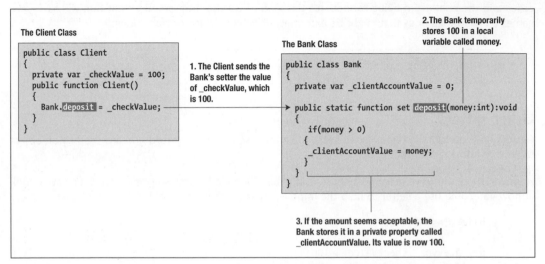

Figure 8-4. Setters allow classes to receive information from other classes and use that information to change their properties if the conditions seem fair.

The wonderful thing about using getters and setters is that objects can communicate without having to directly access or change each other's properties. This helps with encapsulation, which means that the classes are completely sealed off from one another. If they have to communicate, they do so only under strict conditions. If you use getters and setters in your own classes, as in these examples, you're far less likely to encounter bugs that come from objects not being able to make sense of information they weren't programmed to deal with.

Getting started with the object-oriented approach

All you really need to know to get started using object-oriented programming are the techniques and concepts discussed over the last few pages:

- Think of each class as a model of an object. Describe the object using properties and methods.

- Make all your properties and methods private. If ClassA tries to directly change or access the properties in ClassB, you'll begin to weave a tangled web of dependencies that could be very difficult to debug if things go wrong.

- Your classes should communicate with each other using getters and setters.

Object-oriented programming can become quite a big topic, but it doesn't have to be. Start small by using these simple techniques. In the next section, you'll look at a very practical example of these new object-oriented techniques in a game design project.

Case study: Dungeon Maze Adventure

The game you'll build is a very simple adventure game called Dungeon Maze Adventure. It's a tiny game, but don't be fooled—all the elements that go into building a complex, large-scale adventure game are contained in this example.

The best thing to do first is actually play the game, which you'll find as dungeonMaze.swf in the chapter's source files. Figure 8-5 is a map of the game and the objectives the player has to achieve to win.

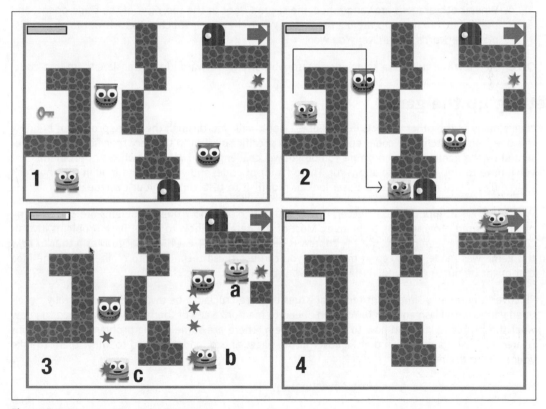

Figure 8-5. Dungeon Maze Adventure map

Here's how the game is played:

1. The player starts at the bottom-right corner of the stage and has to find its way up to the key in the top-left chamber. A dragon is stalking the corridor; if the player touches it, the blue health meter decreases. If the health meter falls to zero during the game, a screen is displayed with the words Game Over, You Lost!

2. When the player touches the key, the player can carry it to the first door. If the player tries to go through the door without the key, the player's movement is blocked. The door opens only with the key, and the player can then move to the right side of the dungeon. When the door is unlocked, a sound plays, and the key disappears.

3. The player's task is to find the star weapon, which can be picked up when it's touched. Pressing the spacebar fires stars, and if the player manages to hit the dragons with five stars each, they disappear from the stage.

4. When both dragons are vanquished, the second door at the top right of the stage opens, and the player can move to the big red arrow. When the player touches the arrow, the screen displays the words Game Over, You Won!

Once you know the rules of a game, it's a reasonably straightforward job to translate them into code.

Setting up the game

Unlike many of the other projects in this book, I won't walk you through the entire process of building this one from scratch. This code represents a very specific solution to the very specific problems presented by the game, and every game you design will challenge you with its own set of problems that you'll have to find creative solutions for. There's a lot of code, and you can find it all in the chapter's source files if you need to take a closer look or modify it to test some of your own ideas.

What is of great importance, however, is that you understand how these problems are solved using object-oriented programming techniques. Most of the details of how to solve these problems involve code that you've seen before, but the context is quite different. Treat this case study as a tour of how this game was made, but keep in mind how you can use these techniques to realize that game idea that might be buzzing around in the back of your brain.

I'll cover a number of important technical issues that are crucial to be aware of to make fully developed games with Flash and AS3.0. You don't need to memorize any of them, but you do need to know what the problems are and how to overcome them. There are some classic problems and solutions related to Flash game design that I'll cover in the pages ahead, and you need to know them to take your skills to the next level.

Here's how to make Dungeon Maze Adventure!

Gathering project files and objects

The files are contained in the chapter's source files. Follow these steps:

1. In Flash, open the file called dungeonMaze.fla.

2. Select Quick Project from the Project panel's drop-down menu. Your project panel will look like Figure 8-6.

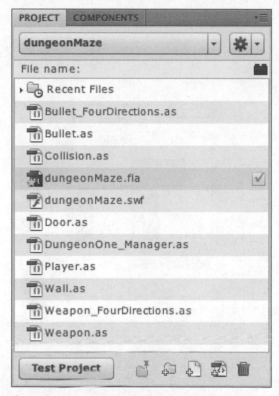

Figure 8-6. Dungeon Maze Adventure's project files

Important objects in the game have their own classes. Also included is the Collision class from the previous chapter, which will be very helpful in this game. One conspicuous absence is the Main.as file. Although you could use a document class in this project, it's not necessary. It will be interesting to see how you get by without one. I'll explain how all these files work together in detail.

Entering the dungeon!

If it's not already open, double-click the dungeonMaze.fla file in the Project panel to open it in the Flash workspace. Let's go on a quick tour of how the game has been built.

Dungeon Maze Adventure has been designed entirely within one symbol: DungeonOne. This game was planned as a multilevel game, and it's much easier to add more levels later if each level is contained within its own symbol. The first thing you see on the stage is an instance of the DungeonOne symbol, as illustrated by Figure 8-7.

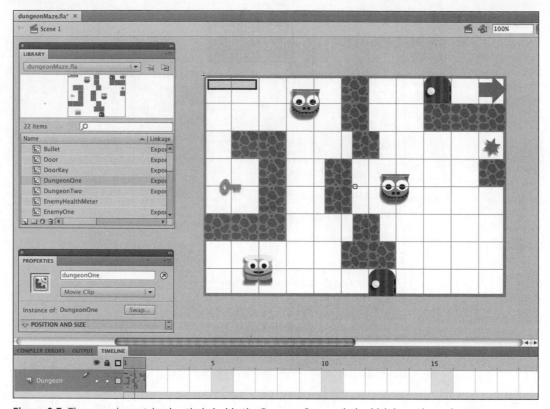

Figure 8-7. The game is contained entirely inside the DungeonOne symbol, which is on the main stage.

Double-click DungeonOne in the Library to open it. It contains all the objects in the game. Like the storybook pages from earlier chapters, the symbol's registration point is at the top-left corner of the stage. Figure 8-8 shows how DungeonOne has been laid out and the instance names of the all objects.

Let's take a quick tour of how DungeonOne has been designed.

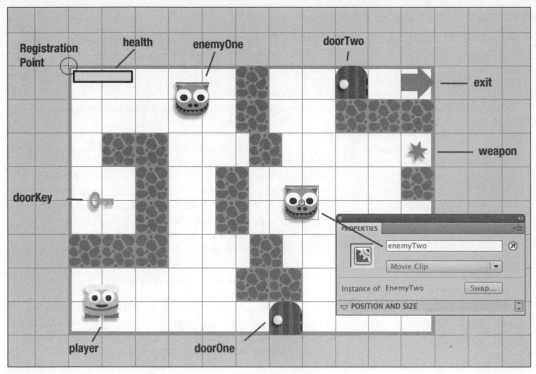

Figure 8-8. Instance names of objects inside the DungeonOne symbol

Laying out the level

The objects and level layout of Dungeon Maze Adventure are designed within a 50-by-50 pixel grid. To switch on the grid view in Flash, select View ➤ Grid ➤ Edit Grid and chose your grid size. Make sure that Show Grid and (optionally) Snap to Grid are selected. Designing levels for your games is often much easier if you work within a grid layout.

All the objects that require collision detection, such as the player, enemies, and walls are centered in the middle of their symbol editing windows. This makes calculating their half-widths and half-heights much easier.

> *It can sometimes be easier to create a game level layout if you switch on **pixel snapping**, which forces Flash's vector objects to conform to fixed pixel widths. Without pixel snapping, objects could have irregular widths and heights, such as 55.3 or 12.1. The problem with this is that when the objects are rendered in the SWF file, these fractional widths and heights will be rounded off to the nearest pixel, which means that an object might end up being wider or narrower by one pixel than you thought it was when you designed it. Switching on pixel snapping solves this problem by forcing vector objects to fixed, whole pixel sizes when you design them. You can switch on pixel snapping by selecting View ➤ Snapping ➤ Snap to Pixels.*

The objects in the game

There are lots of objects on the DungeonOne stage. Some have their own classes, but most don't need them. Table 8-1 lists the objects on the stage with their symbol name, instance name, and class file, if they have one.

Table 8-1. Objects used in the game

Object	Name and file	What it does
	Symbol name: DungeonOne **Instance name**: dungeonOne **Class file**: DungeonOne_Manager.as	The DungeonOne symbol is a container for all objects in the dungeon. It's like one of the pages of the interactive storybook from Chapters 2, 3, and 4. All other objects are inside it. DungeonOne has been planned as the first level of a multilevel game. If you want to create a game that switches levels, it makes sense to keep each level as a separate symbol. This makes it easy to use addChild and removeChild to add the next level and remove the previous one, just as you switched pages in your interactive storybook. The DungeonOne symbol is bound to the DungeonOne_ Manager class. This class contains all the game's logic, such as figuring out whether the player has achieved goals such as winning and losing.
	Symbol name: Player **Instance name**: player **Class file**: Player.as	The Player class uses the keyboard control system from the previous chapters to move the hero around the dungeon. It also keeps track of whether the key has been picked up.
	Symbol name: Wall **Instance name**: Assigned dynamically **Class file**: Wall.as	There are many instances of the Wall symbol in the game. The game never needs to make a specific reference to any of them, so they don't need instance names. They are all bound to the same Wall class. The Wall class blocks the movement of the player character.
	Symbol name: Door **Instance name**: doorOne, doorTwo **Class file**: Door.as	There are two instances of the Door symbol on the stage. The Door class keeps track of whether the doors are open or closed.

Object	Name and file	What it does
	Symbol name: DoorKey **Instance name:** doorKey **Class file:** None	The doorKey object can be picked up by the player to unlock the first door.
	Symbol name: EnemyOne **Instance name:** enemyOne **Class file:** None	The EnemyOne symbol contains a subobject called meter that keeps track of the enemy's health (it is the red bar between the enemy's horns). When the enemy is hit by a bullet five times, its meter drops to zero and it's removed from the stage. The enemy uses motion tween animation to move around the stage.
	Symbol name: EnemyTwo **Instance name:** enemyTwo **Class file:** None	The same as EnemyOne, except that it follows a different motion path.
	Symbol name: Weapon **Instance name:** weapon **Class file:** Weapon.as	When the player touches the weapon, the weapon becomes "armed." The Weapon class then allows the player to fire bullets by pressing the spacebar
	Symbol name: Bullet **Instance name:** bullet **Class file:** Bullet.as	When bullets are created by the weapon, they move up the stage. The Bullet class checks for collisions with enemy objects and reduces their health meters by 10 pixels each time they hit.
	Symbol name: Exit **Instance name:** exit **Class file:** none	When the player touches this object, the GameOver screen is displayed and tells the player that the game has been won.

Continued

Table 8-1. Continued

Object	Name and file	What it does
	Symbol name: Meter **Instance name**: meter **Class file**: None	This is the player's health meter. It's reduced by one each time the player touches one of the enemies. When it falls below one, the GameOver screen is displayed and tells the player that the game has been lost.
Game Over You Won!	**Symbol name**: GameOver **Instance name**: gameOverWon, gameOverLost **Class file**: None	The GameOver symbol is a 550-by-400 white rectangle with a dynamic text field called messageDisplay. It's displayed at the end of the game and tells the player whether the game has been won or lost.
	Symbol name: DungeonTwo **Instance name**: Created dynamically **Class file**: None	The Library also contains a symbol called DungeonTwo. It exists to show you how you can add a new level to the game if you continue building it. Later in the chapter I'll show you how to do this.

Animating with the timeline

Before you start looking at the code for this game, you'll learn how the enemy objects were made. The enemy objects are animated using the timeline. Flash was originally designed as animation software, and there's no reason why you shouldn't use some of its excellent built-in tools to easily add animation to the game. Although it's often preferable to animate game objects using pure AS3.0 code, you'll find that doing the animation manually is often a more straightforward approach.

In this next section, I'll give you step-by-step directions for creating these enemies. If you want to create animated objects for your own games, you can use these instructions as a general model.

Creating the enemies

Before you can start animating, you need to make sure that the enemy objects are set up properly. The first thing you need to understand is that the animation is happening *in the timeline of the enemy objects themselves*. The objects are not being animated on the DungeonOne timeline.

For this to work properly, the EnemyOne and EnemyTwo symbols need to be containers for two other symbols: EnemyOne_SubObject and EnemyTwo_SubObject. These two subobjects will contain the actual graphic design of your enemies and will be animated inside the EnemyOne and EnemyTwo Movie Clip symbols. When that's done, you can drag instances of EnemyOne and EnemyTwo into DungeonOne, along with the rest of your objects.

Here are the steps for creating the enemyOne object (the steps for creating enemyTwo are exactly the same except for the names):

1. Create a new Movie Clip symbol called EnemyOne_SubObject. Design the enemy any way you like.

2. Design a health meter inside EnemyOne_SubObject. A long rectangle without a border works just fine. Convert it to a Movie Clip symbol and give it the instance name meter.

3. Create a new Movie Clip symbol called EnemyOne. Drag an instance of EnemyOne_SubObject into it and give it the instance name subObject. This is the symbol in which you'll be doing the animation. Make sure that it has only one layer.

4. Drag an instance of EnemyOne into the DungeonOne symbol.

Figure 8-9 illustrates these steps.

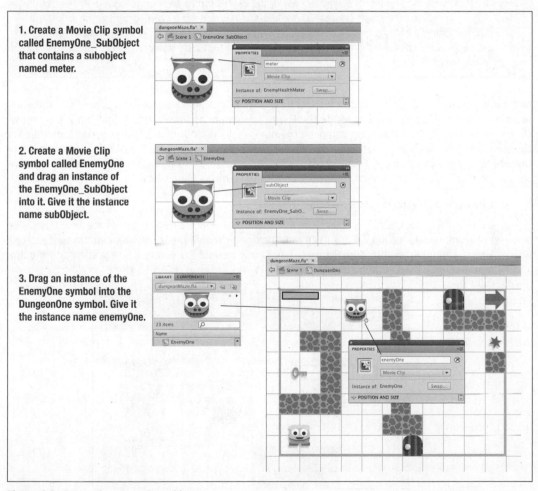

Figure 8-9. Create the enemyOne object.

You can follow exactly the same steps to create enemyTwo; just change the names accordingly.

Animating the object

You'll animate the subObject object inside the EnemyOne symbol. The animation technique you'll use is called **motion tweening**. It works by specifying the frame where the motion starts and then an ending frame where the motion stops. Flash calculates the position of the object for all the frames in between. That's where the *tween* comes from: *between*.

> *If you've used previous versions of Flash, you'll be happy to know that Adobe has completely rede-signed motion tweening for Flash CS4. Surprisingly for an animation tool, Flash always had a very weak animation system: it was finicky and unintuitive, and the fact that every tween had to be between different instances of an object often meant that any associated ActionScript code went haywire if the instance names changed in the middle of a complex tweening sequence. Thankfully, Adobe has remodeled the Flash version 10 animation system on the great-grandfather of all mul-timedia authoring software: Director. Although predating Flash by eight years, it's much superior animation system was based on motion paths, and they have now been incorporated into and supercharged in Flash 10.*

Motion tweening is really easy to do, but you have a small problem you need to solve first. You want to animate the subObject instance inside the EnemyOne symbol. However, this animation will be show-cased in the DungeonOne symbol, so you need to know what the floor plan of DungeonOne looks like for the animation to look appropriate. You don't want to accidentally animate the object through walls or outside the edges of the stage. Fortunately, Flash gives you a way to open a symbol's editing window so that you can still see its context if it's part of another symbol. Here's how:

1. Open the DungeonOne symbol editing window.

2. Double-click the enemyOne object on the stage that you created in the preceding steps. The EnemyOne symbol editing window will open, yet you can still see DungeonOne in the background, which is dimmed slightly (see Figure 8-10). This is perfect for you because you can do the ani-mation inside the EnemyOne symbol with the layout of DungeonOne to guide you.

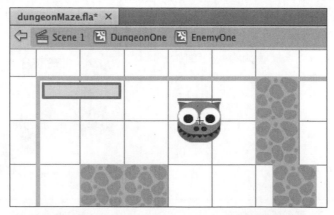

Figure 8-10. Double-click the enemyOne instance to open EnemyOne's symbol editing window with DungeonOne still visible in the background.

Now you're ready to animate:

1. In the EnemyOne symbol, select layer 1 in the timeline. (If the timeline is not visible, select Window ➤ Timeline.)

2. Select Insert ➤ Motion Tween. You'll notice that the frames extend to frame 30 and are colored blue, seen as gray in Figure 8-11.

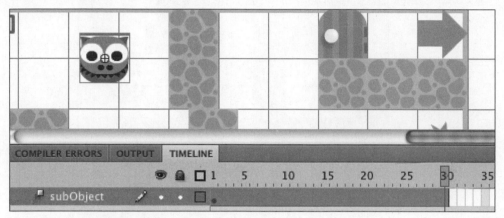

Figure 8-11. Insert a motion tween.

3. Drag the blue bar that represents the motion tween to frame 180.

4. Select frame 90.

5. Move the subObject object to a new position on the stage. You'll notice two things:

   ■ A tiny diamond-shaped dot appears in the timeline. This is called a **property keyframe**. Property keyframes are a special type of keyframe that indicates that the x and y (or even z) position of an object in an animation has changed. Unlike ordinary keyframes, they don't create new instances of the object. You can add property keyframes simply by highlighting the frame you want your object to move to and dragging it there with the mouse.

   ■ A **motion path** appears on the stage, which shows the path that the object has taken. You can actually select this path to bring up the motion path Properties panel, which allows you to apply some extra options such as rotation or **easing**. (Easing refers to how gently the object "eases into" its movement. Play around with it—it's fun!) You can also change the shape of the motion path so the object takes a curved route to its destination. You can select a motion path to delete it as well, and when you do so, its associated property keyframe also disappears.

Figure 8-12 shows what the enemyOne property keyframe and motion path look like.

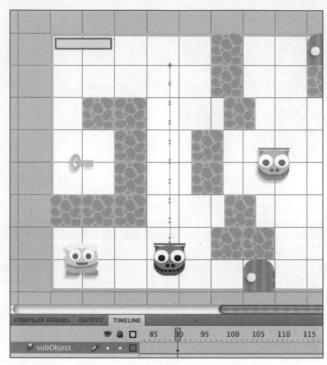

Figure 8-12. The property keyframe and motion path

6. The last step is to highlight frame 180 and move the subObject object back to its start position. (If you centered the object precisely when you added it to EnemyOne, its original x and y positions are 0 and 0.)

There you have it. The object moves back and forth along the motion path when the game runs.

EnemyTwo

The EnemyTwo subObject is animated in a very similar way. Open EnemyTwo_SubObject in the Library and take a look. Its motion path is circular, and its start point and endpoint are at the same spot.

It uses four property keyframes (at frames 60, 120, 180, and 240) to create four connected motion paths. Each motion path has been curved using the Selection Tool so that the object moves in an organic and unpredictable way. Figure 8-13 shows the path that the EnemyTwo subObject takes. To make sure that the animation loops smoothly, the x and y positions of the object on frame 240 are the same as on frame 1.

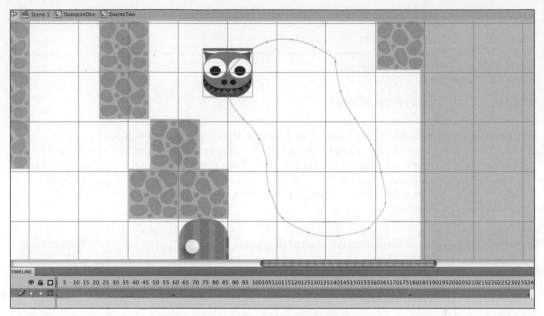

Figure 8-13. The EnemyTwo's subobject follows four connected motion paths.

For fine control over how objects are animated, you can use the Flash Motion Editor. To open the Motion Editor, highlight any layer that uses a motion tween and then select Window ➤ Motion Editor. Many more details of how the object behaves when it moves across the motion path can be controlled from this window.

One of the great things about working with Flash as a game-design platform is how accessible and fun it is to animate objects. I won't discuss Flash's timeline animation capabilities in much more detail than I've done here, so if you're new to Flash, you might want to take a short break from this chapter and do a little more experimenting on your own. Animation is quite a big topic, deserving of a whole book in its own right, but the best way to learn is to dive right in and start playing.

Controlling timeline animations with code

In Chapter 9 and Chapter 10, you'll be looking at techniques for animating objects using pure AS3.0 programming code. However, AS3.0 has quite a few built-in methods and properties that you can use to control objects that are animated on a timeline. With a bit of ingenuity, you can build a quite complex game just using timeline animation and a few of these methods and properties. Table 8-2 describes how to use these methods and properties.

Table 8-2. Methods and properties of Movie Clips animated on the timeline

Method	What it does
play()	Starts the animation.
stop()	Stops the animation.
gotoAndPlay()	Tells the object to move to a specific frame and then play from that point forward. For example, gotoAndPlay (23); moves the timeline's playhead to frame number 23 and starts playing from there. If you use frame labels in your animation, you can insert the frame label name. For example, gotoAndPlay ("nextSection"); starts the animation playing from a frame labeled nextSection.
gotoAndStop()	Stops the animation at a specific frame. gotoAndStop(23) stop the animation at frame 23.

Property	What it does
currentFrame	Tells you the number of the frame where your animated object is.
totalFrames	Gives you a number that is the total number of frames of your animation.

To use these methods and properties with an animated object, you need to know where the object is in its hierarchy of objects and subobjects. Let's say you want to control one of the enemy objects directly inside DungeonOne. You can just add a line of code like this, and the enemy's animation will stop:

```
enemyOne.stop();
```

If in this game you were using a document class (such as the Main.as class you used in previous chapters) and want to access enemyOne inside dungeonOne, you might use code that looks like this:

```
dungeonOne.enemyOne.gotoAndPlay(50);
```

If you want to make an object's animation play and are programming directly inside that object's class, you can use code that looks like this:

```
play();
```

Timeline animation is often the best way to make your game objects move. Lucky for you, Flash happens to be great at doing animation. Have fun with this!

Adding and removing objects from the stage

Before you look at the code of the game, I need to explain the new way in which classes are being initialized. Dungeon Maze Adventure has been planned as a multilevel game. If you want to add another level, it means that you have to remove dungeonOne from the stage and add dungeonTwo. This gets you into a tricky technical situation regarding how AS3.0 initializes objects in the Flash Player when the game runs. It's an extremely important issue to be aware of because it will plague the development of your Flash games and give you countless sleepless nights if you don't understand why it happens and how to solve it.

Let's take a look a look at this problem. When the published SWF of the game runs, it does two things (in this order):

1. It initializes all the objects by running the constructor methods in their classes.

2. It displays the objects on the stage. (It displays them one by one in the order in which they were dragged to the stage from the Library when you designed the game in the FLA.)

Here's the issue: if the class's constructor method includes a reference to the stage or an object that is on the stage that hasn't yet been displayed, you'll get an error message saying this:

```
Error #1009: Cannot access a property or method
of a null object reference
```

If you're adding objects to the game, there's a good chance that many of those objects have to access the stage as soon as they're created. They might need to do this to set stage boundaries or access the properties of other objects that are also on the stage. If they can't find the stage object because they haven't been added to the stage yet, AS3.0's compiler will "throw its hands in the air" and you'll see the preceding error message.

To solve this problem, you need to initialize objects only when they they've been added to the stage, not before.

ADDED_TO_STAGE event

In earlier chapters, you initialized the classes like this:

```
public class Main extends MovieClip
{
  public function Main()
  {
    init();
  }
  function init():void
  {
    //Initialize class...
  }
}
```

This doesn't ensure that the object is on the stage before it's initialized. To do that, you need to use an event called ADDED_TO_STAGE. You can put an ADDED_TO_STAGE event listener in the constructor method. When the object is actually added to the stage, the event handler is triggered and you can use it to initialize the class.

Here's a format you can use:

```
public class GameObject extends MovieClip
{
  public function GameObject()
  {
    addEventListener(Event.ADDED_TO_STAGE, onAddedToStage);
  }
  private function onAddedToStage(event:Event):void
  {
    //Initialize properties
  }
}
```

In this example, the onAddedToStage event handler does the same job as the init method you used in previous chapters. The only difference is that the directives it contains are run only when the object is displayed on the stage.

If you need to be absolutely certain that all the objects are on the stage before you initialize a class, consider using the FRAME_CONSTRUCTED event, which runs only after all the objects have been displayed on the stage. Similar to ENTER_FRAME, it's triggered in every frame.

If you want to use it to initialize a class, you'll probably only want to run once. You can do this by removing the event after the first time it runs. You can use this format:

```
public class GameObject extends MovieClip
{
  public function GameObject()
  {
    addEventListener(Event.FRAME_CONSTRUCTED, onFrameConstructed);
  }
  private function onFrameConstructed(event:Event):void
  {
    //Initialize properties
    removeEventListener(Event.FRAME_CONSTRUCTED, onFrameConstructed);
  }
}
```

If your class needs to access an object on the stage as part of its initialization, FRAME_CONSTRUCTED guarantees that it can to find it. (If you want FRAME_CONSTRUCTED to run every frame, you can leave out the removeEventListener directive from the preceding example.)

REMOVED_FROM_STAGE event

The ADDED_TO_STAGE event has a companion event called REMOVED_FROM_STAGE. The REMOVED_FROM_STAGE event fires when an object is "removed from the stage." This is very useful in a game because objects (like enemies who are hit by bullets) are frequently removed. It allows the object to perform some final tasks, such as updating a score or spawning a new object just before they flicker out of existence.

Also, very importantly, the REMOVED_FROM_STAGE event allows you to remove any event listeners that might be attached to the object. This is particularly important for ENTER_FRAME events. One of AS3.0's little quirks is that even after objects are taken off the stage using removeChild, their ENTER_FRAME events will still run silently in the background. If an ENTER_FRAME event is running and trying to reference objects that no longer exist, it will generate a torrent of error messages in Flash's Compile Errors pane. To prevent this, you can use the REMOVED_FROM_STAGE event to remove the object's onEnterFrame event listener when the object itself is removed.

> *Although manually removing* ENTER_FRAME *events is required, removing other event listeners manually is optional. Flash still deletes objects even if they have listeners on in most cases. However, just to make sure, it's considered best practice to manually remove them so you know with absolute certainty that that there won't be any lingering code running in the background after the object is gone.*

In Dungeon Maze Adventure, I used ADDED_TO_STAGE and REMOVED_FROM_STAGE with all the classes. Using them together is a bulletproof way to make sure that objects initialize properly and don't leave lingering code running in the background when they're removed. Here's the format that all the classes in Dungeon Maze Adventure use:

```
package
{
  import flash.display.MovieClip;
  import flash.events.Event;

  public class GameObject extends MovieClip
  {
    public function GameObject()
    {
      addEventListener(Event.ADDED_TO_STAGE, onAddedToStage);
    }
    private function onAddedToStage(event:Event):void
    {
      //Initialize properties
      //Add event listeners
      addEventListener(Event.ENTER_FRAME, onEnterFrame);
      addEventListener(Event.REMOVED_FROM_STAGE, onRemovedFromStage);
    }
    private function onRemovedFromStage(event:Event):void
    {
      removeEventListener(Event.ENTER_FRAME, onEnterFrame);
      removeEventListener(Event.ADDED_TO_STAGE, onAddedToStage);
      removeEventListener(Event.REMOVED_FROM_STAGE, ➡
        onRemovedFromStage);
```

349

```
    }
    private function onEnterFrame(event:Event):void
    {
      //Directives...
    }
  }
}
```

All the classes follow this same basic structure. Figure 8-14 explains how all these pieces fit together.

```
                                      package
                                      {
                                        import flash.display.MovieClip;
                                        import flash.events.Event;

                                      public class GameObject extends MovieClip
                                      {
When the object's constructor            public function GameObject()
method runs, a listener waits for        {
the object to be added to the stage.       addEventListener(Event.ADDED_TO_STAGE, onAddedToStage);
                                         }
                                         private function onAddedToStage(event:Event):void
                                         {
When the object has been added             //Initialize properties
to the stage, its properties can be        //Add event listeners
initialized and other listeners            addEventListener(Event.ENTER_FRAME, onEnterFrame);
can be added.                              addEventListener(Event.REMOVED_FROM_STAGE, onRemovedFromStage);
                                         }
                                         private function onRemovedFromStage(event:Event):void
                                         {
When the object is removed from the        removeEventListener(Event.ENTER_FRAME, onEnterFrame);
stage, its listeners are also removed.     removeEventListener(Event.ADDED_TO_STAGE, onAddedToStage);
ENTER_FRAME events should always           removeEventListener(Event.REMOVED_FROM_STAGE, onRemovedFromStage);
be removed so that they don't continue   }
to run in the background. Other event   private function onEnterFrame(event:Event):void
listeners also need to be removed         {
so that the object can be completely        //Directives…
cleared from the Flash player's memory.   }
Any other tasks that you want the object  }
to perform when it's removed can also   }
be included here.
```

Figure 8-14. Using the ADDED_TO_STAGE and REMOVED_FROM_STAGE event listeners

Optionally, to make sure that an object isn't reinitialized if it's accidentally added to the stage again, remove the ADDED_TO_STAGE *event listener in the* onAddedToStage *event handler itself:*

```
private function onAddedToStage(event:Event):void
{
  addEventListener(Event.ENTER_FRAME, onEnterFrame);
  addEventListener(Event.REMOVED_FROM_STAGE, onRemovedFromStage);
  removeEventListener(Event.ADDED_TO_STAGE, onAddedToStage);
}
```

I know what you're thinking: it looks like a big mess of code! Unfortunately, it's an essential little technical hoop you need to jump through to safely add and remove objects from your game. If you break it down piece by piece, you'll see that it's not so bad. You can pretty much just copy/paste this code to use with all your classes.

How Dungeon Maze Adventure works

The logic of the game is programmed in the DungeonOne_Manager class. In large-scale games, you'll find that it's usually useful to have one or more classes exclusively handle game logic. Game events such as collision, picking up items, and winning and losing are all handled best if they're kept in a single "manager" class. If all the game's logic is in one place, it makes it easy for you to change and update the code because you don't have to hunt through all your classes to find out where, for example, you added the code that changes the player's health meter. In earlier projects in this book, this was handled by the Main class. DungeonOne_Manager is now taking over that role,

The DungeonOne_Manager class is bound to the DungeonOne symbol. That means that whenever an instance of DungeonOne is on the stage, the DungeonOne_Manager class also runs. Binding the class to the symbol was done in the DungeonOne Properties by assigning DungeonOne_Manager in the Class field. You can open the DungeonOne Properties to see this yourself by the selecting the DungeonOne symbol in the Library and clicking the small Properties button on the Library's bottom menu bar. (The Properties button looks like an *i* enclosed in a circle.) Figure 8-15 shows what you will see.

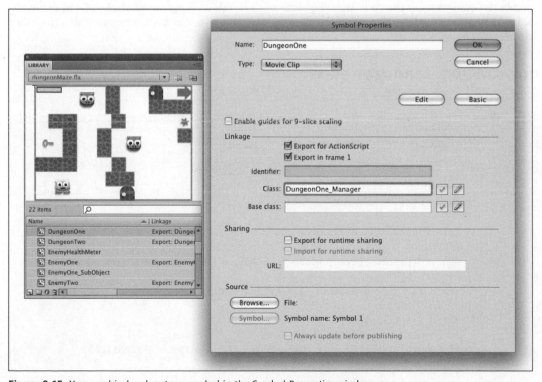

Figure 8-15. You can bind a class to a symbol in the Symbol Properties window.

There are other specialized classes that are working simultaneously with DungeonOne_Manager:

- Player: Contains the player's keyboard control system. It also keeps track of whether the key has been picked up.
- Wall: Sends references of all the wall instances to the DungeonOne_Manager class to help with collision detection between the walls and the player.
- Door: Keeps track of whether the doors are open or closed. It also plays a sound when the door is opened.
- Weapon: Lets the player fire bullets. It creates new instances of the Bullet class and adds them to the stage.
- Bullet: Controls the bullets' movement.

As long as all the classes are in the same project folder, they can communicate with each other.

Let's take a look at the DungeonOne_Manager class. It's a very long class, but don't let that scare you. Most of the game logic is in the onEnterFrame event handler, and I numbered and highlighted each important section with code comments. You'll see that you can break each of the major occurrences in the game down into very manageable and almost mundane if/else statements.

A good way to read the code is while you're playing the game. When you complete a specific task in the game, such as picking up the key, see if you can figure out how code actually makes it work. I used numbered comments in the code to walk you through it. You'll recognize most of this code immediately from other chapters. I'll explain the all-new code, and how this code integrates with the other classes, in the pages ahead.

DungeonOne_Manager class

```
package
{
  import flash.display.MovieClip;
  import flash.events.Event;

  public class DungeonOne_Manager extends MovieClip
  {
    public function DungeonOne_Manager()
    {
      //Initialize the class when the
      //dungeon objects is displayed on the stage.
      addEventListener(Event.ADDED_TO_STAGE, onAddedToStage);
    }
    private function onAddedToStage(event:Event):void
    {
      //Add event listeners
      addEventListener(Event.ENTER_FRAME, onEnterFrame);
      addEventListener(Event.REMOVED_FROM_STAGE, onRemovedFromStage);
```

```
}
private function onRemovedFromStage(event:Event):void
{
  //Remove the onEnterFrame event if
  //this object is removed from the stage
  removeEventListener(Event.ENTER_FRAME, onEnterFrame);
  removeEventListener(Event.ADDED_TO_STAGE, onAddedToStage);
  removeEventListener(Event.REMOVED_FROM_STAGE,➡
    onRemovedFromStage);
}

//Most of game logic is programmed into the
//onEnterFrame event handler
private function onEnterFrame(event:Event):void
{
  //1. If the player is touching the key and
  //doesn't have it, pick it up
  if (player.hitTestObject(doorKey))
  {
    player.hasKey = true;
    player.addChild(doorKey);
    doorKey.x = 0;
    doorKey.y = 0;
    doorKey.rotation = 300;
  }

  //2. If the player is touching the door and has the
  //key, and the door is closed, then open the door.
  //Otherwise, the door must block the player
  if (player.hitTestObject(doorOne))
  {
    if (player.hasKey)
    {
      if(! doorOne.isOpen)
      {
        doorOne.isOpen = true;
        doorKey.visible = false;
      }
    }
    else
    {
      Collision.block(player, doorOne);
    }
  }
```

```
//3. If the enemies still exist on the stage,
//check if the player is touching the
//enemies and reduce the player's health meter
if(enemyOne != null)
{
  if (player.hitTestObject(enemyOne))
  {
    health.meter.width--;
  }
}
if(enemyTwo != null)
{
  if (player.hitTestObject(enemyTwo))
  {
    health.meter.width--;
  }
}

//4. If the player's health meter is less than
//one pixel wide, the player has lost.
//Display the Game Over screen.
//("GameOver" is a symbol in the Libary).
if (health.meter.width < 1)
{
  var gameOverLost:GameOver = new GameOver();
  gameOverLost.messageDisplay.text = "Game Over"➥
    + "\n" + "You Lost!";
  parent.addChild(gameOverLost);
  parent.removeChild(this);
}

//5. If the player is touching the weapon, arm the
//weapon and allow the player to carry it
if (player.hitTestObject(weapon))
{
  weapon.isArmed = true;
  weapon.x = player.x - (player.width/2);
  weapon.y = player.y;
}

//6. If both enemies are dead, open the second door,
//otherwise, the door should block the player
if ((enemyOne == null) && (enemyTwo == null))
{
  if(! doorTwo.isOpen)
  {
    doorTwo.isOpen = true;
  }
}
```

```
  else
  {
    Collision.block(player, doorTwo);
  }


  //7. If the player reaches the exit, the game has been won
  //Display the Game Over screen
  if(player.hitTestPoint(exit.x, exit.y, true))
  {
    var gameOverWon:GameOver = new GameOver();
    gameOverWon.messageDisplay.text = "Game Over"➥
      + "\n" + "You Won!";
    parent.addChild(gameOverWon);
    parent.removeChild(this);
  }
}


//8. Pulic methods that other classes can use to
//check for collisions with objects in the game

//A. Allow the wall objects to check for a collison
//with the player
public function checkCollisionWithPlayer(wall:MovieClip)
{
  if (player != null)
  {
    Collision.block(player, wall);
  }
}
//B. Allow bullet objects to check for
//collisions with the enemies
public function checkCollisionWithEnemies(bullet:MovieClip)
{
  //Enemy One
  if (enemyOne != null)
  {
    if (enemyOne.hitTestPoint(bullet.x, bullet.y,true))
    {
      enemyOne.subObject.meter.width -= 10;
      if (enemyOne.subObject.meter.width < 1)
      {
        enemyOne.subObject.stop();
        removeChild(enemyOne);
        enemyOne = null;
      }
      removeChild(bullet);
      bullet = null;
    }
  }
```

```
                   //Enemy Two
                   if (enemyTwo != null)
                   {
                     if (enemyTwo.hitTestPoint(bullet.x, bullet.y,true))
                     {
                       enemyTwo.subObject.meter.width -= 10;
                       if (enemyTwo.subObject.meter.width < 1)
                       {
                         enemyTwo.subObject.stop();
                         removeChild(enemyTwo);
                         enemyTwo = null;
                       }
                       removeChild(bullet);
                       bullet = null;
                     }
                   }
                 }
               }
             }
           }
```

Let's take a walk through the events of the game, starting with how to make the player object move.

Moving the player

Control of the player object is delegated to the Player class. It's almost identical to code that you looked at in Chapters 6 and 7, except for one important detail. In the previous versions of this code, the player properties were referred to like this:

```
player.x
player.y
```

In this code, it's referred to just like this:

```
x
y
```

All the code in this class is bound directly to the Player symbol in the Library. That means that it's running *inside* the player object itself. Because of that, x and y refer directly to the player object. This is also the same for all the other properties in the Player class, such as _vx and _vy.

You can also use the keyword this to make it clear. The properties in the Player class can also be written like so, making it obvious that you're talking about *this object*:

```
this.x
this.y
this._vx
this._vy
```

Whenever you see the keyword this, remind yourself that it refers to the object the class is bound to: *this object*.

Have a quick look back at the DungeonOne_Manager class and you'll notice that you still use player.x and player.y in this game. That's because the player object is inside the DungeonOne symbol, which the DungeonOne_Manager class is bound to. Figure 8-16 illustrates this.

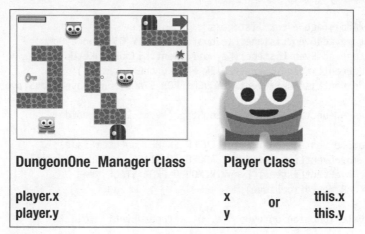

Figure 8-16. The Player class is written from a first-person perspective, so it doesn't need the qualifier "player" to refer to its own properties. The dungeon needs to know which of the many objects it contains you're refering to, so you need to add the object name in front of the property you're targeting.

The other difference is that all properties and methods of the Player class are now private. Here's the player class in its entirety:

```
package
{
    import flash.display.MovieClip;
    import flash.events.KeyboardEvent;
    import flash.ui.Keyboard;
    import flash.events.Event;

    public class Player extends MovieClip
    {
        private var _vx:int;
        private var _vy:int;
        private var _playerHalfWidth:uint;
        private var _playerHalfHeight:uint;
        private var _hasKey:Boolean;

        public function Player()
        {
            addEventListener(Event.ADDED_TO_STAGE, onAddedToStage);
        }
        private function onAddedToStage(event:Event):void
        {
            _vx = 0;
```

```
      _vy = 0;
      _playerHalfWidth = width / 2;
      _playerHalfHeight = height / 2;
      _hasKey = false;

      //Add stage event listeners
      stage.addEventListener(KeyboardEvent.KEY_DOWN,onKeyDown);
      stage.addEventListener(KeyboardEvent.KEY_UP,onKeyUp);
      addEventListener(Event.ENTER_FRAME, onEnterFrame);
      addEventListener(Event.REMOVED_FROM_STAGE, onRemovedFromStage);
}
private function onRemovedFromStage(event:Event):void
{
   removeEventListener(Event.ENTER_FRAME, onEnterFrame);
   removeEventListener(Event.ADDED_TO_STAGE, onAddedToStage);
   removeEventListener(Event.REMOVED_FROM_STAGE, ➡
      onRemovedFromStage);
}
private function onKeyDown(event:KeyboardEvent):void
{
   if (event.keyCode == Keyboard.LEFT)
   {
      _vx = -5;
   }
   else if (event.keyCode == Keyboard.RIGHT)
   {
      _vx = 5;
   }
   else if (event.keyCode == Keyboard.UP)
   {
      _vy = -5;
   }
   else if (event.keyCode == Keyboard.DOWN)
   {
      _vy = 5;
   }
}
private function onKeyUp(event:KeyboardEvent):void
{
   if (event.keyCode == Keyboard.LEFT ||➡
      event.keyCode == Keyboard.RIGHT)
   {
      _vx = 0;
   }
```

```
            else if (event.keyCode == Keyboard.DOWN ||➡
              event.keyCode == Keyboard.UP)
            {
              _vy = 0;
            }
        }
        public function onEnterFrame(event:Event):void
        {
          //Move the player
          x += _vx;
          y += _vy;

          //Stop player at the stage edges
          if (x + _playerHalfWidth > stage.stageWidth)
          {
            x = stage.stageWidth - _playerHalfWidth;
          }
          else if (x - _playerHalfWidth < 0)
          {
            x = 0 + _playerHalfWidth;
          }
          if (y - _playerHalfHeight < 0)
          {
            y = 0 + _playerHalfHeight;
          }
          else if (y + _playerHalfHeight > stage.stageHeight)
          {
            y = stage.stageHeight - _playerHalfHeight;
          }
        }

        //Getters and setters used for keeping
        //track of whether the player has the key

        public function get hasKey():Boolean
        {
          return _hasKey;
        }
        public function set hasKey(keyState:Boolean)
        {
          _hasKey = keyState;
        }
      }
    }
```

This class also has a getter and setter used for keeping track of whether the key has been picked up. You'll look at how it works next.

Picking up the key

You'll see how simple the code of the game really is when you break it up piece by piece. The player's first task is to pick up the key. The DungeonOne_Manager class uses hitTestObject to check for this:

```
if (player.hitTestObject(doorKey))
{
  player.hasKey = true;
  player.addChild(doorKey);
  doorKey.x = 0;
  doorKey.y = 0;
  doorKey.rotation = 300;
}
```

If the player object touches the key, the key becomes a *child object* of the player by using addChild, which allows the player to carry it around.

To center the doorKey object over the player, you have to set its x and y positions to 0. Because it's now a child of the player, 0 refers to position 0 on the player object, not the stage. The Player symbol's center x and y point is 0. The key's rotation is set to 300, which is just a simple effect to highlight that it's been picked up.

A very important thing that this code does is set the player's hasKey setter to true, which will be needed when the player tries to open a door. Figure 8-17 illustrates how the setter is set.

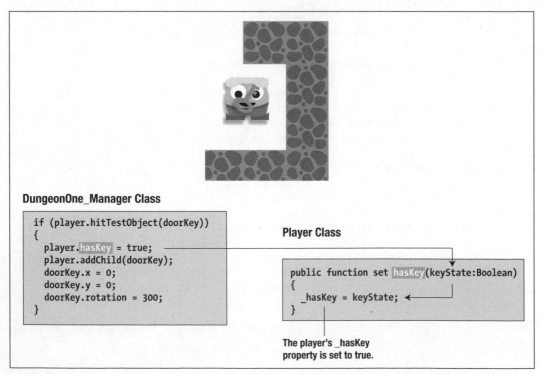

Figure 8-17. The DungeonOne_Manager class sets the player's _hasKey property to true using the Player class's hasKey setter.

Let's now look at how the door is opened.

Opening the first door

If the player object touches doorOne and doesn't have the key, its movement is blocked. If it does have the key, doorOne's isOpen setter is set to true, and the key becomes invisible:

```
if (player.hitTestObject(doorOne))
{
  if (player.hasKey)
  {
    if(! doorOne.isOpen)
    {
      doorOne.isOpen = true;
      doorKey.visible = false;
    }
  }
  else
  {
    Collision.block(player, doorOne);
  }
}
```

Figure 8-18 shows how the DungeonOne_Manager class checks the Player class's getter to find out what the value of hasKey is.

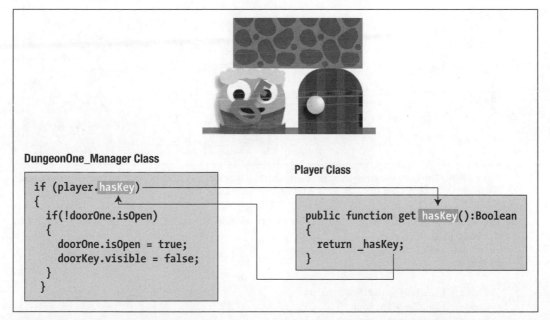

Figure 8-18. The DungeonOne_Manager class checks the Player class's hasKey getter. The getter returns whatever the value of the private _hasKey variable is. It's a Boolean variable, so it will be either true or false.

If the player object's _hasKey property is true, three things happen:

1. The code checks to see whether the door is closed. It checks the value of the doorOne isOpen getter. If it returns false, the door is closed. It checks for a false value by using the not (!) operator.

2. If the door is closed, the doorOne isOpen setter is sent the value of true, which "opens the door." The door becomes invisible, and the chimes sound plays. Figure 8-19 illustrates how this works. I'll explain how the sound works in the section ahead, and you'll find the full Door class listed as follows.

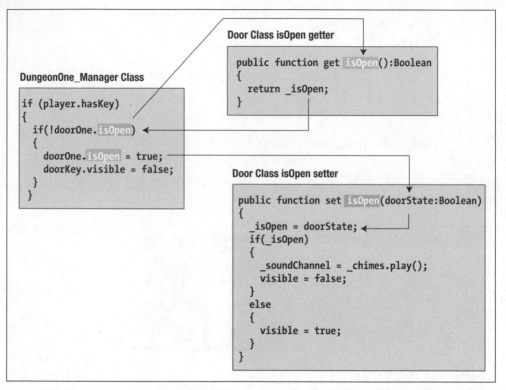

Figure 8-19. The DungeonOne_Manager class finds out whether the door is open by checking the Door class's getter. It opens the door by using a setter to set the Door class's _isOpen property to true.

3. The doorKey's visible property is set to false, so it seems to disappear. doorOne is bound to the Door class:

```
package
{
  import flash.display.MovieClip;
  import flash.media.Sound;
  import flash.media.SoundChannel;
  import flash.events.Event;
```

```
public class Door extends MovieClip
{
  private var _isOpen:Boolean;
  private var _chimes:Chimes;
  private var _soundChannel:SoundChannel

  public function Door()
  {
    addEventListener(Event.ADDED_TO_STAGE, onAddedToStage);
  }
  private function onAddedToStage(event:Event):void
  {
    _isOpen = false;
    _chimes = new Chimes();
    _soundChannel = new SoundChannel();
    visible = true;
    addEventListener(Event.REMOVED_FROM_STAGE, onRemovedFromStage);
  }
  private function onRemovedFromStage(event:Event):void
  {
    removeEventListener(Event.ADDED_TO_STAGE, onAddedToStage);
    removeEventListener(Event.REMOVED_FROM_STAGE,➡
      onRemovedFromStage);
  }
  //Getters and setters
  public function get isOpen():Boolean
  {
    return _isOpen;
  }
  public function set isOpen(doorState:Boolean)
  {
    _isOpen = doorState;
    if(_isOpen)
    {
      _soundChannel = _chimes.play();
      visible = false;
    }
    else
    {
      visible = true;
    }
  }
}
}
```

Both doorOne and doorTwo are instances of the Door class, so they both share this code. The code is general; it doesn't make any reference to any other object and doesn't get involved in the game logic—it's very well encapsulated. You can see here how the class attempts to be a model of a real door. Real doors can be either opened or closed, and they also make sounds. You should be able to use this code equally well with any other door objects in the game you might create, and it will work just fine.

> *In this game, both doorOne and doorTwo are instances of the same class, so it's easy for them to share the same code. What would you do, however, if you had two different symbols that needed to share the same class?*
>
> *In the* Symbol Properties, *assign each symbol a unique class in the* Class *field, such as* EnemyOne *and* EnemyTwo. *Just below the* Class *field is a field called* Base Class. *In the* Base Class *field, assign the common class that you want them to share (for example,* CommonEnemyClass). *You can then control instances of both symbols using this one class.*

Next, I'll show you how to play a sound when the doors open.

Adding sound to the game

To use sound in a game, you need to import the sound file into the Library. Here's how to add the chime sound of the door opening to Dungeon Maze Adventure:

1. Open the game's FLA file.
2. Select File ➤ Import ➤ Import to Library.
3. Find the sound file you want to use and click the Import to Library button. The sound will now appear as a symbol in the Library.
4. Select the sound in the Library by clicking it once. Click the Properties button at the bottom of the Library pane. The Sound Properties window opens.
5. In the Sound Properties window, change the name of the sound so that it doesn't include the file extension. For example, if the sound is called Chimes.mp3, change it so that it's named Chimes.
6. Select Export for ActionScript.
7. Change the name in the Class field so that it matches the name you gave it previously, such as Chimes. Figure 8-20 shows what the Sound Properties of the Chimes sound in Dungeon Maze Adventure looks like.

Any classes that use sounds need to also import the Sound and SoundChannel classes:

```
import flash.media.Sound;
import flash.media.SoundChannel;
```

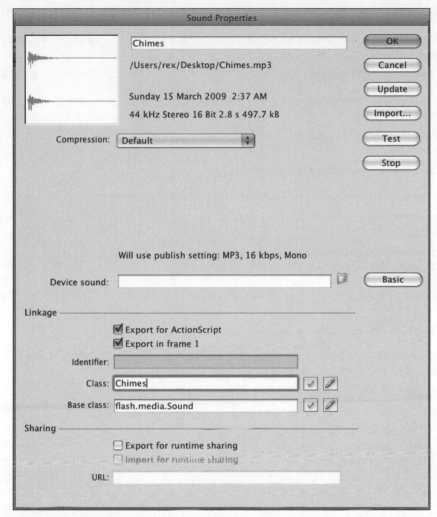

Figure 8-20. The Sound Properties window lets you change the properties of sounds imported into the Library.

Creating the Sound and SoundChannel objects

Creating and playing sounds is a two-step process. That's not as hard as it sounds, but it's potentially a bit confusing. You need to keep in mind that in AS3.0 creating sounds and playing sounds are two separate steps, controlled by two separate objects:

- You first need to create a Sound object. This is the actual sound that you want to play. In this game, it's the Chimes sound that I imported into the Library.
- You then need to create a SoundChannel object to actually play the sound. You can think of this as a "sound player" that actually does the work of playing the sound. You can't play the sound without this SoundChannel object.

Here's how the Sound and SoundChannel objects work together to play the Chimes sound.

1. First, you have to declare the Sound object. In the Door class, the Sound object is called _chimes, and is declared at the beginning of the class definition:

```
private var _chimes:Chimes;
```

This refers to the actual sound file that you imported into the Library. Its type matches its symbol name: Chimes.

2. Next, you have to declare the SoundChannel object. In the Door class, it's called _soundChannel.

```
private var _soundChannel:SoundChannel;
```

It's the job of the _soundChannel object to actually play the sound.

3. Create the Sound and SoundChannel objects. Like any other objects, you create them with the new operator:

```
_chimes = new Chimes();
_soundChannel = new SoundChannel();
```

4. Play the sounds. You do this by assigning the Sound object to the SoundChannel object, like this:

```
_soundChannel = _chimes.play();
```

The Sound object's play method plays the sound. You can use this directive anywhere in the class when you want the sound to play.

In the Door class, the chimes play when the _isOpen property becomes true:

```
if(_isOpen)
{
  _soundChannel = _chimes.play();
  visible = false;
}
else
{
  visible = true;
}
```

This has been a brief introduction to using sound in games, but it's by no means the end of it. For much more information on using sound, visit Adobe's online documentation at http://help.adobe.com/en_US/ActionScript/3.0_ProgrammingAS3/ and see the chapter "Working with Sound."

Colliding with the enemies

If the player touches any of the enemies, the health meter at the top-left corner of the stage is reduced, as shown in Figure 8-21.

Figure 8-21. When an enemy touches the player, the health meter is reduced.

This is the code in the DungeonOne_Manager that causes it to happen:

```
if(enemyOne != null)
{
  if (player.hitTestObject(enemyOne))
  {
    health.meter.width--;
  }
}
if(enemyTwo != null)
{
  if (player.hitTestObject(enemyTwo))
  {
    health.meter.width--;
  }
}
```

Before the meter can be reduced, the code has to check whether the enemy objects are actually on the stage. You can find out if an object exists by checking whether it has a null value like this:

```
enemyOne != null
```

The code needs to find out whether the enemyOne object exists because if it makes a reference to an object that doesn't actually exist, the compiler will generate a deluge of errors when the program runs. The enemy objects can be removed from the game by being shot by the player's bullets, so there's a chance they might not actually exist at some point. You can't take the chance that the code might not be able to find them.

How does the object get a null value? It's given one when it's removed from the game by being hit by a bullet in the checkCollisionWithEnemies method:

```
removeChild(enemyOne);
enemyOne = null;
```

You'll see how this works ahead. There's also a lot more information on removing objects at the end of the chapter in the section called "Removing objects from the game."

Losing the game

When the health meter reaches zero, the Game Over screen is displayed with this message: Game Over, You Lost!

```
if (health.meter.width < 1)
{
  var gameOverLost:GameOver = new GameOver();
  gameOverLost.messageDisplay.text = "Game Over" + "\n" + "You Lost!";
  parent.addChild(gameOverLost);
  parent.removeChild(this);
}
```

The code creates the gameOverLost object, which is an instance of the GameOver symbol.

```
var gameOverLost:GameOver = new GameOver();
```

The GameOver symbol contains a dynamic text field called messageDisplay, which is used to display the message:

```
gameOverLost.messageDisplay.text = "Game Over" + "\n" + "You Lost!";
```

Next, the gameOverLost object is displayed on the stage:

```
parent.addChild(gameOverLost);
```

I want the Game Over screen to be added directly to the main stage. parent refers to the main stage, so I can use the parent keyword to add the Game Over screen to the main stage. Figure 8-22 illustrates what the code does.

Finally, dungeonOne itself is removed:

```
parent.removeChild(this);
```

parent again refers to the stage, and this refers to *this object*, which is dungeonOne. Why is the parent property asked to remove the object?

AS3.0 doesn't permit objects to add or remove themselves. Only an object's container can remove it. This is logical because think how awkward it would be in a real-life situation if your socks removed themselves from your sock drawer instead of removing them yourself?

Figure 8-22. gameOverLost replaces dungeonOne on the main stage.

AS3.0 often tries to model these real-life scenarios. dungeonOne exists as an object on the stage. The stage is the dungeonOne *container*—its parent object. dungeonOne can't remove itself, so it asks its parent to do it. (Besides this change of perspective, the process of adding and removing game screens is exactly the same as the way you added and removed pages in your interactive storybook in Chapters 2, 3, and 4.)

> One nice feature of the parent keyword is that objects don't need to know the exact names of their parent containers. That means that if the dungeonOne parent object ever changes, you won't need to rewrite this code. By using keywords such as this and parent, you keep your code general, flexible, and portable.

This code is a little bit confusing because it's being run from inside the dungeonOne object. It's almost as if one of your socks were calling out to you from the drawer, "Hey, it's dark in here, take me out!" Ideally, you wouldn't want objects to be responsible for adding or removing themselves like this, just as you wouldn't want your socks telling you what to do. It's much better to have the actual object that's doing the adding or removing do it directly itself. That way, the control of the game is more centralized, which can help when you need to make changes.

With a bit more programming, you can create a document class and remove dungeonOne directly, like this:

```
removeChild(dungeonOne);
```

This works because the document class is attached to the stage that contains dungeonOne. You'll find more information on how to add a document class to manage the game near the end of the chapter.

Picking up the star weapon

When the player touches the star weapon, the weapon's x property is positioned on the left side of the player, so it looks like it is being carried:

```
if (player.hitTestObject(weapon))
{
  weapon.isArmed = true;
  weapon.x = player.x - (player.width / 2);
  weapon.y = player.y;
}
```

This code demonstrates another way you can have the player carry an object—without using addChild. The weapon's x and y properties match the player's.

When the weapon's isArmed property is true, the player can fire bullets. Here's the entire Weapon class (I'll show you how it is used to fire bullets next):

```
package
{
  import flash.display.MovieClip;
  import flash.events.KeyboardEvent;
  import flash.ui.Keyboard;
  import flash.events.Event;

  public class Weapon extends MovieClip
  {
    private var _isArmed:Boolean;

    public function Weapon()
    {
      addEventListener(Event.ADDED_TO_STAGE, onAddedToStage);
    }
```

```
      private function onAddedToStage(event:Event):void
      {
        _isArmed = false;
        stage.addEventListener(KeyboardEvent.KEY_DOWN, onKeyDown);
        stage.addEventListener(Event.REMOVED_FROM_STAGE, ➡
          onRemovedFromStage);
        addEventListener(Event.ENTER_FRAME, onEnterFrame);
      }
      private function onRemovedFromStage(event:Event):void
      {
        removeEventListener(Event.ENTER_FRAME, onEnterFrame);
        removeEventListener(Event.ADDED_TO_STAGE, onAddedToStage);
        removeEventListener(Event.REMOVED_FROM_STAGE,➡
          onRemovedFromStage);
      }
      private function onKeyDown(event:KeyboardEvent):void
      {
        if (event.keyCode == Keyboard.SPACE)
        {
          shootBullet();
        }
      }
      private function shootBullet():void
      {
        if (_isArmed)
        {
          parent.addChild(new Bullet());
        }
      }
      private function onEnterFrame(event:Event):void
      {
        rotation += 2;
      }

      //Getters and setters
      public function get isArmed():Boolean
      {
        return _isArmed;
      }
      public function set isArmed(weaponState:Boolean)
      {
        _isArmed = weaponState;
      }
    }
  }
```

Firing bullets

The Weapon and Bullet classes work together to fire bullets. When the player presses the spacebar, the Weapon class's shootBullet method is called:

```
private function shootBullet():void
{
  if (_weaponArmed)
  {
    parent.addChild(new Bullet());
  }
}
```

If _weaponArmed is true, the directive that creates the bullets is run:

```
parent.addChild(new Bullet());
```

This adds a new instance of the Bullet class to the parent container of the Weapon class: dungeonOne. The bullet object is created *without an instance name*.

This is the first time you've seen an object created without an instance name. The format for creating objects that you're more familiar with is this one:

```
var bullet:Bullet = new Bullet();
parent.addChild(bullet);
```

With this format, you can use bullet to refer to the bullet object you just created. With the format used in the Weapon class, the object is created but it isn't given a name. If these objects aren't assigned instance names, what happens to them when they're added to dungeonOne? They actually have instance names, but these names are assigned automatically by AS3.0. That's just fine because you don't need to reference any of the bullet objects specifically in the code.

> *If you want to find out the instance names to which AS3.0 assigns the bullets, drop this directive into the* Bullet *class's* onAddedToStage *event handler:*
>
> ```
> trace("Bullet instance name: " + this.name);
> ```
>
> *When you start firing bullets, you'll see something like this in the* Output *panel:*
>
> ```
> Bullet instance name: instance112
> Bullet instance name: instance114
> Bullet instance name: instance116
> ```
>
> *AS3.0 assigns these names automatically. Interesting!*

Figure 8-23 illustrates how the Weapon class fires bullets.

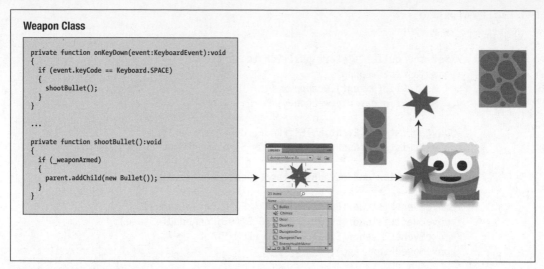

Figure 8-23. Press the spacebar to trigger the shootBullet method and add a bullet to the stage.

You'll see how the bullets actually work next.

Using bullet objects

All the bullet objects use the Bullet class—it positions the bullets on the stage and makes them move. It also sends references of the bullet objects back to the DungeonOne_Manager class so they can be checked for collisions with enemies.

It's important to remember that a new instance of this class is created *every time a bullet is added to the stage*. This one class is shared by countless bullet instances:

```
package
{
  import flash.display.MovieClip;
  import flash.events.Event;

  public class Bullet extends MovieClip
  {
    private var _vx:int;
    private var _vy:int;

    public function Bullet()
    {
      addEventListener(Event.ADDED_TO_STAGE, onAddedToStage);
    }
    private function onAddedToStage(event:Event):void
    {
      //The bullet's velocity
```

```
        _vx = 0;
        _vy = -10;

        //Set the bullet's start position to be the
        //same as the weapon's
        x = MovieClip(parent).weapon.x;
        y = MovieClip(parent).weapon.y;

        addEventListener(Event.ENTER_FRAME, onEnterFrame);
        addEventListener(Event.REMOVED_FROM_STAGE, onRemovedFromStage);
      }
      private function onRemovedFromStage(event:Event):void
      {
        removeEventListener(Event.ENTER_FRAME, onEnterFrame);
        removeEventListener(Event.ADDED_TO_STAGE, onAddedToStage);
        removeEventListener(Event.REMOVED_FROM_STAGE, ➥
          onRemovedFromStage);
      }
      private function onEnterFrame(event:Event):void
      {
        rotation += 20;

        //Move the bullet
        x += _vx;
        y += _vy;

        //send DungeonOne_Manager's checkCollisionWithEnemies
        //method a reference of this object to check
        //for collisions with the enemies
        MovieClip(parent).checkCollisionWithEnemies(this);

        //Remove the bullet if it moves
        //beyond the top of the stage
        if (y + height / 2 < 0)
        {
          parent.removeChild(this);
        }
      }
    }
  }
```

When a new bullet is added to the stage, it is assigned a start position that is the same as the weapon's position:

```
x = MovieClip(parent).weapon.x;
y = MovieClip(parent).weapon.y;
```

weapon is in dungeonOne, which is the bullet's parent. You can refer to dungeonOne from the Bullet class like this:

```
MovieClip(parent)
```

dungeonOne is a Movie Clip object. Sometimes AS3.0's compiler needs your help to tell it exactly what kind of thing an object is. You need to force it to interpret parent as a Movie Clip object by using the previous format. This procedure is called **type casting**.

> *If you ever need to access the document class directly from any other class, you can use this:*
>
> ```
> MovieClip(root)
> ```
>
> *It allows you to access the main timeline, the main stage, any objects on the main stage, and properties of the document class.*

By using MovieClip(parent) to refer to dungeonOne, you can actually access any object in the game from within the Bullet class like this:

```
MovieClip(parent).player
MovieClip(parent).health.meter
MovieClip(parent).doorOne
```

If you ever need to refer to an object in a parent container, use this format.

> *As useful as this technique is, it's actually not a good idea to use it too often in your own projects. It makes the class completely dependent on instances inside another class. If those instance names change or the object no longer exists, the code won't work. This is known as **tight coupling** and it breaks a class's encapsulation. As a general rule, try not to program your classes so that they refer to specific objects inside other classes. It will be harder for you to debug and change your game if you do. I've done so here as an example of how to do it if you need to, but in later chapters the code will avoid this.*

Of course, the most important thing the bullets do is help the player defeat the enemies. Let's look at how this works next.

Bullets vs. enemy collisions

The Bullet class and the DungeonOne_Manager class work together to check whether the bullets are hitting the enemies.

First, the bullet objects need to tell DungeonOne_Manager that they exist. One directive in the Bullet class does this:

```
MovieClip(parent).checkCollisionWithEnemies(this);
```

It might look confusing at first glance, but don't let it scare you. In plain English, it reads as follows:

```
Send a reference of "this bullet object" to the parent class's
checkCollisionWithEnemies method.
```

checkCollisionWithEnemies is a method in DungeonOne_Manager, which is the bullet's parent. It takes one parameter, which is the bullet object itself: this.

this from the Bullet class becomes bullet when it's sent to the checkCollisionWithEnemies method. Figure 8-24 illustrates how it fits together.

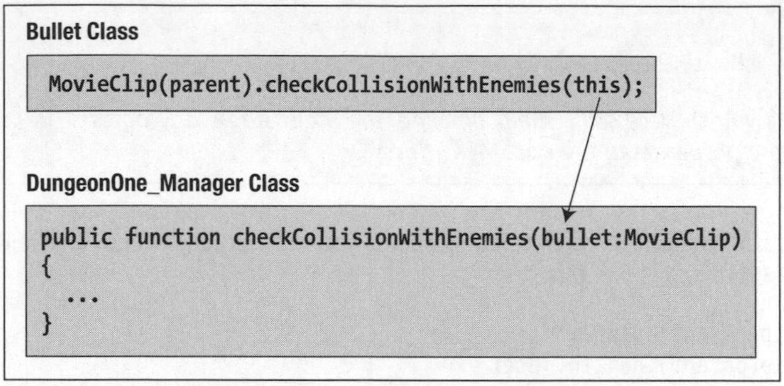

Figure 8-24. The bullet objects send references of themselves to the checkCollisionWithEnemies method. The method can now refer to them by using the variable name bullet, which is assigned in its parameter.

Here's the entire checkCollisionWithEnemies method from the DungeonOne_Manager class:

```
public function checkCollisionWithEnemies(bullet:MovieClip)
{
  //Enemy One
  if (enemyOne != null)
  {
    if (enemyOne.hitTestPoint(bullet.x, bullet.y, true))
    {
      enemyOne.subObject.meter.width -= 10;
      if (enemyOne.subObject.meter.width < 1)
      {
        enemyOne.subObject.stop();
        removeChild(enemyOne);
        enemyOne = null;
      }
      removeChild(bullet);
      bullet = null;
    }
  }
}
```

```
    //Enemy Two
    if (enemyTwo != null)
    {
      if (enemyTwo.hitTestPoint(bullet.x, bullet.y, true))
      {
        enemyTwo.subObject.meter.width -= 10;
        if (enemyTwo.subObject.meter.width < 1)
        {
          enemyTwo.subObject.stop();
          removeChild(enemyTwo);
          enemyTwo = null;
        }
        removeChild(bullet);
        bullet = null;
      }
    }
  }
```

This method is called every time a new bullet is created, which is every time the player presses the spacebar. It's public so that outside classes such as Bullet can access it. The actual instance names of the bullets will be different, but that doesn't matter because the method refers to them all as bullet. The great thing about this system is that it all happens without you needing to know the actual instance names of the bullets themselves. You could have one bullet or 1000, and the code remains the same.

The collision-detection code is very straightforward. When the bullets hit the enemies, they're removed from the stage, and the width of the enemies' health meters are reduced by ten pixels. If the width of the meters becomes less than one pixel, the enemies are removed from the stage.

After the enemy and bullet objects are removed from the stage, the references to them are also assigned a null value, like this:

```
    enemyOne = null;
    enemyTwo = null;
    bullet = null;
```

Assigning a null value to variables that reference objects ensures that Flash will remove the object from the Flash Player's memory.

As it did before, the code needs to first check whether enemyOne and enemyTwo actually exist on the stage by using this check:

```
    if (enemyTwo != null)
```

The code generates errors if the enemy has already been removed and the code can't find it.

> If you think you might use an object again at some point in your game, use `removeChild` without assigning a `null` value. You can then see whether the object is on the stage by checking whether the object's `parent` is `null`. Here are two simple examples:
>
> ```
> if(enemyOne.parent != null)
> {
>   //Then the object must be on the stage...
> }
>
> if(enemyOne.parent == null)
> {
>   //Then the object must have been removed from the stage...
> }
> ```
>
> If the object doesn't have a parent container, then it's not on the stage, and vice versa.
>
> If you don't assign the variable that references the object a `null` value, that object still exists in Flash's memory. You can add it back to the stage again at any time using `addChild`.

Player vs. wall collisions

Exactly the same technique is used to check for collisions between the wall objects and the player:

Here's the Wall class:

```
package
{
  import flash.display.MovieClip;
  import flash.events.Event;

  public class Wall extends MovieClip
  {
    public function Wall()
    {
      addEventListener(Event.ADDED_TO_STAGE, onAddedToStage);
    }
    private function onAddedToStage(event:Event):void
    {
      //Add event listeners
      addEventListener(Event.ENTER_FRAME, onEnterFrame);
      addEventListener(Event.REMOVED_FROM_STAGE, onRemovedFromStage);
    }
    private function onRemovedFromStage(event:Event):void
    {
      removeEventListener(Event.ENTER_FRAME, onEnterFrame);
      removeEventListener(Event.ADDED_TO_STAGE, onAddedToStage);
```

```
        removeEventListener(Event.REMOVED_FROM_STAGE, ➡
          onRemovedFromStage);
      }

      private function onEnterFrame(event:Event):void
      {
        MovieClip(parent).checkCollisionWithPlayer(this);
      }
    }
  }
```

Despite all the code, the Wall class does only one important thing: it sends a reference of itself to the checkCollisionWithPlayer method of the DungeonOne_Manager:

```
        MovieClip(parent).checkCollisionWithPlayer(this);
```

There are 19 wall objects in the game, and this class is attached to each of them. Every one of those wall objects runs this directive. Because it's in an ENTER_FRAME event, it means that the checkCollisionWithPlayer method of the DungeonOne_Manager is called *19 times each frame*.

```
      public function checkCollisionWithPlayer(wall:MovieClip)
      {
        if (player.parent != null)
        {
          Collision.block(player, wall);
        }
      }
```

Figure 8-25 illustrates how the wall objects use this method.

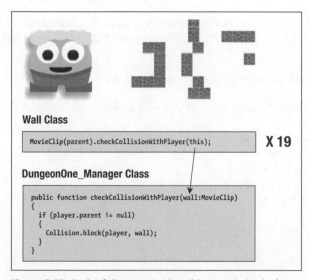

Figure 8-25. Each of the game's 19 wall instances checks for a collision with the player on every frame (30 times per second).

Synchronizing ENTER_FRAME events

There's one extremely important technical detail you need to be aware of for the player vs. wall collision system to work accurately. In this game, there are many ENTER_FRAME events running on many different objects. AS3.0 doesn't run them all at the same time. It runs them in the order in which the objects were added to the stage—either by you dragging them from the Library or adding them with code using addChild. That means if the player object were added to the stage before the wall objects, all its code, including its ENTER_FRAME event, would run before the code in the wall objects does.

Why is this important to be aware of? If the wall objects run their code first and call the Collision.block method before the player's onEnterFrame event runs, the player's _vx and _vy values will be those from the *previous frame*. Yes, the previous frame! This will throw the accuracy of the collision detection off by one frame, and the player will appear to overlap with the walls slightly when it touches them. Figure 8-26 illustrates how this looks.

Figure 8-26. If the collision-detection code runs before the object's positions have been updated, the acccuracy will be off by one frame.

Because the player is a moving object, its ENTER_FRAME event needs to run before the walls' ENTER_FRAME events for the collision detection to be accurate. In Dungeon Maze Adventure, I made sure that the player's code runs first by dragging the player object onto the stage before adding any of the wall objects. This is a very primitive but effective way of making sure it updates its velocity before the walls call Collision.block.

You will invariably run into this problem in your own games at some point. You'll notice that the collision detection is maddeningly off by one frame and you won't know why. Well, now you do! Adding objects to the game in the order you want their code to run is one solution.

Another is this: use only one ENTER_FRAME event in your game in a manager class such as DungeonOne_Manager. Use that event to call methods in other classes that *behave* like ENTER_FRAME events, but aren't.

Here's an example. In the manager class, use code that looks like this:

```
private function onEnterFrame(event:Event):void
{
  objectA.frameEvents();
  objectB.frameEvents();
  objectC.frameEvents();
}
```

In the object classes, use a method that looks like this:

```
public function frameEvents():void
{
   //Add any code that would go into an
   //ENTER_FRAME event here
}
```

It's an ordinary function definition, but it behaves like an ENTER_FRAME event because it's called from inside the manager class's ENTER_FRAME event. This means that you have only one ENTER_FRAME event running for all the objects in the game. You can use it to precisely control the order in which the sub-object's frame events run. If you want the objectC frame events to run before those of objectA, you can change the order like this:

```
private function onEnterFrame(event:Event):void
{
   objectC.frameEvents();
   objectB.frameEvents();
   objectA.frameEvents();
}
```

This system allows you to fine-tune the accuracy of the collision-detection system of your game and avoid off-by-one errors. Remember this solution! It could become a life-saver in some of your own game design projects. For games requiring accurate collision detection, it's essential.

This was a bit of a detour, but an important one. Now let's get back to Dungeon Maze Adventure!

Winning the game

When both enemies are defeated, doorTwo opens:

```
if ((enemyOne == null) && (enemyTwo == null))
{
   if(!doorTwo.isOpen)
   {
      doorTwo.isOpen = true;
   }
}
else
{
   Collision.block(player, doorTwo);
}
```

The player can then reach the exit object, and the Game Over screen is displayed, announcing that the game has been won:

```
if(player.hitTestPoint(exit.x, exit.y, true))
{
  var gameOverWon:GameOver = new GameOver();
  gameOverWon.messageDisplay.text = "Game Over" + "\n" + "You Won!";
  parent.addChild(gameOverWon);
  parent.removeChild(this);
}
```

And there you have it; Dungeon Maze Adventure is solved!

Modifying the game

Dungeon Maze Adventure is designed as a model to introduce you to some basic object-oriented programming techniques and get you thinking about how to distribute the tasks of your game to different classes. You can take some of the ideas from this chapter and run with them in your own projects.

There's a great deal more you can do. To get you started, there are some advanced modifications you can make:

- Add a new level.
- Create a class to manage all the levels in the game.
- Fire bullets in four directions.

Let's take a look!

Adding a new level

It's easy to add a new level to the game. The Library already contains a symbol called DungeonTwo. The following steps describe how to use it to add a new level when the player has reached the dungeonOne's exit:

1. Modify the last code in the previous section so that it looks like this:

```
if(player.hitTestPoint(exit.x, exit.y, true))
{
  var dungeonTwo = new DungeonTwo();
  parent.addChild(dungeonTwo);
  parent.removeChild(this);
}
```

2. Save the DungeonOne_Manager.as file and test the project.

3. Play the game to the end. When the player reaches the exit, dungeonTwo appears. Figure 8-27 illustrates what you'll see.

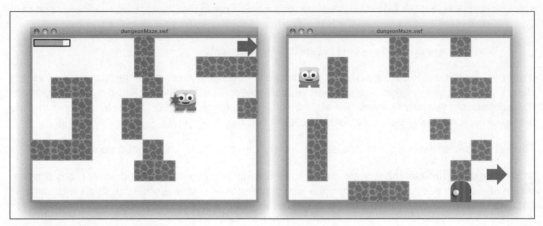

Figure 8-27. Add a second level.

This is just an example of how the new level can be added. I'll leave the design of the new level up to you.

The problem of dependency

Unfortunately, one more thing you'll see when the new level is added is a runtime error in the Output panel:

```
TypeError: Error #1006: checkCollisionWithPlayer
is not a function. at Wall/onEnterFrame()
```

It looks like Figure 8-28.

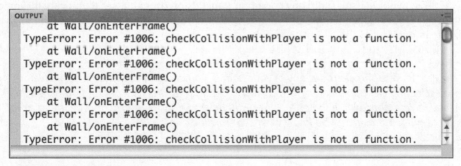

Figure 8-28. A runtime error

Runtime errors happen when the code looks for something that it can't find while the program is running. There's a very good reason for why this runtime error occurs: **dependency**.

The error tells you that the Wall class is looking for a method called checkCollisionWithPlayer and can't find it. Just to refresh your memory, this is the directive in the Wall class that looks for that method:

```
MovieClip(parent).checkCollisionWithPlayer(this);
```

It's looking for this method in the parent object: dungeonOne. dungeonOne contains the DungeonOne_Manager class. When the game switched levels, it removed dungeonOne. The DungeonOne_Manager class is bound to dungeonOne, so it was also removed. The walls are all looking for the checkCollisionWithPlayer method in the DungeonOne_Manager class and, of course, can't find it.

The Wall class *depends* on the checkCollisionWithPlayer method. This is not a good thing!

At this stage in your learning, using dependencies like this helps you understand how classes communicate and allows you to achieve a complex technique such as multiple object collision with minimal code. In Chapter 10, I'll show you how you can use events to avoid this.

For now however, dependency is isn't *too bad* if you manage it carefully. There are a few ways you can solve the runtime error you received:

1. Create a class called DungeonTwo_Manager and bind it to the DungeonTwo symbol. Make sure that it contains a method called checkCollisionWithPlayer. The wall objects in DungeonTwo still look for the parent object, but they then find the code they're looking for in DungeonTwo_Manager. As long as the name of the method hasn't changed, it works. If you'll create a second level of the game, you'll need a DungeonTwo_Manager class anyway, so this solution makes sense.

2. Create a third class, maybe called Collision_Manager, that isn't bound to any objects and is just used for checking collisions in the game. Game objects send references of themselves to this new class. The next section makes one suggestion about how to do this.

This is just a very general description to get you thinking about the problem of code dependency. When you design your classes, avoid any code that depends on other classes if you can. It's impossible to completely remove dependency from your games and programs, but with careful planning you can minimize its impact.

> *If you get a runtime error in any of your games, you can find out where the problem is by selecting* Debug ➤ Debug Movie. *Flash's debugger starts its work and points to the line in your code where the error is. You still have to figure out exactly why the error is occurring, but as least you know where to start looking.*

Creating a game manager

In Dungeon Maze Adventure, all the game logic is attached to dungeonOne in the DungeonOne_Manager class. If you have more than one level in your game, however, it makes sense to have some code that exists outside of the dungeon objects so that you that can manage them (a kind of "Dungeon Master" that isn't removed when the levels are removed).

Hey, you already know how to do this! It's called the document class! Dungeon Maze Adventure doesn't use a document class, but why not? Go ahead and make one; it will open up all sorts of possibilities.

You can put any properties or methods that *all the dungeons can use* in the document class, which will save you having to write the same method over more than once if that method is used in more than one level. And you can use it as a way to keep track of global values, such as a score that persists between levels.

You can use public static methods to do this. You can define a static method using this format:

```
public static function methodName():void
```

Other classes can then access the method like this:

```
Main.methodName(arguments);
```

> Be careful when using public methods because they can break a class's encapsulation and open you up to some of the dependency problems you looked at in the previous section.

You can also create getters and setters in this game manager class to allow the dungeons or the objects in them to communicate with it. One of the dungeon objects can access the game's score with a getter like this:

```
MovieClip(parent).score
```

And set the score like this:

```
MovieClip(parent).score += 10;
```

You can also access the document class from any other class using the format MovieClip(root).

You can easily access all the dungeons and objects in them from the document class like this:

```
dungeonOne.player
dungeonTwo.doorTwo
```

You already know how to do this, so go for it!

Firing bullets in four directions

In the project files, you'll find two classes: Weapon_FourDirections and Bullet_FourDirections. You can use them so that the player can shoot bullets in four directions. Here's how to make them work:

1. Open the dungeonMaze.fla file.

2. Select the Weapon symbol in the Library and open its Symbol Properties window.

3. Enter Weapon_FourDirections in the Class field and click the OK button.

4. Select the Bullet symbol in the Library and open its Symbol Properties window.

5. Enter Bullet_FourDirections in the Class field and click the OK button.

6. Save the dungeonMaze.fla file.

7. Test the project. You can now fire bullets in any of four directions, depending on which arrow key you press. Figure 8-29 illustrates this.

Figure 8-29. Use the arrow keys to shoot bullets in four directions.

The code is provided as follows, and I'll go into some aspects of it in a bit of detail, but here's an overview of how it works.

The Weapon_FourDirections class has a new property called _direction that is assigned the value "up", "down", "left", or "right", depending on which arrow key is pressed. The bullets need to know which direction they need to travel, so the _direction property is passed to them directly as a parameter when they're created. (Have a quick look back at Chapters 3 and 7 if you're a bit hazy on what method parameters are and how they work). The bullets then use that direction to assign the correct horizontal and vertical velocity. The two classes work together to produce the effect you see on the stage. Figure 8-30 illustrates the process, and I'll explain it in detail ahead.

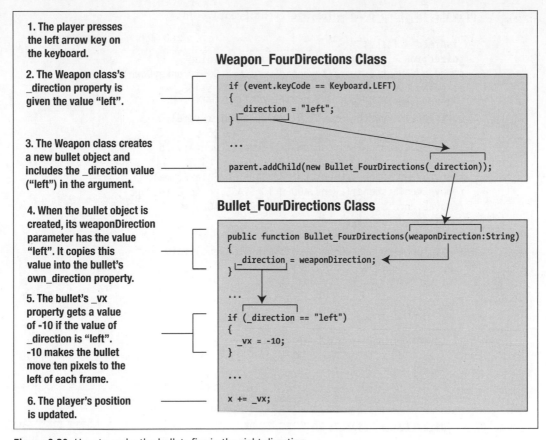

1. The player presses the left arrow key on the keyboard.

2. The Weapon class's _direction property is given the value "left".

3. The Weapon class creates a new bullet object and includes the _direction value ("left") in the argument.

4. When the bullet object is created, its weaponDirection parameter has the value "left". It copies this value into the bullet's own _direction property.

5. The bullet's _vx property gets a value of -10 if the value of _direction is "left". -10 makes the bullet move ten pixels to the left of each frame.

6. The player's position is updated.

Weapon_FourDirections Class

```
if (event.keyCode == Keyboard.LEFT)
{
    _direction = "left";
}

...

parent.addChild(new Bullet_FourDirections(_direction));
```

Bullet_FourDirections Class

```
public function Bullet_FourDirections(weaponDirection:String)
{
    _direction = weaponDirection;
}

...

if (_direction == "left")
{
    _vx = -10;
}

...

x += _vx;
```

Figure 8-30. How to make the bullets fire in the right direction

Here's the entire Weapon_FourDirections class:

```
package
{
  import flash.display.MovieClip;
  import flash.events.KeyboardEvent;
  import flash.ui.Keyboard;
  import flash.events.Event;

  public class Weapon_FourDirections extends MovieClip
  {
    private var _isArmed:Boolean;
    private var _direction:String;

    public function Weapon_FourDirections()
    {
      addEventListener(Event.ADDED_TO_STAGE, onAddedToStage);
    }
```

```
private function onAddedToStage(event:Event):void
{
  _isArmed = false;
  _direction = "up"; //"up" is the default value
  stage.addEventListener(KeyboardEvent.KEY_DOWN, onKeyDown);
  stage.addEventListener(Event.REMOVED_FROM_STAGE, ➥
    onRemovedFromStage)
  addEventListener(Event.ENTER_FRAME, onEnterFrame);
}
private function onRemovedFromStage(event:Event):void
{
  removeEventListener(Event.ENTER_FRAME, onEnterFrame);
  removeEventListener(Event.ADDED_TO_STAGE, onAddedToStage);
  removeEventListener(Event.REMOVED_FROM_STAGE, ➥
    onRemovedFromStage);
}
private function onKeyDown(event:KeyboardEvent):void
{
  if (event.keyCode == Keyboard.SPACE)
  {
    shootBullet();
  }
  if (event.keyCode == Keyboard.LEFT)
  {
    _direction = "left";
  }
  else if (event.keyCode == Keyboard.RIGHT)
  {
    _direction = "right";
  }
  else if (event.keyCode == Keyboard.UP)
  {
    _direction = "up";
  }
  else if (event.keyCode == Keyboard.DOWN)
  {
    _direction = "down";
  }
}
private function shootBullet():void
{
  if (_isArmed)
  {
    parent.addChild(new Bullet_FourDirections(_direction));
  }
}
private function onEnterFrame(event:Event):void
{
  rotation += 2;
```

```
      }

      //Getters and setters
      public function get isArmed():Boolean
      {
        return _isArmed;
      }
      public function set isArmed(weaponState:Boolean)
      {
        _isArmed = weaponState;
      }
    }
  }
```

The most important new directive is this one:

```
    parent.addChild(new Bullet_FourDirections(_direction));
```

It sends the value of the _direction property directly to the Bullet_FourDirections class. That class then uses it ("up", "down", "left", or "right") when it creates the bullet instances to initialize its direction.

For this to work, you need to make an important addition to the Bullet class. It needs a **constructor parameter** so the _direction value can be accepted and used in the class. Here's the Bullet_FourDirections class. The constructor parameter has been highlighted—see if you can figure out how it uses that information in the code:

```
    package
    {
      import flash.display.MovieClip;
      import flash.events.Event;

      public class Bullet_FourDirections extends MovieClip
      {
        private var _vx:int;
        private var _vy:int;
        private var _direction:String;
        private var _stageHeight:uint;
        private var _stageWidth:uint;

        public function Bullet_FourDirections(weaponDirection:String)
        {
          _direction = weaponDirection;
          addEventListener(Event.ADDED_TO_STAGE, onAddedToStage);
        }
        private function onAddedToStage(event:Event):void
        {
          //Set the bullet's start position to be the
          //same as the weapon's
          x = MovieClip(parent).weapon.x;
          y = MovieClip(parent).weapon.y;
```

```
//Initialize direction
if (_direction == "up")
{
  _vy = -10;
}
if (_direction == "down")
{
  _vy = 10;
}
if (_direction == "left")
{
  _vx = -10;
}
if (_direction == "right")
{
  _vx = 10;
}


//Find the stage height and width of the stage
//To use with stage boundaries
_stageWidth = stage.stageWidth;
_stageHeight = stage.stageHeight;

addEventListener(Event.ENTER_FRAME, onEnterFrame);
addEventListener(Event.REMOVED_FROM_STAGE, onRemovedFromStage);
}
private function onRemovedFromStage(event:Event):void
{
  removeEventListener(Event.ENTER_FRAME, onEnterFrame);
  removeEventListener(Event.ADDED_TO_STAGE, onAddedToStage);
  removeEventListener(Event.REMOVED_FROM_STAGE, ➡
    onRemovedFromStage);
}
private function onEnterFrame(event:Event):void
{
  //Move object
  rotation += 20;
  x += _vx;
  y += _vy;

  //Check for collisions with the enemies
  MovieClip(parent).checkCollisionWithEnemies(this);

  //Stage Boundaries:
  //Top
  if (y + height / 2 < 0)
  {
    parent.removeChild(this);
  }
```

```
            //Bottom
            if (y - height / 2 > _stageHeight)
            {
              parent.removeChild(this);
            }
            //Left
            if (x + width / 2 < 0)
            {
              parent.removeChild(this);
            }
            //Right
            if (x - width / 2 > _stageWidth)
            {
              parent.removeChild(this);
            }
          }
        }
      }
```

Let's take a closer look at the constructor method:

```
      public function Bullet_FourDirections(weaponDirection:String)
      {
        _direction = weaponDirection;
        addEventListener(Event.ADDED_TO_STAGE, onAddedToStage);
      }
```

Its parameter is called weaponDirection. When the bullet is created, weaponDirection contains exactly the same value of the _direction variable that was passed to it by the weapon. It has a value of "up", "down", "left", or "right". (The weapon's _direction variable was a string, so weaponDirection needs to be typed as String as well.)

Any parameters that are used in the constructor method are *local to the constructor method*, so the weaponsDirection variable can't be used anywhere else in the class. The first job is to copy its value over into a variable that can be used in the entire class. The Bullet_FourDirections class has its own property called _direction that is used to store this information. When new bullet instances are created, they use this new _direction property to figure out in which direction they should be traveling.

Now that bullet objects know the direction they have to travel, their velocity is simply assigned using the _direction property.

Accessing the stage outside of the document class

There's an extremely important oddity that you might have noticed in the Bullet_FourDirections class: these two lines of code in the onAddedToStage event handler:

```
      _stageWidth = stage.stageWidth;
      _stageHeight = stage.stageHeight;
```

You need to know the stage's height and width to calculate the stage boundaries. But why were those properties copied into variables instead of being accessed directly? It's related to a problem that will cause a lot of frustration if you don't understand it properly.

Here's the problem. Only the document class (for example, Main, which was used in earlier chapters) has direct access to the stage object. If you try to access the stage object in any other class that isn't directly referenced by the document class, that class can't "see" the stage. If you make a reference to the stage object in one of these classes, you'll get an error message: Cannot access a property or method of a null object reference.

There are a few ways to get around this:

- An object that uses an event listener attached to the stage object doesn't have this problem because the stage object is actively involved in that class. Here's an example:

  ```
  stage.addEventListener(KeyboardEvent.KEY_DOWN,onKeyDown);
  ```

  Objects that use code like this have no trouble making references to the stage directly.

- An object doesn't know that the stage exists until it's been *added to the stage*. That's one of the reasons you've been using the ADDED_TO_STAGE event. When the onAddedToStage event handler runs, you can freely access the stage object in the class.

- Even though you can access the stage object directly in the onAddedToStage event handler, you might not be able to access it anywhere else in the class. This could be very important if your game relies on stage.stageHeight and stage.stageWidth to define stage boundaries. The way around this is to create a property in the onAddedToStage event handler, which makes a reference to the stage object. You can then use that property anywhere in the class, and it will behave as if you were accessing the stage object directly.

It's this third scenario that you're dealing with in the Bullet_FourDirections class. You have to copy the stage's stageHeight and stageWidth properties into the class's own _stageHeight and _stageWidth variables so those values can be used elsewhere in the class.

Have a look at the class again and see if you can find the spot where these properties are being used to define stage boundaries. And remember these solutions because this problem is one of the biggest pitfalls programmers new to AS3.0 fall into when they begin game design.

Removing objects from the game

Let's take a more detailed look at what happens when objects are removed from the game. Most of the objects are removed using removeChild, like this:

```
removeChild(objectName);
```

To completely clear the object from memory, give any variables that refer to the object a null value, like this:

```
objectName = null;
```

What actually happens to the object when it's removed? AS3.0 has a **garbage collector** to do the job. You can think of the garbage collector as a little software robot that runs around your game looking for objects and properties that aren't being used or don't have any value, and deletes them for good. This saves memory and processing power—thanks, Flash! One of the jobs of the garbage collector is to find objects that have been removed with removeChild, and wipe them from Flash Player's memory. However, the garbage collector is a bit of a finicky fellow, and very picky about what it chooses to completely delete:

- The garbage collector doesn't delete objects that have an ENTER_FRAME event running. These objects make the garbage collector a bit squeamish, so you have to manually remove the ENTER_FRAME event with removeListener, as you did with the removedFromStage event handlers. Although objects remove their own event listeners (such as ADDED_TO_STAGE and REMOVED_FROM_STAGE) it's considered best practice to also remove them manually.

- The garbage collector doesn't like Movie Clip objects that are animated using a timeline, such as the two enemy objects. It doesn't touch them unless the animation is stopped by using the stop method.

- If any objects have timers running using the Timer class (more on timers in Chapter 10), the garbage collector doesn't delete them.

- The garbage collector doesn't delete an object if there's more than one variable in the game that makes a reference to it. For example, imagine that you have two variables, playerObjectOne and playerObjectTwo, which both contain a reference to the player object:

```
var _playerObjectOne = player;
var _playerObjectTwo = player;
```

Imagine that in your program you try and remove the player object like this:

```
removeChild(_playerOne);
playerOne = null;
```

The player object is removed from the stage, but the garbage collector doesn't delete it from memory because the playerObjectTwo variable still contains a reference to it.

The only way to coerce the garbage collector to completely delete the player object is if every variable that holds a reference to it is assigned a value of null (which is a value used with Movie Clip objects to wipe them clean of all data). It's not hard to do, and a directive like this will do the trick:

```
_playerTwo = null;
```

One more thing: you have to make sure that *every reference* to the player object in *every class* that might have made one also sets those variables to null. Only then does the garbage collector come back with his broom and finish the job. And if that's the case, the player object is then completely deleted.

I went into quite a bit of detail into this issue because if you spend any time working with Flash (which you will!) you'll inevitably come across issues in your games where quirky things start to happen because of objects still actually existing, or running listeners or animations in the background, when you think they're gone.

Using removeChild isn't the only way (or even the best way) to take your objects out of the game. A more low-tech but equally effective method is to set an object's visible property to false. This is how the doorKey object in Dungeon Maze Adventure was removed from the game:

```
doorKey.visible = false;
```

The nice thing about this technique is that the objects still actually exist on the stage the entire time. If you have a game in which you hide and show the same objects over and over again, this is the way to do it.

Finally, I should explain how other objects know that an object is no longer in the game. If you're using the visible property to remove the object, you could use code that looks like this:

```
if (! player.visible)
{
   ... then it means the player object is gone!
}
```

If you use removeChild to get rid of an object, things are a bit more subtle. When you remove an object from the stage with removeChild, the object's parent property is set to null. Think about it this way, if the player object is removed from dungeonOne, it no longer has a parent Movie Clip container. In a nutshell, its parent is null.

Here's what the code that informs other objects that the player object has been removed from the game using removeChild might look like:

```
if (player.parent == null)
{
   ... then it means the player object is gone!
}
```

> If you use a document class and are trying to figure out whether an object has been removed, you can check to see whether its stage property is null. For example:
>
> ```
> if(player.stage == null)
> {
>    //... then it means the object is not on the stage.
> }
> ```

But using removeChild alone isn't enough to make sure that the object is completely deleted from memory. You also have to remove all references to that object. This is done by assigning another value to any variables that refer to it. You can assign any other value, but it often makes sense to assign a null value, like this:

```
player = null;
```

Once that's done, you can check whether or not an object exists in the game using this format:

```
if (player == null)
{
   ... then it means the player object is gone!
}
```

This is the process used in Dungeon Maze Adventure to remove objects.

These are all very important technical details to keep in mind when designing your games.

Summary

This was a big chapter! There was a lot of code and many new concepts to absorb. Everything covered here, however, is absolutely essential to gaining a solid foundation in Flash game design. You'll have to deal with all these issues sooner or later in your game design career. If you didn't understand everything the first time, though, break the chapter down into smaller chunks and work through each section carefully until it makes sense. Compare what you see happening while you play the game with the code that makes it work. The best way to understand this chapter is to create your own version of Dungeon Maze Adventure. You definitely have the skills to do it, and the steps you go through will reinforce all the concepts covered here.

I hope this chapter got you thinking about how to start using classes to help build games. The model you used here can take you quite far if you use it carefully. Just keep in mind the potential risks of code dependency and try to avoid it wherever you can. In Chapter 10, you'll see how you can solve the problem of dependency by having objects communicate by dispatching events.

Until then, have fun with some of the new techniques you looked at in this chapter. How about coming up with a game that combines them with some of the other techniques you learned in earlier chapters? For example, what about a dungeon or space game with huge scrolling levels? That would be amazing! And how about incorporating some puzzle solving using input text, such as the number guessing game from Chapter 5? Don't forget about random numbers—they can give your game a lot of variety. Even at this stage in the book, you have some real game-coding power at your fingertips. The best way to learn is to dive in there and start making a game.

In the next chapter, you'll look at a completely different game genre: a platform game. You'll learn how to make objects move using physics simulations and how to store and analyze data using arrays.

Have fun designing your next great game, and I'll meet you in Chapter 9 when you're done!

Chapter 9

PLATFORM GAME: PHYSICS AND DATA MANAGEMENT

One of the most popular genres of video game is the **platform game**, which also poses some very interesting programming and design challenges. From a programming point of view, if you can program a platform game, you've reached a benchmark in your development as a game designer.

The game you'll create in this chapter is called Bug Catcher, and you'll find the finished SWF file in the chapter's source files. You'll use it to take a detailed look at some core video game design techniques:

- Natural motion using physics simulations
- Complex player character behavior
- Collisions with accurate bounce and friction
- Converting a subobject's local coordinates to global coordinates
- Display list and object stacking order
- Rotating an object toward another object
- Random motion
- Artificial intelligence (AI)
- Arrays

You'll look at these techniques within a practical, real-world context so that you'll have a clear idea of how to apply them to your own games.

Natural motion using physics

When you bump into a wall, what happens? If you are a character in Dungeon Maze Adventure from the previous chapter, absolutely nothing—you just stop moving and that's the end of the story. In real life, things are much more complicated. A bouncy rubber ball traveling at high speed bounces back at an angle. Something heavier, such as a rock, falls with a thud. Here's another example: when you step on a car's accelerator, the car gradually increases in speed and takes a bit of time to slow down after you hit the brakes. These sorts of physical reactions are part of what makes real-world games such as tennis and car racing so much fun.

Over the next few pages, you'll take the venerable `Player` class from Chapter 8 and modify it a step at a time to illustrate the following kinds of motion that simulate real-world physics:

- **Acceleration**: Gradually speeding up
- **Friction**: Gradually slowing down
- **Bouncing**: Changing the direction of motion when the object hits the edge of the stage
- **Gravity**: Adding a force that pulls the object to the bottom of the stage
- **Jumping**: One of the most required abilities for video game characters

Applying physics to games is easy to do. Most of the techniques boil down to a simple calculation that's applied to the vx and vy properties. Although the calculations are simple, it's sometimes far from obvious how they can be used in a practical way. It's exactly this practical application that you'll examine.

> In this book, most of the physics calculations that you'll apply are based on **Euler integration** (its popular name is "easy video game physics"). Video game physics appear to be absolutely precise in the context of a video game, but are actually only approximations of the real thing. You'll use game physics because the CPU power required to process them are far, far less than if you used calculations from a physics textbook. If you need to do precise physical simulations of the real world, Keith Peters's ActionScript 3.0 Animation: Making Things Move and AdvanceED ActionScript 3.0 Animation go into detail on this subject.

Setting up the project files

In the chapter source files, you'll find an FLA file called physics.fla in a folder called Physics. You'll open it as a project:

1. In Flash, select File ➤ Open.
2. Find the physics.fla file in the Chapter 8 Physics folder. Click the Open button.
3. Select Quick Project in the Project panel's drop-down menu.
4. The physics project is created. Your stage and the Project panel should now look something like Figure 9-1.

Figure 9-1. The physics project

You'll notice that the project contains five classes: Player_Acceleration, Player_Friction, Player_ Bounce, Player_Gravity, and Player_Jump. The Library contains a symbol called Cat, which is the player character. You'll see the use of physics in motion by binding the cat symbol to these different classes.

Let's start with the simplest of these types of motion: acceleration.

Acceleration

Acceleration means to gradually increase velocity, just as your car does when you give it some gas. To gradually speed up game objects, you need to add a value to your object's vx or vy properties in an ENTER_FRAME event. You might recall from Chapter 6 that vx refers to "velocity on the x axis" and vy refers to "velocity on the y axis." In a nutshell, these properties represent an object's speed, traveling either horizontally or vertically.

In AS3.0, if you gradually want to increase an object's velocity on the x axis, you need to use an addition assignment operator (+=) to add the value of the acceleration to the vx property. Your code might look something like this:

```
vx += 0.2;
```

On the y axis, your code might look like this:

```
vy += 0.2;
```

Where did 0.2 come from? That's the value of acceleration. Exactly what the number is depends entirely on you and how quickly or slowly you want the object to speed up. A larger number such as 0.6 makes the object accelerate faster, and a lower number such as 0.1 makes it accelerate much more slowly. Choosing the right number is just a matter of trial and error and observing the effect it has on the object.

Let's see this effect on the cat object on the stage:

1. Make sure that the Player_Acceleration class is bound to the Cat symbol. To do that, select the Cat symbol in the Library and click the Properties button. The Symbol Properties window opens.

2. Make sure that the Class field contains the value Player_Acceleration, as shown in Figure 9-2. If it doesn't, change it so that it does.

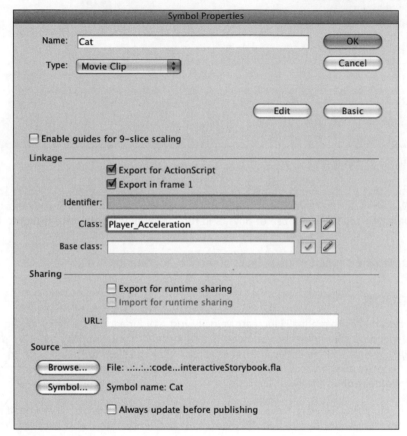

Figure 9-2. Bind the Player_Acceleration class to the Cat symbol.

3. Click the OK button.

4. Move the cat object around the stage with the arrow keys. It gradually speeds up before reaching its maximum speed of 5 pixels per frame.

Player_Acceleration class

This is what the Player_Acceleration class looks like:

```
package
{
  import flash.display.MovieClip;
  import flash.events.KeyboardEvent;
  import flash.ui.Keyboard;
  import flash.events.Event;

  public class Player_Acceleration extends MovieClip
  {
    private var _vx:Number;
    private var _vy:Number;
    private var _accelerationX:Number;
    private var _accelerationY:Number;
    private var _speedLimit:Number;

    public function Player_Acceleration()
    {
      _vx = 0;
      _vy = 0;
      _accelerationX = 0;
      _accelerationY = 0;
      _speedLimit = 5;

      //Stop animation on the object
      this.ears.stop();

      //Add stage event listeners
      stage.addEventListener(KeyboardEvent.KEY_DOWN, onKeyDown);
      stage.addEventListener(KeyboardEvent.KEY_UP, onKeyUp);
      addEventListener(Event.ENTER_FRAME, onEnterFrame);
    }
    private function onKeyDown(event:KeyboardEvent):void
    {
      if (event.keyCode == Keyboard.LEFT)
      {
        _accelerationX = -0.2;
      }
      if (event.keyCode == Keyboard.RIGHT)
      {
        _accelerationX = 0.2;
      }
      if (event.keyCode == Keyboard.UP)
```

```
    {
      _accelerationY = -0.2;
    }
    if (event.keyCode == Keyboard.DOWN)
    {
      _accelerationY = 0.2;
    }
  }
  private function onKeyUp(event:KeyboardEvent):void
  {
    if (event.keyCode == Keyboard.LEFT || ➥
      event.keyCode == Keyboard.RIGHT)
    {
      _accelerationX = 0;
      _vx = 0;
    }
    else if (event.keyCode == Keyboard.DOWN || ➥
      event.keyCode == Keyboard.UP)
    {
      _accelerationY = 0;
      _vy = 0;
    }
  }
  private function onEnterFrame(event:Event):void
  {
    //Initialize local variables
    var playerHalfWidth:uint = width / 2;
    var playerHalfHeight:uint = height / 2;

    //Apply Acceleration
    _vx += _accelerationX;
    if (_vx > _speedLimit)
    {
      _vx = _speedLimit;
    }
    if (_vx < -_speedLimit)
    {
      _vx = -_speedLimit;
    }

    _vy += _accelerationY;
    if (_vy > _speedLimit)
    {
      _vy = _speedLimit;
    }
    if (_vy < -_speedLimit)
```

```
    {
      _vy = -_speedLimit;
    }

    //Move the player
    x += _vx;
    y += _vy;

    //Stop player at stage edges
    if (x + playerHalfWidth > stage.stageWidth)
    {
      _vx = 0;
      _vy = 0;
      x = stage.stageWidth - playerHalfWidth;
    }
    else if (x - playerHalfWidth < 0)
    {
      _vx = 0;
      _vy = 0;
      x = 0 + playerHalfWidth;
    }
    if (y - playerHalfHeight < 0)
    {
      _vx = 0;
      _vy = 0;
      y = 0 + playerHalfHeight;
    }
    else if (y + playerHalfHeight > stage.stageHeight)
    {
      _vx = 0;
      _vy = 0;
      y = stage.stageHeight - playerHalfHeight;
    }
  }
 }
}
```

Despite the length of the code, it's nothing more than the run-of-the mill Player class from Dungeon Maze Adventure that's been adapted to handle acceleration. I'm sure you recognize most of it. Let's look at what's new and see how acceleration works.

> To keep the code as simple as possible, none of the classes in this chapter is initialized using an init method or onAddedToStage event handler. They're all initialized in the constructor method, which is also a perfectly valid way to initialize objects.

The code contains three variables to store the new acceleration data, which are initialized by the constructor method:

```
_accelerationX = 0;
_accelerationY = 0;
_speedLimit = 5;
```

The _accelerationX and _accelerationY variables store the value that determines by how much the object accelerates. Because you don't want the object to move when it first appears on the stage, _accelerationX and _accelerationY are initialized to zero. _speedLimit is the maximum speed that you want the object to travel. A value of 5 means that the object will travel a maximum of no more than 5 pixels per frame.

> *Just below the variable initialization is a directive that reads this.ears.stop();. The Cat symbol contains an animated subobject called ears, which you don't want to play for now. You'll see this in action soon enough.*

The work of assigning a value to the _accelerationX and _accelerationY variables is done by the onKeyDown event handler:

```
private function onKeyDown(event:KeyboardEvent):void
{
  if (event.keyCode == Keyboard.LEFT)
  {
    _accelerationX = -0.2;
  }
  if (event.keyCode == Keyboard.RIGHT)
  {
    _accelerationX = 0.2;
  }
  if (event.keyCode == Keyboard.UP)
  {
    _accelerationY = -0.2;
  }
  if (event.keyCode == Keyboard.DOWN)
  {
    _accelerationY = 0.2;
  }
}
```

If _accelerationX has a positive value, the object moves to the right. A negative value makes it move left. A positive _accelerationY value makes the object move down, and a negative value makes it move up.

When any of the arrow keys is pressed, these new values are assigned. All you need to do to make the object move is to assign these values to the object's _vx and _vy properties. You can do this easily enough with two lines of code:

```
_vx += _accelerationX;
_vy += _accelerationY;
```

However, if you leave things as is, the acceleration values are added to the object's velocity on every frame, without any limit to how fast the object can go. This means that the object eventually moves so fast that it will be nothing more than a blur on the stage. This won't be of much use in most games, so it's usually a good idea to assign a speed limit, which is what this section of code does:

```
if (_vx > _speedLimit)
{
  _vx = _speedLimit;
}
if (_vx < -_speedLimit)
{
  _vx = -_speedLimit;
}

_vy += _accelerationY;
if (_vy > _speedLimit)
{
  _vy = _speedLimit;
}
if (_vy < -_speedLimit)
{
  _vy = -_speedLimit;
}
```

The acceleration values are added to the object's velocity only if the _vx and _vx properties are within the speed limit, which is 5 in this case. This means that the object will accelerate up to 5 pixels per frame and then travel at a constant rate. The logic behind this is exactly the same logic used to set stage boundaries.

The next step is to add these new velocity values to the object's x and y positions. That's done with some venerable old friends—the same directives you've been using since Chapter 6:

```
x += _vx;
y += _vy;
```

In fact, these two directives are all you will *ever* need to move the objects, even though the physics involved in making them move become quite complex. All the physics calculations are applied to the _vx and _vy variables; they are then simply assigned to the object's x and y properties to make the object move.

So how does this actually work to accelerate the object? Let's trace the output and find out:

1. Add the following trace directive to the `Player_Accelerate` class in the `onEnterFrame` event handler:

```
//Move the player
x += _vx;
y += _vy;
trace("_vx: " + _vx);
trace("x: " + x);
trace("----------");
```

2. Save the `Player_Accelerate.as` file.

3. Test the project.

4. Press the right arrow key and check the trace in the Output window. When the object starts moving, you'll see something that looks like this:

```
_vx: 0
x: 275
----------
_vx: 0.2
x: 275.2
----------
_vx: 0.4
x: 275.55
----------
_vx: 0.6000000000000001
x: 276.15
----------
_vx: 0.8
x: 276.95
```

These are the first 5 frames of movement, but this pattern continues until _vx reaches a maximum value of 5, which is what the _speedLimit property is set to.

The numbers with the large number of decimal places are a byproduct of the way the CPU's binary number system stores fractions. For all practical purposes, you can ignore the strings of zeros and round off to two decimal places.

> The smallest unit into which Flash can divide a pixel is 0.05. This unit is known by the whimsical name **twip** (20 twips equal 1 pixel). That's why all the x and y values you see in the trace output are multiples of 0.05.

On the second frame, the accelerationX initial value of 0.2 is added to the object's current x position, resulting in a new x value of 275.2. Because the right arrow key is still being held down, this code is then run:

```
else if (event.keyCode == Keyboard.RIGHT)
{
  _accelerationX = 0.2;
}
```

It adds an *additional* 0.2 to the _vx value, giving it a new value of 0.4. (You can see this new value reflected in the third trace.) 0.4 is then added to the object's x position, resulting in a new position of 275.55.

Strange! 275.55 doesn't equal 272.2 plus 0.4, so logically the new value should be 275.6. But why is it 0.05 less? This again has to do with the way binary systems deal with fractional numbers. Behind the scenes, the CPU actually represents 272.2 plus 0.4 as 275.59999999999997. Almost 275.6, but not quite. Flash therefore decides to round this down to the nearest multiple of 0.05, which is 275.55. It's not completely accurate, but remember that I'm talking about 1/20 of a pixel here! The difference is so small that it's absolutely imperceptible when the object moves across the stage.

You can see from this trace that the _accelerationX value continues to compound by adding 0.2 to its value each frame until it finally reaches 5, and the object is clipping along at quite a quick pace. All this adds up to a very neat illusion that the object is accelerating.

The last thing that the code does is stop the object, which is handled by the onKeyUp event handler:

```
private function onKeyUp(event:KeyboardEvent):void
{
  if (event.keyCode == Keyboard.LEFT || ➡
    event.keyCode == Keyboard.RIGHT)
  {
    _accelerationX = 0;
    _vx = 0;
  }
  else if (event.keyCode == Keyboard.DOWN || ➡
    event.keyCode == Keyboard.UP)
  {
    _accelerationY = 0;
    _vy = 0;
  }
}
```

This sets the object's acceleration and velocity to zero when the appropriate keys are released.

Friction

Friction is the exact opposite of acceleration: it causes the object to gradually slow down. Let's see how it works with the cat:

1. Select the Cat symbol in the Library and click the Properties button. Change the Class field to Player_Friction and click the OK button.

2. Test the project.

3. Move the cat around the screen with the arrow keys. You can move it in delightfully smooth swoops and arcs, as if it were floating.

The Player_Friction class is almost identical to Player_Acceleration except for a few small additions. Double-click it in the Project panel to open it and take a look.

First, is the new variable, _friction, which is initialized to 0.96:

```
_vx = 0;
_vy = 0;
_accelerationX = 0;
_accelerationY = 0;
_speedLimit = 5;
_friction = 0.96;
```

A value of 1 amounts to "no friction," so anything less than 1 gradually slows the object down. Values from 0.94 to 0.98 apply friction very gradually, for very fluid movement. Values such as 0.7 or 0.6 slow the object very quickly.

All you need to do now is add the _friction value to the _vx and _vy properties:

```
_vx *= _friction;
_vy *= _friction;
```

It multiplies the velocities by a number less than 1, which gradually reduces them. It's very simple and very effective. There's one technical detail you have to fix, however.

Here's the scenario. Imagine that the object's velocity is 5. Its friction is 0.6. The object needs a velocity of zero to stop completely. You apply some friction every frame, multiplying the velocity by 0.6, hoping to finally reach zero. Here's what the first five frames might look like.

5 * 0.6 = 3

3 * 0.6 = 1.8

1.8 * 0.6 = 1.08

1.08 * 0.6 = 0.648

0.648 * 0.6 = 0.3888

But you're not at zero yet. How long do you think it will take before you get there? Well, you can keep going all day—you never will!

This is an effect known as **Xeno's paradox**. It goes something like this. Let's say you have a slice of cake, which you cut in half. You cut one of those slices in half once more. Then do the same to the third slice. The pieces of cake keep getting thinner and thinner. How many times can you slice them until there's nothing left to slice? Xeno's paradox is that you never reach an end—the pieces of cake just become infinitely thin, and you can go on slicing them forever. Crazy as it sounds, the math actually backs this up, and even more crazily, you have to deal with it in AS3.0!

This means that when you apply friction, _vx and _vy never reach zero. The object will never stop completely. What you need to do then is *force a value of zero* when _vx and _vy fall below a certain threshold. This is what this next bit of new code does:

```
if (Math.abs(_vx) < 0.1)
{
  _vx = 0;
}
  if (Math.abs(_vy) < 0.1)
{
  _vy = 0;
}
```

If _vx and _vy fall below an absolute value of 0.1, it forces them a value of 0, thus halting Xeno in his tracks. 0.1 is low enough that it won't have any observable effect on the motion of the object and the object appears to stop very naturally, even at low friction values such as 0.99. Without this code, your objects will creep slightly up and to the left on the stage, and never actually stop.

> As a quick refresher, Math.abs forces the value in its argument to be positive ("absolute"). It simplifies the code because you don't have to check for negative values.

One final small change to the code is that onKeyUp now no longer sets _vx and _vy to zero. That job is left for the friction calculation to do. All onKeyUp needs to do is stop the object's acceleration:

```
private function onKeyUp(event:KeyboardEvent):void
{
  if (event.keyCode == Keyboard.LEFT || ➡
    event.keyCode == Keyboard.RIGHT)
  {
    _accelerationX = 0;
  }
  if (event.keyCode == Keyboard.UP || ➡
    event.keyCode == Keyboard.DOWN)
  {
    _accelerationY = 0;
  }
}
```

And that's it for friction!

Bouncing

After acceleration and friction happen, bouncing is a piece of cake (the un-infinite kind!).

Bind the Cat symbol to the Player_Bounce class using the same steps you followed earlier. Move the cat around the stage with the arrow keys and you'll notice that you can bounce it off the stage edges, as shown in Figure 9-3.

Figure 9-3. Bounce the cat off the edges of the stage.

Double-click the Player_Bounce class in the Project panel to open it. You'll notice that it's remarkably similar to Player_Friction, except for the addition of a new _bounce variable and few other small changes.

The _bounce variable is declared with a value of -0.7:

```
_vx = 0;
_vy = 0;
_accelerationX = 0;
_accelerationY = 0;
_speedLimit = 5;
_friction = 0.96;
_bounce = -0.7;
```

The bounce value has to be negative because bouncing works by *reversing* the object's velocity. You'll see how this happens in a moment. A value of -0.7 creates the effect of a moderate bounce. A value of -1 makes the object super bouncy. A value of 1 makes the object completely bounce-less. Any value less than -1 makes the object look like it's hitting an extremely springy surface, such as a trampoline. This is important to keep in mind if you want to make a springing platform in a game.

The _bounce variable doesn't make a further appearance until the section of code that handles stage boundaries:

```
if (x + playerHalfWidth > stage.stageWidth)
{
  _vx *= _bounce;
  x = stage.stageWidth - playerHalfWidth;
}
else if (x - playerHalfWidth < 0)
{
  _vx *= _bounce;
  x = 0 + playerHalfWidth;
}
if (y - playerHalfHeight < 0)
{
  _vy *= _bounce;
  y = 0 + playerHalfHeight;
}
  else if (y + playerHalfHeight > stage.stageHeight)
{
  _vy *= _bounce;
  y = stage.stageHeight - playerHalfHeight;
}
```

All that's happening is that the object's velocity is being multiplied by the _bounce value, which is negative. If you reverse an object's velocity, it looks as if it is bouncing!

Gravity

Gravity is just as easy to implement as the other physical forces. All you need to do is create one more value and add it to the object's _vy velocity.

To see gravity at work, bind the Player_Gravity class to the Cat symbol. Test the project. The cat drops to the bottom of the stage. If you press the up arrow key, the cat moves up. When the up arrow is released again, the cat falls to the ground. When the cat reaches its maximum speed, terminal velocity displays in the Output panel.

The cat's ears now also flap when it moves. At last, a use for those long ears—the cat can fly! Figure 9-4 illustrates what you'll see.

Figure 9-4. Use the arrow keys to make the cat fly.

Double-click the `Player_Gravity` class to take a quick look at it. Even though the code is very simple, the result is a very convincing simulation of the real world. In fact, it's almost scarily realistic! Let's see how it works.

The new _gravity variable is nothing special:

```
_vx = 0;
_vy = 0;
_accelerationX = 0;
_accelerationY = 0;
_speedLimit = 5;
_friction = 0.96;
_gravity = 0.3;
```

Like the other values, 0.3 is just one that came about through trial and error, and it looks natural in this context. A higher number increases gravity, and a lower number decreases it.

Applying gravity to the object is simply a matter of adding it to the _vy value, which this directive does:

```
_vy += _gravity;
```

That's it! That's all you need to do to implement gravity.

The Player_Gravity class goes a little bit further, however. You want to allow the player to make the cat move up when the up arrow is pressed. There is actually more than one way to do this, and this class represents the slightly more complex way.

The way this works is that when the player presses the up arrow key, _gravity is set to 0 in the onKeyDown event handler:

```
private function onKeyDown(event:KeyboardEvent):void
{
  if (event.keyCode == Keyboard.LEFT)
  {
    _accelerationX = -0.2;
  }
  else if (event.keyCode == Keyboard.RIGHT)
  {
    _accelerationX = 0.2;
  }
  else if (event.keyCode == Keyboard.UP)
  {
    _accelerationY = -0.2;
    _gravity = 0;
    this.ears.play();
  }
}
```

This allows the cat object to move up the stage freely and also triggers its ears subobject to start its animation. The ears are animated using a simple motion tween. Have a look at the Ears symbol in the Library to take a closer look at how this works. (Notice that there's also no code for the down arrow key. You don't need it—gravity takes care of moving the object down.)

When the keys are released, the _gravity variable is set back to its original value of 0.3.

```
private function onKeyUp(event:KeyboardEvent):void
{
  _accelerationX = 0;
  _accelerationY = 0;
  _gravity = 0.3;
  this.ears.gotoAndStop(1);
}
```

The ears are also stopped and returned to their starting frame. You can create this same effect by just giving _accelerationY a positive value when you need gravity applied. (A positive y value pulls the object to the bottom of the stage.) It means that you could dispense with having to create the _gravity variable altogether, and the class would contain a bit less code. However, the nice thing about using a separate _gravity variable is that it makes the code easier to understand, and it keeps your options open for mixing and matching the _gravity force with other physical forces that you might add later.

There are two other bits of fine-tuning done to this code. I want the object to fall at a faster rate than it ascends. I modified the speed limit in the `if` statement that checks to see how fast the object is moving down the stage:

```
if (_vy > (_speedLimit * 2))
{
  _vy = (_speedLimit * 2);
  trace("terminal velocity");
}
if (_vy < -_speedLimit)
{
  _vy = -_speedLimit;
}
```

Multiplying it by 2 makes it fall twice as fast as it climbs. It also displays terminal velocity when it reaches its maximum speed. You could use this in a Lunar Lander–type game to figure out whether the space-craft is going too fast when it hits the planet surface.

The other small change is that friction isn't added to the _vy property—gravity takes care of that as well.

Jumping

Probably half of all video games ever made use jumping as a primary character action. All it boils down to is a temporary increase in the object's y velocity. Once you understand how acceleration, friction, and gravity work, jumping is not at all difficult to implement. However, there are a few additional things to keep in mind that make it a little more complex:

- You want your object to be able to jump when it's on the ground, and only on the ground. But how will your object know that it's on the ground? And what is the ground, anyway? The code has to be able to figure these things out.

- You need to prevent the jump keys from triggering a jump more than once if they're held down.

Let's look at an example of jumping in action and how to solve these problems. Bind the `Player_Jump` class to the Cat symbol. Test the project. The left and right arrow keys move the cat horizontally, and pressing the up arrow key or the spacebar makes it jump. While the cat is moving up, its ears flap, but they stop flapping when it's moving down toward the ground. Figure 9-5 illustrates this.

Figure 9-5. Press the spacebar or up arrow key to make the cat jump.

To implement jumping, you need two new variables:

```
_vx = 0;
_vy = 0;
_accelerationX = 0;
_accelerationY = 0;
_speedLimit = 5;
_friction = 0.96;
_gravity = 0.3;
_isOnGround = undefined;
_jumpForce = -10;
```

_isOnGround is a Boolean value that tells the class whether the object is on the ground. It's initialized as undefined because you might not always know whether the object will be on the ground when the game starts.

_jumpForce is the force with which the object will jump. It needs to project upward toward the top of the stage, so it has a negative value. The actual value that you give it is again a matter of trial and error. You'll need to make sure that its value is enough to counteract gravity and any other forces that might be acting on the object.

How does the object know whether it's on the ground? This is something that could become quite complex, depending on the game you're designing, so you'll need to think about this carefully when you start any project that uses jumping. In this simple example, the cat object is on the ground when it's at the bottom of the stage. So all you need to do is set _isOnGround to true in the same section of code that checks for the bottom stage boundary:

```
if (x + playerHalfWidth > stage.stageWidth)
{
  _vx = 0;
  x = stage.stageWidth - playerHalfWidth;
}
  else if (x - playerHalfWidth < 0)
{
  _vx = 0;
  x = 0 + playerHalfWidth;
}
if (y - playerHalfHeight < 0)
{
  _vy = 0;
  y = 0 + playerHalfHeight;
}
else if (y + playerHalfHeight > stage.stageHeight)
{
  _vy = 0;
  y = stage.stageHeight - playerHalfHeight;
  _isOnGround = true;
}
```

That's pretty straightforward. In most games that use jumping, game characters also need to know when they're standing on platforms. That makes detecting the ground a little more complex, but you'll be looking at a solution in the Bug Catcher game that you'll build later in the chapter.

Making the object actually jump happens in the onKeyDown event handler:

```
private function onKeyDown(event:KeyboardEvent):void
{
  if (event.keyCode == Keyboard.LEFT)
  {
    _accelerationX = -0.2;
  }
  if (event.keyCode == Keyboard.RIGHT)
  {
    _accelerationX = 0.2;
  }
  if ((event.keyCode == Keyboard.UP)
```

```
      || (event.keyCode == Keyboard.SPACE))
    {
      if (_isOnGround)
      {
        _accelerationY = _jumpForce;
        _isOnGround = false;
        this.ears.play();
      }
    }
  }
```

If the spacebar or up arrow key is pressed, the code checks to see whether the object is on the ground. If it is, it adds the jump force value to the vertical acceleration. It also sets the _isOnGround variable to false. In this example, it also makes the cat's ears flap.

The last little technical issue that you need to solve is that after the preceding code sets _accelerationY to -10, it remains that way until the jump keys are released. That means that if the keys are held down, _accelerationY will remain at -10, and the object will keep jumping. To fix this, you need to give _accelerationY a value of zero if the object is not on the ground. This section of code in the onEnterFrame event handler accomplishes this:

```
    if (! _isOnGround)
    {
      _accelerationY=0;
    }
```

One more little detail prevents the cat's ears from flapping when it descends from the apex of the jump. This is easy to do:

```
    if (_vy > 0)
    {
      this.ears.gotoAndStop(1);
    }
```

The animation stops if the cat's vertical velocity is less than 0, which means it's moving toward the bottom of the stage.

Finally, there's no speed limit set if the object ascends because that would conflict with the value of _jumpForce.

Stage boundaries and subobjects

There's another feature in the Player_Jump class that will get you thinking about some of the other issues you'll be looking at in the example Bug Catcher game, coming up next. If you move the cat to the left or right side of the stage, its ears extend beyond the stage boundaries. It is, in fact, the cat's body that's being blocked at the edges.

This happens because the cat has a subobject called body. It's a round black circle that defines the main area of the cat. It seemed to me that it looked more natural to use it as the cat's collision area instead of using its overlong ears. The ears are great for flying, but seem to get in the way of everything else!

To use the cat's body to define the player's collision area, all I needed to do was modify the variables that describe the player's dimensions to specify the body as the primary object:

```
var playerHalfWidth:uint = this.body.width / 2;
var playerHalfHeight:uint = this.body.height / 2;
```

The keyword this is optional, but it does help to clarify "the body of *this* object."

Figure 9-6 illustrates the effect of using the cat's body subobject as the collision area for stage boundaries. This is important to note because in the upcoming example game, you'll be taking a detailed look at how to properly use and target subobjects in your games.

Figure 9-6. The cat's body subobject is used as the collision area for checking stage boundaries.

Case study: Bug Catcher

I'm sure you have quite a few ideas about how you can use some of these new techniques in your games. You'll take a look at how you can use them to build a simple game called Bug Catcher. In the Bug Catcher Finished folder of the chapter's source files is a file called bugCatcher_Finished.swf, which looks something like Figure 9-7 when it runs.

Figure 9-7. Bug Catcher

The objective of Bug Catcher is to catch three bugs and bring them to the frog. (But the frog doesn't like mice, so be careful not to catch him one of those!) Bug Catcher is a platform game, one of the most popular genres of video game. Platform games feature characters that run and jump across surfaces on different planes known as **platforms**.

The game will use every detail of motion physics that you've looked over the first part of this chapter. It will introduce an advanced collision detection utility that you can use to bounce a player object off a platform. You'll also use scripted animation, arrays, artificial intelligence, and a bit of trigonometry. Oh yes, and did I also mention it was going to be a very easy game to create? You'll be surprised!

The object of this project is to illustrate specific techniques that you can use to build your own platform game. Feel free to follow along, step by step, but I'm treating this project more as a discussion of how the game was made instead of something you should copy outright. Many of the problems you'll solve by building this game are absolutely central to video game design, so you have to learn about them. And the best way to learn is to dive in and start experimenting with these new techniques in your own way.

A good approach for completing this chapter is to follow along and use these techniques to build a similar game of your own, in parallel with my explanation.

Setting up the project files

To get you started, you'll find a basic setup file called bugCatcher.fla in the Bug Catcher Setup folder of the Chapter 9 source files. In the same folder are three other classes: Player_Platform.as, Collision.as, and Main_BugCatcher.as. You'll need all these files as a starting point for this project.

Let's create the project. Follow these steps:

1. Select File ➤ Open.

2. Navigate to the bugCatcher.fla file in the Chapter 9 Bug Catcher Setup folder. Click the Open button.

3. Select Quick Project in the Project panel's drop-down menu.

4. The bugCatcher project is created. The stage, Library, and Project panel should now look something like Figure 9-8.

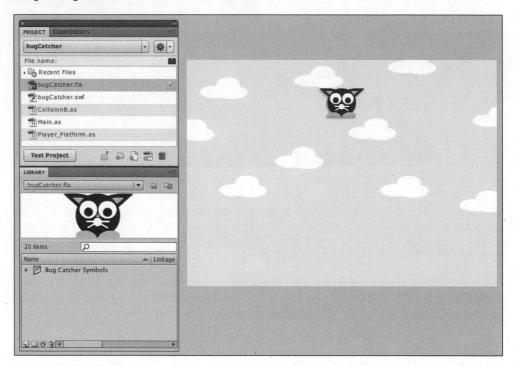

Figure 9-8. Bug Catcher project

5. Test the project. When the SWF file runs, the cat drops to the ground, and you can use the arrow keys to make it move and jump. The cat bounces slightly when it hits the ground. (In this class, the ground is actually defined as a point 10 pixels above the bottom of the stage. I did this so I can add a 10-pixel-high solid ground graphic a little later in the project.)

If this process doesn't work, double-check that the Cat symbol is bound to the Player_Platform class by selecting the Cat symbol in the Library *and clicking the* Properties *button. Also, check that Main_BugCatcher is set as the bugCatcher.fla document class.*

This puts you at a starting point that's just about where you left off with the Player_Jump class. The player object is now bound to the Player_Platform class, which is extremely similar to Player_Jump. Let's take a closer look at it.

Using the Player_Platform class

This class is long, but it is almost functionally identical to Player_Jump. The biggest difference is a string of getters and setters at the end of the class that allow it to communicate with other classes and objects. There are also a few modifications, such as the _bounceX and _bounceY variables that you need for the player object to interact with the platforms. The class also introduces a new concept: constants. You'll look at all of this in detail.

For now, this is what the class looks like. It's long, but you've seen most of it before:

```
package
{
  import flash.display.MovieClip;
  import flash.events.KeyboardEvent;
  import flash.ui.Keyboard;
  import flash.events.Event;

  public class Player_Platform extends MovieClip
  {
    //Constants
    private const FRICTION:Number = 0.60;
    private const SPEED_LIMIT:int = 7;
    private const GRAVITY:Number = 0.8;
    private const ACCELERATION:Number = 1.5;
    private const BOUNCE:Number = -0.3;
    private const JUMP_FORCE:Number = -16;
    private const BOTTOM_OF_STAGE:uint = 10;

    //Variables:
    private var _vx:Number;
    private var _vy:Number;
    private var _accelerationX:Number;
    private var _accelerationY:Number;
    private var _frictionX:Number;
    private var _isOnGround:Boolean;
    private var _bounceX:Number;
    private var _bounceY:Number;
    private var _collisionArea:MovieClip;
```

```
public function Player_Platform()
{
  _vx = 0;
  _vy = 0;
  _accelerationX = 0;
  _accelerationY = 0;
  _frictionX = FRICTION;
  _isOnGround = undefined;
  _bounceX = 0;
  _bounceY = 0;
  _collisionArea = this.body;
  this.ears.stop();

  //Add stage event listeners
  stage.addEventListener(KeyboardEvent.KEY_DOWN,onKeyDown);
  stage.addEventListener(KeyboardEvent.KEY_UP,onKeyUp);
  addEventListener(Event.ENTER_FRAME, onEnterFrame);
}
private function onKeyDown(event:KeyboardEvent):void
{
  //Remove friction if the object is moving
  _frictionX = 1;

  if (event.keyCode == Keyboard.LEFT)
  {
    _accelerationX = -ACCELERATION;
  }
  if (event.keyCode == Keyboard.RIGHT)
  {
    _accelerationX = ACCELERATION;
  }
  if ((event.keyCode == Keyboard.UP)
  || (event.keyCode == Keyboard.SPACE))
  {
    if (_isOnGround)
    {
      _accelerationY = JUMP_FORCE;
      this.ears.play();
      _isOnGround = false;
    }
  }
}
private function onKeyUp(event:KeyboardEvent):void
{
  if ((event.keyCode == Keyboard.LEFT)
  || (event.keyCode == Keyboard.RIGHT))
  {
    _accelerationX = 0;
```

```
        //Apply friction when the keys are no longer being pressed
        _frictionX = FRICTION;
    }
    if ((event.keyCode == Keyboard.UP)
    || (event.keyCode == Keyboard.SPACE))
    {
        _accelerationY = 0;
    }
}
private function onEnterFrame(event:Event):void
{
    //Initialize local variables
    var playerHalfWidth:uint = _collisionArea.width / 2;
    var playerHalfHeight:uint = _collisionArea.height / 2;

    //Apply Acceleration
    _vx += _accelerationX;
    if (_vx > SPEED_LIMIT)
    {
        _vx = SPEED_LIMIT;
    }
    if (_vx < -SPEED_LIMIT)
    {
        _vx = -SPEED_LIMIT;
    }

    _vy += _accelerationY;
    if (_vy > SPEED_LIMIT * 3)
    {
        _vy = SPEED_LIMIT * 3;
    }
    //No speed limit for jumping

    //Apply Friction
    if (_isOnGround)
    {
        _vx *= _frictionX;
    }
    if (Math.abs(_vx) < 0.1)
    {
        _vx = 0;
    }
    if (Math.abs(_vy) < 0.1)
    {
        _vy = 0;
    }

    //Apply Gravity
    _vy += GRAVITY;
```

```
//Apply Bounce from collision with platforms
x += bounceX;
y += bounceY;

//Move the player
x += _vx;
y += _vy;

//Reset platform bounce values so that they
//don't compound with the next collision
_bounceX = 0;
_bounceY = 0;

//Prevent object from moving up if it's not on the ground
if (! _isOnGround)
{
  _accelerationY = 0;
}

//Flap ears only when going up
if (_vy >= 0)
{
  this.ears.gotoAndStop(1);
  _isOnGround = false;
}

//Stage boundaries
if (x + playerHalfWidth > stage.stageWidth)
{
  _vx = 0;
  x = stage.stageWidth - playerHalfWidth;
}
else if (x - playerHalfWidth < 0)
{
  _vx = 0;
  x = 0+playerHalfWidth;
}
if (y - playerHalfHeight < 0)
{
  _vy = 0;
  y = 0 + playerHalfHeight;
}
else if (y + playerHalfHeight > stage.stageHeight ➥
  - BOTTOM_OF_STAGE)
{
  _vy *= BOUNCE;
  y = stage.stageHeight - playerHalfHeight - BOTTOM_OF_STAGE;
  _isOnGround = true;
```

```
        }
    }

    //Getters and Setters
    public function get isOnGround():Boolean
    {
        return _isOnGround;
    }
    public function set isOnGround(onGround:Boolean):void
    {
        _isOnGround = onGround;
    }
    public function set vx(vxValue:Number):void
    {
        _vx = vxValue;
    }
    public function get vx():Number
    {
        return _vx;
    }
    public function set vy(vyValue:Number):void
    {
        _vy = vyValue;
    }
    public function get vy():Number
    {
        return _vy;
    }
    public function get bounceX():Number
    {
        return _bounceX;
    }
    public function set bounceX(bounceXValue:Number):void
    {
        _bounceX = bounceXValue;
    }
    public function get bounceY():Number
    {
        return _bounceY;
    }
    public function set bounceY(bounceYValue:Number):void
    {
        _bounceY = bounceYValue;
    }
    public function get collisionArea():MovieClip
    {
        return _collisionArea;
    }
    }
}
```

Constants

The first thing you'll probably notice about this class is the use of words that are fully capitalized, such as BOUNCE and GRAVITY. They are called **constants**, which are used exactly like variables, except that their values never change. Their values are *constant*.

Constants are declared and initialized in the class definition using the keyword const. Here are the constants used in the class:

```
private const FRICTION:Number = 0.60;
private const SPEED_LIMIT:int = 7;
private const GRAVITY:Number = 0.8;
private const ACCELERATION:Number = 1.5;
private const BOUNCE:Number = -0.3;
private const JUMP_FORCE:Number = -16;
private const BOTTOM_OF_STAGE:uint = 10;
```

After the values of constants are assigned, they can never be changed. This is helpful because it means that your program will be free of errors that result from values being accidentally overwritten by other values when your program depends on them to remain unchanged.

Constants also make it easy to quickly change the functioning of the program. By changing the values of the constants at the top of the class, you can completely change the physical forces that affect the player character, from the strength of gravity to the height of each jump. It makes the class very customizable by just changing a few simple values.

By convention, constants are always written in full uppercase characters, which make them easy to spot in your code. If the name of a constant is made up of two or more words, the convention is to separate the words with an underscore character, like this: TWO_WORDS. Like variables, constants are also referred to as **properties**.

One small change to this code is the use of the _frictionX variable, which is used as the value of friction on the x axis. Because in this game the player object moves only left and right along the ground, you don't need to account for friction on the y axis. This is just a slightly more specific way of dealing with friction than in the previous examples, but the effect is exactly the same.

Player friction

The other slight modification is that friction on the x axis is completely removed when the keys are pressed. You can see this at the beginning of the onKeyDown event handler:

```
private function onKeyDown(event:KeyboardEvent):void
{
    //Remove friction if the object is moving
    _frictionX = 1;
```

A value of 1 means the value of _vx is multiplied by 1, so the value doesn't change. Friction is returned to its initial value (the value of the FRICTION constant, which is 0.6) when the keys are released.

```
private function onKeyUp(event:KeyboardEvent):void
{
  if ((event.keyCode == Keyboard.LEFT)
  || (event.keyCode == Keyboard.RIGHT))
  {
    _accelerationX = 0;
    //Apply friction when the keys are no longer being pressed
    _frictionX = FRICTION;
  }
...
```

I included this bit of fine-tuning in the class because if no friction is being applied while the character is moving, its movement is a little more fluid and a little more responsive. It's entirely up to you whether you'll feel the same way about the characters in the games you'll be designing.

Bounce variables

There are two new variables in this class that you haven't used before: _bounceX and _bounceY. These variables are used to accept bounce values that will be sent to the class by the platforms that the player object will be jumping on. Without these values available, the player object can't bounce on platforms. You'll use a special collision utility to control how the player interacts with platforms (discussed later).

The variables _bounceX and _bounceY are unrelated to the BOUNCE constant. The BOUNCE constant is used to define the "bounciness" of the player object. In the game that you'll be designing, the BOUNCE constant is used only to define by how much the player object will bounce when it hits the bottom of the stage.

```
else if (y + playerHalfHeight > stage.stageHeight - BOTTOM_OF_STAGE)
{
  _vy *= BOUNCE;
  y = stage.stageHeight - playerHalfHeight - BOTTOM_OF_STAGE;
  _isOnGround = true;
}
```

Notice that the bottom of the stage is offset by 10 pixels, which gives you some space to add the 10-pixel-high ground graphic. This offset is defined by the BOTTOM_OF_STAGE constant, which is defined at the beginning of the class definition.

Player collision area

Another small but important change is that the cat's body subobject, which will be used as the collision area, is now assigned to a _collisionArea variable.

```
_collisionArea = this.body;
```

This is important because the code will access this property to check which part of the player object should be checked for collisions with platforms.

Adding Platforms

Cats love to jump, so let's give the cat character something to jump on!

1. Create a 50-by-50 pixel square Platform symbol in the Library. (Feel free to create your own graphics and symbols for this game, but if you're feeling a bit lazy, you'll find all the symbols for the original Bug Catcher game in the Bug Catcher Symbols folder in the Library.)

2. Drag as many instances of the Platform symbol onto the stage as you like, in any arrangement that you think will be fun to jump on. You can also use the free-transform tool to stretch these platform instances to any rectangular shape that you like. The platform collision code that you'll be adding can handle rectangular-shaped platforms of any size.

3. Give all your platforms instance names. Name them in this format: platform0, platform1, platform2, platform3, and so on. It's very important to give them all the same root name, such as platform, and start the numbering at zero (you'll see why very soon). My arrangement of platforms looks like Figure 9-9.

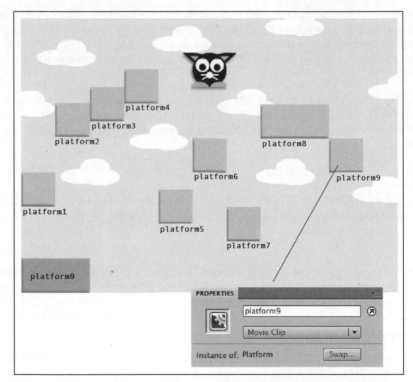

Figure 9-9. Give your platforms instance names in the format platform0, platform1, platform2, and so on.

Beveling

In this example, the platforms have a slight 3D effect, as if they extend up above the surface of the stage. This effect is called **beveling**. Bevel is one of the filters that can be assigned to an object in the Filters section of the Properties panel.

To bevel an object, select it, and choose Bevel from the Add filter button at the bottom of the panel. There are many settings that you can adjust until the object looks the way you want it to. Figure 9-10 shows the setting used for the platforms in Bug Catcher.

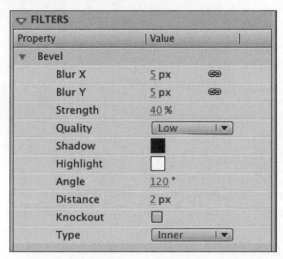

Figure 9-10. Bevel objects for a shallow 3D raised-surface effect.

Filters are a quick and easy way to add surface texture to games. The cat and frog use slight drop-shadow filters, which contrast well with the beveled platforms.

Tinting

The Properties panel has a section called Color Effect. One of the effects that you can choose from its Style drop-down menu is called Tint. Tinting an object allows you to change the color of an instance without affecting the color of its parent symbol. This process is very useful because it means that you can have many instances of the same symbol, each with a unique color or **tint**, without having to create a new symbol to accommodate for it.

In the Bug Catcher game, I used the Tint color effect to make the platform on the bottom-left corner of the stage a darker shade of green than the other platforms. To tint an object, select it, choose Tint from the Style drop-down menu, and play with the options until you find a color that you're happy with. Figure 9-11 shows the settings used to tint the bottom-left platform.

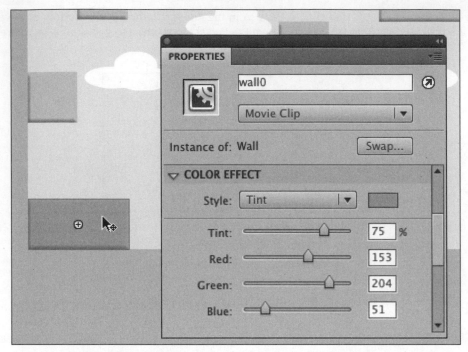

Figure 9-11. Tinting allows you to give instances a unique color without changing the color of the parent symbol.

Now that the platforms have been plotted on the screen, you can put them to work.

Detecting platform collisions

In the Project panel, you'll find the Collision class. This is the same class used in previous chapters, but in this chapter you'll use one of its methods: playerAndPlatform. Like the block method, it prevents two rectangular objects from intersecting. However, it's been upgraded with some fancy new features that allow it to handle physics. When two rectangular objects collide, you can specify whether the first object bounces back when it hits. You can also specify whether it loses some additional momentum when it does so, by adding some extra friction into the mix.

The Collision.playerAndPlatform method requires four arguments:

- The first object, which is the player object
- The second object, which is the platform
- The amount you want the player to bounce when it hits the platform
- The amount of friction, which is lost momentum when the player object hits

Here's the basic model for using it:

```
Collision.playerAndPlatform(player, platform, bounceValue, ➥
    frictionValue);
```

Let's say you want to set up a collision between the player object and platform0. You want to give the collision a bounce value of 0.6 and a bit of friction. Friction is calculated in a different way in this method, so a low friction would be a value of 0.1. The method might look something like this:

```
Collision.playerAndPlatform(player, platform0, 0.6, 0.1);
```

To use the Collision.playerAndPlatform method with your games, you need to be aware of the following:

- The Collision class must be in the same directory as the rest of the code or imported into a class using the import statement.

- The first object in the argument, player, has to have _vx and _vy properties that are accessible by getters and setters called vx and vy. Have a look at the Player_Platform class to see how it is implemented. If the object doesn't have these properties assigned, the method will try to create them dynamically, although you won't have much control over how the collision behaves. It's usually better to plan for this and establish the _vx and _vy properties in the object's class, like you have in Player_Platform.

- If you want the player to bounce when the collision occurs, it needs to have properties called _bounceX and _bounceY that are accessible by getters and setters called bounceX and bounceY. If your object doesn't have these properties, the blocking feature of the method still works, but the bounce effect doesn't. This is implemented in the Player_Platform class, so check out the code if you're unsure about how to do this.

- You can assign a subobject to be used as the collision area. If the player contains a property called _collisionArea that's accessible by a getter called collisionArea, that object will be used as the collision object. If you don't have a _collisionArea property assigned, the entire object is used in the collision detection.

The method has been written as an easy-to-use utility that you'll find a use for in countless game projects. As such, you don't need to know how it works; just how to implement in your games. For the curious, however, you'll be taking a detailed look at its inner workings at the end of this chapter. Take a sneak peek if you want to!

But without much further ado, let's put this new collision method to work for you in the game-to-be:

1. Open the project's Main_BugCatcher class by double-clicking it in the Project panel. When it opens, you'll see that the basic framework of the class has already been written for you, so you can quickly get to the fun part of actually programming the game.

2. You need to check for a collision between the player object and each of the new platform objects using the new Collision.playerAndPlatform method. This means writing out almost the same directive for as many times as you have platform objects and changing the name of the platform object for each new line. You'll give the collision a mild bounce, for which a value of 0.2 works pretty well. The friction value is additional friction to the friction that you've already assigned in the Player_Platform class. You don't really need it in this game, so you'll give it a value of zero. Change the Main_BugCatcher.as file by adding the following code to

the onEnterFrame event handler (if you added more or fewer platform objects in your own project, make sure that the number and names match what you created):

```
package
{
  import flash.display.MovieClip;
  import flash.events.Event;
  import flash.geom.Point;

  public class Main_BugCatcher extends MovieClip
  {
    public function Main_BugCatcher ()
    {
      addEventListener(Event.ENTER_FRAME, onEnterFrame);
    }
    private function onEnterFrame(event:Event):void
    {
      //Player vs platform collision
      Collision.playerAndPlatform(player, platform0, 0.2, 0);
      Collision.playerAndPlatform(player, platform1, 0.2, 0);
      Collision.playerAndPlatform(player, platform2, 0.2, 0);
      Collision.playerAndPlatform(player, platform3, 0.2, 0);
      Collision.playerAndPlatform(player, platform4, 0.2, 0);
      Collision.playerAndPlatform(player, platform5, 0.2, 0);
      Collision.playerAndPlatform(player, platform6, 0.2, 0);
      Collision.playerAndPlatform(player, platform7, 0.2, 0);
      Collision.playerAndPlatform(player, platform8, 0.2, 0);
      Collision.playerAndPlatform(player, platform9, 0.2, 0);
    }
  }
}
```

3. Save the Main_BugCatcher.as file.

4. Check to make sure that Main_BugCatcher is set as the document class in the bugCatcher.fla file.

5. Check to make sure that the cat on the main stage has the instance name player.

6. Save the bugCatcher.fla file.

7. Test the project. Wow, the cat can now hop around the stage from platform to platform! Figure 9-12 illustrates this.

If the process didn't work, make sure that you named the platform instances correctly and also used the correct instance names in the previous code. With so many similar instance names, it's very easy to make a small mistake here.

Figure 9-12. The cat can jump from platform to platform.

The cat's body subobject is being used for collision, as Figure 9-13 illustrates. This is another feature of the Collision. playerAndPlatform method. The subobject that is specified in the collisionArea property of the player is used as the object in the collision detection. You'll look at exactly how this works at the end of the chapter.

If you added the platforms on the same layer as the cat object, the cat's ears are behind the platform, which looks a little awkward. Don't worry; you'll be fixing this in the pages ahead.

Figure 9-13. Finally, the cat's long ears don't get in the way!

To finish off the platforms, let's create some ground for the cat to walk on. For the Bug Catcher game, I decided to make the ground a shallow pond:

1. Use the Rectangle tool to draw a 10-pixel-high blue rectangle across the bottom of the stage. You might want to put it on a layer behind the foreground objects.

2. Above this blue rectangle, create a blue, 20-pixel-high drawing of waves. Convert it to a Movie Clip symbol and give it an alpha of 40 in the Color Effect section of the Properties panel. (You'll find a symbol called Water in the Bug Catcher Symbols folder in the Library if you don't feel like making the waves yourself.) I gave it the instance name water.

3. Test the project and try out the new ground you've created. Figure 9-14 shows what this might look like.

A little later in the project, you'll use some code to make the transparent waves appear in front of the cat, which will make the cat look like it's actually sitting in the pond.

Figure 9-14. Some ground for the cat to walk on

Using for loops

If you're like me, you probably found that writing out or copying/pasting those ten lines of repetitive code a terrible chore. Aren't computers supposed to be miraculous time-saving devices designed to spare you this sort of drudge work? Yes they are, and yes there is a better way.

Those ten directives were exactly the same in every way, except for one thing: the number of the platform instance. Could you make some kind of basic template of the directive and tell AS3.0 to repeat it ten times, just inserting the correct number? Yes, you guessed it, you can! It's a programming device called a **loop**.

Loops are used to repeat a section of code a specific number of times. There are quite a few different kinds of loops you can create in AS3.0, and even though they all do almost the same thing, some are slightly more appropriate in different situations than others. Far and away the most commonly used loop is the for loop, which is a block statement that begins with the keyword for (meaning *for* this many number of times). Any directives inside the for loop are repeated as many times as the loop specifies—from once to hundreds or thousands of times.

The structure of the for loop might look weird and confusing at first because its arguments actually contain three separate statements:

- A variable that's used to track the number of times the loop has repeated. This is known as the **loop index variable**, which is usually represented by the letter *i* (it stands for *index*).

- A conditional statement that tells the loop when it should stop.

- A statement that adds 1 to the index variable every time the for loop repeats. (Although 1 is usually added, you can add or subtract numbers in many different ways to fine-tune the loop if you need to.) Each of these statements is separated by a semicolon.

Here's an example of a for loop that displays the numbers from 0 to 4 in the Output panel.

```
for(var i:int = 0; i < 5; i++)
{
   trace(i);
}
```

If you use this code in the class's constructor method, you'll see this in the Output panel when you publish the SWF:

```
0
1
2
3
4
```

In the chapter's source files you'll find a file called forLoop.fla in the For Loop folder. Open it in Flash and choose Quick Project from the Project panel's drop-down menu. Double-click the Main_ForLoop. as file to view the code. Test the project; you'll see the same result as shown previously.

It's easy to understand how a for loop works if you break down what it does into smaller parts. The first thing it does is declare the variable that will be used to count the number of loops:

```
for(var i:int = 0; i < 5; i++)
```

This creates a local integer variable called i, which is initialized to 0. The next statement tells the loop how many times it should repeat:

```
for(var i:int = 0; i < 5; i++)
```

This is a conditional statement. It tells the loop to repeat "while the index variable is less than 5." In this example, the index variable is initialized to zero, so the loop will repeat until it reaches 4. You can use any kind of conditional statement you want here.

The last statement increases the index variable by 1 each time the directives in the loop are run:

```
for(var i:int = 0; i < 5; i++)
```

The first time the loop runs, i starts with its initialized value, which is zero. The next time it repeats, the ++ operator adds a value of 1. That means that i then equals 1 (because 0 plus 1 equals 1, of course). The next time the loop repeats, 1 is added to i again, which results in a value of 2. This repeats while i is less than 5. As soon as it gets a value of 5, the loop stops dead in its tracks.

Although i++ is the most common way to increase the value of the index variable, you can use any statement you like to increase or decrease it. For example, i += 2 will increase the index variable by 2 each time the loop repeats. i-- will decrease it by 1 if you want your loop to count backward.

If you opened the forLoop project, experiment with a few different values and conditional statements and see what the output looks like when you test it. You can initialize i to any number you like, and use any condition to quit the loop. Here's another example: i is initialized to 1, and the loop repeats until it becomes 5:

```
for(var i:int = 1; i <= 5; i++)
{
    trace(i);
}
```

This produces the following output:

```
1
2
3
4
5
```

Initializing the index variable to 1 and quitting the loop on 5 is particularly useful because it makes it very clear where the loop starts and ends.

You'll look at a few different ways to use for loops over the course of this chapter. Figure 9-15 is a quick-reference diagram of the way for loops work.

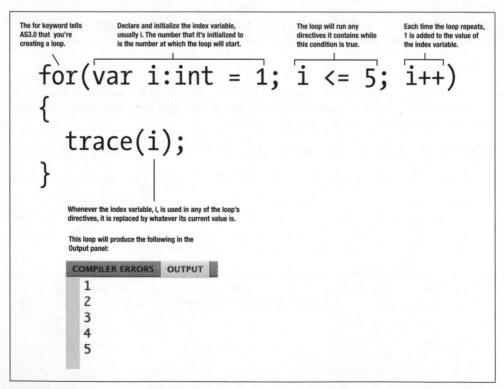

Figure 9-15. The for loop in detail

Although the for loop is a perennial favorite, AS3.0 allows you to create loops in a few other ways as well. You can also create a while loop or a do-while loop. They all do the same things as the for loop, although they have nuances that might be useful in certain situations.

The while loop can be particularly useful for games. It looks like this:

```
while(a certain condition is true)
{
  //...do this
}
```

The while loops don't run for a set number of times; they run as many times as they need to until the condition becomes false. When you use while loops in your programs, you have to make sure that the condition eventually will become false. If it doesn't, the loop will run "forever" and the Flash Player might hang. The Flash Player usually quits the loop itself if it runs for 15 seconds without ending, but sometimes it doesn't! Use while loops with caution and always save your work before you test them.

I won't be covering while and do-while loops in detail in this book, but it's worth doing a bit of further research into them just to see what they're capable of. For more information, see the section titled "Looping" in the chapter "ActionScript Language and Syntax," from Adobe's online document, Programming Adobe ActionScript 3.0 for Adobe Flash *(http://help.adobe.com/en_US/ActionScript/3.0_ProgrammingAS3/).*

Looping through platforms

The platforms all share the same instance name, except for the number that appears at the end of their name. You can make the platform collision detection code much more efficient by putting one directive inside a for loop and then repeating that directive for as many times as there are platform instances. All you need to do is replace the number in the instance name with the for loop's index variable.

If that sounds confusing, it's actually much easier to understand when you see it put into practice:

1. In the Main_BugCatcher.as file, change the onEnterFrame event handler so it looks like this:

```
private function onEnterFrame(event:Event):void
{
  //Player vs platform collision
  for (var i:int = 0; i <= 9; i++)
  {
    Collision.playerAndPlatform(player, this["platform" + i], 0.2, 0);
    trace("platform" + i);
  }
}
```

2. Save the Main_BugCatcher.as file and test the project. The cat can still jump across every platform, but the code is much more efficient.

Before you look at how this is working, let's first examine the result of the trace directive. This is what it looks like:

```
trace("platform" + i);
```

And this is what it displays in the Output panel:

```
platform0
platform1
platform2
platform3
platform4
platform5
platform6
platform7
platform8
platform9
```

As you can see, the string "platform" has the value of the loop's index variable, i, appended to it. i starts with a value of zero the very first time the loop runs, but it's increased by 1 every time the loop repeats. This allows you to dynamically create the names of all the platform instances, from platform0 to platform9.

The code that actually checks for a collision between the player and the platform instances works in exactly the same way as the trace directive:

```
Collision.playerAndPlatform(player, this["platform" + i], 0.2, 0);
```

The key to making it work is this section of code:

```
this["platform" + i]
```

The name of the instance is created by taking the base name, platform, adding the current value of the index variable to it, and surrounding the whole thing in square brackets. You use this because the platform instances are a property of "this class."

Because *Main_BugCatcher* is the document class, you can read this to mean "in this object." When the SWF runs, it creates an instance of the *Main_BugCatcher* class, which is an object just like any other in your game. Any objects that are on the stage become internal properties of the document class. You can refer to any of the class's internal properties with the this keyword. The player and platform objects are all properties of the class, so they can be referred to as this.player and this. platform3, for example.

This is also the first time you've used square brackets in the code:

```
[]
```

Square brackets are called an **array access operator**, which has a few different uses. One use is to refer to instance or property names dynamically, as in the previous code. It also refers to elements in an array. You haven't seen this second use yet, but will very soon. Stay tuned!

Finding the global x and y position of a subobject

The Bug Catcher game includes a frog character that sits on the platform in the bottom-left corner of the stage. If you look at the frog closely while you're playing the game, you'll notice that its eyes follow the cat wherever it goes.

To implement this little trick, you need to know the exact x and y position of the frog's leftEye and rightEye subobjects, and then rotate the eyes so that they point in the correct direction.

There's one big problem, however. Flash and AS3.0 interpret the x and y positions of subobjects according to the subobject's **local coordinates**. It doesn't know what the x and y coordinates are that they occupy on the stage. The stage's coordinates are known as the **global coordinates**. Before you can make the frog's eyes rotate correctly, you need to know what their global x and y positions are.

Let's first take a closer look at the problem, and then how you can solve it. The Frog symbol has two Movie Clip subobjects: leftEye and rightEye. If you double-click the Frog symbol in the Library and then click the rightEye instance, you'll notice that the Properties panel says it has an x position of 18.8. Figure 9-16 illustrates this. This is the eye's local coordinate. Keep this in mind!

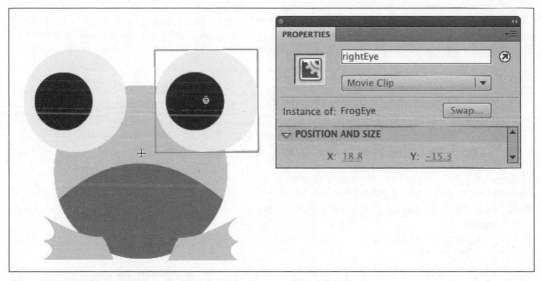

Figure 9-16. The frog's rightEye subobject has a local x coordinate of 18.8.

Let's add the frog object to the stage and find out what its position is:

1. Drag an instance of the Frog symbol onto the stage and give it the instance name frog.

2. Select the frog instance and check its x position in the Properties panel. My frog's x position is 50, which you can see in Figure 9-17.

Figure 9-17. The frog's global x position is 50.

Okay, that's interesting. That must mean that the frog's right eye should have a global x position of around 68.8 (or 68.75 to account for binary rounding). Adding 50 to 18.8 equals 68.8, which should be its global position on the stage.

Does it actually have that x value? You can find out:

1. Add the following trace statement to the Main_BugCatcher class's constructor method:

```
public function Main_BugCatcher()
{
  addEventListener(Event.ENTER_FRAME, onEnterFrame);
  trace(frog.rightEye.x);
}
```

2. Save the Main_BugCatcher.as file and test the project. You'll see this displayed in the Output panel:

```
18.75
```

That's its local position! So if you refer to the right eye's x position using the format frog.rightEye.x, AS3.0 can only tell you where it is in relation to its parent object. If you want the eye to interact in any useful way with the objects on the stage, you need its global x position—and you can't access it.

AS3.0 has a system for converting local coordinates to global coordinates. As a game designer, this is something you'll find yourself needing to do all the time. Strangely, however, AS3.0 doesn't make this easy, and converting local to global coordinates is something that has stumped even very experienced developers new to AS3.0. To make matters worse, Adobe's documentation on this is far from clear, especially in the practical usage that you need to put it to in everyday situations such as these.

You won't like this system; it's cumbersome and convoluted. But it's the only way of converting coordinates, it works, and you have to learn to live with it. Don't worry, though; just bookmark this page and refer to these directions every time you need to do this. It's actually not so bad once you get used to it!

Here's the process you need to follow to convert local coordinates to global coordinates (don't let this long list scare you; you'll soon see that it's not quite as hard to implement as it might seem):

1. Import AS3.0's Point class with the import directive import `flash.geom.Point;`. This import directive should be part of the class definition, along with all the other import directives.

2. Create a new Point object to store the x and y positions of the subobject whose local coordinates you want to convert to stage coordinates. In this example, the line of code might look like this:

```
var frogsRightEye:Point = new Point(frog.rightEye.x, frog.rightEye.y);
```

Point objects contain two built-in properties: x and y. The x and y coordinates of the object that you specify in the arguments when you create the Point object are copied into the Point object's own x and y properties. (Don't worry if this is confusing! You'll look at this in more detail in a moment.)

3. Use AS3.0's built-in localToGlobal method to convert the new Point object's local coordinates to global coordinates. localToGlobal is a method of the MovieClip class, so it needs to be called by a Movie Clip object. Usually, the object that calls it is the parent of the subobject. In the example, the parent is the frog object. So to convert the x coordinate, you can use some code that looks like this:

```
frog.localToGlobal(frogsRightEye).x;
```

4. You need to store this new global coordinate in yet another variable so that you can put it to some practical use in the program. You can convert the Point object's x coordinate and store it in a new variable with a single line of code that looks like this:

```
var frogsRightEye_X:Number = frog.localToGlobal(frogsRightEye).x;
```

5. After all that trouble, you have a variable called frogsRightEye_X. It contains the global coordinate of the subobject's x position. That's the variable you use if you want to refer to the right eye's global x position.

6. Hey, not so fast! You're not done yet! You've only converted the x position's coordinate. Repeat steps 3 to 5 to convert the y position as well. Rinse thoroughly and blow dry.

Apart from the fact that I do believe a letter is in order to Adobe before they let AS4.0 pass without simplifying this, let's not let this get you down. You can do it!

Let's try and implement this system in the program so far to see if you can actually find the x value of 68.75 that you're looking for:

1. Enter the following code into the Main_BugCatcher class's constructor method (delete the trace statement from the earlier steps if you added it):

```
public function Main_BugCatcher()
{
  addEventListener(Event.ENTER_FRAME, onEnterFrame);

  var frogsRightEye:Point = new Point➥
    (frog.rightEye.x, frog.rightEye.y);
  var frogsRightEye_X:Number = frog.localToGlobal(frogsRightEye).x;
  var frogsRightEye_Y:Number = frog.localToGlobal(frogsRightEye).y;

  trace("Right Eye X: " + frogsRightEye_X);
  trace("Right Eye Y: " + frogsRightEye_Y);
}
```

2. Save the Main_BugCatcher.as file and test the project. You'll see the following displayed in the Output panel:

```
Right Eye X: 68.75
Right Eye Y: 304.25
```

68.75! That's it! That's the global coordinate you need! Any place in the code in which you need to refer to the global x and y position of the frog's left and right eyes, you can use these two new variables: frogsRightEye_X and frogsRightEye_Y.

> Remember that to use this code, you had to create a Point object. Point objects can be created only if you import Flash's Point class with an import flash.geom.Point directive. This class was added to the Main_BugCatcher.as file for you when it was set up, but you need to remember to do it if you want this code to work in your own projects.

The process of converting local to global coordinates like this is neither obvious nor intuitive. Just a glance at the code involved is enough to stun an ox. The one saving grace is that you don't need to memorize any of this. That's what this book is for!

Figure 9-18 takes you on a tour of how to convert a subobject's local to global coordinates.

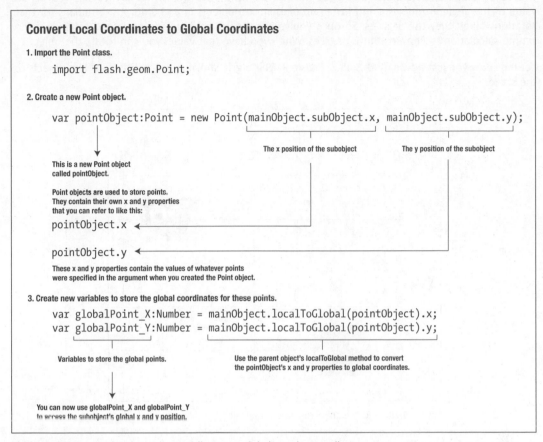

Figure 9-18. Convert local x and y coordinates to global x and y coordinates.

Now that you can access the global coordinates of the frog's left and right eyes, you can use these values to rotate them.

Rotating toward an object

You'll make the frog's eyes follow the player object as it moves around the stage. To do this, you need to apply a bit of trigonometry to the eyes' rotation properties.

If you're a mathophobe, rest assured that you don't need to necessarily *understand* the trigonometry you'll look at to be able to use it. If fact, you won't even see it. AS3.0 does the math for you—you just need to give it the correct numbers. And once you see it in use, you'll see how easy it is to apply whenever you need to rotate an object toward another object. It's a walk in the park compared with converting coordinate systems.

AS3.0 has a built-in method called `Math.atan2` that will give you the correct angle of rotation between two objects. One little technical detail you need to deal with, though, is that `Matn.atan2` returns the value of the angle in *radians*, and Movie Clip (and Sprite) objects in AS3.0 don't use radians for their rotation values; they use degrees. So once you've got the value in radians, you need to apply a very simple calculation to convert it into degrees. When you have that value, you can rotate the object.

Let me show you just how easy this all is. Figure 9-19 is a grid showing the positions of two objects on the stage.

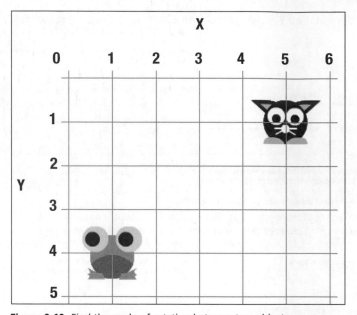

Figure 9-19. Find the angle of rotation between two objects.

Here's how to find out the angle of rotation, from the point of view of the frog:

1. Find the positions of the objects:

   ```
   cat.x = 5
   cat.y = 1

   frog.x = 1
   frog.y = 4
   ```

2. Subtract the x and y positions of the target object, from the x and y position of the object that will be doing the rotating:

   ```
   frog.x - cat.x = -4
   frog.y - cat.y = 3
   ```

3. Plug these numbers into the `Math.atan2` function. Very importantly, the y value has to come first:

   ```
   Math.atan2(3, -4)
   ```

This returns a number in *radians*. Unfortunately, this is not useful for rotating Movie Clip objects. You need to convert this number to *degrees*, which is the type of value expected by the rotation property.

To convert radians to degrees, you can use a simple calculation: multiply the value in radians by 180 divided by Pi (3.14). AS3.0 has a built-in function called Math.PI that returns the value of Pi, just to make things easier for you. Here's what the final line of code might look like:

```
Math.atan2(1, -4) * (180/Math.PI)
```

This gives you a rounded-off value in degrees:

143

Figure 9-20 shows what this looks like in the example.

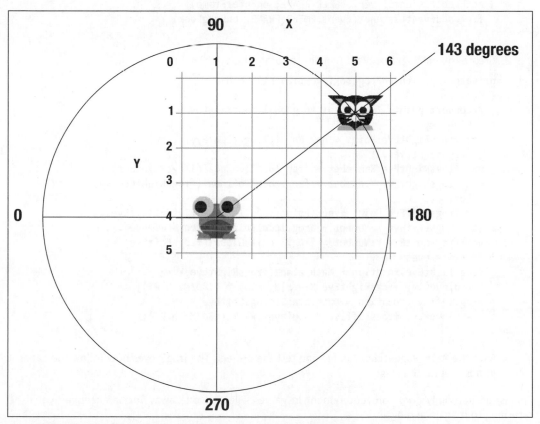

Figure 9-20. Use AS3.0's built-in Math.atan2 function to find the angle of rotation.

Great! You now have a number you can use to rotate the frog. You can use it in a directive like this:

```
frog.rotation = Math.atan2(1, -4) * (180/Math.PI);
```

Whenever you need to rotate an object toward another object, this is formula you need to use. It's probably about 50% of the trigonometry you'll ever need to know for your games, and you didn't actually have to do the math yourself! In Chapter 10, you'll look at a few more of AS3.0's trigonometry functions.

Rotating the frog's eyes toward the player object

Of course, you don't want to rotate the frog; you want to rotate its eyes, which are subobjects. You need to put together the rotation code with the earlier code to convert an object's local coordinates to global coordinates. Here's how:

1. Add an ENTER_FRAME event handler to the frog object in the constructor method:

```
public function Main_BugCatcher()
{
    addEventListener(Event.ENTER_FRAME, onEnterFrame);
    frog.addEventListener(Event.ENTER_FRAME, onFrogLook);
}
```

2. Create the onFrogLook event handler to rotate the eyes:

```
private function onFrogLook(event:Event):void
{
    //Convert points from local to global coordinates
    //Right eye
    var frogsRightEye:Point = new Point(frog.rightEye.x, ➥
      frog.rightEye.y);
    var frogsRightEye_X:Number = frog.localToGlobal(frogsRightEye).x;
    var frogsRightEye_Y:Number = frog.localToGlobal(frogsRightEye).y;
    //Left eye
    var frogsLeftEye:Point = new Point(frog.leftEye.x,frog.leftEye.y);
    var frogsLeftEye_X:Number = frog.localToGlobal(frogsLeftEye).x;
    var frogsLeftEye_Y:Number = frog.localToGlobal(frogsLeftEye).y;
    //Rotate eyes
    frog.rightEye.rotation = Math.atan2(frogsRightEye_Y ➥
      - player.y, frogsRightEye_X - player.x) * (180/Math.PI);
    frog.leftEye.rotation = Math.atan2(frogsLeftEye_Y ➥
      - player.y, frogsLeftEye_X - player.x) * (180/Math.PI);
}
```

3. Save the Main_BugCatcher.as file and test the project. The frog's eyes now follow the cat as it jumps around the stage.

This is an incredibly common requirement in games. File this one away for safekeeping; you'll be returning to it again and again.

Changing the stacking order

You might have noticed that the cat appears behind the frog and that its ears appear behind the platforms, as shown in Figure 9-21. In this game, it will appear more natural for the cat to appear above these objects. You can add a simple line of code to fix it.

When objects are added to the stage by dragging them from the Library or by using addChild, AS3.0 adds them to something called the **display list**, which is just a list of all the objects on the stage. The first objects on the list appear *behind* objects that are added after them. Because the cat was one of the first objects added to the stage in this game, the platforms and the frog appear in front of it.

To make the cat appear in front of all the other objects, it needs to be the last item on the display list. The number of objects on the stage is stored in a built-in property called numChildren. If you add the following directive in the constructor method, it will actually tell you the number of objects on the stage:

Figure 9-21. The cat is one of the first objects on the display list, so it appears behind the other objects.

```
trace(numChildren);
```

This displays 15 for me at this point of the project. There are 15 objects, but the display list starts numbering objects from 0, which means that the last object on the list is actually object number 14.

You can find out the number of any object on the list by using another built-in method called getChildAt. I know that my cat object happens to be number 3 on the list (which actually means it's the fourth object, if you start counting from zero). I can use a method called getChildAt to make sure:

```
trace(getChildAt(3));
```

In my game, this displays as follows:

```
[object Player_Platform]
```

Player_Platform is the class that the cat belongs to. You can append the name property to getChildAt to find out the object's actual instance name. For example, getChildAt(3).name has the value of cat.

Let's combine this with numChildren inside a for loop to view the instance names of all the objects on the stage:

1. Add the following code to the constructor method:

```
public function Main_BugCatcher()
{
  addEventListener(Event.ENTER_FRAME, onEnterFrame);
  frog.addEventListener(Event.ENTER_FRAME, onFrogLook);
  for (var i:int = 0; i < numChildren; i++)
  {
    trace(i + ". " + getChildAt(i).name);
  }
}
```

2. Save the Main_BugCatcher.as file and test the project. This loop runs for as many times as there are objects in the display list, which is the number provided by numChildren. You'll see something that looks similar to this in the Output panel:

```
0. instance1
1. instance8
2. water
3. player
4. platform4
5. platform8
6. platform9
7. platform3
8. platform6
9. platform5
10. platform1
11. platform2
12. platform7
13. platform0
14. frog
```

You can see from this list that in order to get the cat to appear above the other objects, you need to move it to the end of the list, to position 14. Another built-in method called setChildIndex can do this for you.

To move the cat to the end of the display list, you can use setChildIndex to give it a position number that is one less than the number provided *by* numChildren (it has to be one less to compensate for the fact that the list starts at zero). setChildIndex takes two arguments: the name of the object and the position you want to move it to.

1. Add the following to the constructor method:

```
public function Main_BugCatcher()
{
  addEventListener(Event.ENTER_FRAME, onEnterFrame);
```

```
    frog.addEventListener(Event.ENTER_FRAME, onFrogLook);
    setChildIndex(player, numChildren - 1);
    for (var i:int = 0; i < numChildren; i++)
    {
      trace(i + ". " + getChildAt(i).name);
    }
  }
```

2. Save the Main_BugCatcher.as file and test the project. The cat will now be the last item on the list in the Output panel. The cat now appears above the frog and the platforms on the stage.

One last thing in the stacking order that I want to fix is to make the cat appear behind the transparent water graphic so it looks like it's standing in water when it's on the ground. To do this, I'll give the water object a position index number of numChildren-1 and the player object a position number of numChildren-2.

1. Update the constructor method:

```
public function Main_BugCatcher()
{
  addEventListener(Event.ENTER_FRAME, onEnterFrame);
  frog.addEventListener(Event.ENTER_FRAME, onFrogLook);
  setChildIndex(water, numChildren - 1);
  setChildIndex(player, numChildren - 2);
  for (var i:int = 0; i < numChildren; i++)
  {
    trace(i + ". " + getChildAt(i).name);
  }
}
```

2. Save the Main_BugCatcher.as file and test the project. The cat now appears in front of all the other objects, but behind the water object, as shown in Figure 9-22.

Figure 9-22. The cat appears in front of the frog but behind the water.

The appearance of objects being in front of or behind other objects has nothing to do with which layer they were created on in the FLA. Once their position on the display list is altered, that position takes precedence over the layer position in the FLA. You can make an object from a bottom layer appear above all other objects just by changing its position on the display list.

Another of AS3.0's built-in methods that you'll certainly find use for in your games is swapChildren. You can swap the position of two objects in the display list by using a line of code that looks like this:

```
swapChildren(frog, player);
```

This code makes the two objects change places in the list. You're not using swapChildren in this game, but it's important to keep it in mind. It's always useful when you need to make one object appear above or below another object without having to know their actual positions in the list.

Adding some bugs to the code—literally!

Now that you have a fun environment to play in, let's start to turn this into a real game. In my Bug Catcher game, I created three little bug Movie Clip symbols: Fly, Bee, and Mosquito. These symbols are all exactly the same except for their colors. They each contain a one-frame animation that flaps their wings. I added them to the stage and gave them the instance names fly, bee, and mosquito.

In the Dungeon Maze Adventure game from Chapter 8, all the important game objects had their own class. Although that's probably a preferable approach to take for most games because it really does help to break down complexity into manageable chunks, it can be overkill for a very small game such as Bug Catcher. In Bug Catcher, all the objects, except from the player, are programmed in the Main_BugCatcher class. There are a few reasons for this:

- You need to see how this can be done. It's often quicker and easier to work through ideas with all the code in one big class, such as Main. Once you understand how some of the code is working, you can then break it down into classes. It's a good experimental lab.

- You're learning a few new techniques, and their effects will be clearer if all the code is in one place.

- Truth be told, this is a better way to work for very small games. It's much less code and it can be easier to make quick changes than working with many classes. The chance of bugs occurring (programming bugs!) because of code dependency is mitigated by the fact that the game is so small.

When you're designing your games, you'll need to decide whether you want to take a more object-oriented route, as with Dungeon Maze Adventure, or a more procedural route, as with Bug Catcher. If Bug Catcher were even just slightly bigger, I would have broken it down into smaller classes.

Here's how to program the bugs in the game:

- Dynamically create vx and vy properties for each of the bugs, directly in the constructor method.

- Attach an ENTER_FRAME event to each bug to control the bug's movement and artificial intelligence.

Let's first add the bugs to the stage, create the properties, and add the event listeners:

1. Add instances of the three bugs to the stage and give them the instance names fly, bee, and mosquito.

2. Add the following code to the constructor method:

```
public function Main_BugCatcher()
{
  addEventListener(Event.ENTER_FRAME, onEnterFrame);
  frog.addEventListener(Event.ENTER_FRAME, onFrogLook);
  setChildIndex(water, numChildren - 1);
  setChildIndex(player, numChildren - 2);
  for (var i:int = 0; i < numChildren; i++)
  {
    trace(i + ". " + getChildAt(i).name);
  }

  //Initialize objects
  //fly
  fly.vx = 0;
  fly.vy = 0;
  fly.addEventListener(Event.ENTER_FRAME, onBugMove);

  //bee
  bee.vx = 0;
  bee.vy = 0;
  bee.addEventListener(Event.ENTER_FRAME, onBugMove);

  //mosquito
  mosquito.vx = 0;
  mosquito.vy = 0;
  mosquito.addEventListener(Event.ENTER_FRAME, onBugMove);
}
```

3. Add the onBugMove event handler just below onFrogLook:

```
private function onBugMove(event:Event):void
{
  //Create a variable to store a reference to the bug object
  var bug:MovieClip = event.target as MovieClip;

  //Add Brownian motion to the velocities
  bug.vx += (Math.random() * 0.2 - 0.1) * 15;
  bug.vy += (Math.random() * 0.2 - 0.1) * 15;

  //Add some friction
  bug.vx *= 0.95;
  bug.vy *= 0.95;

  //Move the bug
  bug.x += bug.vx;
  bug.y += bug.vy;

  //Stage Boundaries
  if (bug.x > stage.stageWidth)
```

```
  {
    bug.x = stage.stageWidth;
    //Reverse (bounce) bug's velocity when it hits the stage edges
    bug.vx *= -1;
  }
  if (bug.x < 0)
  {
    bug.x = 0;
    bug.vx *= -1;
  }

  //Keep the bug above the water
  if (bug.y > stage.stageHeight - 35)
  {
    bug.y = stage.stageHeight - 35;
    bug.vy *= -1;
  }
  if (bug.y < 0)
  {
    bug.y = 0;
    bug.vy *= -1;
  }

  //Apply collision with platform
  for (var i:int = 0; i < 10; i++)
  {
    Collision.playerAndPlatform(MovieClip(bug), ➥
      this["platform" + i], 0.2, 0);
  }
}
```

4. Save the Main_BugCatcher.as file and test the project. The three bugs flutter randomly around the stage and bounce off the edges very realistically (like flies bumping into windows).

There's no magic to any of this. You just combined a few things that you already know how to do in ways you haven't seen before.

Dynamic instance variables

In the constructor method, you declared and initialized vx and vy variables for the bugs and added ENTER_FRAME event listeners like this:

```
fly.vx = 0;
fly.vy = 0;
fly.addEventListener(Event.ENTER_FRAME, onBugMove);
```

The vx and vy variables were created **dynamically** (they're called **dynamic instance variables**). All that means is that you needed these variables, so you created them on the spot without checking with the object's class whether it was okay to do so. In fact, the bug objects don't belong to any special class, except the general MovieClip class.

The MovieClip class is a **dynamic class**, which means that new properties added to objects that are descended from the MovieClip class don't have to be declared within the class itself. You can create them anywhere in any class that references these objects.

> *If a class is not declared as dynamic, you can't create variables on objects like this; you need to do it within the object's own class. To make a class dynamic, declare it with the dynamic keyword. Here's an example:*
>
> ```
> public dynamic class ClassName extends MovieClip
> ```

Being able to create properties dynamically on objects like this is very convenient. It saves you the trouble of having to create an entire class around an object. However, it comes with the same danger of breaking encapsulation that public properties pose. (Encapsulation, as you might recall from Chapter 8, is the programming practice of striving to keep objects as self-contained as possible so they're not dependent on other objects.) If you're not careful, you might create properties that are assigned values that the object doesn't know how to deal with, and this could cause weird things to happen in your code that might be very difficult to debug. So my advice is that when you use dynamic instance variables, do so only in very small games such as Bug Catcher, and keep a careful eye on the values you assign them. If you can do that, they're a big time-saver.

> *You might have noticed that vx and vy properties are named without being preceded by an underscore character. That is because they're technically public properties. In the naming conventions that you're following in this book, public property names aren't preceded with an underscore.*

You'll also notice that all three bug objects share exactly the same ENTER_FRAME event handler. You'll see how you're able to do this next.

Multiple objects sharing one event handler

One great feature of the AS3.0 event listeners is that when events are created, an awful lot of information about that event is stored in a special event object. (Refer to Chapter 3 if you need a quick refresher on this topic.) One of the properties of the event object is called target. The target property stores a reference to the object that called the event. That means that you can access these objects in the event handler with code that looks like this:

```
event.target
```

That's really useful for you in the current situation. Each of the bugs in the game uses the same event handler, onBugMove, but they call the event handler at different times. By using the event.target property you can find out which bug object is currently calling the event and store this object in a local variable. That's what the first line of code in the onBugMove event handler does:

```
var bug:MovieClip = event.target as MovieClip;
```

Whichever object is currently calling the event is referenced in this local bug variable. You can now use the bug variable to refer to whichever bug object is running the event at the moment. This saves you the trouble of having to write three identical event handlers for each bug. They all do exactly the same thing, so this is just fine.

The only little technical detail you have to be aware of is that you need to use "as MovieClip" to tell AS3.0, "Yes, don't worry, you know what you're doing, this is a Movie Clip object." The event sends the target property as a String, so you need to cast it as a MovieClip to be able to access the actual object it refers to.

Making the bugs move

You want the bugs to move like bugs, so some kind of random motion might be a good idea. There is a formula for random motion that makes objects dither about in no particular direction called **Brownian motion**. The formula for Brownian motion looks like this:

```
(Math.random() * 0.2 - 0.1)
```

It uses the Math.random method to generate a random number between -0.1 and 0.1 (Refer to Chapter 5 if you need a refresher on how to generate random numbers.) This number is too small to be much use for moving an object on the stage, so you need to multiply it by another number to amplify the effect. Through trial and error, I noticed that multiplying it by 15 looked good for my bugs.

This new formula is then added to the bugs' vx and vy properties:

```
bug.vx += (Math.random() * 0.2 - 0.1) * 15;
bug.vy += (Math.random() * 0.2 - 0.1) * 15;
```

Add a bit of friction and then add the vx and vy velocities to the bugs' x and y properties.

```
//Add some friction
bug.vx *= 0.95;
bug.vy *= 0.95;

//Move the bug
bug.x += bug.vx;
bug.y += bug.vy;
```

This amazingly mundane code is all that's needed to make the bug object move like a real bug. Makes you think!

> Brownian motion is great if you want to make objects that move in a way that mimic the organic randomness of insects, dust particles, or snow. Experiment with the friction value and change the multiplier from 15 to something like 9 or 3.

The next section of code simply sets the stage boundaries. It uses the simple bounce formula you looked at earlier in the chapter to bounce the bugs off the stage edges when they get too close, like this:

```
bug.vx *= -1;
```

Another very simple bit of code that results in surprising complexity! The last thing you did was set up the collision detection code for the platforms:

```
for (var i:int = 0; i <= 9; i++)
{
  Collision.playerAndPlatform(bug, this["platform" + i], 0, 0);
}
```

This is the same as the code you used to detect a collision between the platforms and the player, except that there has been no bounce value assigned.

Artificial intelligence

The next step is to make the bugs aware of their environment. Bugs don't like frogs, so let's make them fly away if they come within 50 pixels of the frog.

The collision detection follows the same logic that you used in the original collision detection code from Chapter 7. It checks whether a bug is within 50 pixels of the frog on the x axis. If it is, it checks whether the bug is within 50 pixels of the frog on the y axis. If that's true as well, the bug is too close to the frog, and it changes its direction.

1. Add the following code to the onBugMove event handler:

```
//Artificial intelligence
//Frog
if ((Math.abs(bug.x - frog.x) < 50)   )
{
  if (Math.abs(bug.y - frog.y) < 50)
  {
      bug.x += -bug.vx;
      bug.y += -bug.vy;
      bug.vx *= -1;
      bug.vy *= -1;
      trace(bug.name + ": Frog!");
  }
}
```

2. Save the `Main_BugCatcher.as` file and test the project. When the bugs come within 50 pixels of the frog, they fly away quickly and display the word Frog! in the Output window, as shown in Figure 9-23.

Figure 9-23. The bugs reverse direction if they come within 50 pixels of the frog.

The code pushes the bug out of the collision area and then reverses its velocity using the bounce formula. Again, this is simple code, but the effect is startlingly realistic.

The way that the bugs interact with the cat is only slightly more complex. The bugs have two different behaviors, depending on whether the cat is moving or not moving. When the cat's velocity is less than 1 on either axis, the bugs have the same behavior as they have with the frog. When the cat is moving, however, the bugs enter panic mode. They add the player's velocity to their own and multiply their random motion by 30, which makes their movement much more erratic.

1. Add the following code just below the preceding code you added:

```
//Player
if ((Math.abs(bug.x - player.x) < 60))
{
  if (Math.abs(bug.y - player.y) < 60)
  {
    //If the player is moving...
    bug.vy += player.vy + ((Math.random() * 0.2 - 0.1) * 30);
    bug.vx += player.vx + ((Math.random() * 0.2 - 0.1) * 30);
    trace(bug.name + ": Cat!");
    if ((Math.abs(player.vy) < 1) && (Math.abs(player.vx) < 1))
    {
      //If the player is sitting still...
      bug.y += -bug.vy;
      bug.x += -bug.vx;
      bug.vy *= -1;
      bug.vx *= -1;
    }
  }
}
```

2. Save the `Main_BugCatcher.as` file and test the project. The bugs will flee wildly from the cat if it chases them, and bob around it complacently if it sits still.

All this adds up to very realistic bug behavior. In fact, the bugs almost seem to have some kind of intelligence. That's why this kind of programming is called **artificial intelligence**, known as **AI** for short.

As you can see, there's nothing too special about his code, and there's certainly no magic formula for writing it. I wrote this code with a vague idea of how I wanted the bugs to behave and spent an hour or so playing around with a few different combinations of directives until I found something I was happy with. To say that there are as many different ways the code could be written as there are readers of the book is an understatement. There are millions of ways this code could have been written, and the example I present here is just one possibility I dreamed up on a snowy afternoon. When you're programming objects that need some sort of awareness of the environment they inhabit, try and break down their behavior into small steps. Solve one step and build from there. With just a few lines of code and a few simple `if` statements you can create something that appears alive and truly intelligent. It's really not hard; try it!

Although it works well enough for me, there's one weakness in this code that you'll discover if you play the game long enough. Because the bugs add the exact value of the cat's velocity to their own, they *always* outrun the player. The only way you can catch one of the bugs is to trap it in a corner. To make the game a little more realistic, you could add an extra bit of randomness, more or less, to the value of the velocity obtained from the `player` object. But I'll leave that for you to figure out!

Using arrays

The next phase in the game is to actually catch the bugs. You need some kind of container to store them in, such as a collection jar. In AS3.0, a collection jar for objects is known as an **array**.

Arrays can actually be used to store anything: variables, numbers, strings, objects, methods, or even other arrays. You can think of arrays as big storage containers in which everything inside is indexed with a number. You'll take a look at some practical examples of how this works.

Before you can use an array, you need to instantiate it using the new keyword. If you want to create an empty collection jar for the cat to collect bugs with, you can create one like this:

```
private var _collectionJar:Array;
_collectionJar = new Array();
_collectionJar = [];
```

Arrays contain their objects using square brackets (the array access operator) that you looked at earlier in the chapter. A pair of empty brackets means that the array is empty.

You can initialize the array so that it's already filled with objects:

```
_collectionJar = [fly, mosquito, bee];
```

All objects in an array are numbered sequentially, starting with zero. These numbers are called **index numbers**. In the preceding example, fly has an index number of 0, mosquito has an index number of 1, and bee has an index number of 2.

You can find out which object is at which index number using the array access operator. Here's an example:

```
_collectionJar[1]
```

This has the value of mosquito because mosquito has an index number of 1.

It's really very simple. An array is just a numbered list of things known as **elements**. Figure 9-24 illustrates an empty array compared with an array with three elements.

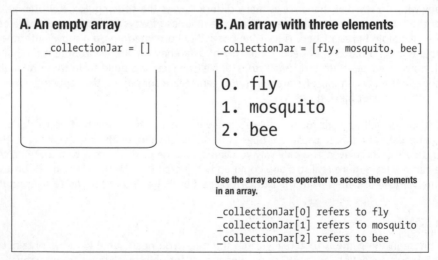

A. An empty array

```
_collectionJar = []
```

B. An array with three elements

```
_collectionJar = [fly, mosquito, bee]
```

```
0. fly
1. mosquito
2. bee
```

Use the array access operator to access the elements in an array.

```
_collectionJar[0] refers to fly
_collectionJar[1] refers to mosquito
_collectionJar[2] refers to bee
```

Figure 9-24. Arrays and array elements

There are several ways to put elements into arrays. In the previous example, three elements were added to the array when it was initialized. You'll usually start with an empty array and add elements to it as you need to.

One way to put elements into an array is to assign elements directly to a position in the array's index:

```
_collectionJar[2] = fly;
```

So whenever your code sees _collectionJar[2] it returns the value of fly.

Let's look at a slightly more concrete example. The chapter source files include a folder called Array Basic, which contains an FLA file called arrayBasic.fla. Open it is as a project and have a look at the Main_ArrayBasic.as file:

```
package
{
  import flash.display.MovieClip;

  public class Main_ArrayBasic extends MovieClip
  {
    //Declare array
    private var _collectionJar:Array;

    public function Main_ArrayBasic()
    {
      //Instantiate array
      _collectionJar = new Array();

      //Add elements to array
      _collectionJar[0] = "fly";
      _collectionJar[1] = "mosquito";
      _collectionJar[2] = "bee";

      //Trace array entire contents
      trace("Entire Array: " + _collectionJar);

      //Trace individual elements
      trace("Element 0: " + _collectionJar[0]);
      trace("Element 1: " + _collectionJar[1]);
      trace("Element 2: " + _collectionJar[2]);
    }
  }
}
```

If you test this, the trace displays this:

```
Entire Array: fly,mosquito,bee
Element 0: fly
Element 1: mosquito
Element 2: bee
```

459

> *In this example, "fly", "mosquito", and "bee" are stored in the array as strings, not objects.*

Pushing elements into an array

Another very common way to get elements into an array is to use an array's built-in push method. You can use push to literally "push" an element into an array by using this format:

```
arrayName.push(elementName);
```

When you push an object into an array, it gets an index number that's one higher than the last element added. This means that if the last element has an index number of [2], the object that you push into it will have an index number of [3].

Using push is really helpful because you don't need to worry about which index number to add the element to. The array figures this out for you.

The chapter source files include a folder called Array Push that contains an FLA called arrayPush. Open it as a project and have a look at Main_ArrayPush.as. It's identical to the first example, except that it uses push to add the elements to the array:

```
_collectionJar.push("fly");
_collectionJar.push("mosquito");
_collectionJar.push("bee");
```

The trace output is exactly the same as the first example. The fact that you don't need to worry about the index numbers is very convenient.

> *To remove an element from an array, you can use the array's pop method. The following code uses pop to remove the last element from an array and assign it to a variable:*
>
> *removedElement = _collectionJar.pop();*
>
> *If the last element was "bee", removedElement has the value of "bee". It also means that _collectionJar now contains only two elements: "fly" and "mosquito".*
>
> *You can also add and remove elements to an array using the splice method. I'll cover it in detail in the next chapter.*

Looping arrays

You might have noticed something familiar: arrays look an awful lot like the display list discussed earlier. This is no accident; the display list is an array!

You used a for loop to display the contents of the display list and you can use one to display the contents of any array in this way. In fact, arrays and for loops tend to go hand in hand.

Arrays have a built-in property called length, which tells you how many elements the array has. You can access an array's length property like this:

```
arrayName.length
```

It is the same as the display list's numChildren.

> *Just like numChildren, the numbering starts at zero. length doesn't give you the last element in the array; it gives you the total number of elements. To find the index number of the last element you would need to use this:*
>
> ```
> arraryName.length-1
> ```

You can use an array's length property to control the number of times a for loop repeats. Here's a basic example of the format you can use:

```
for (var i:int = 0; i < arrayName.length; i++)
{
  trace(arrayName[i]);
}
```

This code displays all the elements in the array, starting with element 0 and running through all the way to the end of the array, however long it happens to be.

The chapter's source files include a folder called Array Loop that contains a file called arrayLoop.as. It contains an example of how to use a for loop to list the contents of an array. Open it as a project and test it to see the effect. The Main_ArrayLoop.as file of arrayLoop looks like this:

```
package
{
  import flash.display.MovieClip;

  public class Main_ArrayLoop extends MovieClip
  {
    //declare array
    private var _collectionJar:Array;
```

```
public function Main_ArrayLoop()
{
  //Instantiate array
  _collectionJar = new Array();

  //Add elements to array
  _collectionJar.push("fly");
  _collectionJar.push("mosquito");
  _collectionJar.push("bee");

  //Trace entire array contents
  for (var i:int = 0; i < _collectionJar.length; i++)
  {
    trace("Element " + i + ": " + _collectionJar[i]);
  }
}
}
}
```

This displays the following in the Output panel:

```
Element 0: fly
Element 1: mosquito
Element 2: bee
```

Searching arrays

Another interesting feature of this system is that you can create basic search functionality by throwing an if statement into the mix. It's really simple; you just check to see whether an array element in the loop matches a certain search term. If you have a match, the element you're looking for has been found.

Here's the basic format for searching an array:

```
for (var i:int = 0; i < arrayName.length; i++)
{
  if(arrayName[i] == "searchTerm")
  {
    trace("Search term found.");
    break;
  }
}
```

One new thing here is the keyword break, which is used to stop a loop immediately without waiting for it to complete. When you use loops to search through arrays, you're often looking for only one item. Once that item has been found, it doesn't make sense to continue the loop, so you can use break to stop it early. Because your program doesn't have to do any unnecessary checking, your game will run faster.

You'll find a file called arraySearch.fla in the Array Search folder of the chapter's source files. Open it as a project and take a look at its Main_ArraySearch.as file. It uses an if statement inside a for loop to check whether the array contains an element called "mosquito". Once the if statement finds the correct element, a break directive runs to stop the loop from continuing:

```
package
{
  import flash.display.MovieClip;

  public class Main_ArraySearch extends MovieClip
  {
    //declare array
    private var _collectionJar:Array;

    public function Main_ArraySearch()
    {
      //Instantiate array
      _collectionJar = new Array();

      //Add elements to array
      _collectionJar.push("fly");
      _collectionJar.push("mosquito");
      _collectionJar.push("bee");

      //Search array
      for (var i:int = 0; i < _collectionJar.length; i++)
      {
        if(_collectionJar[i] == "mosquito")
        {
          trace("Mosquito found at position " + i);
          break;
        }
      }
    }
  }
}
```

If you test it, you'll see this output:

```
Mosquito found at position 1
```

Because you include a break directive, the loop stops at that point. It never checks element [2], which is a good thing. The loop has found what it's looking for, so it doesn't need to check. Using for loops to search arrays is a basic programming technique that you'll be using frequently from now on.

You'll need a bit of practice with arrays before you start to feel comfortable using them in your own code. Spend a bit of time with these example files, make some changes, and follow the way your changes affect the output.

Collecting bugs

Now that you know how to use arrays, let's collect some bugs!

1. Create a dynamic text field named `instructions` to display the game's instructions.

2. Create some boxes to visually display the bugs you collect. Give the boxes these instance names: `itemBox0`, `itemBox1`, and `itemBox2`.

3. Add a mouse object to the stage. The mouse doesn't actually do anything in the game; it's added as an obstacle for the player. If the player collects the mouse, the game is lost. The frog doesn't like mice! Figure 9-25 shows what these new objects look like.

4. Save the `bugCatcher.fla` file.

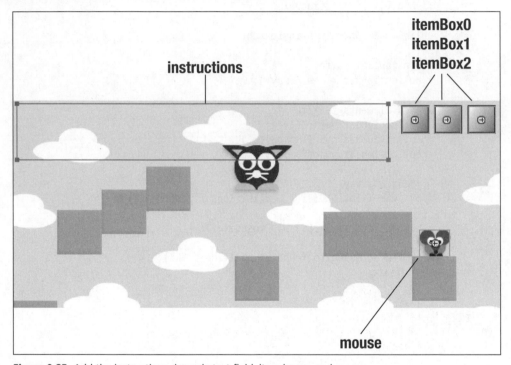

Figure 9-25. Add the instructions dynamic text field, item boxes, and mouse.

5. You need to declare an array to collect the bugs and a variable to tell you whether the mouse has been collected. Add the following declarations at the top of the class definition:

```
private var _collectionJar:Array;
private var _mouseFound:Boolean;
```

6. Initialize the array, variable, and dynamic text field in the constructor method:

```
_collectionJar = new Array();
_collectionJar = [];
_mouseFound = false;
instructions.text = "Catch 3 bugs for the frog.";
```

7. Add an onCollisionWithPlayer event listener to the fly, bee, mosquito, and mouse objects in the constructor method (these objects all share the same event listener):

```
fly.vx = 0;
fly.vy = 0;
fly.addEventListener(Event.ENTER_FRAME, onBugMove);
fly.addEventListener(Event.ENTER_FRAME, onCollisionWithPlayer);

//bee
bee.vx = 0;
bee.vy = 0;
bee.addEventListener(Event.ENTER_FRAME, onBugMove);
bee.addEventListener(Event.ENTER_FRAME, onCollisionWithPlayer);

//mosquito
mosquito.vx = 0;
mosquito.vy = 0;
mosquito.addEventListener(Event.ENTER_FRAME, onBugMove);
mosquito.addEventListener(Event.ENTER_FRAME, onCollisionWithPlayer);

//mouse
mouse.addEventListener(Event.ENTER_FRAME, onCollisionWithPlayer);
```

8. Add the onCollisionWithPlayer event handler:

```
private function onCollisionWithPlayer(event:Event):void
{
  var collectionItem:MovieClip = event.target as MovieClip;
  if (_collectionJar.length < 3)
  {
    if (player.hitTestPoint(collectionItem.x, collectionItem.y, true))
    {
      this["itemBox" + _collectionJar.length].addChild(collectionItem);
      collectionItem.x = 0;
      collectionItem.y = 0;
      _collectionJar.push(collectionItem);
      //Remove listeners of collected items
      if (collectionItem != mouse)
      {
        collectionItem.removeEventListener(Event.ENTER_FRAME, ➡
          onBugMove);
      }
      collectionItem.removeEventListener(Event.ENTER_FRAME, ➡
        onCollisionWithPlayer);
    }
  }
}
```

9. Save the `Main_BugCatcher.as` file and test the project. Chase the bugs around the stage. When you catch them, they'll appear in the item boxes on the top-right corner, as shown in Figure 9-26. The game allows you to catch only three objects.

Figure 9-26. Catch the bugs (and maybe a mouse, too)!

The job of collecting the bugs falls to the `onCollisionWithPlayer` event handler. The first thing it does is create a local variable to store a reference to the object that's calling the event:

```
var collectionItem:MovieClip = event.target as MovieClip;
```

> *Remember that there are four objects that are calling this event: the bee, fly, mosquito, and mouse. The code in onCollisionWithPlayer applies to all of them.*

The code then checks to see whether the collection jar is full. Because you want to allow the player to collect only 3 items, the code should run only if the `length` of the `_collectionJar` array is less than 3:

```
if (_collectionJar.length < 3)
{
```

If the jar isn't full yet, the code checks whether the object is colliding with the `player`:

```
if (player.hitTestPoint(collectionItem.x, collectionItem.y, true))
{
```

If it passes this second test, the main part of the event handler is allowed to run. The first thing that happens is that the object is made a *child* of the first next available item box. This places the object into one of the item boxes at the top-right corner of the stage:

```
this["itemBox" + _collectionJar.length].addChild(collectionItem);
```

Let's break this down into two smaller parts. First, there's this bit of code:

```
this["itemBox" + _collectionJar.length]
```

It figures out which item box is free by finding out how long the _collectionJar array currently is. If no objects have yet been collected, the array's length property is zero. This means that the item box that is used to store the object is itemBox0. "itemBox" + 0 equals itemBox0. itemBox0 is the first box.

Let's look at another example. If 2 objects have *already been collected*, then the length of the _collectionJar array is 2. Because you started naming the item boxes at zero (0), 2 is the last box, the third one. That means that "itemBox" + 2 equals itemBox2, which is the third box.

I know; it's confusing! But run it through a few times in your head or on a piece of paper, and it will start to make sense.

An important thing to keep in mind is that this bit of code uses square brackets, [ ], to dynamically create the name of the item box that you want to move the collected object to. When two bugs have been collected, for example, the code interprets this:

```
this["itemBox" + _collectionJar.length]
```

to mean this:

```
itemBox2
```

Make sense?

Once you have the name of the object, you can trigger one of that object's methods. That's what the second bit of code is:

```
.addChild(collectionItem);
```

It adds the collected object as its child, which causes the object to attach itself to the item box. You can see this happening visually on the stage when one of the bugs is caught.

To make a bit more sense of this, imagine that the fly object called this event and happened to be the second object collected. The entire directive would be interpreted like this:

```
itemBox1.addChild(fly);
```

The next job is to center the object in the item box. That's the work of these two lines:

```
collectionItem.x = 0;
collectionItem.y = 0;
```

Why are you setting the object to an x and y position of zero? Remember that the object is now a *child* of one of the item boxes. The coordinates it uses no longer refer to coordinates on the main stage. 0 is a *local coordinate*: the center of the item box.

Next, you push the object into the _collectionJar array:

```
_collectionJar.push(collectionItem);
```

The last job is to remove the event listeners. You have a small problem because the bugs all use the onBugMove event listener, but the mouse doesn't. onBugMove is what makes the bugs move and also includes their artificial intelligence. Remember, the mouse doesn't do anything; it's just an obstacle for the player to avoid. You have to be careful not to try to remove the onBugMove listener from the mouse; otherwise, the code will generate an error.

An easy way around this is just to run the code if the object that's called the onCollisionWithPlayer event is not a mouse. A simple if statement takes care of that:

```
if (collectionItem != mouse)
{
   collectionItem.removeEventListener(Event.ENTER_FRAME, onBugMove);
}
```

Finally, you have to remove the onCollisionWithPlayer event itself:

```
collectionItem.removeEventListener(Event.ENTER_FRAME, ➥
   onCollisionWithPlayer);
```

Now that you can collect bugs, you need to find out how to end the game.

Winning and losing conditions

The best place to check for the end of the game is in the onCollisionWithPlayer event handler.

1. Add the following code just before the directives that remove the event listeners:

```
...
_collectionJar.push(collectionItem);
//Check for end of game
if (_collectionJar.length == 3)
{
   addEventListener(Event.ENTER_FRAME, onEndGame);
}
//Remove listeners of collected items
if (collectionItem != mouse)
{
...
```

If the length of the _collectionJar is 3, all the objects have been collected, and the onEndGame event listener is added.

2. Create the onEndGame event handler. Add it below onCollisionWithPlayer:

```
private function onEndGame(event:Event):void
{
  instructions.text = "Visit the frog to tell him ➡
    what you've collected.";
  if (player.collisionArea.hitTestObject(frog))
  {
    for (var i:int = 0; i < _collectionJar.length; i++)
    {
      if (_collectionJar[i] == mouse)
      {
        _mouseFound = true;
        break;
      }
    }
    if (_mouseFound)
    {
      instructions.text = "I don't like mice!";
    }
    else
    {
      instructions.text = "Thanks very much!";
    }
      removeEventListener(Event.ENTER_FRAME, onEndGame);
  }
}
```

3. Save the Main_BugCatcher.as file and test the project. Now when you collect three items, you can visit the frog. (The frog will you whether he's happy with what you caught.)

onEndGame implements the array search system that you looked at earlier. As soon as the player touches the frog, these lines of code are run:

```
for (var i:int = 0; i < _collectionJar.length; i++)
{
  if (_collectionJar[i] == mouse)
  {
    _mouseFound = true;
    break;
  }
}
```

This code is almost identical to the code that you looked at earlier. If mouse turns up as an element in the array, the _mouseFound variable is set to true, and the loop quits. Depending on the value of _mouseFound, a different message is displayed. Finally, the onEndGame listener is removed, and the game finishes.

Complete Main_BugCatcher class

In case you need to double-check anything, here's the complete Main_BugCatcher class:

```
package
{
  import flash.display.MovieClip;
  import flash.events.Event;
  import flash.geom.Point;

  public class Main_BugCatcher extends MovieClip
  {
    private var _collectionJar:Array;
    private var _mouseFound:Boolean;

    public function Main_BugCatcher()
    {
      addEventListener(Event.ENTER_FRAME, onEnterFrame);
      frog.addEventListener(Event.ENTER_FRAME, onFrogLook);

      setChildIndex(water, numChildren - 1);
      setChildIndex(player, numChildren - 2);
      for (var i:int = 0; i < numChildren; i++)
      {
        trace(i + ". " + getChildAt(i).name);
      }

      //Initialize objects
      //fly
      fly.vx = 0;
      fly.vy = 0;
      fly.addEventListener(Event.ENTER_FRAME, onBugMove);
      fly.addEventListener(Event.ENTER_FRAME, onCollisionWithPlayer);

      //bee
      bee.vx = 0;
      bee.vy = 0;
      bee.addEventListener(Event.ENTER_FRAME, onBugMove);
      bee.addEventListener(Event.ENTER_FRAME, onCollisionWithPlayer);

      //mosquito
      mosquito.vx = 0;
      mosquito.vy = 0;
      mosquito.addEventListener(Event.ENTER_FRAME, onBugMove);
      mosquito.addEventListener(Event.ENTER_FRAME, ➥
        onCollisionWithPlayer);

      //mouse
      mouse.addEventListener(Event.ENTER_FRAME, onCollisionWithPlayer);
```

```
  //Initialise array and variables
  _collectionJar = new Array();
  _collectionJar = [];
  _mouseFound = false;
  instructions.text = "Catch 3 bugs for the frog."
}
private function onEnterFrame(event:Event):void
{
  //Player vs platform collision
  for (var i:int = 0; i <= 9; i++)
  {
    Collision.playerAndPlatform(player, this["platform" + i], ➡
      0.2, 0);
     //trace("platform" + i);
  }
}


private function onFrogLook(event:Event):void
{
  //Convert points from local to global coordinates
  //Right eye
  var frogsRightEye:Point = new Point(frog.rightEye.x, ➡
    frog.rightEye.y);
  var frogsRightEye_X:Number = frog.localToGlobal(frogsRightEye).x;
  var frogsRightEye_Y:Number = frog.localToGlobal(frogsRightEye).y;
  //Left eye
  var frogsLeftEye:Point=new Point(frog.leftEye.x,frog.leftEye.y);
  var frogsLeftEye_X:Number=frog.localToGlobal(frogsLeftEye).x;
  var frogsLeftEye_Y:Number=frog.localToGlobal(frogsLeftEye).y;
  //Rotate eyes
  frog.rightEye.rotation = Math.atan2(frogsRightEye_Y - player.y, ➡
    frogsRightEye_X - player.x) * (180/Math.PI);
  frog.leftEye.rotation = Math.atan2(frogsLeftEye_Y - player.y, ➡
    frogsLeftEye_X - player.x) * (180/Math.PI);
}


private function onBugMove(event:Event):void
{
  //Create a variable to store a reference to the bug object
  var bug:MovieClip = event.target as MovieClip;

  //Add Brownian motion to the velocities
  bug.vx += (Math.random() * 0.2 - 0.1) * 15;
  bug.vy += (Math.random() * 0.2 - 0.1) * 15;

  //Add some friction
  bug.vx *= 0.95;
  bug.vy *= 0.95;
```

```
//Move the bug
bug.x += bug.vx;
bug.y += bug.vy;

//Stage Boundaries
if (bug.x > stage.stageWidth)
{
  bug.x = stage.stageWidth;
  //Reverse (bounce) bug's velocity when it hits the stage edges
  bug.vx*=-1;
}
if (bug.x < 0)
{
  bug.x = 0;
  bug.vx *= -1;
}

//Keep the bug above the water
if (bug.y > stage.stageHeight - 35)
{
  bug.y = stage.stageHeight - 35;
  bug.vy *= -1;
}
if (bug.y < 0)
{
  bug.y = 0;
  bug.vy *= -1;
}

//Apply collision with platform
for (var i:int = 0; i <= 9; i++)
{
  Collision.playerAndPlatform(bug, this["platform" + i],0,0);
}

//Artificial intelligence
//Frog
if ((Math.abs(bug.x - frog.x) < 50)   )
{
  if (Math.abs(bug.y - frog.y) < 50)
  {
    bug.x += -bug.vx;
    bug.y += -bug.vy;
    bug.vx *= -1;
    bug.vy *= -1;
    //trace(bug.name + ": Frog!");
  }
}
```

```
      //Player
      if ((Math.abs(bug.x - player.x) < 60)    )
      {
        if (Math.abs(bug.y - player.y) < 60)
        {
          //If the player is moving...
          bug.vy += player.vy + ((Math.random() * 0.2 - 0.1) * 30);
          bug.vx += player.vx + ((Math.random() * 0.2 - 0.1) * 30);
           //trace(bug.name + ": Cat!");
          if ((Math.abs(player.vy) < 1) && (Math.abs(player.vx) <1 ))
          {
            //If the player is sitting still...
            bug.y += -bug.vy;
            bug.x += -bug.vx;
            bug.vy *= -1;
            bug.vx *= -1;
          }
        }
      }
    }

    private function onCollisionWithPlayer(event:Event):void
    {
      var collectionItem:MovieClip = event.target as MovieClip;
      if (_collectionJar.length < 3)
      {
        if (player.hitTestPoint(collectionItem.x, ➡
          collectionItem.y, true))
        {
          this["itemBox" + _collectionJar.length].addChild ➡
            (collectionItem);
          collectionItem.x = 0;
          collectionItem.y = 0;
          _collectionJar.push(collectionItem);
          //Remove listeners of collected items
          if (_collectionJar.length == 3)
          {
            addEventListener(Event.ENTER_FRAME, onEndGame);
          }
          if (collectionItem != mouse)
          {
            collectionItem.removeEventListener(Event.ENTER_FRAME, ➡
              onBugMove);
          }
          collectionItem.removeEventListener(Event.ENTER_FRAME, ➡
            onCollisionWithPlayer);
          //trace("Bugs Collected: " + _collectionJar);
        }
      }
    }
```

```
    }
    private function onEndGame(event:Event):void
    {
      instructions.text = "Visit the frog to tell him ➡
        what you've collected.";
      if (player.collisionArea.hitTestObject(frog))
      {
        for (var i:int = 0; i<_collectionJar.length; i++)
        {
          if (_collectionJar[i] == mouse)
          {
            _mouseFound = true;
            break;
          }
        }
        if (_mouseFound)
        {
          instructions.text = "I don't like mice!";
        }
        else
        {
          instructions.text = "Thanks very much!";
        }
        removeEventListener(Event.ENTER_FRAME, onEndGame);
      }
    }
  }
}
```

New Collision.playerAndPlatform utility

You'll take a look at the Collision.playerAndPlatform collision utility that you used for platform collisions. Make sure that you are familiar with Collision.block (refer to Chapter 7). The basic logic is exactly the same, but it's a bit more detailed because it's been designed to handle bounce and friction.

Collision.playerAndPlatform does the job of checking for collisions between two rectangles. When it finds a collision, it separates the objects and applies bounce and friction forces.

playerAndPlatform method

This code is pretty complex, so don't feel you have to understand exactly how it works any time soon. It's the most complex code in the entire book. I included it as a useful extra that you might find helpful in some of your own games. This is definitely not code that you need to understand at this stage in your learning.

In fact, you can even skip this section of the chapter and simply go on using the Collision. playerAndPlatform method as a utility without ever worrying about how it works. It's presented only so that you can see the underlying collision system involved. Also, this code is tailored specifically for this project, so feel free to change it as much as you like for your own games. With time, you might want to revisit this code when you understand it a bit better and then rewrite it so it's more general and easier to adapt to a wider range of situations. In fact, I hope you'll eventually do this. General code tends to be very complex, so the present version is written as a learning tool to be as simple as possible while still retaining a good degree of flexibility for many different kinds of games.

To use this code in your games, you need the following:

1. The first object involved in the collision, player, needs publicly accessible vx and vy properties. The vx and vy getters and setters in the Player_Platform class accommodate for this.

2. The player object optionally needs publicly accessible bounceX and bounceY properties if you want it to be able to bounce off platforms.

3. If the player object has a subobject assigned through a publicly accessible collisionArea property, that subobject is used as the collision object. In Bug Catcher, the cat's body subobject was assigned to the collisionArea property. It's available to the code through the Player_ Platform class's getter.

4. If you're programming a platform game and need to know whether the player is on top of any of the platforms, the code will look for a publicly accessible property called isOnGround and set it to true.

I won't discuss this code in detail, but I'll give you a general map of how it works. Each section of the code contains comments that explain what it does. I'll leave it up to you to check the specifics on the code and put all the pieces together. You won't understand all the code immediately, but it's something you can come back to as your programming experience increases over the weeks and months ahead. If you feel a bit overwhelmed when you first look at it, don't let it scare you. It's a lot of code, but you've actually seen all of it in different contexts before. The only really new things are the three formulas used to calculate bounce and friction, and you'll be looking at them in the pages ahead.

Here's how the playerAndPlatform method works:

- It accepts four parameters:
  - The first object involved in the collision (the player object)
  - The second object (the platform)
  - A bounce value
  - A friction value

- If the player object has a collisionArea subobject assigned, its width and height are used to define the player collision area. Its x and y coordinates are also converted to global coordinates using the localToGlobal method.

- The code checks for a collision on each axis; if it finds one, it determines which side of the platform the collision is occurring on. This is exactly the same system used in the Collision. block method. After it finishes, it separates the player from the collision with the platform and applies bounce and friction forces.

Here's what playerAndPlatform looks like:

```
static public function playerAndPlatform(player:MovieClip, ➥
  platform:MovieClip, bounce:Number, friction:Number):void
{
  //This method requires the following getter and
  //setter properties in the player object:
  //objectIsOnGround:Boolean, vx:Number, vy:Number,
  //bounceX:Number, bounceY:Number

  //Decalre variables needed for the player's
  //position and dimensions
  var player_Halfwidth:Number;
  var player_Halfheight:Number;
  var player_X:Number;
  var player_Y:Number

  //Decalre variables needed for the physics calculations
  var bounceX:Number;
  var bounceY:Number;
  var frictionX:Number;
  var frictionY:Number;

  //Find out whether the player object has a collisionArea
  //subobject defined
  if(player.collisionArea != null)
  {
    //If it does, find out its width and height
    player_Halfwidth = player.collisionArea.width / 2;
    player_Halfheight = player.collisionArea.height / 2;

    //Convert the collisionArea's local x, y coordinates
    //to global coordinates
    var player_Position:Point = new Point(player.collisionArea.x, ➥
      player.collisionArea.y);
    player_X = player.localToGlobal(player_Position).x;
    player_Y = player.localToGlobal(player_Position).y;
  }
  else
  {
    //If there's no collisionArea subobject
    //use the player's main height, width, x and y
    player_Halfwidth = player.width / 2;
    player_Halfheight = player.height / 2;
    player_X = player.x;
    player_Y = player.y;
  }
  //Find the platform's dimensions
  var platform_Halfwidth:Number = platform.width / 2;
```

```
var platform_Halfheight:Number = platform.height / 2;

//Find the distance between the player and platfrom on the x axis
var dx:Number = platform.x - player_X;

//Find the amount of overlap on the x axis
var ox:Number = platform_Halfwidth + player_Halfwidth - Math.abs(dx);

 //We have all the values we need, now
 //we can start checking for a collision

//Check for a collision on the x axis
if (ox > 0)
{
  //If the objects overlap on the x axis, a collision might be
  //occuring  Define the variables you need to check for
  //a collision on the y axis
  var dy:Number = player.y - platform.y;
  var oy:Number = platform_Halfheight + player_Halfheight ➡
    - Math.abs(dy);

  //Check for a y axis collision. We know a collision must be
  //occuring if there's a collision on both the x and y axis
  if (oy > 0)
  {
    //Yes, a collision is occuring!
    //Now you need to find out on which side
    //of the platform it's occuring on.
    if (ox < oy)
    {
      if (dx < 0)
      {
        //Collision on Right
        oy = 0;
        dx = 1;
        dy = 0
      }
      else
      {
        //Collision on Left
        oy = 0;
        ox *= -1;
        dx = -1;
        dy = 0
      }
    }
    else
    {
      if (dy < 0)
```

```
    {
      //Collision on Top
      ox = 0;
      oy *= -1;
      dx = 0;
      dy = -1;
      //set the player's isOnGround property to
      //true to enable jumping
      player.isOnGround = true;
    }
    else
    {
      //Collision on Bottom
      ox = 0;
      dx = 0;
      dy = 1;
    }
  }

  //Calculate the bounce and friction:
  //Find the direction of the collision
  var directionOfCollision:Number = player.vx * dx ➡
    + player.vy * dy;

  //Calculate the new direction for the bounce
  var newDirection_X:Number = directionOfCollision * dx;
  var newDirection_Y:Number = directionOfCollision * dy;

  //Find the "tangent velocity":
  //the speed in the direction that the object is moving.
  //It's used for calculating additional platform friction.
  var tangent_Vx:Number = player.vx - newDirection_X;
  var tangent_Vy:Number = player.vy - newDirection_Y;

  //Apply collision forces if the object is moving into a collision
  if (directionOfCollision < 0)
  {
    //Calculate the friction
    frictionX = tangent_Vx * friction;
    frictionY = tangent_Vy * friction;

    //Calculate the amount of bounce
    bounceX = newDirection_X * bounce;
    bounceY = newDirection_Y * bounce;
  }
  else
  {
    //Prevent forces from being applied if the object is
    //moving out of a collision
```

```
                    bounceX = 0;
                    bounceY = 0;
                    frictionX = 0;
                    frictionY = 0;
                }
                //Apply platform friction
                player.vx += ox - frictionX;
                player.vy += oy - frictionY;

                //Move the player out of the collision
                player.x += ox;
                player.y += oy;

                //Bounce the player off the platform
                player.bounceX = bounceX;
                player.bounceY = bounceY;
            }
        }
    }
}
```

Platform bounce and friction

Although finding out on which side of the platform a collision is occurring is reasonably straightforward, applying the right physics is a little a bit more complex. You need to find out in what direction the object is traveling so that it can bounce away at the correct angle.

Lucky for you, you can borrow some formulas used in a branch of mathematics called **vector math** to help you sort this out.

To apply the correct bounce and friction when the player hits the platforms, you need to know three things:

- The direction the player is traveling in. You can figure this out by using a vector math formula that calculates a value known as a **dot product**:

```
var directionOfCollision:Number = player.vx * dx + player.vy * dy;
```

- The new direction the player needs to travel in when it bounces on the platform. In vector math, this is called the **projection**:

```
var newDirection_X:Number = directionOfCollision * dx;
var newDirection_Y:Number = directionOfCollision * dy;
```

- The player's speed, in the direction that it's bouncing. This is known as the **tangent velocity** and it's used to calculate the platform's friction.

```
var tangent_Vx:Number = player.vx - newDirection_X;
var tangent_Vy:Number = player.vy - newDirection_Y;
```

Figure 9-27 illustrates a simple example of how these three values can describe an object bouncing on a surface.

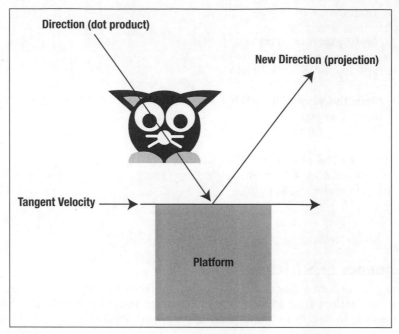

Figure 9-27. Use some vector math to help with bounce and friction.

These formulas will work no matter which side and from which direction the player is hitting the platform. Vector math is very helpful for these sorts of physics calculations in games. If you go on to do much more game design outside the pages of this book, consider studying a bit of vector math in more detail.

Now that you have those values, you can multiply them with the bounce and friction values that were supplied to the method as parameters. An important thing about the next bit of code is that it applies the forces only if the player is moving into a collision with the platform. Without this check, the player will appear to be fixed to the platform with glue when it lands on it:

```
//Apply collision forces if the object is moving into a collision
if (directionOfCollision < 0)
{
  //Calculate the friction
  frictionX = tangent_Vx * friction;
  frictionY = tangent_Vy * friction;

  //Calculate the amount of bounce
  bounceX = newDirection_X * bounce;
  bounceY = newDirection_Y * bounce;
}
else
```

```
    {
      //Prevent forces from being applied if the object is
      //moving out of a collision
      bounceX = 0;
      bounceY = 0;
      frictionX = 0;
      frictionY = 0;
    }
```

When the bounce and friction forces are calculated, they can be applied to the player object:

```
    //Apply platform friction
    player.vx += ox - frictionX;
    player.vy += oy - frictionY;

    //Move the player out of the collision
    player.x += ox;
    player.y += oy;

    //Bounce the player off the platform
    player.bounceX = bounceX;
    player.bounceY = bounceY;
```

Remember that ox and oy are the amount by which the player overlaps the platform when the collision occurs. The player is separated from the platform by that amount.

Detecting the top of the platform

There's one other detail I need to point out. The Player_Platform class needs to know when the player is on the ground so that it can be permitted to jump. It contains a private Boolean variable called _isOnGround that's accessed by a getter and setter called isOnGround. When the player is on the bottom of the stage, _isOnGround is set to true, and the player can jump.

The player needs to be able to jump not only when it's on the bottom of the stage but also when it's on top of a platform. Fortunately, the collision code is able to tell you which side of the platform the player is colliding with. All you need to do is set isOnGround to true when the code detects a hit with the top side of a platform:

```
    if (dy < 0)
    {
      //Collision on Top
      ox = 0;
      oy *= -1;
      dx = 0;
      dy = -1;
      //set the player's isOnGround property to
      //true to enable jumping
      player.isOnGround = true;
    }
```

Summary

I covered a number of new techniques in this chapter, all of which you'll find a use for in your own game projects. The specific game logic that you use to solve the conditions for winning and losing, as well as artificial intelligence for your game characters, will be different with every project. But hopefully this chapter has shown you some approaches to tackling these issues and some of the things that you'll need to think about to solve these problems in your own games.

This has been a basic introduction to platform games, but you'll find all the building blocks here to start you off building a game that could become quite complex with a bit of planning and imagination. Add a bit of the puzzle solving and task completion that you looked at in Dungeon Maze Adventure, and maybe a few animated enemies, and you'll be well on your way to building a really fun game. You could also add a weapon, some sound, and even some scrolling so the player could explore a large area. What about items that give the player some special abilities, or maybe some vehicles to drive?

One bonus of the collision code that you're using is that it tells you which side of the platform the player is hitting. You can adapt it for enemy collisions to find out whether the player was jumping on an enemy's head, which is the classic way of vanquishing enemies in platform games. You can also adapt the physics code to create a flight-based action game such as Joust; or a flight rescue or exploration game such as Lunar Lander, Choplifter, or Defender. Actually, just about any 2D platform game is within your reach. And what about moving platforms? It could be interesting!

In the next chapter, you'll take a closer look at enemy artificial intelligence and scripted motion. I'll show you player control schemes that use the mouse, how to move objects and fire bullets in 360 degrees, and one of the most useful programming techniques in a game designer's arsenal: dispatching events.

Chapter 10

ADVANCED OBJECT AND CHARACTER CONTROL

In this final chapter of the book, I'll show you a wide variety of useful techniques you'll need to know to get started on your own professional-level game design projects:

- Dragging and dropping objects with the mouse
- Using easing for smooth motion
- Controlling game characters with the mouse
- Moving objects in the direction of their rotation
- Firing bullets in all directions
- Using dynamic filters
- Making objects with the switch statement and the simple factory system
- Learning basic enemy artificial intelligence (AI): following, running away, and firing bullets in the direction of the player
- Using a timer
- Using keyboard-driven spaceship and mouse-driven platform game controls
- Dispatching events

This is quite a big and dense chapter, so don't feel you need to absorb all these techniques at one sitting. This chapter has been designed as a toolbox for you to delve into when you're trying to solve a particular problem in your own game design projects. Take it one small bite at a time and try to apply the techniques to your projects as much as possible.

The one must-read section, however, is the "Dispatching events" section at the end of the chapter. Learning to dispatch events is such a useful skill for a game designer that it could become the primary technique that you use for structuring your games from now on, no matter what kind of game you're designing.

So, without further ado, on with the game!

Dragging and dropping objects

To create any kind of game that involves matching objects, such as puzzle or board games, you need to create objects that can be dragged and dropped with the mouse. Lucky for you, any objects that inherit AS3.0's Sprite class, such as Movie Clip objects, have some built-in properties and methods that are specialized for drag-and-drop interfaces:

- startDrag: Makes an object dragable
- stopDrag: Stops dragging
- dropTarget: Tells you which object is under the mouse when an object is being dragged

You'll take a look at two contrasting examples of how to program a basic drag-and-drop game: a procedural approach and an object-oriented approach. Highlighting the differences between these approaches will illustrate some important aspects about drag-and-drop objects and be an interesting look at the way procedural programs differ from object-oriented ones.

Dragging and dropping the procedural way

Let's have a look at a simple example of a drag-and-drop interface.

1. In this chapter's source files, you'll find a folder called Drag and Drop 1. Open this folder as a project in the Project panel.

2. Test the project. You can drag the red and blue squares around the stage. When you release them over the corresponding empty red or blue squares, they snap into place. If you release the left mouse button over an object, the name of the object is displayed in the Output panel.

The dragAndDrop1.fla file contains four objects: blueSquare, redSquare, blueTarget, and redTarget (see Figure 10-1).

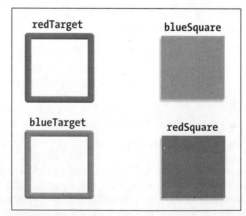

Figure 10-1. Drag-and-drop objects

The code that makes all this work is in the Main_DragAndDrop1.as file:

```
package
{
  import flash.display.MovieClip;
  import flash.events.Event;
  import flash.events.MouseEvent;

  public class Main_DragAndDrop1 extends MovieClip
  {
    //Declare variables
    private var _isDragging:Boolean;

    public function Main_DragAndDrop1()
    {
      //Initialize variables
      _isDragging = false;

      //Add event listeners
      redSquare.addEventListener(MouseEvent.MOUSE_DOWN, onMouseDown);
      blueSquare.addEventListener(MouseEvent.MOUSE_DOWN, onMouseDown);
      addEventListener(Event.ENTER_FRAME,onEnterFrame);
    }
    private function onEnterFrame(event:Event):void
    {
      if (redSquare.hitTestObject(redTarget))
      {
        if (! _isDragging)
        {
          redSquare.x = redTarget.x;
          redSquare.y = redTarget.y;
        }
      }
      if (blueSquare.hitTestObject(blueTarget))
      {
        if (! _isDragging)
        {
          blueSquare.x = blueTarget.x;
          blueSquare.y = blueTarget.y;
        }
      }
    }
    private function onMouseDown(event:Event):void
    {
      var currentDragObject:MovieClip = event. currentTarget ➥
        as MovieClip;
      currentDragObject.startDrag();
      setChildIndex(currentDragObject, numChildren - 1);
      _isDragging = true;
```

487

```
        currentDragObject.addEventListener(MouseEvent.MOUSE_UP, ➥
          onMouseUp);
      }
      private function onMouseUp(event:Event):void
      {
        var currentDragObject:MovieClip = event. currentTarget ➥
          as MovieClip;
        currentDragObject.stopDrag();
        _isDragging = false;
        currentDragObject.removeEventListener(MouseEvent.MOUSE_UP, ➥
          onMouseUp);

        //Display the name of object that mouse is released over
        if(currentDragObject.dropTarget != null)
        {
          trace(currentDragObject.dropTarget.parent.name);
        }
      }
    }
  }
```

Much of this code is quite familiar to you by now, but there are a few new things here that require some explanation.

The class uses a Boolean variable called _isDragging to keep track of whether you are dragging any objects. You need this variable to prevent the squares from snapping to their targets before the mouse button is actually released.

At the heart of the program, however, are the onMouseDown and onMouseUp events. This program again illustrates how two or more objects can share the same event handler. When the program is initialized, both the redSquare and blueSquare objects add the very same onMouseDown event listener:

```
redSquare.addEventListener(MouseEvent.MOUSE_DOWN, onMouseDown);
blueSquare.addEventListener(MouseEvent.MOUSE_DOWN, onMouseDown);
```

When the mouse button is pressed down over either of these objects, the onMouseDown event handler is called:

```
private function onMouseDown(event:Event):void
{
  var currentDragObject:MovieClip = event.currentTarget as MovieClip;
  currentDragObject.startDrag();
  setChildIndex(currentDragObject, numChildren-1);
  _isDragging = true;
  currentDragObject.addEventListener(MouseEvent.MOUSE_UP, onMouseUp);
}
```

This event handler does a number of interesting things:

- It figures out which object has been clicked by accessing the event's event.currentTarget property and assigning it to a variable called currentDragObject (more on the currentTarget property ahead):

```
var currentDragObject:MovieClip = event.currentTarget as MovieClip;
```

- It then invokes the startDrag method of the object. This starts the object dragging, with the effect you can clearly see on the stage:

```
currentDragObject.startDrag();
```

- You want the object that you're dragging to be above all the other objects on the stage. This creates the illusion that it's being picked up. To do this, you need to move it to the highest position in the display list. setChildIndex(currentDragObject, numChildren-1) takes care of that quite nicely:

```
setChildIndex(currentDragObject, numChildren - 1);
```

- It sets the _isDragging variable to true:

```
_isDragging = true;
```

- It adds the onMouseUp listener to the object. You could have easily added this event to the object in the constructor method, but, for performance reasons it's generally a good idea to create listeners only when you need them. You don't need to listen for a MOUSE_UP event before the MOUSE_DOWN event is triggered, so it makes sense to add it here:

```
currentDragObject.addEventListener(MouseEvent.MOUSE_UP, onMouseUp);
```

Now that you can happily drag the object around the stage, what happens when the mouse is released? The onMouseUp event handler is called:

```
private function onMouseUp(event:Event):void
{
  var currentDragObject:MovieClip = event.currentTarget as MovieClip;
  currentDragObject.stopDrag();
  _isDragging = false;
  currentDragObject.removeEventListener(MouseEvent.MOUSE_UP, ➥
    onMouseUp);

  //Display the name of object that mouse is released over
  if(currentDragObject.dropTarget != null)
  {
    trace(currentDragObject.dropTarget.parent.name);
  }
}
```

This event listener uses the target object's stopDrag method to stop the drag effect. It sets _isDragging to false and then removes itself after completing the job.

Using target or currentTarget properties

In previous chapters, the target of an event using the event object's target property was referred to like this:

    event.target

The target object is the object that triggered the event. In the Bug Catcher game from the previous chapter, for example, you used event.target to find out which bug was currently calling the onEnterFrame event.

In this drag-and-drop example, a property called currentTarget is used to find which object the mouse is clicking:

    event.currentTarget

What's the difference between target and currentTarget?

Figure 10-2 illustrates an example. Imagine that you have an object called square that contains a subobject called triangle. You registered the event listener with the square object like this:

    square.addEventListener...

currentTarget refers to the object that the event is registered with. In this example, it's the square object. If you click and drag anywhere on the square object, the whole square object moves, including the triangle subobject.

target refers to the actual object that the mouse clicked. If you click the triangle subobject, you can drag only the triangle; the parent square doesn't move. (If you click an area of the square that doesn't include the triangle, however, the two objects move together).

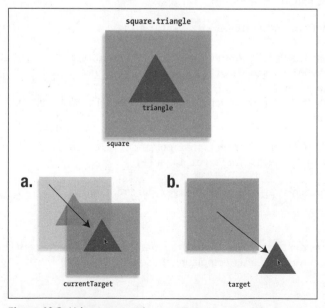

Figure 10-2. Using target and currentTarget

Using dropTarget

The last thing the code does is to display the name of the object that the mouse is released over by using the dropTarget property. If you test the project, you'll notice that when you release the mouse, the name of the object that is directly under the tip of the mouse pointer is displayed in the Output panel. This doesn't have any functional purpose in the program except to illustrate how the dropTarget property works.

This is the line of code that displays the name of the object that dropTarget references:

```
trace(currentDragObject.dropTarget.parent.name);
```

Have a look at the object path:

```
currentDragObject.dropTarget.parent.name
```

Do you notice something odd there? Why do you need to access the parent property? If you're anything like me, you might have thought that the path should have more logically read something like this:

```
currentDragObject.dropTarget.name
```

But it doesn't. An extra parent has been slipped in there just to keep you on your toes. The reason why is worth explaining—if you ever use the dropTarget property in any of your games, you'll have a few sleepless nights if you don't understand it.

dropTarget is a property of the MovieClip class. dropTarget.name gives you the name of the object that the mouse is over *inside* that Movie Clip object. However, in almost any drag-and-drop scenario imaginable, you don't need to know the name of that object (which will usually be a drawing shape from the Shape class or a Movie Clip subobject). What's important to know is the name of the object that the mouse is over in the *parent container*.

In this case, the parent container is an object that's on the main stage. The stage is at the root of the hierarchy for display objects, so it's also the parent container for any object on the main stage, including the dropTarget object in this case. Only when your dragable object doesn't contain any other subobjects (or even drawing shapes) can you get by without referencing the parent object.

Remember this if you ever have problems with code that depends on being able to access the dropTarget object. More than one experienced Flash game designer has been tripped up by this! A very useful strategy to follow while building drag-and-drop games is to set a trace for both the parent and dropTarget properties. This will help you keep things straight in your own mind while negotiating this little minefield.

A further word of caution about using dropTarget: it returns only the name of the object that the mouse is currently *directly over*. If part of the object that you're dragging is touching another object when you release the mouse, but the tip of the mouse pointer isn't, dropTarget doesn't register that object. This is a limitation that could scuttle its use in many drag-and-drop games. Figure 10-3 illustrates some cases in which dropTarget doesn't return any value, even though the object being dragged is clearly over another object.

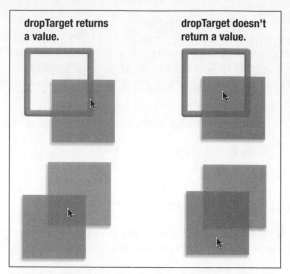

Figure 10-3. dropTarget returns only a reference to the object that mouse is directly over.

Because of this limitation, you might find yourself using dropTarget infrequently, and it might be little or no use at all for sophisticated drag-and-drop games. Instead, you might want to consider using hitTestObject to find the names of the objects that the drag object is passing over. This will be a bit more work to set up because you need to store the names of all possible targets in an array and loop through each frame to check whether they're colliding with the drag object. You don't quite have the skills to do this yet, but you will by the end of this chapter.

Snapping the object to the target

The code that actually snaps the drag objects to their targets sits in an ENTER_FRAME event handler:

```
private function onEnterFrame(event:Event):void
{
  if (redSquare.hitTestObject(redTarget))
  {
    if (! _isDragging)
    {
      redSquare.x = redTarget.x;
      redSquare.y = redTarget.y;
    }
  }
  if (blueSquare.hitTestObject(blueTarget))
  {
    if (! _isDragging)
    {
      blueSquare.x = blueTarget.x;
      blueSquare.y = blueTarget.y;
    }
  }
}
```

The code uses hitTestObject to check whether the object is over its target. If it is, it then checks to see whether the object is currently being dragged. You need to check for this so that the object doesn't snap to the target before the mouse button is released. If it all seems fine, the dragable objects are assigned the exact same x and y positions as the targets. The result is that the objects appear to snap into place.

Centering the drag object to the mouse

The startDrag method has two optional parameters that give you a little more fine control over how your dragable objects behave.

The first parameter is called lockCenter. It's a Boolean value that tells AS3.0 whether the object should be centered over the mouse. To use it, just add true as an argument in the startDrag method, like this:

```
startDrag(true);
```

Try it in the example and you'll notice that the object snaps to the mouse center when you click it.

Confining the drag area

You might find in some circumstances that you want to contain dragging to a certain area of the stage. The startDrag method has a second optional parameter called bounds that accepts a Rectangle object as an argument. The Rectangle object defines the area that the object will be confined to.

First, however, you need to actually make a Rectangle object, which is an abstract bit of code that defines an area of a rectangle. Creating one is about as easy or difficult as it is to create a Point object (pretty easy!):

1. Import the Rectangle class with the following import statement:

   ```
   import flash.geom.Rectangle;
   ```

2. Next, declare a Rectangle object in your class (you can give this variable any name you like; you don't have to call it _rectangle):

   ```
   private var _rectangle:Rectangle;
   ```

3. Define the rectangle by specifying x, y, height, and width values (you can do this anywhere in your program, but it probably makes sense to do it in the constructor method):

   ```
   _rectangle = new Rectangle();
   _rectangle.width = 200;
   _rectangle.height = 200;
   _rectangle.x = 100;
   _rectangle.y = 100;
   ```

4. After the _rectangle variable is defined, you can use it as the second argument in the startDrag method, like this:

   ```
   startDrag(false, _rectangle);
   ```

> *Because you have to specify the rectangle as the second argument, you also have to supply a first argument, which is where* false *comes from.* false *refers to the* lockCenter *parameter that you looked at in the previous section. Setting it to* false *tells the program that you don't want the object to snap to the mouse's center point. You can set it to* true *if you want to; it's entirely up to you.*

After you follow those steps, you'll have an invisible rectangle that you can't drag your object out of. If you create a Rectangle object the same size as the stage, the object will be confined within the stage boundaries.

Dragging and dropping the object-oriented way

When you design drag-and-drop environments and interfaces, you'll almost certainly find the object-oriented way a little more flexible, easier to code, and easier to manage than the procedural approach you just looked at. I could have left you on your own after the first example, but there are some important quirks regarding AS3.0's drag-and-drop system that you need to know in order to get an object-oriented drag-and-drop system working in the way that you might expect it to. I'm also going to show you how you can use some of the techniques you looked at earlier, such as using an ENTER_FRAME event, to put you on the path to creating quite complex drag-and-drop objects if you need to.

1. In this chapter's source files, you'll find a folder called Drag and Drop 2. Open it as a project in the Project panel.

2. Test the project. It works exactly the same as the first example except for two improvements:

   - The objects ease gently into position over the targets.
   - The objects are prevented from moving beyond the edges of the stage.

In this example, both the redSquare and blueSquare objects have been bound to the same class: DragableObject. You can check this by doing the following:

1. Open the dragAndDrop2.fla file.

2. Select either the redSquare or blueSquare symbol in the Library.

3. Click the small Properties button at the bottom of the Library panel.

4. You'll see a window open that looks something like Figure 10-4. Both symbols have DragableObject as their base class, which allows both objects to use the same class.

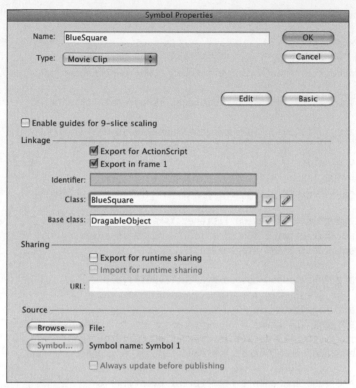

Figure 10-4. Both blueSquare and redSquare share the same base class: DragableObject.

DragableObject class

The code that makes both objects work is the DragableObject class:

```
package
{
  import flash.display.MovieClip;
  import flash.events.Event;
  import flash.events.MouseEvent;

  public class DragableObject extends MovieClip
  {
    //Initialize variables
    private var _isDragging:Boolean;
```

```
public function DragableObject()
{
  //Add listeners
  addEventListener(Event.ENTER_FRAME, onEnterFrame);
  addEventListener(MouseEvent.MOUSE_DOWN, onMouseDown);

  //Important: onMouseDown listener is added to this object
}
private function onMouseUp(event:Event):void
{
  stopDrag();
  _isDragging = false;
  stage.removeEventListener(MouseEvent.MOUSE_UP, onMouseUp);

  //Important: onMouseUp listener is added to the stage
  //so that it will function if the mouse is released
  //outside the SWF stage area.
}
private function onMouseDown(event:Event):void
{
  startDrag();
  _isDragging = true;
  parent.setChildIndex(this, parent.numChildren - 1);
  stage.addEventListener(MouseEvent.MOUSE_UP, onMouseUp);
}
private function onEnterFrame(event:Event):void
{
  //Stage boundaries
  var halfWidth:uint = width / 2;
  var halfHeight:uint = height / 2;

  if (x + halfWidth > stage.stageWidth)
  {
    x = stage.stageWidth - halfWidth;
  }
  else if (x - halfWidth < 0)
  {
    x = 0 + halfWidth;
  }
  if (y - halfHeight < 0)
  {
    y = 0 + halfHeight;
  }
  else if (y + halfHeight > stage.stageHeight)
  {
    y = stage.stageHeight - halfHeight;
  }
}
```

```
        //Getter
        public function get isBeingDragged():Boolean
        {
          return _isDragging;
         }
      }
    }
```

As you can see, all the drag-and-drop functionality has been pushed into this class. The `_isDragging` variable is accessed with a getter so it can be used by the Main class to find out whether the object is being dragged.

The class also uses an ENTER_FRAME event that prevents the object from moving past the edges of the stage. I used it in this simple example just to show you how it can be done, but there's no reason for you to stop here. You can use any other code you like here (including code for friction, acceleration, and gravity) and also build in a collision detection system if you need to.

One very important thing to understand is that when you drag objects using startDrag, the object's position on the stage is not updated by an ENTER_FRAME event. In fact, it even updates at a different rate from the movie's frame rate. This means that any physics simulations you might want to implement won't work while the object is being dragged. This might not be a problem for you, but if it is, you'll be looking at some techniques in the following pages that will help you build your own custom drag-and-drop engine if you need to.

> A drag-and-drop engine? **Engines** are what programmers like to call self-contained systems that perform a specialized job. Phrases such as "collision detection engine" or "drag-and-drop engine" have nothing to do with exhaust pipes and fan belts. It's just another way of saying "integrated system."

Releasing the mouse outside the stage area

There is an extremely important detail that you need to make note of in this code. The onMouseDown listener is added directly to the object, but the onMouseUp listener is added to the stage object. If you don't add the onMouseUp listener to the stage, your drag-and-drop programs will encounter a peculiar glitch that is due to the way the Flash Player interacts with the rest of your computer's operating system.

For "security reasons" (which means to prevent someone using Flash and AS3.0 to write a destructive virus or worm that could damage your computer), the Flash Player does not allow anything that goes on within the confines of the SWF to interact with the rest of the computer's operating system, including the position of the mouse on the screen. If the computer mouse is interacting with objects inside the Flash Player or web browser window, everything works the way you expect it to. However, as soon as the mouse moves away from the player window, the player can no longer receive instructions from the mouse.

This is a problem for drag-and-drop games. What happens if the player clicks an object, drags it to the edge of the screen, and then releases the mouse button *outside* the Flash Player window? The Flash Player isn't informed that the button was released and still thinks that the object is being dragged. This

497

translates to an annoying glitch where the dragable object appears hopelessly stuck to the mouse, and only clicking another drag-and-drop object will set it free. So the Flash Player allows for one special circumstance where it allows you to track mouse activity that happens outside the boundaries of the stage. However, it works *only* if the mouse listener is added to the stage object. If you design a drag-and-drop game, you're sure to encounter this problem, so bookmark this page in case you do!

Main_DragAndDrop2 class

The Main_DragAndDrop2 class takes care of the program's administrative work, which amounts to making sure the right object lands on the right target:

```
package
{
  import flash.display.MovieClip;
  import flash.events.Event;
  import flash.events.MouseEvent;

  public class Main_DragAndDrop2 extends MovieClip
  {
    private var _easing:Number;

    public function Main_DragAndDrop2()
    {
      //Initialize variables
      _easing = 0.3;

      //Add event listeners
      addEventListener(Event.ENTER_FRAME,onEnterFrame);
    }
    private function onEnterFrame(event:Event):void
    {
      if (redSquare.hitTestObject(redTarget))
      {
        if (! redSquare.isBeingDragged)
        {
          redSquare.x += (redTarget.x - redSquare.x) * _easing;
          redSquare.y += (redTarget.y - redSquare.y) * _easing;
        }
      }
      if (blueSquare.hitTestObject(blueTarget))
      {
        if (! blueSquare.isBeingDragged)
        {
          blueSquare.x += (blueTarget.x - blueSquare.x) * _easing;
          blueSquare.y += (blueTarget.y - blueSquare.y) * _easing;
        }
      }
    }
  }
}
```

The program figures out whether the object is being dragged by accessing the object's getter. isBeingDragged is true when the object "is being dragged" and false when it isn't.

You should also see the great advantage of using object-oriented programming: the work of the program is distributed between two classes. Each class is responsible for handling only those tasks that directly relate to it. Although the overall structure is more complex because you're dealing with two classes rather than just one, the individual complexity of those classes is much less. In the long run, this saves you much more time when it comes to changing features and debugging.

Easing

Another little trick introduced in this example is a scripted motion technique called **easing**, which is the effect that you can see as objects gently "ease" into position over the targets.

Easing is very easy to implement using a simple formula inside an ENTER_FRAME event:

*(origin - destination) * easingValue;*

You can make the animation happen faster or slower by changing the easing value. In the program, this value is stored in a variable called _easing and has a value of 0.3. Changing it to a higher number, such as 0.5, makes the easing effect happen much more quickly. Changing it to a lower number, such as 0.1, creates a much slower effect. The code that makes the objects ease into position over the target looks like this:

```
redSquare.x += (redTarget.x - redSquare.x) * _easing;
redSquare.y += (redTarget.y - redSquare.y) * _easing;
```

The code adds the easing formula to the x and y positions of the object to make it move to the new position. Easing is a basic technique in game design to move objects, and you'll be looking at many more examples throughout this chapter.

An alternative to inheritance: Composition

Up until now, you've been creating objects using inheritance. You might recall that inheritance is the system of extending a class to create a new class. All the classes so far have been created by extending the MovieClip class. When you see the keyword extends in the class definition, you know that inheritance is at work:

```
public class NewClass extends MovieClip
```

This allows the new class to "inherit" all the properties and methods of the class it extends. The new class can then use all those properties and methods in addition to any new properties and methods that the new class defines. Inheritance is a quick, easy, and flexible way to make new objects based on old ones.

There is an alternative way to creating objects using classes called **composition**. To get more insight into object-oriented programming, you'll take a brief look at how composition works.

In the example drag-and-drop program you just examined, both the redSquare and blueSquare objects share the same class. Although binding symbols to a common base class is usually the simplest way for symbols to share a class, you can also do it directly with code using composition.

Composition allows many objects to share the same class. The great thing is that you don't need to hard-code the class you want them to use into the symbol's properties. You can decide when you write the program which object should use which class, and even switch the class it uses at any time you like. Composition requires a bit more code and a bit more structural planning than inheritance, but ultimately gives you a greater flexibility when you build your games.

Let's look at a very simple example. You could create a very basic class called DragableObject that accepts one parameter: the name of any Movie Clip instance that wants to use the class. The class might look like this:

```
package
{
 import flash.display.MovieClip;

 public class DragableObject
  {
    var _dragableObject:MovieClip

    public function DragableObject(anyObject:MovieClip)
    {
      _dragableObject  = anyObject;
    }

    //Getter
    public function get dragObject():MovieClip
    {
      return _ dragableObject;
    }
  }
}
```

Imagine that you have an object on the stage called square that you want to make dragable. In your Main document class, you then create the dragable _square object like this:

```
private var _square:DragableObject = new DragableObject(square);
```

In the Main document class you can then access the actual object you want to drag through the DragableObject class's getter, like this:

```
_square.dragObject
```

You can access any of the object's properties like this:

```
_square.dragObject.x
_square.dragObject.width
```

Figure 10-5 illustrates this simple example of how composition works.

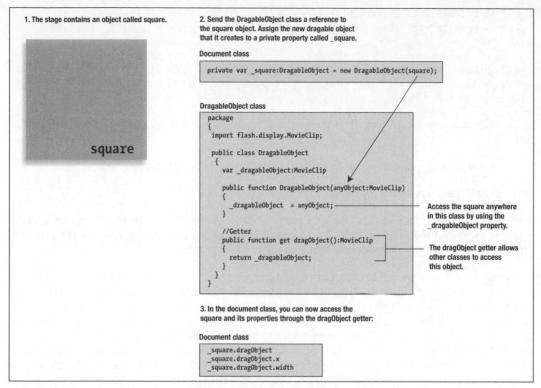

Figure 10-5. Composition allows any object to acquire the properties and methods of any other class.

You could make your code a little more readable by adding another getter in the DragableObject class that returns any of the dragable object's properties, such as the x property:

```
public function get x():Number
{
  return _ dragableObject.x;
}
```

In the document class, you could access the object's property like this:

```
_square.x
```

This is a bit more code to write in the DragableObject class, but it makes your code much more readable because it mimics the way you would normally access an object's properties. If your objects need a reference to the stage (to set stage boundaries, for example), you need to pass the DragableObject class a reference to the stage object as one of its parameters when you instantiate the object. You need to do this because the DragableObject class itself is never added to the stage, so it has no other way to access the stage's properties. To do this, you can change the DragableObject constructor method so that it looks like this:

```
public function DragableObject(anyObject:MovieClip, stage:Object)
{
```

```
        private var _dragableObject:MovieClip = anyObject;
        private var _stage:Object = stage;
    }
```

The stage object has to be typed as Object and not Stage. Because the DragableObject class isn't on the stage, it can't access the Stage class, even if the Stage class is just needed to assign the object's type.

In the Main document class, you then create the dragable _square object with two arguments, like this:

```
        private var _square = new DragableObject(anyMovieClipInstance, stage);
```

This includes the stage as one of the arguments.

If you want to take a look at how the little drag-and-drop sample looks written entirely using composition, open up the Drag and Drop 3 – Composition folder in this chapter's source files. It's very interesting to compare how it works with the previous two examples.

Composition is a very powerful object-oriented technique because any objects can share a class at any time in your program without having to hard-code the class into the symbol properties. This also means that if you decide, for example, that you want any of your enemy objects to suddenly take on all the qualities of the player's class in the middle of a game, you can just feed them into that class using composition. Another not-so-obvious advantage is that the class your objects use can extend any class they choose (or none at all). They don't have to extend the class of the containing object, such as MovieClip. This gives your classes more flexibility to extend whatever other classes they please. All this helps to whittle away at the problem of code dependency discussed in Chapter 8. Composition rocks!

This has been an extremely brief and very condensed introduction to composition, so don't worry too much if you don't understand it thoroughly right away. Spend a bit of time looking at the example in the source files, mull over them a bit and do a bit of experimenting on your own. You'll soon get an appreciation for the beauty of this system.

Moving objects with the mouse

The AS3.0 drag-and-drop system is very convenient, but it has some limitations. Because the object's position is updated independently of the movie's frame rate, all the little bells and whistles (such as physics simulations and collision detection) that you expect to be able to apply to an object while it's being dragged won't work. Because of this, many developers of drag-and-drop games end up building their own drag-and-drop engines using the AS3.0 Mouse and MouseEvent classes.

But aside from drag-and-drop interfaces, games that use the mouse are just so much fun to play! In fact, if you start designing Flash games professionally, your clients will probably expect that the game controls rely on the mouse instead of the keyboard, and if you can design game controls using the mouse exclusively, you're only a small step away from designing games for touch screen interface devices, such as the iPhone or Nintendo DS. One of the most sophisticated 2D games ever designed, The Phantom Hourglass for the Nintendo DS uses what amounts to just a simple point-and-click interface for its entire control scheme. With thoughtful and clever design of your games, you can completely eliminate reliance on the keyboard, and your players will thank you for it.

So let's take a step-by-step look at how to control objects with the mouse.

Fixing an object to the mouse's position

Let's start by fixing an object to the mouse's x and y positions using the Mouse class. In the chapter's source files is a folder called Mouse Pointer. Open it as a project and test it. You'll see that you can control the up-and-coming star of this chapter, Button Fairy, just by moving the mouse around the stage. Figure 10-6 illustrates what you will see.

Figure 10-6. Move the mouse to make Button Fairy fly around the stage.

When you move the mouse, the mouse pointer disappears, but the object remains fixed to the exact position where it would be. This is a technique that you can use to create a custom mouse pointer for any of your games.

The code also adds a dynamic drop-shadow filter to Button Fairy, which I'll discuss in a bit. All the code is in the Main_MousePointer class:

```
package
{
  import flash.display.MovieClip;
  import flash.events.Event;
  import flash.ui.Mouse;
  import flash.filters.DropShadowFilter;
  import flash.filters.BitmapFilterQuality;

  public class Main_MousePointer extends MovieClip
  {
```

```
            //Declare variables
            private var _player:Player;
            private var _shadow:DropShadowFilter;

            public function Main_MousePointer()
            {
              //Create a new instance of the Player class
              //and add it to the stage
              _player = new Player();
              addChild(_player);

              //Hide the mouse
              Mouse.hide();

              //Configure drop shadow filter
              _shadow = new DropShadowFilter();
              _shadow.distance = 4;
              _shadow.angle = 120;
              _shadow.strength = 0.6;
              _shadow.quality = BitmapFilterQuality.LOW;
              //Add drop shadow to player
              _player.body.filters = [_shadow];

              //Add listeners
              addEventListener(Event.ENTER_FRAME,onEnterFrame);
            }
            private function onEnterFrame(event:Event):void
            {
              _player.x = mouseX;
              _player.y = mouseY;
            }
        }
    }
```

This code relies on the use of the Mouse class, so the first thing you need to do is import it into the program:

```
import flash.ui.Mouse;
```

The Library contains a symbol called Player. The program creates an instance of the Player class called _player and adds it to the stage:

```
_player = new Player();
addChild(_player);
```

It then hides the mouse using the Mouse class's hide method:

```
Mouse.hide();
```

Finally, it fixes the _player object's position to the now invisible mouse by using the stage's mouseX and mouseY properties:

```
_player.x = mouseX;
_player.y = mouseY;
```

And there you have a custom mouse pointer!

> Because mouseX and mouseY are properties of the stage, you need to preface them with stage if you use them in any class that isn't the document class (for example, you would need to use stage.mouseX and stage.mouseY).

Adding a dynamic filter

Button Fairy casts a slight shadow, as shown in Figure 10-7. This is a **drop shadow filter** that is added dynamically by the code. Filters allow you to apply a special visual effect to Movie Clip objects. In previous chapters, you learned how to add filters to selected objects on the stage by using the Filters pane in the Properties panel. In many of your games, you'll be adding objects to the stage using addChild, so you can't add filters to them in this way. AS3.0 allows you to create and apply filters using code, so you can add them to an object in your game any time you like.

To use a filter, you need to first import the filters package and then the filter class you need to use. Here's how the DropShadowFilter class was imported:

```
import flash.filters.DropShadowFilter;
```

Optionally, if you want to control the quality of the filter, you need to import the BitmapFilterQuality class:

```
import flash.filters.BitmapFilterQuality;
```

Being able to control the quality of the filter is very important for games. High-quality filters consume more of the Flash Player's resources to produce, so you generally want the filter's quality setting to be low, especially for any objects that are moving.

Figure 10-7. A drop shadow filter was added dynamically.

Filters are independent objects, just like any other objects you create in AS3.0. To use a filter, you first need to create the filter object, set its properties, and then add it to the object that you want to apply the filter to. Here are the steps to create and apply the drop shadow filter:

1. To use a filter, you need to declare a variable to contain the new filter object:

   ```
   private var _shadow:DropShadowFilter;
   ```

2. Create the filter object with the new operator:

   ```
   _shadow = new DropShadowFilter();
   ```

3. Set any of the filter's properties. Most of the properties for most filters match those that you can set in the Filters pane of the Properties panel. You can set as many or as few of these properties as you need to:

   ```
   _shadow.distance = 4;
   _shadow.angle = 120;
   _shadow.strength = 0.6;
   ```

4. Set the optional quality property of the filter by applying LOW, MEDIUM, or HIGH from the BitmapFilterQuality class:

   ```
   _shadow.quality = BitmapFilterQuality.LOW;
   ```

5. Every Movie Clip object has a special property called filters. Unlike any other property you've looked at before, the filters property is actually an array. You apply a filter to an object by adding the filter as an element to the filters array (which is the same way elements were added to an array in Chapter 9). In this example, I want the shadow to be applied only to the _player object's body subobject:

   ```
   _player.body.filters = [_shadow];
   ```

Adding filters as array elements is very useful because it means that you can apply more than one filter to an object at a time. If you want to also add a bevel or glow filter to the same object, you can create those filter objects and add them to the filters array, like this:

```
_player.body.filters = [_shadow, _bevel, _glow];
```

To remove all the filters from an object, give the filters array a null value, like this:

```
_player.body.filters = null
```

Table 10-1 lists the basic filter classes and their uses.

Table 10-1. Basic filters classes available

Filter class	What it does
BevelFilter	Creates a shallow 3D raised surface effect.
BlurFilter	Blurs the object slightly, giving the impression that it's out of focus or moving quickly.
DropShadowFilter	Casts a shadow.
GlowFilter	Makes it appear as if a light is being cast from underneath the object.
GradientBevelFilter	An enhanced bevel effect that improves its 3D appearance by allowing you to add a gradient color to the bevel.
GradientGlowFilter	An enhanced glow effect that allows you to add a gradient glow to the edges of an object. This filter optionally requires that you import the BitmapFilterType class so you can specify where on the object to apply the filter.

This has been a very brief introduction to AS3.0 filters, but it's enough to get you started. All the filters have a great number of properties that can be set. You can find them all, including more specific information on these filters, in the chapter "Filtering Display Objects" in Adobe's online document, Programming ActionScript 3.0 (http://help.adobe.com/en_US/ActionScript/3.0_ProgrammingAS3/). Also, there are some specific issues that you need to be aware of if you want to change an object's filter or make specialized adjustments to it while the SWF is running. The "Potential Issues for Working with Filters" subchapter from the "Filtering Display Objects" chapter outlines some of these problems and how to overcome them.

Other advanced filters that have more specialized uses: the color matrix filter, convolution filter, displacement map filter, and shader filter. I won't be discussing these filters in this book, but you should know that they allow for very fine control over color and alpha effects.

Moving an object with easing

It's likely that in a game scenario you will want your player character to move with a little more grace than simply staying fixed to the mouse position exactly. Using the simple easing formula discussed earlier, you can create some very elegant systems to move objects.

In this chapter's source files, you'll find a folder called Easing With Mouse. Open it as a project and test it. If you click anywhere on the stage, Button Fairy serenely flutters to that spot, gradually easing into position (see Figure 10-8).

Figure 10-8. Click anywhere on the stage, and Button Fairy eases to that position.

When Button Fairy has reached her destination point, you'll see the words Player reached target displayed in the Output panel.

Here's the code that makes this happen:

```
package
{
  import flash.display.MovieClip;
  import flash.events.Event;
  import flash.events.MouseEvent;

  public class Main_EasingWithMouse extends MovieClip
   {
    //Declare constants
    private const EASING:Number = 0.1;

    //Declare variables
    private var _targetX:Number;
    private var _targetY:Number;
```

```
public function Main_EasingWithMouse ()
{
  //Initialize variables
  _targetX = player.x;
  _targetY = player.y;

 //Add event listeners
 stage.addEventListener(MouseEvent.MOUSE_DOWN, onMouseDown);
}
private function onEnterFrame(event:Event):void
{
  //Calculate the distance from the player to the mouse
  var dx:Number = _targetX - player.x;
  var dy:Number = _targetY - player.y;
  var distance = Math.sqrt(dx * dx + dy * dy);

  //Move the object if it is more than 1 pixel away from the mouse
  if (distance >= 1)
  {
    player.x += (_targetX - player.x) * EASING;
    player.y += (_targetY - player.y) * EASING;
  }
  else
  {
    trace("Player reached target")
    removeEventListener(Event.ENTER_FRAME, onEnterFrame);
  }
}
private function onMouseDown(event:Event):void
{
  _targetX = mouseX;
  _targetY = mouseY;
  addEventListener(Event.ENTER_FRAME, onEnterFrame);
}
    }
  }
}
```

When the player clicks anywhere on the stage with the mouse, the onMouseDown event handler is called. It stores the mouse's position in two variables: _targetX and _targetY. It also adds the onEnterFrame event listeners. (This is another example of the listener not being added until it's needed.)

It then becomes the job of onEnterFrame to move the object. Don't worry too much about the complex-looking code that it contains. Most of that code is there to solve a small technical problem that you have to deal with whenever you use easing. The essence of the onEnterFrame event handler, the code that actually makes the object move, is in these two lines:

```
player.x += (_targetX - player.x) * EASING;
player.y += (_targetY - player.y) * EASING;
```

These directives use *exactly* the same formula as that in the drag-and-drop example. In fact, if these were the only two lines in the onEnterFrame event handler, the class would still work perfectly well.

What is the rest of the code for? The easing formula invokes another example of Xeno's Paradox, which I discussed in the previous chapter. The object slows down gradually as it approaches its target, but although it appears to eventually stop moving, the numbers in the background still try to calculate ever-smaller divisions of a pixel for it to move toward. As far as AS3.0 is concerned, the final destination is never actually reached. You might think that this might not matter because you can't see the effect of it on the stage, but it's not a good idea to allow mathematical processes like that running in the background—they consume precious CPU power that could used to improve the performance of other aspects of the game. Preventing this from happening is like sealing a window in a drafty old house.

A good solution is to find out whether the object is less than 1 pixel from its destination. If it is, you know that the object is close enough, and you can quit the easing motion. One pixel is the smallest amount visible on the stage, so even if the easing formula is still calculating farther smaller fractions of a pixel, stopping it at this point won't matter.

But how can you calculate how far the object is from the target destination? You could compare the absolute values of the x and y positions of the object and its target, as you did in the Bug Catcher game, to find out how close the bugs were from the cat. However, there's another way:

1. Calculate the distances between the object and the target on the x and y axes, and store these values as variables called dx and dy (you saw this approach in the collision detection code used in the Collision class):

```
var dx:Number = destinationX - originX;
var dy:Number = destinationX - originX;
```

2. Apply a simple formula, the Pythagorean Theorem, and copy the result into a variable called distance:

```
var distance:Number = Math.sqrt(dx * dx + dy * dy);
```

The Pythagorean Theorem states that "the square of the hypotenuse of a right triangle is equal to the sum of the squares on the other two sides." Translated into practical AS3.0 code, this means you need to use the built-in Math.sqrt function to find the square root of the sum of the dx and dy values, which are then multiplied by each other. Luckily for you, Pythagoras was right! Whenever you need to find the distance between two points, use his formula. It will become a regular in your arsenal of game design tricks, and you'll be using it a lot in this chapter.

Now that the program knows what the distance is between the two points, you simply need to set up an if/else statement to move the object when the distance is greater than 1 pixel, and stop moving it by removing the onEnterFrame event listener if it's less than 1 pixel:

```
if (distance >= 1)
{
  player.x += (_targetX - player.x) * EASING;
  player.y += (_targetY - player.y) * EASING;
}
else
{
  trace("Player reached target")
  removeEventListener(Event.ENTER_FRAME, onEnterFrame);
}
```

Easy easing!

Following the mouse with a bit of delay

Another little twist to the code will give you an object that follows the mouse with a slight bit of drag, as if it's being pulled by a spring. In the chapter's source files, find the folder called Mouse Follow and open it as a project. Test it to see the effect.

The code is very similar to the previous example, except that the mouseX and mouseY target variables are updated directly in the onEnterFrame event handler. This makes the object update its destination every time the mouse moves. It's a very organic and pleasing effect, and you're sure to find this useful for the basis of many games:

```
package
{
  import flash.display.MovieClip;
  import flash.events.Event;
  import flash.events.MouseEvent;

  public class Main_MouseFollow extends MovieClip
  {
    //Declare constants
    private const EASING:Number = 0.1;

    //Declare variables
    private var _targetX:Number;
    private var _targetY:Number;
    private var _vx:Number;
    private var _vy:Number;
```

```
public function Main_MouseFollow()
{
  //Initialize variables
  _targetX = mouseX;
  _targetY = mouseY;
  _vx = 0;
  _vy = 0;

  //Add event listeners
  addEventListener(Event.ENTER_FRAME,onEnterFrame);
}
private function onEnterFrame(event:Event):void
{
  _targetX = mouseX;
  _targetY = mouseY;

  //Calculate the distance from the player to the mouse
  var dx:Number = _targetX - player.x;
  var dy:Number = _targetY - player.y;
  var distance = Math.sqrt(dx * dx + dy * dy);

  //Apply easing if the player is more than 1 pixel away from
  //the mouse
  if (distance >= 1)
  {
    _vx = (_targetX - player.x) * EASING;
    _vy = (_targetY - player.y) * EASING;
  }

  //Move player
  player.x += _vx;
  player.y += _vy;
}
}
}
```

A slight modification is that the easing is applied to the _vx and _vy variables. This gives you a bit more flexibility because it means that you can easily add physical forces or collision detection to the code if you need to. I hope you'll find this a useful starting point for your own customized character control scheme or drag-and-drop engine.

One pitfall is that the Math.sqrt is one of the most CPU-intensive math functions you can call. If you can avoid using it, you'll save a great deal of processing power. In the case study ahead, you'll look at a way to optimize this code so that it achieves the same thing without using Math.sqrt.

Easing—advanced

In the previous examples, the player object moved by speeding up really quickly and then gradually coming to a stop. This is a nice effect and is probably the most common easing effect you'll use in your games, but what if you need something a little more complex? Wouldn't it be nice if the object could gradually speed up when it starts moving and then gradually come to a stop as it approaches its destination?

Easing effects like that can be achieved very easily using the AS3.0 Tween class. The Tween class allows you to create a special "tween object" that will animate an object based on specific information that you supply.

Let's take a look at a very simple example of the Tween class at work. In this chapter's source files, you'll find a folder called Basic Tween. Open it as a project and test it. It features Button Fairy's arch-nemesis: Bucket Robot. You'll see the robot at the left side of the stage gradually speed up, reach a maximum speed, and then slowly come to a stop at the right side of the stage. The robot object is using the Regular.easeInOut method from the easing package. Figure 10-9 illustrates what you'll see.

speeds up... ... reaches peak speed... ... slows down

Figure 10-9. The robot object gradually speeds up and slows down using the the Regular.easeInOut method of the Tween class.

The code that makes this work is in the Main_BasicTween.as file:

```
package
{
  import flash.display.MovieClip;
  import flash.events.Event;
  //Import classes and packages required for Tweening
  import fl.transitions.Tween;
  import fl.transitions.easing.*;
```

513

```
public class Main_BasicTween extends MovieClip
{
  //Declare variables
  private var _tween:Tween;

  public function Main_BasicTween()
  {
    //Create an instance of the Tween class
    _tween = new Tween(robot, "x", Regular.easeInOut, robot.x, 450, ➡
      60, false);
  }
}
}
```

To use the Tween class, you need to import some new packages and classes into the Main_BasicTween class. The Tween class and the easing package that contains the formulas create the easing effects:

```
import fl.transitions.Tween;
import fl.transitions.easing.*;
```

You might be wondering what the asterisk is doing after the dot in the directive that imports the easing package. It instructs the program to import *every* class in the easing package. Normally you would not want to do this. For matters of clarity, it's usually best just to import the classes you need, but in this case, there are a lot of classes in the easing package that you'll want to experiment with, so it saves you a bit of trouble of having to import them one at a time.

In the preceding class, an instance of the Tween class called _tween was created. You need to provide the Tween class with six parameters when you create a new Tween instance:

```
_tween = new Tween(robot, "x", Regular.easeInOut, robot.x, 450, ➡
  60, false);
```

As you can see, it's packed with information. It might look a bit disorienting at first glance, but it's pretty straightforward if you break down the arguments it contains one piece at a time. Figure 10-10 is a diagram that explains what the information in the arguments represents.

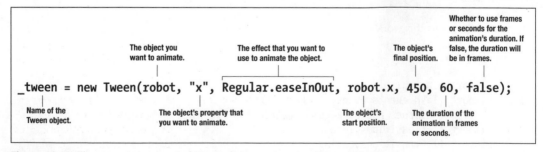

Figure 10-10. The arguments you need to supply to create a new Tween instance

As you can see, it's really just a detailed list of information that the Tween object needs to create the animation.

Properties and methods of the Tween class

Each argument also represents a property in the Tween class. Table 10-2 is a plain-English breakdown of what the arguments are, what they tell the _tween object, and which Tween class properties that they refer to.

Table 10-2. Tween class properties

Argument	What it tells the Tween object	Tween class property it represents	Kind of information it can contain
robot	Use the robot object on the stage for the animation.	obj	Any object—it does not just have to be a display object. You can even use the Tween class to "animate" numerical data if you want to.
x	You want to animate the robot's x property.	prop	The string that represents the property you want to animate. It can be any property at all; it doesn't just have to be an x or y property.
Regular. easeInOut	The formula that you'll use to animate the robot is Regular. easeInOut, which is part of the easing package you imported earlier.	func	The easing formula used to animate the object.
robot.x	The starting position for the robot is the robot's x position.	begin	The value where you want to start the animation. This should be a Number.
450	The finish position on the stage is position number 450. Because you're animating the object's x position, this refers to an x value of 450.	finish	Where you want the animation to end; it should also be a Number.
60	The duration of the animation: 60 frames.	duration	A number that indicates how long the animation lasts. It can represent seconds or frames.
false	Tells the Tween object that the duration should be in frames, not seconds.	useSeconds	A Boolean value that determines whether the duration should be measured in frames or seconds. If true, seconds are used; if false, frames are used.

As you can see, it's very compact information, but it all relates very clearly to things you can see happening on the stage when the animation plays.

After you create a Tween object, you can still access its properties anywhere in the class and change them if you need to. For example, if you want to change the duration of the animation, you can change it like this:

```
_tween.duration = 25;
```

If you need to change the endpoint of the animation, you can change it like this:

```
_tween.finish = 200;
```

To find out the name of the object that is being animated (robot in this case), you can use this:

```
_tween.obj;
```

Being able to access and change all these properties means that you can change the animation after you create it, change it while it's running, or access any of the Tween object's properties for use in other parts of your program. This is the same as the way you can change properties of filter objects that you looked at in the previous section.

Tween objects also contain many more properties that you can change and access. Table 10-3 lists them and explains what they do.

Table 10-3. Additional Tween class properties

Tween property	What it does
FPS	The frames per second (fps) at which the animation takes place. This is the same fps as the main movie's frame rate by default, but you can change it to a higher or lower frame rate without affecting the frame rate of the rest of the movie. This is really useful for games because you can set lower-priority animations (such as background animations) to a lower frame rate. That might give your game a performance boost because it means that there's more processing power available to animate important foreground objects.
isPlaying	Returns true or false, depending on whether the animation is currently playing.
looping	Set this to true to make the animation loop infinitely. A value of false stops the loop.
position	Tells you the current value of the property that is being animated. For example, if you use the following line of code in an ENTER_FRAME event in the current example program, it displays the x position of the robot every frame: trace(_tween.position);
time	Allows you to get or set the current time that has elapsed since the animation started. The value it uses is related to the duration property.

Hey, is that not enough for you? You're far from done yet! The Tween class also has many methods that you can use to control the animation in exactly the same way you can control an animation in the timeline. Table 10-4 shows methods you can use with your Tween objects.

Table 10-4. Tween class methods

Tween method name	What it does
stop();	Stops the animation at its current position.
start();	Starts the animation from its beginning point.
continueTo()	Tells the animation to continue from its current position to a new finish point with a new duration. Takes two arguments: the new finish point and the new duration. You could use it like this: tween.continueTo(150, 20); You can use continueTo to alter the direction and duration of an animation after it has started.
fforward()	Fast forwards the animation directly to the end.
prevFrame()	Plays the previous frame in the animation.
resume()	Resumes the animation after it's been stopped using the stop() method.
rewind()	If the animation is playing, rewinds it to the beginning and starts it playing once more. If the animation has been stopped, the animation is rewound to the beginning but not restarted.
yoyo();	Plays the animation back in reverse. It's usually used in conjunction with the MOTION_FINISH event from the TweenEvent class.

You can use any of these methods the same way you use methods in other classes, like this:

```
_tween.start();
_tween.yoyo();
```

I won't go into any of these properties or methods in any detail, but there's quite a treasure trove of material here to keep a creative programmer busy for a long, long time. And you'll soon see that using properties and methods from the Tween class is often easier and quicker than creating animations manually on the timeline.

Easing package classes and methods

The property that actually does the job of animating the object is the `func` property. In the example, this is `Regular.easeInOut`. It's highlighted in bold in the following code:

```
_tween = new Tween(robot, "x", Regular.easeInOut, robot.x, 450, ➥
  60, false);
```

`Regular`, a class in the easing package, contains a method called `easeInOut`. `easeInOut` eases the object into the animation and then eases it to a gradual stop.

The `Regular` class contains two more methods:

- `easeIn`: Accelerates the object and stops it abruptly
- `easeOut`: Starts the object abruptly and gradually slows it down

The best way to understand how this works is to see its actual effect on the stage:

1. Open the `Basic Tween` folder as a project if it isn't already open.
2. Double-click the `Main_BasicTween.as` file so it opens in the workspace.
3. Change the constructor method so that it looks like this:

```
public function Main_BasicTween()
{
  _tween = new Tween(robot, "x", Regular.easeOut, robot.x, 450, ➥
    60, false);
}
```

4. Save the `Main_BasicTween.as` file and test the project. The robot starts quickly and gradually slows down.
5. Change the code again so it looks like this:

```
_tween = new Tween(robot, "x", Regular.easeIn, robot.x, 450, ➥
  60, false);
```

6. Save the `Main_BasicTween.as` file and test the project. The robot gradually speeds up and stops suddenly.

The motion isn't dependent on an ENTER_FRAME event. Although the animation happens within the context of the movie's frame rate, it's completely orchestrated by the Tween object. This is helpful because you can initialize different Tween objects containing different animations, stop them with the stop method, and trigger them with a start method whenever you need them in your program.

In addition to the Regular class, the easing package contains five other classes. Table 10-5 describes all these classes, the methods they contain, and the effect they have on the object that's being animated.

Table 10-5. Easing classes

Easing class name	Methods it contains	How it behaves
Back	easeIn easeInOut easeOut	The object reverses when it eases into the motion and slightly overshoots the target when it eases out.
Bounce	easeIn easeInOut easeOut	The object appears to bounce toward the target when it eases in and bounces against it when it eases out.
Elastic	easeIn easeInOut easeOut	The object wobbles back and forth around the begin and finish points of the animation.
None	easeIn easeInOut easeNone easeOut	Surprise! No easing! If you don't want any easing, use None.caseNone. The object simply moves from the start to finish point without changing its speed at all. The None class also contains easeIn and easeInOut methods, but they have the same effect: none! Why then are they there? They were added by Adobe engineers for consistency with the other classes.
Regular	easeIn easeInOut easeOut	The standard easing effect.
Strong	easeIn easeInOut easeOut	Very similar to Regular, except that the effect is slightly exaggerated.

> All the methods of these classes—easeIn, easeInOut, *and* easeOut—*can be supplied with additional arguments to fine-tune how they behave. Check Adobe's online documentation at* http://help.adobe.com/en_US/AS3LCR/Flash_10.0/fl/transitions/easing/package-detail.html *for more information if you need it.*

Try out some of these classes and methods in the example program:

- _tween = new Tween(robot, "x", **Bounce.easeOut**, robot.x, 450, 60, false);
- _tween = new Tween(robot, "x", **Back.easeInOut**, robot.x, 450, 60, false);
- _tween = new Tween(robot, "x", **Elastic.easeIn**, robot.x, 450, 60, false);

It's like being nine years old again!

Tween events

Tween objects come with their own sets of events. Let's take a look at practical example of how you can use the MOTION_FINISH event along with the delightful yoyo method.

Open the folder Yoyo Tween from the chapter's source files as a project. Test it and you'll see that the robot now oscillates back and forth across the screen like a yoyo! Here's what the Main_YoyoTween.as file looks like that makes this happen:

```
package
{
  import flash.display.MovieClip;
  import flash.events.Event;
  import fl.transitions.Tween;
  import fl.transitions.TweenEvent;
  import fl.transitions.easing.*;

  public class Main_YoyoTween extends MovieClip
  {
    //Declare variables
    private var _tween:Tween;

    public function Main_YoyoTween()
    {
      _tween = new Tween(robot, "x", Regular.easeInOut, robot.x, 100, ➥
        60, false);
      _tween.addEventListener(TweenEvent.MOTION_FINISH, ➥
        onMotionFinish);
    }
    private function onMotionFinish(event:Event)
    {
      event.target.yoyo();
    }
  }
}
```

This code relies on the TweenEvent class, so it needs to be imported with this directive:

```
import fl.transitions.TweenEvent;
```

The code adds a MOTION_FINISH event to the _tween object:

```
_tween.addEventListener(TweenEvent.MOTION_FINISH, onMotionFinish);
```

MOTION_FINISH is one of the events from the TweenEvent class. It's triggered when the animation is finished. In this case, it's set up to call the onMotionFinish event handler:

```
private function onMotionFinish(event:Event)
{
  event.target.yoyo();
}
```

event.target refers to the _tween object, *not the object that's being animated*. This is important to remember. The yoyo method tells the _tween object to play its animation in reverse. Because this event handler is called every time the animation finishes, the direction is reversed each time. Very easy to implement, and it's a great effect.

There are six events in the TweenEvent class that you can use with Tween objects (see Table 10-6).

Table 10-6. TweenEvent class events

TweenEvent class events	It's triggered when . . .
MOTION_CHANGE	The object being animated moves.
MOTION_FINISH	The animation is finished.
MOTION_LOOP	The animation is started from the beginning again.
MOTION_RESUME	The animation is started after having been stopped.
MOTION_STOP	The animation stops playing.
MOTION_START	The animation starts playing.

As you can see, with a bit of imagination there's quite a bit of untapped power here at your disposal to build very sophisticated scripted animation environments for games. You can use these events to start, stop, and change an object's animation based on any conditions in your game.

Easing to random positions and calculating velocity

Let's look at another practical example. In the chapter source files, open the Random Tween folder as a project and test it. The robot object eases to random positions on the stage. In addition, a dynamic text field displays the robot's vx and vy velocities. Figure 10-11 illustrates what you'll see.

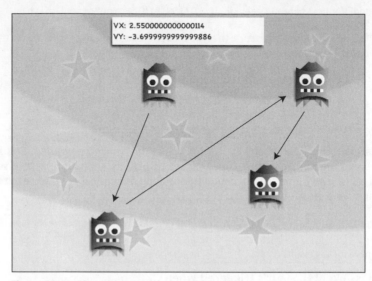

Figure 10-11. The robot eases to a random position on the stage, and a dynamic text field displays its velocity.

Here's the code that makes it work. Except for the robot's velocity calculation, there's nothing really new here. Read through the comments in the code, and see if you can match the way it's working with what you see on the stage when the SWF runs:

```
package
{
  import flash.display.MovieClip;
  import flash.events.Event;
  import fl.transitions.Tween;
  import fl.transitions.TweenEvent;
  import fl.transitions.easing.*;

  public class Main_RandomTween extends MovieClip
  {
    //Declare variables
    private var _tweenX:Tween;
    private var _tweenY:Tween;
    private var _randomX:uint;
    private var _randomY:uint;
```

```
public function Main_RandomTween ()
{
  //Initialize dynamic instance variables in the robot
  //object to help calculate the robot's velocity
  robot.vx = 0;
  robot.vy = 0;
  robot.oldX = 0;
  robot.oldY = 0;

  //Select a random stage position
  _randomX = Math.ceil(Math.random() * 550);
  _randomY = Math.ceil(Math.random() * 400);

  //Create Tween objects for the x and y axes
  _tweenX = new Tween(robot, "x", Regular.easeInOut, robot.x, ➥
    _randomX, 60, false);
  _tweenY = new Tween(robot, "y", Regular.easeInOut, robot.y, ➥
    _randomY, 60, false);

  //Add listeners that are triggered when the animation finishes
  _tweenX.addEventListener(TweenEvent.MOTION_FINISH, ➥
    onMotionFinishX);
  _tweenY.addEventListener(TweenEvent.MOTION_FINISH, ➥
    onMotionFinishY);

  //Add an ENTER_FRAME listner to help
  //calculate the object's velocity
  addEventListener(Event.ENTER_FRAME, onEnterFrame);
}
private function onMotionFinishX(event:Event)
{
  var tweenObject:Tween = event.target as Tween;

  //Calculate new start and finish positions
  tweenObject.begin = robot.x;
  tweenObject.finish = Math.ceil(Math.random() * 550);

  //Start the Tween object playing again
  tweenObject.start();
}
private function onMotionFinishY(event:Event)
{
  var tweenObject:Tween = event.target as Tween;
  tweenObject.begin = robot.y;
  tweenObject.finish = Math.ceil(Math.random() * 400);
  tweenObject.start();
}
private function onEnterFrame(event:Event)
{
```

```
            robot.vx = robot.x - robot.oldX;
            robot.vy = robot.y - robot.oldY;
            robot.oldX = robot.x;
            robot.oldY = robot.y;

            //Display robot's velocity in a dynamic text field
            display.text = String("VX: " + robot.vx + "\n" + "VY: " ➥
              + robot.vy);
        }
      }
    }
```

The code uses a lot of the little techniques you've been looking at over the last few pages. Tween class methods, properties, and TweenEvent class events—they're all in here, playing their little parts.

Notice that there are separate Tween objects for each axis: _tweenX and _tweenY. They also each have their own listeners. (I could have used a bit of programming gymnastics to make them use one listener, but I kept them separate for the sake of clarity.)

The onMotionFinishX and onMotionFinishY are called when the object completes its animation sequence. Let's take a quick look at onMotionFinishY because it's making use of the Tween object's properties in a way that you haven't yet seen:

```
    private function onMotionFinishY(event:Event)
    {
      var tweenObject:Tween = event.target as Tween;
      tweenObject.begin = robot.y;
      tweenObject.finish = Math.ceil(Math.random() * 400);
      tweenObject.start();
    }
```

Remember that the event.target object is the _tweenY object, so it needs to be cast as a Tween using the as operator:

```
    var tweenObject:Tween = event.target as Tween;
```

This is the first time you've seen an object being cast as a type other than MovieClip.

The onMotionFinishY event handler assigns the _tweenY object a new begin and finish point and then starts the animation again based on those new values:

1. It sets the Tween object's begin property as the robot's current y position. That's the position where the last animation ended. So it makes sense that the animation should begin again from that point:

```
    tweenObject.begin = robot.y;
```

2. Next, you need to assign a new random finish point to the finish property:

```
    tweenObject.finish = Math.ceil(Math.random() * 400);
```

3. Finally, you need to restart the animation using the start method:

```
tweenObject.start();
```

There's a bit of a conceptual leap you have to make here because you need to keep in mind that the entirety of the robot's animation is contained with the Tween objects as abstract code. There's no timeline, Movie Clip, or ENTER_FRAME loop that is making the animation happen. The animation is completely created and runs within the Tween object itself.

This is actually very convenient because it takes the responsibility of managing the animation away from the rest of the code. You can create as many Tween objects as you like and then just let them lose to do their thing. The code that actually makes the animation work is neatly hidden from you in the inner workings of the Tween class.

Calculating velocity

There's one weakness in this system that you might have already noticed. In the previous chapter, all the physics and collision detection code were dependent on knowing the objects' vertical and horizontal velocities: _vx and _vy. It's easy to calculate velocity in the context on an ENTER_FRAME event. But there are no vx and vy properties you can access on Tween objects. This means that if you want to change something about the game based on how quickly the object is moving or have it react to a collision with another object, you can't do that directly.

The solution is to create an ENTER_FRAME event handler that tracks the object being animated and calculates its velocity. You can use a very simple system to calculate the object's velocity. Here's a simplified version of what these calculations look like:

```
vx = x - oldX;
vy = y - oldY;
oldX = x;
oldY = y;
```

You'll see how this is used and why it works in a moment.

In the example code, you created all the variables you need to do this directly in the robot object as dynamic instance variables:

```
robot.vx = 0;
robot.vy = 0;
robot.oldX = 0;
robot.oldY = 0;
```

> *As discussed in the previous chapter, dynamic instance variables are properties that can be created on objects as you need them. To be able to do this, the class that the object extends needs to be declared as* dynamic. *The MovieClip class is a dynamic class, so you can create dynamic instance variables on all Movie Clip objects. It's generally considered risky programming, but it is undoubtedly convenient in small programs like this one.*

The onEnterFrame event handler is responsible for using these variables to calculate velocity:

```
private function onEnterFrame(event:Event)
{
  robot.vx = robot.x - robot.oldX;
  robot.vy = robot.y - robot.oldY;
  robot.oldX = robot.x;
  robot.oldY = robot.y;

  //Display robot's velocity in a dynamic text field
  display.text = String("VX: " + robot.vx + "\n" + "VY: " + robot.vy);
}
```

It might look a little convoluted, but what's happening is really very mundane:

1. The object's velocity is calculated by comparing its current position with the position that it was at in the previous frame. oldX and oldY store the object's previous position. For example, if the object was at position 100 in the previous frame and at 105 in the current frame, its velocity would be 5.

```
robot.vx = robot.x - robot.oldX;
robot.vy = robot.y - robot.oldY;
```

2. You need to store the object's current position in the oldX and oldY variables so that you can access these values in the next frame. The object's current position becomes its old position when the frame advances:

```
robot.oldX = robot.x;
robot.oldY = robot.y;
```

With this system, you can capture an animated object's velocity and use it for any other calculations or collision detection that your game might need to do.

Although this system for calculating velocity will hold you in good stead in a situation like this, you might work on a game in which you need to calculate velocity and update the player's position at the same time. In that case, you need to use additional variables that temporarily store the current x and y values. This is necessary so that current x and y values aren't lost when the new velocity is added to the object's position.

```
//Temporarily store the player's current position
temporaryX = x;
temporaryY = y;

//Calculate velocity
vx = x - oldX;
vy = y - oldY;

//Update player's position
x += vx;
y += vy;
```

```
//Capture the current position in the oldX and oldY variables
oldX = temporaryX;
oldY = temporaryY;
```

Implementing a chase feature

With just a very small change to the code, you can implement the basis of a simple but very effective enemy artificial intelligence system. In the code you're using, a random x and y position were assigned for the animation's new finish point. But what if you assigned a value that isn't random? You can give the robot the appearance of intelligently moving around the stage:

1. Make the following changes to the onMotionFinishX and onMotionFinishY event handlers:

```
private function onMotionFinishX(event:Event)
{
  var tweenObject:Tween = event.target as Tween;
  tweenObject.begin = robot.x;
  tweenObject.finish = mouseX;
  tweenObject.start();
}
private function onMotionFinishY(event:Event)
{
  var tweenObject:Tween = event.target as Tween;
  tweenObject.begin = robot.y;
  tweenObject.finish = mouseY;
  tweenObject.start();
}
```

2. Save the Main_RandomTween.as file and test the project. The robot sets its destination to the mouse's position each time the animation restarts and it chases the mouse around the stage (see Figure 10-12).

Figure 10-12. Each time the robot starts its new animation sequence, the mouse's position becomes the new finish point.

You can substitute the mouse's position for the position of any object in a game, such as the player's position. Using the Tween class and its related methods, properties, and events, you have the basis of an effective enemy AI system without an if/else statement in sight. (Remember to use stage.mouseX and stage.mouseY if you use this technique in a class other than the document class.)

You've only just scratched the surface of what you can do with Tween objects in your games. I hope this will inspire you to push the boundaries even farther. There's a rich vein of untapped potential here that can be put to some fantastic use in games. Go forth and conquer!

Case study: Complex mouse-driven player control

To round off this discussion of mouse-driven player control systems, you'll look at a real-world example that takes into account the kind of complexity some of your games will demand.

Many of the games you'll be designing won't need this level of detail in player control; you can get by just fine using some of the systems discussed earlier in the chapter. For those games that require subtle detail in the way the player character is controlled, however, you'll need to put on your thinking cap and work out how you can use a combination of the techniques you've been looking at in the past two chapters.

When you're just learning programming and game design, it won't be obvious at all. So, to make the process a little easier for you, you'll take a detailed look at a player control system that's very much an everything-but-the-kitchen-sink example. I'll throw in as many techniques as can fit, and I'll leave it up to you to deconstruct the examples to make them work the way you might need them to in your own games.

The example you'll look at is a control system for Button Fairy. It implements a classic spaceship-style control scheme using a mouse-based control system instead of a keyboard-based one. You'll also implement a system to allow you to fire bullets in all directions by using some new Math class functions, which isn't necessarily the best way for this control scheme to be built. But it's a good starting point for you to create your own control systems by giving you an inside look at how it's been done.

Player.as

Take a look at how this control scheme works. Find the Character Control folder in the chapter's source files, open it as a project, and take Button Fairy for a test drive. You can fly her around the stage by moving the mouse. The mouse also controls the position of a yellow "wand." If you click the left mouse button, the wand fires red stars in the direction of the mouse.

Button Fairy can be tricky to control at first because her movements are not based on easing. She uses acceleration and friction (discussed in the previous chapter) to regulate her speed. If the mouse is greater than 75 pixels from Button Fairy's center position, she'll accelerate toward it. If the mouse is less than 75 pixels away, acceleration stops and friction kicks in. With a bit of practice, you'll find you can have quite a bit of subtle control. Figure 10-13 illustrates how Button Fairy behaves.

Figure 10-13. Steer Button Fairy with the mouse and
click the left mouse button to fire stars in any direction.

Here's the code that makes Button Fairy work:

```
package
{
  import flash.display.MovieClip;
  import flash.events.Event;
  import flash.events.MouseEvent;
  import flash.events.KeyboardEvent;
  import flash.ui.Keyboard;
  import flash.geom.Point;

  public class Player extends MovieClip
  {
    //variables
    private var _vx:Number;
    private var _vy:Number;
    private var _accelerationX:Number;
    private var _accelerationY:Number;
    private var _acceleration:Number;
    private var _friction:Number;
    private var _angle:Number;
    private var _shotFired:Boolean;

    public function Player()
    {
      //Initialize variables
      _vx = 0;
      _vy = 0;
      _acceleration = 0;
      _friction = 0.96;
      _angle = 0;
      _shotFired = false;
```

```
      //Add listeners
      stage.addEventListener(MouseEvent.MOUSE_DOWN, onMouseDown);
      stage.addEventListener(MouseEvent.MOUSE_UP, onMouseUp);
      addEventListener(Event.ENTER_FRAME, onEnterFrame);
    }
    private function onMouseDown(event:MouseEvent):void
    {
      if (! _shotFired)
      {
        shootBullet();
        _shotFired = true;
      }
    }
    private function onMouseUp(event:MouseEvent):void
    {
      _shotFired = false;
    }
    private function onEnterFrame(event:Event):void
    {
      _angle = Math.atan2(y - stage.mouseY, x - stage.mouseX);
      _accelerationX = Math.cos(_angle) * _acceleration;
      _accelerationY = Math.sin(_angle) * _acceleration;

      //Calculate the distance to the mouse
      var dx:Number = stage.mouseX - this.x;
      var dy:Number = stage.mouseY - this.y;
      var distance:Number = Math.sqrt(dx * dx + dy * dy);

      //Increase acceleration if the mouse is more than 75 pixels away
      if (distance >= 75)
      {
        _acceleration = -0.5;
        _friction = 1;
      }
      else
      {
        _acceleration = 0;
        _friction = 0.96;
      }

      //Apply acceleration
      _vx += _accelerationX;
      _vy +=_accelerationY;

      //Apply friction
      _vx *= _friction;
      _vy *= _friction;

      //Move the player
      x += _vx;
```

```
      y += _vy;

      //Move the wand
      var radius:int = -50;
      wand.x = radius * Math.cos(_angle);
      wand.y = radius * Math.sin(_angle);
    }
    private function shootBullet():void
    {
      //Bullet's velocity
      var bullet_Vx:Number = Math.cos(_angle) * -10;
      var bullet_Vy:Number = Math.sin(_angle) * -10;

      //Bullet's start position
      var radius:int = -50;
      var bullet_StartX:Number = x + radius * Math.cos(_angle);
      var bullet_StartY:Number = y + radius * Math.sin(_angle);

      //Create bullet instance and add it to the stage
      var bullet:Bullet = new Bullet(bullet_Vx, bullet_Vy, ➡
        bullet_StartX, bullet_StartY, "star");
      parent.addChild(bullet);
    }
  }
}
```

You'll look at each aspect of the code one bit at a time.

Moving the player

Button Fairy moves by accelerating toward the mouse. So the first thing the code needs to do is find out where the mouse is. In the onEnterFrame event handler, the first directive finds the direction from the object to the mouse, using the same formula used in Bug Catcher to rotate the frog's eyes:

```
_angle = Math.atan2(y - stage.mouseY, x - stage.mouseX);
```

This is a number in **radians**, which is the system AS3.0's trigonometry functions use to measure angles. One radian equals about 57.2958 degrees.

> *If you need to use an angle to rotate an object in your game, you need to convert the value in radians to a value in degrees. The Movie Clip* rotation *property only understands values in degrees.*
>
> *To convert radians to degrees, multiply the value in radians by 180 divided by PI, like this:*
>
> ```
> radians * (180 / Math.PI)
> ```
>
> *If you want the* _angle *variable in this example code to contain a value in degrees, the directive looks like this:*
>
> ```
> _angle = Math.atan2(y - stage.mouseY,x - stage.mouseX) * (180/Math.PI);
> ```

Once you have that value, you can use it with the Math.cos and Math.sin functions, which are two specialized trigonometry functions that return the ratio of two sides of the triangle formed by the measurement of the angle in the preceding step. If you multiply these numbers by an acceleration value, you can apply the resulting number to the _accelerationX and _accelerationY variables:

```
_accelerationX = Math.cos(_angle) * _acceleration;
_accelerationY = Math.sin(_angle) * _acceleration;
```

These two variables are the basis of what you need to start moving the object in the right direction. You just need to apply them to the _vx and _vy variables, which in turn are applied to the x and y positions:

```
//Apply acceleration
_vx += _accelerationX;
_vy += _accelerationY;

//Apply friction
_vx *= _friction;
_vy *= _friction;

//Move the player
x += _vx;
y += _vy;
```

The code does one more thing. You want the object to move only if the mouse is farther than 75 pixels from Button Fairy's center point. To do this, you first need to find out the distance of her center point from the mouse. You can calculate it using the same formula you used earlier in the chapter:

```
var dx:Number = stage.mouseX - this.x;
var dy:Number = stage.mouseY - this.y;
var distance:Number = Math.sqrt(dx * dx + dy * dy);
```

Once you've got the distance, the rest is easy. You just need to find out whether the distance is greater than or equal to 75. If it is, you can accelerate the object. If it's less, you can cut the acceleration to zero and put on the brakes with a bit of friction (remember that a friction value of 1 means that no friction is being applied):

```
if (distance >= 75)
{
  _acceleration = -0.5;
  _friction = 1;
}
else
{
  _acceleration = 0;
  _friction = 0.96;
}
```

And that's all there is to making Button Fairy move around the stage. To keep the code simple in this example, I haven't implemented any speed limit checks, but you could easily do that based on the examples from the previous chapter.

I mentioned earlier that Math.sqrt *is one of the most processor-intensive of AS3.0's math functions, so if you can avoid using it in your code, you'll give your games a noticeable performance boost.*

How can you avoid it? By exchanging CPU power for brain power: use a hand-held calculator and precalculate the value yourself!

Here's how to change the code in this example to avoid using Math.sqrt:

```
var distanceSquared:Number = (dx * dx + dy * dy);
if (distanceSquared >= 5625)
{
    //Directives to run if object is within range...
}
```

Where does 5625 *come from? It's 75 times 75 (75 squared). By calculating the value yourself, you can drop* Math.sqrt, *and the effect will be exactly the same, except that you'll probably notice that your object moves a little more smoothly across the stage.*

Of course, 5625 *is not really a very understandable number to work with, especially while you're designing and testing a game, but you should always consider optimizing any code that uses* Math.sqrt *like this in the final stages of polishing up.*

Rotating the wand

Button Fairy's wand is the yellow dot that fires stars in the direction of rotation. It's a separate subobject called wand in the Player symbol. It's centered at an x and y position of zero, directly in the center of the symbol, so it's easy for you to make it move around the center of the player object. To do this, you first need to define the radius of the imaginary circle that you want the wand to move in:

```
var radius:int = -50;
```

I gave it a negative value so the wand will point in the direction of the mouse instead of away from it.

The wand's x and y position is obtained by multiplying the radius by the same angle ratios obtained using Math.cos and Math.sin that you looked at earlier. The work of calculating the angle has already been done for you earlier in the code, so you can just reuse the same _angle variable here:

```
wand.x = radius * Math.cos(_angle);
wand.y = radius * Math.sin(_angle);
```

The result is exactly as you see it on the stage.

Firing bullets in 360 degrees

The system you're using to fire bullets (or stars) is the same as the system you used in Dungeon Maze Adventure. The Player class creates new instances of the Bullet class. The only real difference is that because you want the bullets to fire in 360 degrees, you need to supply the Bullet class with extra information as parameters. I also added a feature that lets the player fire star-shaped bullets, round bullets, or squares.

Clicking the left mouse button fires the bullets:

```
private function onMouseDown(event:MouseEvent):void
{
  if (! _shotFired)
  {
    shootBullet();
    _shotFired = true;
  }
}
private function onMouseUp(event:MouseEvent):void
{
  _shotFired = false;
}
```

The _shotFired variable keeps track of whether a shot has been fired. This prevents a bullet from being fired more than once each time the left mouse button is clicked. You could actually have left out this check, and the code would have worked pretty well, but occasionally a mouse click results in more than one bullet being fired. Using a Boolean variable to limit bullets to one per mouse click is a fail-safe system.

The shootBullet method actually does the work of firing the bullet:

```
private function shootBullet():void
{
  //Bullet's velocity
  var bullet_Vx:Number = Math.cos(_angle) * -10;
  var bullet_Vy:Number = Math.sin(_angle) * -10;

  //Bullet's start position
  var radius:int = -50;
  var bullet_StartX:Number = x + radius * Math.cos(_angle);
  var bullet_StartY:Number = y + radius * Math.sin(_angle);

  //Create bullet instance and add it to the stage
  var bullet:Bullet = new Bullet(bullet_Vx, bullet_Vy, bullet_StartX, ➥
    bullet_StartY, "star");
  parent.addChild(bullet);
}
```

First, its velocity is calculated:

```
var bullet_Vx:Number = Math.cos(_angle) * -10;
var bullet_Vy:Number = Math.sin(_angle) * -10;
```

These directives reuse the _angle variable that you calculated earlier. Math.cos and Math.sin are used to find the ratio of two sides of the triangle formed by the angle, the same way you used them to help move Button Fairy. These numbers are then multiplied by -10, which is the effective velocity of the bullets: 10 pixels per frame. These numbers need to be negative so the bullets move in the right direction. The results of these calculations are stored in bullet_Vx and bullet_Vy. You'll soon be passing these variables to the Bullet class, which uses this information to help make the bullets.

Now that you've found out the bullet's velocity, the next thing you need to do is find out what its starting position on the stage should be. This is just a slight modification to the same calculations that you used to find the position of the wand. That's because you want the bullets to appear in exactly the same spot on the stage as the wand.

```
var radius:int = -50;
var bullet_StartX:Number = x + radius * Math.cos(_angle);
var bullet_StartY:Number = y + radius * Math.sin(_angle);
```

The values for the bullet's starting x and y position are stored in the bullet_StartX and the bullet_StartY variables. The only difference between these calculations and the ones you used to set the position of the wand is that you need to add the x and y position of the player object into the mix. They represent the center of the imaginary circle that you're describing with these calculations. (The wand is a subobject of the player and shares the same center x and y position as the player object, so you didn't need to specify this extra information when you calculated its position.)

You can now use all this information, the bullet's start position and velocity, to create the bullet:

```
var bullet:Bullet = new Bullet(bullet_Vx, bullet_Vy, bullet_StartX, ➥
  bullet_StartY, "star");
parent.addChild(bullet);
```

You can see that all the variables you've just created are arguments used to create the bullet. But there's an odd one out: "star".

I created this player control system so that the player has the choice of firing three types of bullets: stars, circles, or squares. You can see this in effect by changing the previous directive so it looks like this:

```
var bullet:Bullet = new Bullet(bullet_Vx, bullet_Vy, bullet_StartX, ➥
  bullet_StartY, "circle");
```

If you save the Player.as file and test the project with this change, you'll see something like Figure 10-14. Button Fairy can now fire blue circles.

Figure 10-14. Change "star" to "circle" to make Button Fairy fire blue circles.

Button Fairy can fire green squares if you change the directive to look like this:

```
var bullet:Bullet = new Bullet(bullet_Vx, bullet_Vy, bullet_StartX, ➥
    bullet_StartY, "square");
```

Figure 10-15 illustrates this. You'll take a detailed look at how this works in the next section.

Figure 10-15. Use "square" as an argument to enable Button Fairy to fire rotating green squares.

Bullet.as

Here's the Bullet class in its entirety:

```
package
{
  import flash.display.MovieClip;
  import flash.events.Event;
  import flash.filters.BevelFilter;
  import flash.filters.BitmapFilterQuality;

  public class Bullet extends MovieClip
  {
    //Constants
    private const STAR:uint = 1;
    private const CIRCLE:uint = 2;
    private const SQUARE:uint = 3;

    //Variables
    private var _vx:Number;
    private var _vy:Number;
    private var _ax:Number;
    private var _ay:Number;
    private var _angle:Number;
    private var _stageHeight:uint;
    private var _stageWidth:uint;
```

```actionscript
private var _bevel:BevelFilter;

public function Bullet(vx:Number, vy:Number, startX:Number, ➥
  startY:Number, bulletType:String)
{
  //Assign velocity and start position using values
  //supplied to the parameters
  this._vx = vx;
  this._vy = vy;
  this.x = startX;
  this.y = startY;

  //Find bullet type
  switch (bulletType)
  {
    case "star" :
      gotoAndStop(STAR);
      break;

    case "circle" :
      gotoAndStop(CIRCLE);
      break;

    case "square" :
      gotoAndStop(SQUARE);
      break;

    default:
      gotoAndStop(CIRCLE);
  }

  //Add an "ADDED_TO_STAGE" listener
  addEventListener(Event.ADDED_TO_STAGE, onAddedToStage);

  //Add the bevel filter
  _bevel = new BevelFilter();
  _bevel.distance = 3;
  _bevel.angle = 120;
  _bevel.quality = BitmapFilterQuality.LOW;
  this.filters = [_bevel];
}
private function onAddedToStage(event:Event):void
{
  //Find the stage's height and width
  _stageHeight = stage.stageHeight;
  _stageWidth = stage.stageWidth;
```

```
      //Add listeners
      addEventListener(Event.ENTER_FRAME, onEnterFrame);
      addEventListener(Event.REMOVED_FROM_STAGE, onRemovedFromStage);
      removeEventListener(Event.ADDED_TO_STAGE, onAddedToStage);
    }
    private function onRemovedFromStage(event:Event):void
    {
      removeEventListener(Event.ENTER_FRAME, onEnterFrame);
      removeEventListener(Event.REMOVED_FROM_STAGE,➡
        onRemovedFromStage);
    }
    private function onEnterFrame(event:Event):void
    {
      //Rotate bullet
      rotation += 20;

      //Move bullet
      x += _vx;
      y += _vy;

      //Stage Boundaries:
      //Top
      if (y + height / 2 < 0)
      {
        parent.removeChild(this);
      }
      //Bottom
      else if (y - height / 2 > _stageHeight)
      {
        parent.removeChild(this);
      }
      //Left
      else if (x + width / 2 < 0)
      {
        parent.removeChild(this);
      }
      //Right
      else if (x - width / 2 > _stageWidth)
      {
        parent.removeChild(this);
      }
    }
  }
}
```

Much of this code you will recognize from previous examples, so if you're unsure about how the ADDED_TO_STAGE and REMOVED_FROM_STAGE events are working, refer to Dungeon Maze Adventure, in which you took an in-depth look at these events and why you need to use them. What's very important here, however, is the system of "manufacturing" bullets.

The Bullet class is bound to the Bullet symbol in the Library. The Bullet symbol is made up of three frames: on the first frame is a graphic of a red star, on the second is a blue circle, and on the third is a green square (see Figure 10-16).

Figure 10-16. The three frames of the Bullet symbol

In the Bullet class, these three frames are represented by constants:

```
private const STAR:uint = 1;
private const CIRCLE:uint = 2;
private const SQUARE:uint = 3;
```

These constants simply represent numbers that relate to the frames on the bullet's timeline: 1, 2, and 3. I could have easily dropped these constants from the class and just used the frame numbers directly in the code. The code would have worked just fine. But you'll soon see how using constants like this makes the code much more readable and easier to understand.

The Bullet class creates bullets by accepting the values that you supplied it in the Player class. Do you remember this directive from the Player class?

```
var bullet:Bullet = new Bullet(bullet_Vx, bullet_Vy, bullet_StartX, ➡
    bullet_StartY, "square");
```

Those variables from the Player class are sent to the Bullet class. They appear as parameters in the Bullet class's constructor method:

```
public function Bullet(vx:Number, vy:Number, startX:Number, ➡
    startY:Number, bulletType:String)
```

The parameters are local variables that the class can use. They contain the same values that were passed to it when the bullets were created in the Player class. The Bullet class needs the values of these variables to make bullets. I could have used the same variable names, but I changed their names to stress the point that they are new variables that are being created in the Bullet class.

These are the values you need, but there's a snag. Those variables in the parameters are available only to be used in the constructor method; they can't be used anywhere else in the class. To get around this, you can copy their values into instance variables. Instance variables *are* available everywhere in the class.

> As a quick refresher, **instance variables** are the variables that you declared at the beginning of the class definition, such as _vx and _vy. They can be used by all methods in the class.

In a nutshell, if you want to use the values from the parameters anywhere else in the class, you need to immediately copy their values into other variables that can be accessed across the entire class. That's fine. I declared _vx and _vy variables in the Bullet class to capture the bullet's velocity when it's created. You can assign the bullet's start position directly to its x and y properties. All you need to do is assign the variables from the constructor method's parameters like this:

```
this._vx = vx;
this._vy = vy;
this.x = startX;
this.y = startY;
```

I prefaced the bullet's properties with this to help you distinguish between the properties of "this bullet object" and the variables being assigned from the parameters. It's helpful to do this sometimes because these situations can become very confusing. Are you referring to variables in the bullet object or to the variables from the parameters that were sent from the Player class? If the variable names are very similar (_vx and vx in this case), it can become pretty confusing pretty quickly! Using this clarifies that you're referring to the properties in "this class."

Now the bullet's velocities and start position are copied into variables that are accessible everywhere in the class. Happy days!

Using a bevel filter

The bullets use a dynamic bevel filter to give them a slight 3D look. Here's how the bevel effect is created:

1. Import the BevelFilter and BitmapFilterQuality classes:

```
import flash.filters.BevelFilter;
import flash.filters.BitmapFilterQuality;
```

2. Declare the bevel object:

```
private var _bevel:BevelFilter;
```

3. Create the bevel object and assign its properties:

```
_bevel = new BevelFilter();
_bevel.distance = 3;
_bevel.angle = 120;
_bevel.quality = BitmapFilterQuality.LOW;
```

4. Add the bevel object to the filters array:

```
this.filters = [_bevel];
```

These steps are identical to adding a dynamic drop shadow filter.

Bullet factory: Using switch

The Bullet class now knows the velocities it needs to make bullets fly in the right direction, but there's still the question of that mysterious fifth parameter in the constructor method:

```
public function Bullet(vx:Number, vy:Number, startX:Number, ➡
  startY:Number, bulletType:String)
```

This is a String variable called bulletType. It contains whatever you supplied as the fifth argument in the directive that created the bullet (it can be "star", "circle", or "square"). It tells the Bullet class what kind of bullet you want to create.

The class needs to do something with this information. It needs to match the name of the shape to the correct frame in the timeline shown in Figure 10-16.

There is more than one way to do this. The "lazy" way is to use an if/else statement. The slightly better way is to use a switch statement, which works by selecting (or "switching between") one option from many, depending on a value supplied to it. Although the syntax is different, the switch statement has exactly the same function as an if/else statement.

Here's the switch statement that finds out what the value of bulletType is and moves the timeline to the frame that displays the correct bullet shape:

```
switch (bulletType)
{
  case "star" :
    gotoAndStop(STAR);
    break;

  case "circle" :
    gotoAndStop(CIRCLE);
    break;

  case "square" :
    gotoAndStop(SQUARE);
    break;

  default:
    gotoAndStop(CIRCLE);
}
```

The switch keyword accepts one argument, which in this example is bulletType:

```
switch (bulletType)
```

You know that bulletType can have three possible values: "star", "circle", or "square". In a switch statement, the value is known as a case, and each case can have a different outcome. Let's look at the first case, "star":

```
case "star" :
    gotoAndStop(STAR);
    break;
```

541

Any directives that come after the colon are the actions the program should take. In this case, the bullet Movie Clip object should stop at frame 1. (Remember that the constant STAR has the value of 1.)

```
gotoAndStop(STAR);
```

The last thing the case does is run a break directive:

```
break;
```

This stops the switch statement from continuing. It's found what it's looking for, so it doesn't need to check any of the other cases. If bulletType isn't "star", however, the switch statement continues to run and checks the remaining cases.

The next two cases do exactly the same thing, but check for different values:

```
case "circle" :
    gotoAndStop(CIRCLE);
    break;

  case "square" :
    gotoAndStop(SQUARE);
    break;
```

If bulletType happens not to be "star", "circle", or "square", the switch statement can implement a backup plan:

```
default:
    gotoAndStop(CIRCLE);
```

The default keyword tells the switch statement that if it doesn't find what it's looking for, it should just run whatever this last directive is. In this case, it stops the playhead at frame 2 in the timeline.

> In this example, "star", "circle", and "square" *happen to be strings, so they're surrounded by quotation marks. If you were using values that were not strings, such as numbers or other variables that represent object names, you would not surround them with quotation marks.*

Figure 10-17 illustrates how all the values in switch statements fit together. You should be able to see that the switch statement is just another way of writing a long if/else statement. In fact, you can actually replace the entire switch statement with an if/else statement, and the result would be exactly the same. Here's what it might look like:

```
if (bulletType == "star")
{
    gotoAndStop(STAR);
}
else if(bulletType == "circle")
{
  gotoAndStop(CIRCLE);
```

```
}
else if(bulletType == "square")
{
  gotoAndStop(SQUARE);
}
else
{
 gotoAndStop(CIRCLE);
}
```

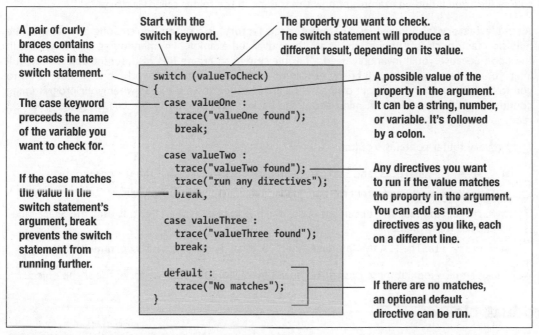

A pair of curly braces contains the cases in the switch statement.

Start with the switch keyword.

The property you want to check. The switch statement will produce a different result, depending on its value.

The case keyword preceeds the name of the variable you want to check for.

A possible value of the property in the argument. It can be a string, number, or variable. It's followed by a colon.

If the case matches the value in the switch statement's argument, break prevents the switch statement from running further.

Any directives you want to run if the value matches the property in the argument. You can add as many directives as you like, each on a different line.

If there are no matches, an optional default directive can be run.

```
switch (valueToCheck)
{
  case valueOne :
     trace("valueOne found");
     break;

  case valueTwo :
     trace("valueTwo found");
     trace("run any directives");
     break;

  case valueThree :
     trace("valueThree found");
     break;

  default :
     trace("No matches");
}
```

Figure 10-17. The switch statement

If there is no functional benefit to using a switch statement, why bother using one? It's purely a stylistic difference—switch statements are a little easier to read. They clearly stand out in your code, and you don't need to navigate through a tangle of disorienting curly braces to clearly see which conditions result in which outcomes. If you have more than two conditions that you're checking for, try to implement a switch statement.

Object factories

The kind of system you've just implemented is a very common one in computer programming. It's a very basic example of what's known as a factory. The Bullet class represents one type of object: a bullet. But it can actually manufacture many different types of bullets, depending on the value that's supplied to it as a parameter. It's a bullet factory!

You'll find many uses for factories in your games. You can, for example, store all the enemies in one Enemy symbol, each on a different frame on the timeline. You can bind them to an Enemy class and manufacture them in a factory, as is done here with the bullets.

You can also go much further. Instead of just displaying different graphics, you can give your enemies completely different behaviors by attaching different ENTER_FRAME event handlers to them when the class creates them. Can you see where this is heading?

When you start to become really confident as a programmer, you'll be able to use this system to actually create completely new instances of classes inside a specialized **factory class**. In the chapter's source files, you'll find an example of how this is done in the folder called Factory.

A **simple factory** (also known as a **parameterized factory**) is a system for creating objects with the help of a factory class. Although this is a rather advanced example, I'm mentioning it at this stage in the book because you'll invariably need a flexible system to create lots of different objects and still keep your code manageable. I'll briefly explain how the example project works, but I'll leave it up to you to try implementing it in your own games a little further down the road when your programming confidence grows. Keep this in mind and come back to this section in the chapter when you feel ready.

The Factory folder contains six files:

- Circle.as, Square.as, and Star.as: Represent the products that the factory produces.
- ShapeMaker.as: The factory class. Its job is to make the shapes.
- Main_Factory.as: The document class, which is known as the **client**. It uses the ShapeMaker class to make shapes.
- factory.fla: The FLA that produces the SWF. Main_Factory.as is its document class.

You'll take a quick look at these classes and how they all work together to make the shape objects.

Product classes

The product classes are the "things" that are made. To keep this example as simple as possible, the product classes don't do anything except display a trace statement, which tells you which shape they are. I'll leave it up to you to make these classes actually display shapes on the stage if you want them to. All three product classes are exactly the same except for their names and the messages they display.

Here's the Circle class:

```
package
{
  import flash.display.MovieClip;

  public class Circle extends MovieClip
  {
    public function Circle()
    {
      trace("Hello from the Circle class! Circles are fun!");
```

```
        }
      }
    }
```

Here's the Square class:

```
    package
    {
      import flash.display.MovieClip;

      public class Square extends MovieClip
      {
        public function Square ()
        {
          trace("It's me, Square! Thanks for making me!");
        }
      }
    }
```

And here's the Star class:

```
    package
    {
      import flash.display.MovieClip;

      public class Star extends MovieClip
      {
        public function Star ()
        {
          trace("Hello, I'm a star! I'm much better than circles ➥
            or squares!");
        }
      }
    }
```

Factory class

ShapeMaker is the class that produces the shape objects. It contains a static method called makeShape. makeShape takes one parameter: a String that represents the shape you want to make. Because the method is static, you can access this method from any other class using this format:

```
    ShapeMaker.makeShape("circle");
```

This is the same way you access methods in the Collision class that you've been using, which also contains static methods.

Here's the ShapeMaker class:

```
    package
    {
      import flash.display.MovieClip;
```

```
public class ShapeMaker
{
  public function ShapeMaker()
  {
  }
  static public function makeShape(shape:String):MovieClip
  {
    switch (shape)
    {
    case "star" :
      return new Star();
      break;

    case "circle" :
      return new Circle();
      break;

    case "square" :
      return new Square();
      break;

    default :
      return new Circle();
    }
  }
}
```

The ShapeMaker class's only job is to create instances of the product classes. Depending on the parameter supplied to the makeShape method, it uses a switch statement to find out what kind of shape it should make. It then uses the return keyword to "return" the instance back to whatever class requested it. The instance of the shape classes is created using the new keyword. Here's an example:

```
return new Circle();
```

new creates a new instance of the Circle class, and return sends that instance back to the class that requested it.

For return to be able to send the instance back successfully, the makeShape method needs a **return type**. You looked at this before, but just as a refresher, the return type is specified by the "type" name after the method's parameters. In this example, the return type is MovieClip:

```
static public function makeShape(shape:String):MovieClip
```

Circle, Square, and Star all extend the MovieClip class, which is why it is the return type used.

Client class

The client class is any class that uses these classes to do something useful. In this example, it's the Main_Factory class. Here's what the Main_Factory class looks like:

```
package
{
  import flash.display.MovieClip;
  import flash.events.Event;

  public class Main_Factory extends MovieClip
   {
    public function Main_Factory()
    {
      var shape:MovieClip = ShapeMaker.makeShape("star");
      trace("The shape object created is: " + shape);
    }
   }
}
```

To see what this actually does, test the project. The Output panel displays the following:

```
Hello, I'm a star! I'm much better than circles or squares!
The shape object created is: [object Star]
```

The shape object is now an instance of the Star class, and the first trace statement is being produced directly by the Star class. The second trace statement comes from the Main class. Can you see how it all fits together? The ShapeMaker class is an intermediary that helps the Main class create the kind of object it needs.

If you change the argument in the ShapeMaker.makeShape method from "star" to "square", you'll see the following trace output:

```
It's me, Square! Thanks for making me!
The shape object created is: [object Square]
```

The advantage of using the simple factory system is that the client class has a common interface for creating any type of shape. It also doesn't need to know anything about the details of how the shapes are made or how they work to be able to make them. This responsibility is offloaded to the ShapeMaker class and the product classes.

File all this away for later because you're certainly going to need a system like this to manage the production of objects later in your game design career. The simple factory that you just looked at is actually a very lightweight introduction to an area of object-oriented programming called **design patterns**, which are systems of organizing classes to help build complex applications. There has been a great deal written on design patterns in AS3.0, and you'll want to take a closer look at this topic as your programming skills increase and your projects become more ambitious. The combination of a factory to produce objects, with a design pattern called a **singleton** to manage them, can form the basis of a very solid system for managing and maintaining games of all kinds.

> *From a technical point of view, the simple factory that you've looked at here is not regarded as a full-blown design pattern in the strictest sense. It's certainly very helpful and will help train you to get used to using helper classes in your programs. However, for a truly bullet-proof elaboration of this system, do a bit of research into the "factory pattern" or "factory method." Although similar to a simple factory, the factory pattern has a few more checks and balances that make it much more robust. The trade-off, of course, is added complexity. You'll need to decide for yourself whether it's a fair trade based on the project you're working on.*

Enemy AI systems

You might be surprised to learn that if you can create an object that follows the mouse, you've already got the basis of an artificial intelligence (AI) system that you can modify for use in a wide variety of game situations. All you need to do is mix and match some of the techniques you learned about in this chapter, and you can design enemies that do the following:

- Follow the player
- Run away from the player
- Aim and fire bullets at the player

You'll find the source files for these examples in a folder called AI Systems.

In the Library of the aiSystems.fla file is a symbol called Robot. I'll demonstrate the three AI examples by asking you to bind the following classes to the Robot symbol as you need them:

- Robot_Follow
- Robot_Run
- Robot_Shoot

These classes contain the logic that the robot will need.

Following the player

Open the aiSystems.fla file. Select the Robot symbol in the Library and bind it to the Robot_Follow class.

Test the project. You'll see that the robot follows the player around the stage if the player is within a 200-pixel range. Figure 10-18 illustrates what you will see.

Figure 10-18. The robot rotates toward Button Fairy and follows her around the stage.

Here's the Robot_Follow class:

```
package
{
  import flash.display.MovieClip;
  import flash.events.Event;

  public class Robot_Follow extends MovieClip
  {
    //Constants
    private const SPEED:Number = 3;
    private const TURN_SPEED:Number = 0.3;
    private const RANGE:Number = 200;
    private const FRICTION:Number = 0.96;

    //Variables
    private var _vx:Number;
    private var _vy:Number;

    public function Robot_Follow()
    {
      //Initialize variables
      _vx = 0;
      _vy = 0;

      //Add listeners
      addEventListener(Event.ENTER_FRAME, onEnterFrame);
    }
    private function onEnterFrame(event:Event):void
    {
```

```
        //Get the target object
        var target = MovieClip(root).player;

        //Calculate the distance
        var dx:Number = target.x - this.x;
        var dy:Number = target.y - this.y;
        var distance:Number = Math.sqrt(dx * dx + dy * dy);

        if (distance <= RANGE)
        {
          //Find out how much to move
          var moveX:Number = TURN_SPEED * dx / distance;
          var moveY:Number = TURN_SPEED * dy / distance;

          //Increase velocity
          _vx += moveX;
          _vy += moveY;

          //Find total distance to move
          var moveDistance:Number = Math.sqrt(_vx * _vx + _vy * _vy);

          //Apply easing
          _vx = SPEED * _vx / moveDistance;
          _vy = SPEED * _vy / moveDistance;

          //Rotate towards the target
          rotation = 180 * Math.atan2(_vy, _vx) / Math.PI + 90;
        }

        //Apply friction
        _vx *= FRICTION;
        _vy *= FRICTION;

        //Move
        x += _vx;
        y += _vy;
      }
    }
  }
```

The constants declared at the top of the class contain the values that the code needs to make the robot move. You can fine-tune how the robot moves just by making small adjustments to these constants.

```
    private const SPEED:Number = 3;
    private const TURN_SPEED:Number = 0.3;
    private const RANGE:Number = 200;
    private const FRICTION:Number = 0.96;
```

The root property

The robot needs to know what it should follow. The following directive in the onEnterFrame event handler assigns the player object as its target:

```
var target = MovieClip(root).player;
```

This is something you haven't seen before. The directive uses the root object.

As you know, stage represents the main stage of the Flash movie. However, AS3.0 also allows you to access the movie's main timeline. You can access the timeline by using the keyword root. The player object is a property of the stage, but it's also a property of the main timeline. That means you can access the player object using the dot notation, like this:

```
root.player
```

For the AS3.0 compiler to be happy with this, however, you have to cast root as a MovieClip. So all you need to do is force its type, like this:

```
MovieClip(root).player
```

Using this format, you can access any object on the main stage. It's important to remember, however, that this works *only* for objects that are on the main stage. If the player object is a child of another Movie Clip object, such as dungeonOne.player, using root won't work. You'll need to use MovieClip(parent) like this:

```
MovieClip(parent).player;
```

The preceding directive also works in the current code.

> root *also refers to the document class. If you want to access your document class from another class, target it as* MovieClip(root). *If you don't have a document class, AS3.0 automatically creates one for you called* MainTimeline. *You don't need to worry much about this, but it's interesting to know that it happens behind the scenes.*

Moving the object

Once the robot knows what its target is, it calculates the distance between itself and the target using the formula you looked at earlier in the chapter. If the distance is less than the RANGE value (which is 200), the robot moves.

It moves using a variation of the easing formula discussed earlier in the chapter. It's a little more complex, however, because you want to limit the robot's speed and the rate at which it turns. Here are the steps the code takes and the formulas it uses to accomplish each task:

1. The code finds out how far to move the object and assigns these values to moveX and moveY variables:

```
var moveX:Number = TURN_SPEED * dx / distance;
var moveY:Number = TURN_SPEED * dy / distance;
```

2. The values of these new variables are used to modify the velocity:

```
_vx += moveX;
_vy += moveY;
```

3. Use these new _vx and _vy values to help you find the total distance required to move:

```
var moveDistance:Number = Math.sqrt(_vx * _vx + _vy * _vy);
```

4. You can use this new distance value along with the SPEED constant to find the correct velocity:

```
_vx = SPEED * _vx / moveDistance;
_vy = SPEED * _vy / moveDistance;
```

5. Finally, you can rotate the object toward the target. This is the same formula you've been using for rotation throughout the book. The addition of + 90 is there to offset the rotation of the robot object by 90 degrees. Without that, the leading edge of the robot would be its right side because of the way the object was drawn in the symbol (with its "front" being the cone on the robot's head). Any objects you use with this code might be oriented differently, so you'll probably want to adjust 90 to another number that you can figure out by trial and error when you see the direction toward which your object rotates:

```
rotation = 180 * Math.atan2(_vy, _vx) / Math.PI + 90;
```

If the object is *not* within the robot's range, these directives kick in, which gradually slow it down by using friction:

```
//Apply friction
_vx *= FRICTION;
_vy *= FRICTION;

//Move
x += _vx;
y += _vy;
```

A bit of simple logic, a few careful adjustments to the easing formula, and you have a very effective following behavior.

Running away from the player

It's very easy to create the exact opposite behavior: make the robot run away from the player. To see this at work, bind the Robot symbol to the Robot_Run class. Test the project and you'll see the robot flee from the player, as illustrated in Figure 10-19.

When I say that this is an opposite behavior, I mean that in the most literal sense imaginable. The Robot_Run class is exactly the same as Robot_Follow, except that three plus signs have been made negative.

The rotation is negative so that the robot points in the opposite direction:

```
rotation = 180 * Math.atan2(_vy, _vx) / Math.PI - 90;
```

And the velocity is negative:

```
x -= _vx;
y -= _vy;
```

That's it!

Figure 10-19. Get too close and the robot flies away.

Rotating and shooting toward the player

In the final AI system, the robot turns and fires bullets toward the player if the player is within range. Bind the Robot_Shoot class to the Robot symbol to see this work. The robot fires bullets in one-second intervals. Figure 10-20 illustrates what you will see when you test the project.

Figure 10-20. The robot rotates and fires bullets at the player.

You'll be happy to know that you already know 90% of the code in this class. In fact, everything from how the object rotates to the method that fires bullets is virtually identical to the code in the Player class. The only really new thing is the introduction of AS3.0's built-in Timer class, which is used to time the firing of the bullets. You'll look at how the Timer class works in detail ahead.

Here's the entire Robot_Shoot class:

```
package
{
  import flash.display.MovieClip;
  import flash.events.Event;
  import flash.events.TimerEvent;
  import flash.utils.Timer;

  public class Robot_Shoot extends MovieClip
  {
    //Constants
    private const RANGE:Number = 250;

    //Variables
    private var _vx:Number;
    private var _vy:Number;
    private var _angle:Number;
    private var _direction:Number;
    private var _shotFired:Boolean;
    private var _timer:Timer;

    public function Robot_Shoot()
    {
      //Initialize variables
      _vx = 0;
      _vy = 0;
      _angle = 0;
      _direction = 0;
      _shotFired = false;

      //Initialize timer
      _timer = new Timer(1000);
      _timer.addEventListener(TimerEvent.TIMER, onShootBullet);
      _timer.start();

      //Add listeners
      addEventListener(Event.ENTER_FRAME, onEnterFrame);
    }
    private function onEnterFrame(event:Event):void
    {
      //Find the target
      var target = MovieClip(root).player;

      //Find the direction of rotation
      _direction = Math.atan2(y - target.y, x - target.x) ➥
        * (180/Math.PI);
      _angle = _direction * Math.PI / 180;

      //Rotate the object
      rotation = _direction - 90;
```

```
        //Calculate the distance to the target
        var dx:Number = target.x - this.x;
        var dy:Number = target.y - this.y;
        var distance = Math.sqrt(dx * dx + dy * dy);

        //fire bullet if target is within range
        if (distance <= RANGE)
        {
          _timer.start();
        }
        else
        {
          _timer.stop();
        }
      }
    private function onShootBullet(event:TimerEvent):void
    {
      //Bullet's velocity
      var bullet_Vx:Number = Math.cos(_angle) * -10;
      var bullet_Vy:Number = Math.sin(_angle) * -10;

      //Bullet's start position
      var radius = -50;
      var bullet_StartX = x + radius * Math.cos(_angle);
      var bullet_StartY = y + radius * Math.sin(_angle);

      //Create bullet instance and add it to the stage
      var bullet:Bullet = new Bullet(bullet_Vx, bullet_Vy, ➥
        bullet_StartX, bullet_StartY, "circle");
      parent.addChild(bullet);
    }
  }
}
```

As you can see, it's pretty familiar. But what's up with all that timer stuff?

Timer and TimerEvent classes

In the chapter's source files, you'll find a folder called Timer. Open it as a project to see a simple example of how the Timer and TimerEvent classes work. When you test the project, you'll see a number counter that updates by one each second. Here's the code that makes it work:

```
package
{
  import flash.display.MovieClip;
  import flash.events.Event;
  import flash.events.TimerEvent;
  import flash.utils.Timer;

  public class Main_Timer extends MovieClip
```

```
  {
    private var _timer:Timer;

    public function Main_Timer ()
    {
      //Initialize timer
      _timer = new Timer(1000);
      _timer.addEventListener(TimerEvent.TIMER, onUpdateTime);
      _timer.start();
    }
    private function onUpdateTime(event:Event):void
    {
      timeDisplay.text = String(_timer.currentCount);

      //Stop timer when it reaches 10
      if(_timer.currentCount == 10)
      {
        _timer.reset();
        _timer.start();
      }
    }
  }
}
```

To use timers in your class, you need to import the Timer and TimerEvent classes:

```
import flash.events.TimerEvent;
import flash.utils.Timer;
```

Timers are objects, so you need to create them in the same way you create other objects, such as Tween, Rectangle and Point objects, by using the new keyword:

```
_timer = new Timer(1000);
```

The Timer class requires one argument, which is a number that represents milliseconds. (One millisecond represents 1/1000th of a second. One thousand milliseconds, as in this example, equals 1 second.)

Timers in AS3.0 work by triggering an event at regular intervals. In this example, you want to trigger an event to fire every second. The event's job is to update the dynamic text field on the stage by one. To set this in place, however, you need to add a TimerEvent event listener to the new _timer object that you just created:

```
_timer.addEventListener(TimerEvent.TIMER, onUpdateTime);
```

Next, you need to use the Timer class's start method to actually start the timer working:

```
_timer.start();
```

The _timer object now triggers the onUpdateTime event handler every second:

```
private function onUpdateTime(event:Event):void
{
  timeDisplay.text = String(_timer.currentCount);

  //Stop timer when it reaches 10
  if(_timer.currentCount == 10)
  {
    _timer.reset();
    _timer.start();
  }
}
```

Timer objects have a property called currentCount that tells you how many times the timer event has fired since it started. The onUpdateTime event copies the value of currentCount to the timeDisplay dynamic text field on the stage:

```
timeDisplay.text = String(_timer.currentCount);
```

You can use currentCount as done here: to display the number of times the event has been triggered. The if statement uses currentCount to check whether ten seconds have elapsed; if they have, it calls the Timer class's reset and start methods:

```
_timer.reset();
_timer.start();
```

reset stops the timer and also resets currentCount to zero. To start the timer again, you need to use the start method once more. (If you need to stop the timer completely in any of your games, you can use the stop method. stop stops the timer without resetting currentCount.)

When you create a Timer object, you can add a second argument, which is known as repeatCount. This is a number that tells the timer how many times it should repeat. You can see the effect of using repeatCount by updating the directive that creates the _timer object so that it looks like this:

```
_timer = new Timer(1000, 5);
```

If you test the project, you'll see that the numbers count up to five. After that, the event is no longer called.

There are a few more Timer class properties that you should know about. If you need to change the interval between events, you can use the delay property. For example, if you want the timer event to be triggered every one-half second, you can set the delay to 500 milliseconds, like this:

```
_timer.delay = 500;
```

If you need to know whether a timer is currently running, you can use the running property. running returns true when the timer is running and false when it isn't.

Finally, you can use the TimerEvent class's TIMER_COMPLETE property to trigger an event when the timer finishes:

```
_timer.addEventListener(TimerEvent.TIMER_COMPLETE, onTimerComplete);
```

This is a very basic introduction to how timers work, but I'm sure you can see that they are used often in games. You can use a Timer object to create a countdown timer, make an object mover intermittently, or calculate a player's score based on how long it takes to complete a task.

Using a timer to fire bullets

Now that you know how a timer works, it should be quite obvious how one has been used in the Robot_Shoot class. The _timer object has been set up to trigger an event every second. However, it's not started when the class is initialized. Instead, it waits until the target object is within range (which is 250 pixels).

```
if (distance <= RANGE)
{
  _timer.start();
}
else
{
  _timer.stop();
}
```

The event that the timer calls is the onShootBullet bullet event. It's identical to the onShootBullet method from the Player class, except that "circle" is provided as an argument instead of "star". It's no more difficult than that!

Shooting at random intervals

There's one small modification you can make that will make the robot's shooting behavior much more realistic. As it's been coded, the robot shoots right on cue every 1000 milliseconds. You can use the Timer class's delay property to randomize this. Add the following code to the onShootBullet event handler to see the effect:

```
private function onShootBullet(event:TimerEvent):void
{
//Bullet's velocity
var bullet_Vx:Number = Math.cos(_angle) * -10;
var bullet_Vy:Number = Math.sin(_angle) * -10;

//Bullet's start position
var radius = -50;
var bullet_StartX = x + radius * Math.cos(_angle);
var bullet_StartY = y + radius * Math.sin(_angle);
```

```
//Create bullet instance and add it to the stage
var bullet:Bullet = new Bullet(bullet_Vx, bullet_Vy, bullet_StartX, ➥
  bullet_StartY,"circle");
parent.addChild(bullet);

//Find a random start time for the next bullet
var randomFireTime:Number = Math.round(Math.random() * 1000) + 200;
_timer.delay = randomFireTime;
}
```

The robot now fires randomly between 200 and 1200 milliseconds.

Using other player control systems

When I introduced the example of Button Fairy's mouse control scheme, I mentioned that it was an everything-but-the-kitchen-sink example. You can rip it apart, take what you need, and build your own system to meet the needs of whatever kind of game you're designing.

However, it might not always be that obvious as to how to go about making a control scheme that's more specialized, especially if you're new to programming. To help you out, in the chapter's source files I included two more complete examples of player control systems that you're free to use and modify for the basis of any of your games:

- **Keyboard-controlled spaceship** is in a folder called Spaceship. It uses the basic techniques outlined in this chapter to control a spaceship. Use the left and right arrow keys to turn, the up arrow keys for thrust, and the spacebar to shoot. Figure 10-21 shows an example. With very little work, you can also turn this into a control scheme for an overhead car driving game.

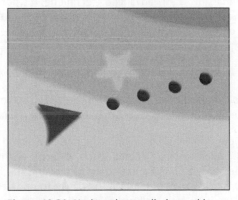

Figure 10-21. Keyboard controlled spacehip

■ **Mouse-controlled platform game character** is in a folder called Platform Mouse Control. Although platform game characters are traditionally controlled with a keyboard or keypad, why not implement a mouse-based control scheme? I modified the cat character's control scheme from Bug Catcher so that it's entirely mouse-based (see Figure 10-22). Move the mouse left and right to move the cat left and right. (Cats usually follow mice, so this makes perfect sense!) Press the left mouse button to make the cat jump when the mouse is above it. Feel free to modify this as much as you like so that it works the way you want it to for your games.

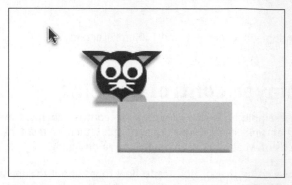

Figure 10-22. A mouse-controlled platform game character

Dispatching events

Dispatching events is one of most useful things you can learn how to do as a game programmer. Just because this topic happens to be the last section of the last chapter of the book, I want to dispel any notion that you might have that this is an "advanced" technique. It's not; for a game designer, it's as basic as fresh air and sunshine. Dispatching events is so useful that you'll want to use it with every game you design from now on.

You've seen events used in almost every chapter in this book. Button clicks, frames, timers—almost every important thing in an AS3.0 program seems to happen because of an event.

So far, all the events that you've used have been built into AS3.0. Did you know that you can create your own events and then trigger them whenever anything important happens in your game?

For example, imagine that you're making an adventure game in which the hero or heroine needs to steal a magical gingerbread cookie from a sleeping witch. As soon as the cookie has been stolen, it might be very useful for other objects in the game to know that this has happened. You could inform a game manager to update a score, you could inform the player to update its inventory, and you could even inform the sleeping witch who may well wake up if the player isn't tip-toeing quietly enough. Instead of informing each of these objects individually, however, the gingerbread cookie needs to broadcast only one event to the entire game: "I've been picked up!" This known as *dispatching an event*. Other objects can then choose whether they want to listen to this event or take any action if it concerns them.

The elegance of this system is that the event isn't dispatched to a specific object, and the objects that are listening for the event don't need to know anything about the object that sent the event.

Here's a quick-start guide to dispatching events:

1. Import the Event class:

```
import flash.events.Event;
```

2. When something happens that any objects in your game might be interested in, create an event for it using the dispatchEvent method. The basic format for creating an event looks like this:

```
dispatchEvent(new Event("eventName", true));
```

This directive broadcasts to the rest of your program that an event has occurred. You can give the event any name you like, such as "eventName", as in this example.

3. Any other class can now listen to this event by adding an event listener, like this:

```
stage.addEventListener("eventName", onEventNameHandler);
```

In your games, you'll probably want to add the event listener to the stage for reasons I'll explain ahead. You can attach event listeners to any object, however.

4. You then need to create the event handler to make something happen when the event occurs:

```
private function onEventNameHandler(event:Event)
{
  trace(event.target);
}
```

In the event handler, you can use the event object's target to access the object that called the event and all its properties. If you want to access the object with which the event was registered, such as the stage in this example, use the currentTarget property.

5. Wait for the event to occur.

You can create events for anything in your game that you think other objects should know about, such as a door opening, an enemy being destroyed, or a variable changing its value. Any objects can then choose to listen to those events if they want to, and take actions based on them.

By using events, objects can communicate without having to use setters (and sometimes even getters) in most cases. You can create classes that are completely encapsulated and don't depend on other classes to function properly. They can listen for events that interest them and change their own private properties internally.

Let's take a closer look at how dispatching events works.

Event "bubbling"

When events are dispatched, they travel through three different states: **capture**, **target**, and **bubbling**. The state that I'll explain in detail is the *bubbling* state, which is most useful in the kinds of game design scenarios that you've seen at work in this book.

When an object dispatches an event, the object broadcasts the event like a radio station broadcasts a news item. Other objects can then "tune in" to the event if they want to listen to it.

Events aren't broadcast to every object in the program at the same time, however. They either travel up or down through the hierarchy of objects. You can listen to events at any point in this journey.

If an event is set to bubble, it means that the event travels up through the hierarchy. It starts with the child object and then informs the parent object. If other objects want to listen to that event, they have to do it by attaching their event listeners to the parent object. Often, that object will be stage, which is the common parent of all display objects. Figure 10-23 illustrates a simple example.

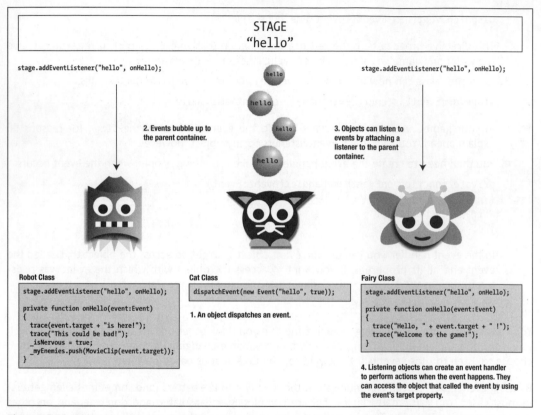

Figure 10-23. Objects can listen to bubbling events from other objects by attaching event listeners to a common parent object, such as the stage.

The dispatchEvent method has one argument, which is called the **event constructor**:

```
dispatchEvent(new Event("eventName", true));
```

The event constructor creates the event. Events can be made to bubble by setting the second argument in the event constructor to true:

```
new Event("eventName", true)
```

If you change it to false or leave it out entirely, the event doesn't bubble.

Let's look at a practical example of how to dispatch events in a game.

Case study: Space Shooter

The chapter's source files contain a folder called Space Shooter. Open it as a project and test it. It's a very simple prototype of a space-shooter game. Figure 10-24 shows what the Space Shooter game looks like.

Figure 10-24. Space Shooter prototype

The player can fly around the screen and shoot the robot. The robot rotates toward and then follows the player; and fires bullets. The scoreboards at the top of the stage keep track of the number of hits each has achieved. The number of bullets on the stage is also displayed.

The Player class uses a control scheme that is based on the easing system you looked at earlier in the chapter. In this system, the fairy's wand is used as the point that follows the mouse.

The Robot class makes the robot follow the player and also rotate toward and shoot at it. This is one more combination of the two techniques discussed earlier in the chapter.

Take a look at both these classes to see how they work. In both cases, they use no new techniques. What is new in this game, however, is the way events are used.

The most important thing about this game is how the bullet objects are being managed with the use of events. Let's take a detailed look at how this works.

563

Game structure

The game is made up of four classes:

- Main_SpaceShooter: The document class that handles all the game logic. It stores all the bullet objects in an array and checks whether any of them are hitting the player or robot. It updates the scores and removes bullets when they hit either object. It also removes the bullets if they reach the stage boundary.
- Player: The player's class. It's completely self-contained but uses the Bullet class to fire bullets.
- Robot: Self-contained, but also uses the Bullet class to fire bullets.
- Bullet: When a new bullet is created, it dispatches an event to tell the game, "Hey, I've been created!" The document class listens to these events and uses them to add the new bullets to an array.

Figure 10-25 illustrates how these classes work together.

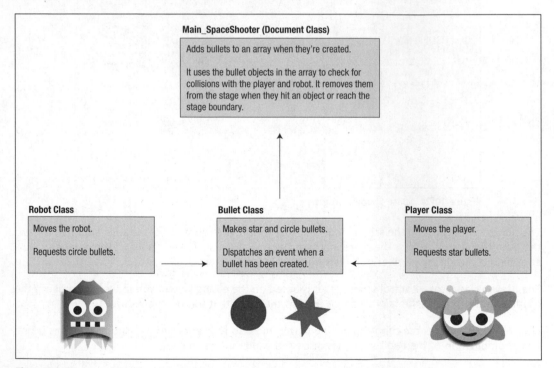

Figure 10-25. Space Shooter game structure

There are quite a few ways that this game could have been structured. The version presented here is not the best for keeping the classes entirely encapsulated or for code efficiency, but it's the clearest demonstration of how dispatching events works with the simplest code. I intentionally opted for some redundant code so that you can clearly see what's happening. Once you see how it works, I'm sure you'll have some clever ideas for improving the code even further.

In Chapter 8, I described the bullet firing system used in Dungeon Maze Adventure as having a few weaknesses. The biggest weakness was that the Bullet class and game manager classes were completely dependent on one another. What's most important about this game is that, unlike Dungeon Maze Adventure, the bullet objects don't know or care what happens to them after they're created. And the document class that manages the game doesn't depend on them because of the use of events for communication.

Let's look at how dispatching events works to manage the bullets on the stage.

Creating bullets

Here's how new bullets are added to the stage:

1. When new bullets are added to the stage, the Bullet class dispatches a bulletCreated event:

```
private function onAddedToStage(event:Event):void
{
    dispatchEvent(new Event("bulletCreated", true));
}
```

2. The document class has a listener that listens for a bulletCreated event:

```
stage.addEventListener("bulletCreated", onBulletCreated);
```

3. When the event occurs, the document calls its onBulletCreated event handler. It copies a reference to the bullet that triggered the event into an array called bullets:

```
private function onBulletCreated(event:Event)
{
    _bullets.push(MovieClip(event.target));
}
```

The _bullets array keeps a list of all the bullets currently on the stage. Figure 10-26 illustrates this process.

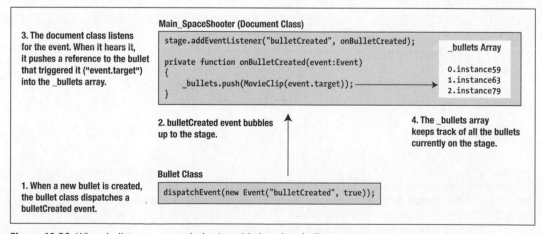

Figure 10-26. When bullets are created, they're added to the _bullets array.

When the game runs, the number of bullets on the stage is displayed in the bottom-right corner of the stage. The number comes from the _bullet array's length property. This is the line of code in the document class's onEnterFrame event that produces it:

```
bulletDisplay.text = "Bullets on the stage: " + ➡
    String(_bullets.length);
```

Now that you have a list of all the bullets on the stage, you can check whether they're colliding with any other objects.

Checking for bullet collisions with objects

The document class checks for collisions between bullets, player, and robot in the onEnterFrame event. Here's the entire code (I'll explain how each part works ahead):

```
for (var i:int = 0; i < _bullets.length; i++)
{
  switch (_bullets[i].bulletType)
  {

    case "circle" :

      //Check for a collision with the player
      if (player.hitTestPoint(_bullets[i].x,_bullets[i].y,true))
      {
        //Remove the bullet from the stage
        removeChild(_bullets[i]);

        //Remove bullet from array
        _bullets.splice(i,1);

        //Subtract 1 from the counter to compensate
        //for the removed element
        i--;

        //Update the robot's score
        _robotScore++;

        //Update the robot's score display on the stage
        robotScoreDisplay.text = String(_robotScore);
      }
      break;

    case "star" :

      //Check for a collision with the robot
      if (robot.hitTestPoint(_bullets[i].x,_bullets[i].y,true))
      {
        //Remove the bullet from the stage
        removeChild(_bullets[i]);
```

```
        //Remove bullet from array
        _bullets.splice(i,1);

        //Subtract 1 from the counter to compensate
        //for the removed element
        i--;

        //Update the enemy's score
        _playerScore++;

        //Update the player's score display on the stage
        playerScoreDisplay.text = String(_playerScore);
      }
      break;

  }
}
```

A for loop checks whether any of the bullets in the array are colliding with either the player or robot:

```
for (var i:int = 0; i < _bullets.length; i++)
{
    //Collision detection here.
}
```

Similar to the examples from Chapter 9, the loop uses the array's length property to find out how many times it should loop. If there are four bullets in the array, this loop will run four times each frame—once for each bullet.

Inside the loop is a switch statement that finds what type of bullet is currently being checked. It can be "star" or "circle". The Bullet class has a getter called bulletType that provides this information. The switch statement uses it to switch between the two cases:

```
switch (_bullets[i].bulletType)
```

If the case is "circle", it means that it's one of the robot's bullets. In that case, the code has to check for a collision between the bullet and the player:

```
if (player.hitTestPoint(_bullets[i].x,_bullets[i].y,true))
{
    //Remove the bullet from the stage
    removeChild(_bullets[i]);

    //Remove bullet from array
    _bullets.splice(i,1);

    //Subtract 1 from the counter to compensate
    //for the removed element
    i--;
```

```
        //Update the robot's score
        _robotScore++;

        //Update the robot's score display on the stage
        robotScoreDisplay.text = String(_robotScore);
    }
```

It should be pretty obvious what this code does. But there's something new here that you haven't seen before:

```
    _bullets.splice(i, 1);
```

splice is used to remove an element from an array. It uses two arguments: the first is the index number of the element to remove, and the second is the number of elements it should remove from that point onward.

In this case, you want to remove the current bullet, which is at index number i. If the loop is in its third repetition, that would be element number 2. (Remember, array elements are numbered starting at zero.)

In the second argument, 1 is the number of elements to remove. In this case, you want to remove only one element.

What splice does in this program is to remove the bullet from the array so the program no longer has to check it for a collision. Without it, the array will just get bigger and bigger, and the program will start to generate errors because it would check for collisions with bullets that have been removed from the stage with removeChild.

> You can also use splice to insert elements into an array. For example, if you want to add an object called box to an array as the third element, you can use a line of code that looks like this:
>
> ```
>         array.splice(2, 0, box);
> ```
>
> This adds the box object at index position 2. 0 means that you didn't delete the element that was originally at position 2. That object will be pushed up to position 3, and any objects that come after it would also be renumbered.
>
> If you want to insert an object into an array and replace the existing element, you can use this format:
>
> ```
>         array.splice(2, 1, box);
> ```
>
> The box object will now be inserted at position 2, but 1 indicates that one element should be deleted from the array. That would be the original element at position number 2. It's now gone for good, replaced by box, and the rest of the elements in the array won't be renumbered.

splice is a very versatile method to use with arrays, and you'll certainly find many occasions when it will help manage game objects.

An important thing to know is that if you remove an element from an array in the middle of a loop, you also need to subtract 1 from the counter variable, i. If you don't do this, it throws the counter off by one and the loop will skip the next item. That's what this directive does:

```
i--;
```

The rest of the code in the switch statement checks for collisions between "star" bullets and the player. It's almost identical to the code you just looked at.

Removing bullets at the stage boundaries

The last thing the document class does is remove the bullets when they reach the stage boundaries. I added this code in the Main_SpaceShoooter class because I want the document class to be entirely responsible for removing objects from the game. It makes it easier to manage the _bullet array.

This code is also in the onEnterFrame event handler, and like the collision detection code, it runs inside a for loop. It checks each bullet in the _bullets array, one at time, to see whether it's crossed the stage boundaries. (The loop counter variable is j to avoid conflicting with i in the previous loop.)

```
for (var j:int = 0; j < _bullets.length; j++)
{
    //Top
    if (_bullets[j].y + _bullets[j].height / 2 < 0)
    {
        removeChild(_bullets[j]);
        _bullets.splice(j, 1);
        j--;
    }
    //Bottom
    else if (_bullets[j].y - _bullets[j].height / 2 > stage.stageHeight)
    {
        removeChild(_bullets[j]);
        _bullets.splice(j, 1);
        j--;
    }
    //Left
    else if (_bullets[j].x + _bullets[j].width / 2 < 0)
    {
        removeChild(_bullets[j]);
        _bullets.splice(j, 1);
        j--;
    }
    //Right
    else if (_bullets[j].x - _bullets[j].width / 2 > stage.stageWidth)
    {
        removeChild(_bullets[j]);
        _bullets.splice(j, 1);
        j--;
    }
}
```

If a bullet crosses a boundary, it's removed from the stage and then from the _bullets array.

Classes and events

This was a very condensed explanation of how the Space Shooter game works, so make sure that you check out the complete code in the source files to see all this code in its proper context.

Space Shooter is a good model for you to base your game projects on because it shows quite clearly how you can distribute different kinds of tasks among classes. The game logic and important game actions, such as removing objects and updating scores, is handled by the document class. (It could also be a manager class, as in Dungeon Maze Adventure.) The object classes don't know much about what's going on in the game, but when something important happens to them, they can announce it to the game by dispatching an event. Other objects can then decide whether that event is important to them or whether they should ignore it. The key thing is that the no other objects are dependent on those events or the objects that are dispatching them to function correctly, and this goes a long way to solving the problem of tight coupling, discussed in Chapter 8.

There's one very important thing you should keep in mind when you design classes: make the classes do as much work with the information they have instead of requesting more information from other classes. Try to keep getters and setters to a minimum or avoid them altogether if you can, and use events to notify objects of things that happen in your game.

With this in mind, the structure of the Space Shooter game could be fine-tuned much more. Instead of registering the bullets in an array in the document class, you could design the game so that the Player class registers circle bullets and checks for collisions with them itself. The player could then notify the rest of the game by dispatching an event if a collision occurs. This would take much of the work off the shoulders of the document class, which would then only have to update the score and do general game administration. Figure 10-23 is a good map to help you design a game structured like this.

Summary

Hey, is the book finished already? It is, but it seemed like the all fun was only just starting! If you've reached this last page in the book, congratulate yourself: You're a game designer! With the skills you've acquired over these ten chapters, there are few game design scenarios that you won't be able to approach with confidence.

But if you're like everyone else who's ever started learning game design, you'll find that the desire to learn more is insatiable. Although you've accomplished so much already, there's a great universe of learning ahead of you. Here's a quick roundup of some of the areas you might want to explore:

- **Adobe's online help documentation**: Adobe maintains excellent online documents detailing most aspects of Flash CS4 and AS3.0 programming. You can access these documents by selecting Help ➤ Flash Help in Flash, or pointing your web browser to http://help.adobe.com/en_US/Flash/10.0_UsingFlash/. I've made numerous references to sections of these documents throughout this book, and they remain the most comprehensive primary source for all things Flash and AS3.0. Although many of the topics they deal with and the approaches they take are reasonably advanced, they should match your current level of ability. Spend some time going through some of the hundreds of articles and you're sure to find great food to fuel your developing programming skills.

- **3D**: Flash is getting better and better at producing interactive 3D environments. There are a few competing systems for implementing 3D in Flash. They all require that you import specialized 3D classes and learn how to use them. If you have a thorough understanding of how AS3.0 works and how to structure programs using classes, you won't find it difficult. However, you'll need to commit to learning how these 3D classes work. Here are the current 3D class packages for AS3.0: Papervision (and PapervisionX), Alternativa3D, Away3D, Sandy 3D Engine, and FIVe3D.

- **Physics**: There are some excellent packages of classes available for doing precise physics simulations with AS3.0. They include Box2D, Motor2, APE, Foam, and Glaze.

- **Tile-based games**: A style of game design in which all objects on the stage are assigned to squares in a grid. The code then creates an abstract model of the game behind the scenes in arrays, and that model is used to update the objects on the stage. Board games, strategy games, and certain puzzle games really benefit from the tile-based approach. Tile-based games run very efficiently, use relatively little CPU power and memory, and are easy to extend if you want to add new game levels. Because of this, the tile-based approach also works well for platform and adventure games.

- **Vector math and geometry**: If you'll create games that involve some degree of physics simulation, it is really beneficial to spend a bit of time learning some vector math and 2D geometry. Even if you don't think you're good at math, give it a try—you might just surprise yourself. You can immediately apply what you learn to your games.

- **Saving game data**: If you want to save some data in your game (such as a score or a game level) so the player can quit the game and continue it later, you need to create a **shared object.** This is covered in detail in the subchapter "Storing local data" in the chapter "Networking and Communication" from Adobe's online document *Programming ActionScript 3.0 for Flash*.

- **Multiplayer games**: It's always more fun to play games with friends. To make multiplayer games you need to store game data on a server on the Web so that other players can access that data to update their own game screens. There are quite a few ways you can do this, but all require some research into additional "server-side technologies." Your Flash games will be able to communicate with these server-side technologies, but to implement most of them you'll need to learn new programming languages such as PHP or Java. Do a bit of research into Java socket servers such as SmartFoxServer, ElectroServer, and Pulse, among many others. (Java is very closely related to AS3.0, so you won't find it completely unfamiliar.) You can create a high-score list for your games using PHP, and you can store game data using a MySQL database. You can avoid Java and PHP directly by storing game data in a content management system (CMS) and accessing the data in Flash using XML. Adobe also provides its own Flash Media Servers. The Media Development Server is free, and although limited, is a great way to get your feet wet with multiplayer technologies in a familiar environment. As you can see, there's a lot to learn! But it's all well worth the time you'll put into it.

As every game designer knows, making games is much more fun than playing them. Like an artist who's just learned how to mix paints and sketch out a few simple scenes, a bit of practice is all you'll need, and you'll be well on your way to creating that masterpiece. You've now got a solid foundation in game design with Flash and AS3.0—go and make some great games!

INDEX

N

W

wall object, Dungeon Maze Adventure game and, 338, 378
wand object (of Button Fairy character), 528, 533
warnings, 233. *See also* error messages
weapon object, Dungeon Maze Adventure game and, 339, 370
Webding font, 57
while loop, 304, 437
whole numbers, 180
width of objects, adjusting, 59
width property, 117
   health meters and, 273
   vs. scaleX property, 138
Wingding font, 57
workspace. *See* Developer workspace
workspaces, 10
wrapping text, 170

X

Xeno's paradox, 409, 510
x position, 123
   acceleration and, 405, 532
   finding for coordinates, 439
x property, 117, 137, 148, 515

Y

yoyo() method, 517, 520
y position, 123
   acceleration and, 405
   finding for coordinates, 439
y property, 117, 137

Z

z 3D property, 118, 148
Zoom tool, 61